DOUBLE LIVES

Also published by Enigma Books

STEPHEN KOCH

DOUBLE LIVES

Stalin, Willi Münzenberg, and the Seduction of the Intellectuals

Completely revised and updated

With an introduction by
Sam Tanenhaus
Author of *Whittaker Chambers*

Enigma Books

Enigma Books
580 Eighth Avenue, New York, NY 10018
www.enigmabooks.com

ISBN 1-929631-20-0

Library of Congress Cataloging in Publication Data

Koch, Stephen.
Double lives : Stalin, Willi Münzenberg and the seduction of the
intellectuals / Stephen Koch ; with an introduction by Sam
Tanenhaus.— Completely rev. and updated.
p. cm.
Originally published: New York : Free Press, c1994.
Includes bibliographical references and index.
ISBN: 1-929631-20-0 (pbk.)
1. Communist strategy—History—20th century. 2. Commu-
nism—History—20th century. 3. Espionage, Communist—
History—20th century. 4. Propaganda, Communist—History—
20th century. 5. Münzenberg, Willi. 6. Communists—Germany—
Biography. 7. Communism—Germany—History—20th century.
I. Tanenhaus, Sam. II. Title.

HX518.S8 K63 2004
327.1247'009'043—dc21

To the memory of my father

ROBERT FULTON KOCH

1907–1951

CONTENTS

Acknowledgments

When I started writing *Double Lives*, the world it explores still lay covered by the darkness of secrecy, disinformation, and neglect. With this new edition I must again thank the many people who were my initial guides to the murky regions and to the strangely fated human beings I found myself trying to understand. I've put a list of those guides at the end of this text. It is a long and, if I may say so, distinguished list: an inventory of very special people to whom I feel, even these many years later, enduring gratitude.

For this revised edition, I must once again pay grateful tribute to the memory of Babette Gross, the widow of Willi Münzenberg, who in the summer of 1989 granted me a week of indispensable interviews. Those memorable exchanges were made possible only through the good offices of Dr. Peter Lübbe, who persuaded a skeptical Babette to speak with me, and made the contact possible. But this was only the most significant of many kindnesses. Dr. Lübbe, with his encyclopedic erudition about the history of German communism, assisted me many times.

I am especially grateful to Sam Tanenhaus for his reflections here. Grateful and proud. To have the masterful author of *Whittaker Chambers: A Biography* introduce this revised edition of *Double Lives* is no small honor.

It was Franklin Dennis whose steadfast belief in *Double Lives* brought the book to Enigma Books, and so made this revised edition possible. I doubt it would ever have happened without his persistence and integrity. It was Franklin's shrewd dual insight into both the book and the book publishing industry that has guided *Double Lives* into its ideal second home.

Among friends, Tzvetan Todorov has steadily nourished my thinking from the beginning of this project until the day before yesterday. And it was during a conversation with Michael Scammell over a long-ago lunch in London that I suddenly glimpsed the outline of this book—like a night landscape made white by lightning.

Among authorities, I am particularly grateful to a cordial correspondence with the Soviet archivist, Frederikh Firsov, and to a trenchant exchange of letters and e-mails with the Russianist and translator Timothy Sergay. My exchange with both these men guided me when I began to reshape the book.

Finally, I must end with a sad backward glance. The editor of the first version of *Double Lives* was the late Erwin Glikes at the Free Press. If only Erwin were here to see the book reach this fresh new phase of its life! Diana Trilling was my literary confidante and guide as I wrote it: Diana is gone too. And while it is unusual to speak about a review on an acknowledgments page, I cannot forbear noting that as the storm of criticism howled around the original *Double Lives*, the late François Furet's gracious review in *La Nouvelle Observateur* was one of the signal events in my writing life.

SK
New York, December 2003

INTRODUCTION

by Sam Tanenhaus

I t may seem odd to say of a work of history that it was ahead of its time, but this formulation applies to *Double Lives*, Stephen Koch's original and arresting account of literary Stalinism in the 1930s. In 1994, when the book first appeared, America's political culture was in a period of transition: global Communism had ended but the "post-Communist" world had yet to take shape. In some quarters the fellow traveling impulse still obtained, particularly among intellectuals, many of whom were slow to rethink the politics they had embraced for much of their lives.

Double Lives, appearing at this awkward moment, demanded just such rethinking. Its biting account of the Communist International's "cultural and intellectual apparatus" did not simply point up (yet again) the duplicities of Soviet Communism. It reminded us that the twentieth century had been an age in which the Romantic ideal of the artist or writer as a sovereign being, answerable only to his own conscience, had given way to a new, diminished ideal of the "intellectual" as member of a politically informed (and sometimes driven) "class."

This transformation was not an abrupt one. It happened over time. In fact Romanticism itself, born in the eighteenth century, was closely tied to politics. Many of the leading Romantic figures in France and England were radicals, at least for a time. The identification was reinforced in the next century, when Karl Marx became the great dramaturge of class conflict. This idea, and its offshoots, attracted a number of literary artists (Zola and Shaw are two examples) for whom politics became the instrument for fashioning a more compelling realism.

But it was the twentieth century that solidified the alliance of politics and art, chiefly through two events, the Russian Revolution of 1917 and the roughly simultaneous "revolution" of Modernism. In tandem the new politics and the new aesthetics offered exciting deliverance from the narrow proscriptions of the previous (Victorian) age-or perhaps, as some said, simply replaced one set of dubious certitudes with another. Either way, when the twentieth century's great crisis came, in the 1930s—with totalitarianism on the rise, "bourgeois capitalism" on the wane, a new world war on the horizon—intellectuals were pulled more deeply than ever into the tides of history and sink into irrelevance. A war had broken out, and one must choose sides. To do otherwise would be to stand against the tides of history, to slip over the edge into irrelevance.

The thirties was the decade of Alger Hiss and Whittaker Chambers, of the Cambridge spies, and of the central figure in *Double Lives*, the ingenious German propagandist Willi Münzenberg who, Koch suggests, "developed what may well be the leading moral illusion of the twentieth century: the notion that in the modern age the principal arena of the moral life, the true realm of good and evil, is politics."

This theme will be familiar to readers of mid-century classics like Lionel Trilling's novel *The Middle of the Journey* and Murray Kempton's account of American communists, *A Part of Our Time*. Like those earlier writers, Koch is interested in the dilemma that political engagement—"commitment"—imposes on the sentient person who must now accept the terms of a world in which power itself has become a romantic ideal.. This theme courses as well through the work of major thirties' writers who were drawn to radicalism even though as modernists they recoiled from the rawer imperatives of "the State," whether capitalist or communist, totalitarian or democratic. Some of W. H. Auden's poetry can be read as a gloss on the theory of the modern state as described by theorists like Mosca, Pareto, and Burnham, only Auden's concern is with the pressure the "managerial society" exerts on individual consciousness and the interior life.

Others faced more practical considerations. How, for instance, could the educated person remain true to the Romantic ideal of intellectual sovereignty and at the same time submerge his ego into the radical cause, taking orders from leaders of party cells and union factions? More baldly, did the new socialist utopia even have a place for privileged denizens of Oxbridge and Bloomsbury or Harvard and Provincetown?

Sometime the confusions were comical. Consider the case, discussed in *Double Lives*, of Michael Straight, the very wealthy young American recruited for underground "special work" while a student Communist at Cambridge in 1937. His recruiter, the art historian Anthony Blunt, startled Straight by telling him that unnamed "friends" in the Comintern had decreed he could best serve the cause by making "a brilliant career" on Wall Street, where his family was well established. Straight was indignant: he wanted to be a revolutionist, not a bourgeois banker. Blunt, reporting back to his superiors, was told Straight needn't worry: his "family connections in Washington would serve as well as those on Wall Street." Eventually Straight would get a desk in the State Department, just as another earnest young Communist, Alger Hiss, would do.

But the awkwardness wasn't only between intellectuals and their masters. The intellectual was just as likely to be at odds with himself, especially once he realized, as so many did, that Communism was usually more attractive in theory than in practice. This, the age-old complication of "revolutionary justice," in Koch's phrase, could result in self-deceptions, most notoriously the theoretical justifications of Stalin's atrocities so commonplace in the 1930s.

Ritual apologetics did not end with that decade. They dominated French intellectual thought for much of the cold war, just as American New Leftists were dogmatic defenders of Castro's Cuba.

In some quarters this still goes on. Not long ago an American writer explained to me that the murder of millions in Communist China was justified by the improved official status Chinese women now enjoy. No matter that the legions of the dead included numberless women, who presumably did not realize they were being martyred in the cause of sisterhood. Or perhaps they did. It would have been in keeping with the canons of "revolutionary justice," with its message that might not only makes right but also defines the good.

These were the sentiments the Comintern exploited so deftly during the peak years (1935-1939) of the Popular Front when some of the most gifted men and women of the day eagerly took up the cause of Stalin's "antifascism." How did Münzenberg and company manage this? The answer is unclear, though I think Koch is right to note that a dual appeal was made-in the first instance to the intellectual's sincere feelings of sympathy, his solidarity with the downtrodden; in the second to his equally sincere snobbery, his psychological estrangement from "bourgeois" culture.

George Orwell, writing in the 1940s, observed that many British intellectuals who had been unmoved by the USSR in its initial Bolshevik phase grew captivated later, after Stalin had established Russia as a totalitarian state. "These people look toward the USSR and see in it, or think they see, a system which eliminates the upper class, keeps the working class in its place, and hands unlimited power to people very similar to themselves," Orwell wrote. The "secret wish" of this "English Russophile intelligentsia," was "to destroy the old, equalitarian version of Socialism and usher in a hierarchical society where the intellectual can at last get his hands on the whip." (An almost identical attraction held as well for artists, like Wyndham Lewis and Ezra Pound, who were drawn to fascism.)

Orwell didn't add that the affinity was not really surprising. Artists and thinkers may well feel a kinship with dictators. Didn't Joseph Conrad, in his famous credo, explain that his objective was to "make" us see? Doesn't the sovereign intellectual also attempt a kind of coercion, first conceiving grand visions and then imposing them, in the form of novels or canvases or symphonies or theories, on a resistant or intractable humanity, through manipulative and often deceptive means? Why shouldn't such a person be attracted to the strong-armed leader, so "creative" and "original" in his approach to the problems of governance?

The transactions Koch describes came to an end with World War II. But the ideal of the intellectual as political actor did not. The radical temper was revived in the 1960s, when a new generation of "political pilgrims" traveled to Hanoi or Havana. It was revived too in the more extreme protests of the anti-war movement and in the political assumptions of the counterculture. The rebellion was short-lived, but its impact was profound. It is quite true, as is often said, that we still inhabit a "post-60s" America.

Politically the consequences are harder to read. Nowadays much attention is paid to the anti-communist upheavals of the 1980s, which caught so many off guard: the great dissident rebellions in Central And Eastern Europe, the historic protest at Tiananmen Square, and, climactically, the Soviet implosion of 1989. This period saw the emergence of intellectual heroes who seemed to defy the radical model established in the 1930s. Some (Joseph Brodsky, Milan Kundera) were ambivalent about politics itself. Others (Andrei Sakharov, Václav Havel) personified the archaic ideal of the intellectual as responsible citizen and member of the broad community.

It is all the more remarkable, then, that in our own moment it is the 1930s ideal of the intellectual as revolutionary has regained its status, owing to the events of September 11, 2001. Once again we inhabit a time in which men of ideas and words have made themselves the instruments of very specific, highly charged, policies. The Iraq campaign is perhaps the first war in American history conceived and orchestrated in large part by intellectuals, in this case neo-conservatives who are in many instances ideological descendants of the 1930s radicals. Some now staff the upper levels of the Bush administration. Others, outside the administration, confidently expound theories of Islamic "fascism" in tones that echo the old, and half-forgotten, calls to arms sounded by Willi Münzenberg.

Indeed the war "for democracy" in the Middle East is strikingly similar to another episode explored in *Double Lives*, the "last stand" of the Spanish Civil War. The cause of universal democracy required the purging of sentiment in the interests of power, which in turn meant, as Auden explained in 1937,

> *. . . the deliberate increase in the chances of death,*
> *The conscious acceptance of guilt in the necessary murder.*

Precisely what forces will be unleashed by this latest union of ideology and aesthetic no one can predict, just as no one could foretell the consequences of Münzenberg's recruitment of intellectuals seventy years ago. We do know what became of that first blaze of muddled intellectual passions, however. It gave us a conflagration. That is the story told in *Double Lives*, a book whose time has decidedly come.

PREFACE TO THE REVISED EDITION

You hold in your hands a shortened, clarified and, I hope, more compelling version of a book first published in the United States in early 1994. I have revised *Double Lives* for three reasons. First, the world has changed since 1994. Second, what we know about Stalinism, about its propaganda juggernaut and totalitarianism generally, has changed. Finally, I have changed.

What has not changed is the essential tale told in *Double Lives*. The terrible story of Willi Münzenberg's rise to power and his descent through terror toward death is intact. So is my account of Willi's founding role in the culture war between Soviet totalitarianism and liberal democracy, the battle that became a seventy-year struggle for the soul of the twentieth century. My account of how Willi organized that epochal argument in all its force and fraudulence is still pretty much as I wrote it—only more so. My outline of the Comintern's co-option of Western antifascism at the very moment Stalin was courting—not confronting, *courting*—Hitler is if anything more emphatically told this time round, as is my narrative of how an idealistic yet fundamentally mendacious network of political fronts became a tool for co-opting the Western response to the Nazi menace in the thirties. Finally, I have expanded on how all this was transformed into the vast political deception known as the Popular Front. In all this, *Double Lives* remains much as it was.

Yet I am retelling this tale of fraud and collusion in a changed world. Some of those changes—like the end of the Cold War—are too obvious to invoke. Others are subtler. Chief among them is that the propaganda argument that Willi Münzenberg injected into the mainstream of twentieth century discourse is at long last at an end. Unlike the Cold War itself, the war between democratic and totalitarian ideas was never exactly won. But neither was it exactly lost, either. It was abandoned. At some point around the turn of the twenty-first century, the battle-weary partisans of that seven-decade slanging match suddenly paused in mid-slander, glanced around at a changed world, and walked away, looking for some newer war somewhere.

In 1994, this desertion of the field was not yet quite complete, and *Double Lives* got swept into the last skirmishes of an old battle. Its many reviews were sadly polarized between right and left, and the negative response, above all the response to my discussion of the Popular Front, was often all but hysterical. Times have changed. I doubt any new response will be so polarized, or that the classic hysteria will resurface in quite the same way. Even the most devout second-generation—or is it third? fourth?—defenders of the old Stalin-derived dispensation have fallen silent. Some have even found their way to.... second thoughts.

Meanwhile the new assessment of the totalitarian catastrophe has only begun, and yet scholarship has been transformed. In the United States, Anne Applebaum's *Gulag: A History* sustains Solzhenitsyn's great polemic in ways that have reduced all but the most committed gulag-minimizers to silence. In 1997, Sam Tanenhaus's biography of Whittaker Chambers at last resolved the epochal personal drama between Chambers and Alger Hiss that for many Americas served as *the* symbol of Cold War divisions. The dreary standard cant about American Communism is pretty much done for, thanks above all to the work of Harvey Klehr, John Haynes, and their collaborators, published mainly in the "Annals of Communism" series of Yale University Press. The old sententious evasions of Stalin's role in the Spanish Civil War have been blown aside, first in Burnett Bolloten's massive *Spanish*

Civil War and later in Ronald Radosh and Mary Halleck's *Spain Betrayed.*

One addition to the Yale series is Sean McMeekin's impressively researched *The Red Millionaire: A Political Biography of Willi Münzenberg* Everyone interested in the Comintern will prize this book. *The Red Millionaire* is a biography of Münzenberg. *Double Lives* is not. I am only secondarily interested most details of Willi's life. My book is about the Soviet co-option of liberalism between the wars, and above all the Soviet co-option of liberal antifascism. Münzenberg played an exemplary role in this sinister drama, but long passages in *Double Lives* are only remotely connected to him.

So, though Professor McMeekin and I have one story in common, and agree about much of it, we tell it very differently. His book, which appeared just as this revised edition was going to press, overflows with new facts, and they have helped me root out, at the last minute, at least one blunder. I now see that Willi's role in the Sacco-Vanzetti campaign was not what I earlier claimed for it. In the United States anyway, it was not Willi but a rival propaganda organization—Red Aid—that really ran the Communist co-option of the great case.

On the other hand, Professor McMeekin and I are essentially different writers. *Double Lives* is filled with speculation. I would never have written it otherwise. To me a fact is alive almost to the degree that it stirs a speculative impulse, and I prize my amateur status precisely because it permits me the full freedom of that impulse. There is not a speculative line in *The Red Millionaire.* Its sterling strength is that it contains facts and only facts. I sense that for Professor McMeekin, the facts end the discussion. For me, they begin it.

American scholarship has been especially adept at straightening out the facts—no minor achievement. In my opinion it has lagged behind other countries in the larger task of assimilating the consequences of the totalitarian collapse. Consider France, for example, where François Furet's dazzling *The Passing of an Illusion,* a great historian's devastating study of Communist thinking in the twentieth century, appeared shortly before that relentless reassessment of Communist practice, *The Black Book of Communism*, put together by the intrepid Stephane Courtois and the argumentative circle of scholars around him. Americans have been slow to look quite so straightforwardly at the tremendous moral and intellectual challenge these impressive works confront.

Yet my own most moving encounter with the new scholarship has come from Russia itself. No writer has been more important to my revision of *Double Lives* than Arkady Vaksberg, an indefatigable student of the Stalinist lie, a master-mover within the Soviet archives, sometime President of Moscow PEN, and author of (among many others) *Hotel Lux* and *The Gorky Mystery*. Where Furet is magisterial and Courtois relentless, Vaksberg wrestles with the new truth-telling driven by a grieving personal passion that transcends scholarship even as it encompasses it. Here is an historian who can open his searing biography of Andrei Vyshinsky, Stalin's prime legal hatchet-man in the Great Terror, with an account of his own mother standing, knees shaking, before Vyshinsky himself, pleading (successfully) with the old monster to issue the one curt command needed to rescue the menaced education of her brilliant young son. Here is a Russian who knew (and liked) that Comintern *apparatchik*, Maria Pavlovna Koudachova, Romain Rolland's wife and Soviet keeper, and who in *Hotel Lux* summons up a Parisian evening in 1968 spent with the old lady, sitting in the vesper light, feeling their through the old falsehoods. Vaksberg was there. Vaksberg lived it. And now the man will not settle for anything less than the truth.

Finally, I myself have changed. *Double Lives* is a work of history, but I am not a professional historian. I am a novelist, and I hope that fact shines through here. I wrote *Double Lives* in the grip of a story—I see it as a war story, a great war story—that I quickly understood *had* to be told in strict obedience to factual accuracy. I also soon saw that to write about this war, I would have to join it. I *had* to take sides. I would have suffocated behind the dreary mask of "objectivity."

And yet a life spent fighting in that war—my voice ringing changes in the endless yammering of the *Kulturkampf*—is close to my idea of a life spent in hell. This version of *Double Lives* is cluttered with much less opinion than the first. I am still partisan of course, and I hope—I know—it shows. To be a human being is to think morally, and this is a moral drama. Yet this is not merely a story about opinion and opinion making. It is a *tragedy* about opinion and opinion making.

When I was an undergraduate, my old teacher, the late Alfred Kazin, used to sit an the end of a long table at the City College in New York and expectorate the word "opinion" with a sneer of contempt that sang in my nineteen-year-old brain with a force that has lasted a lifetime. "Opinion," Kazin used to snap, "is *cheap*"— especially after one of us happened to venture one that Alfred found particularly cheap. Yet Kazin himself was a mightily opinionated man, and his point was not that we shouldn't *have* opinions. He wanted us to avoid mistaking them for *serious* thinking. He warned us against trusting opinions as a guide for anything that *mattered*.

Well, Alfred, I finally take your point. Maybe I had to slog through the full foul swamp of totalitarian propaganda to earn the disdain for opinion I first heard on your lips so long ago. These days, I can spit out the word with a contempt almost equal to your own. I still have plenty of opinions, of course. But I am struck by how little they matter in the real business of thinking and living. Maybe even the real business of *political* thinking and living.

As the opinion-*meister*, Willi Münzenberg made his way south through the valley of the Isère in 1940, trying to escape a falling France, how much did opinion—*any* opinion—guide him? In 1952, as Otto Katz stood clutching the rail of the prisoner's dock of a court in Prague, trying to shape his plea for death through his smashed dentures, did some opinion serve him in his abjection? As Maxim Gorky lay dying in his palace in the Crimea, cynically watched over by the lovely liar who claimed to love him, did the murmur of opinion comfort him? These three men had lived on opinion. They knew better than anyone what a dangerous drug opinion really is, what a cheap substitute for insight—or for goodness, or for action, or for truth—it can be. It is an exhilarating, addictive toxic substance, and they had trafficked in it all their lives. The dark dance of their futility—I see it now—is no small part of what this story has been struggling to tell me since the day I began to write it. If *Double Lives* strikes you as another face-off in the culture wars, if it leaves you with nothing but some new opinions—or old ones confirmed—I have failed. I want to leave you with something very different than an opinion. I want to leave you with a shiver of pity and terror.

Yes, I have my opinions, and to hell with them. Never trust the teller. Trust the tale.

Stephen Koch

Again, ye have heard that it hath been said by them of old time, Thou shalt not forswear thyself, but shalt perform unto the Lord thine oaths:

But I say unto you, Swear not at all; neither by heaven, for it is God's throne:

Nor by the earth; for it is his footstool: Neither by Jerusalem; for it is the city of the great King.

Neither shall thou swear by thine head, because thou canst not make one hair white or black.

But let your communication be, Yea, Yea; Nay, nay: for whatsoever is more than these cometh of evil.

—MATTHEW 5:33–37

As cited by Arthur Koestler at the opening session
of the Congress for Cultural Freedom, June 25, 1950

Chapter 1

LYING FOR THE TRUTH

On October 22, 1940, not far from a tiny French hamlet near Grenoble called Montagne, two hunters out with their dogs stumbled across something gruesome hidden in a small stand of woods. At the foot of a fine old oak sat, upright, the decomposing body of a man. The man had been dead for a long time, and he appeared to have been hanged.

What the hunters found that day would become more than a legend of their town; it would take its place among the enduring mysteries of modern politics. For this was the body of a man named Willi Münzenberg, and Willi Münzenberg had lived and died as one of the unseen powers of twentieth-century Europe. When the hunters found it, his corpse was almost entirely covered with fallen leaves. Only the vile face and the popped stare of strangulation were visible—that and the noose. The reek was awful; the body had plainly been there for months. The knotted cord around its neck seemed to have snapped, probably quite soon after he had been hanged, and when it broke, the body had apparently dropped to the base of the tree. There it had stayed, knees up, all through that summer of the French defeat, sitting oddly undetected until October began to cover it with the drift of autumn and the hunters' dogs, yelping and whining, discovered the thing.

The French villagers knew nothing about Willi Münzenberg. Münzenberg was and is not a famous name, though this man's power had given him a potent grip on the workings of fame. Since his radical youth in 1917, Münzenberg had been a largely covert but major actor in the politics of the twentieth century. As a founding organizer of the Communist International and a leader in the structure of Marxist-Leninist power outside Russia, Münzenberg had played an especially influential part in the conspiracies, the maneuvers, the propaganda, the secret policies and the public spins on opinion that had led to this very spot: here to the fall of France; here to Hitler's war on the West; here to these woods, and this death.

October 1940 came in the bitter first autumn following the French debacle at the hands of the Nazi *Wehrmacht*. France was huddled in the morose stillness of defeat. The nation's downfall seemed complete; for the moment, the war had finished its vicious business in France and moved on.

For the dictators, all was going well. Stalin had consolidated his alliance with Hitler. After years of secret contacts made behind a smokescreen of co-opted antifascism—a smokescreen significantly created by Willi himself—the two totalitarian secret services were working in a sinister collaboration that was defined by their gangster enmity, bound tight in a brotherhood of loathing. Poland had been successfully partitioned between the two; Finland was in Stalin's hands. The Nazis were driving west, and the war in all its horror was focused on England.

For this was also the autumn of the Battle of Britain. All through the months since France had fallen, the *Luftwaffe* had been carpet-bombing the cities of England. Every night the London sky was lit with tracers and fire; the air was filled with the shattering scream of bombs and the pounding of anti-aircraft defense. The prospect of an English defeat was imminent and real.

But in that French valley of the Isère River, the only gunfire being heard was the occasional muted crack of a hunter's shotgun kicking its echo across the lovely wooded countryside. And through that countryside the two men from Montagne now rushed back into town, along with their dogs, to alert the gendarmerie to what they had found.

Almost certainly, Willi Münzenberg had died in those woods five months before, on June 21, 1940. Whether he died by suicide or murder is not clear. June 21, 1940, however, was the day that the French government fell to the Nazis, and as we shall see, much rests on this exact coincidence of one man's death with the nation's fall. In those days of the French collapse, the countryside around Montagne had been filled with exiles and refugees streaming southward. Everyone was in flight. Yet Willi Münzenberg's flight differed from most. For one thing, it was being tracked by the secret services of at least three nations. It seems that even in those worst of times, certain important players were exceptionally interested in whether this one man, running, left France alive.[1]

***

Why, in a collapsing world, would several governments have been so interested in this middle-aged man from Germany? Who was Willi Münzenberg?

He was a major German communist, but he was more. Since around 1921, Lenin had empowered Münzenberg in a series of tasks, some very public, some very secret, that left this dynamic man the *de facto* director of the Soviet Union's covertly directed propaganda operations in the West.

The field of covertly directed propaganda operations is an area in the world of secret services which until now has rarely been mapped, and the role of such operations in both the cultural politics of modern life has rarely been understood. In the twenty-first century, we live in a world all-too-obviously influenced by carefully networked power-conferences, by ideologically directed think tanks, by relentless "spinmeisters" stirring the press-pool, by culture warriors and celebrity pundits of both left and right, all driven by a perpetual lunge for the jugular, all struggling to seize ideological control of what used to be called public opinion and is now called "the discourse." Whatever their hidden or overt ideological agenda, the modern managers of "spin" stand, like it or not, in uneasy indebtedness to Münzenberg. He is one of the founding geniuses of their trade.

If we follow Münzenberg from Lenin's side to the forest where he died, his path will serve as an Ariadne's thread through much in twentieth-century politics. The byways of his career link the most secret operations of revolutionary politics to central cultural events of the century. We will see the Kremlin tied to Bloomsbury; we will watch the effects of his operations move from the Elysée to Hollywood and back to the Left Bank; from the life of Ernest Hemingway in Spain to André Gide speaking at the state funeral of Maxim Gorky. It is a thread that snakes through many mysteries, and across many encounters with betrayal, terror, and murder, not least of which is the possible murder of Münzenberg himself. It leads to the primal encounter between Hitler and Stalin. It leads to the Second World War. It leads to the founding events of the Cold War.

Münzenberg was a companion of Lenin during their pre-revolutionary days in Switzerland, and he was an important personality in the original Bolshevik circle. In 1915, Lenin was cooling his heels in Bern, fretful and furious as he waited for War to become Revolution. Münzenberg was then a young German radical, unaffiliated except through his talents and his rage. In 1914 he had met Leon Trotsky, and Trotsky, taking his measure, decided to bring him to Lenin himself.

What Trotsky had spotted in the cocky 26-year-old German hothead was a talent for secret work. Münzenberg was presented to the future dictator as a wunderkind, a kid with a knack, like a computer whiz of a later age. Beginning in his teens, Willi had been promiscuously supplying all kinds of revolutionary groups with freelance clandestine networks: undercover systems for transmitting information, laundering money, forging passports, and beaming people across heavily guarded borders as if by magic. It seemed the boy could spin a network out of nothing. When Lenin met him, Willi's information was already speeding around Europe totally undetected: Conspiracies traveled in jam jars and cigar boxes; forged papers arrived in food parcels; plans for covert action stayed concealed, but moved. Münzenberg even had managed, quite on his own, to place an operative inside the Vatican. Trotsky understood that here was a young radical Lenin could *use*.[2]

Lenin was duly impressed and introduced his discovery to Karl Radek, his answer-man for the bourgeois press. Münzenberg and Radek became a kind of team. Karl Radek was an exceptionally talkative and calculating Polish radical and literary intellectual, destined to become the Revolution's slickest rationalizer. He was brilliant and glib, the cynically amused protégé of another Pole, Count Felix Dzerzhinsky, that man without humor whom infamy will forever remember as the inventor of the police state.[3]

Among Lenin's men, the bond that held Dzerzhinsky, Radek, and Stalin together is an affiliation of great interest. Taken in their ensemble, they represent three of the essential strands that bind the knot of the terror state. Dzerzhinsky was the true believer, the sanctified fanatic of absolute state power. Stalin on the other hand was its ultimate politician, its grand tactician and bureaucrat. Radek was the new state's propagandist and apologist, the creator of its intellectual rationale, the man who fabricated its "human face," and much of its lie.

Dzerzhinsky was the founder of the Cheka, later to be renamed the OGPU, then the NKVD, then the KGB, the man who made the secret police the prime instrument of revolutionary justice. It is therefore especially fitting that in the great days of August 1991, the liberation from Marxism-Leninism in Russia should have been celebrated by the crowd tearing down the monumental statue to this monster of sanctimony where it stood in front of KGB headquarters.

Count Felix was an ideologist of hatred and as such he is easy to hate. The difficult thing, and the more troubling thing, is to imagine how he was able to marshal so very much commitment and love. For Dzerzhinsky was far from being a mere brute; he was not an empty monster. He was a man whose passion, self-sacrifice, and faith won to the Revolution the allegiance of people driven by what were surely among the highest moral aspirations of their time. For

7

the young Whittaker Chambers, as for the young Isaac Babel, Felix Dzerzhinsky was a visionary, a being who was bringing real justice to the real world, empowering life's highest ideals.[4] In the glory days of the Revolution, when Dzerzhinsky and Lenin were laying the foundations of the totalitarian police state, life in the Cheka seemed invested with the prestige of a righteous elect, both at home and abroad. Abroad, what was "secret work" but the business of the ultimate liberation of humanity? And at home, who were agents of the Cheka but the Revolution's avenging angels? Indeed, in the days of its innocence, before it became so very obviously the province of murderers and thugs, the revolutionary secret police looked like the natural habitat of the new clerisy, a puritan high priesthood, devout in its atheism. Here were the avengers of all the ancient evils; here were the enforcers of new heaven, new earth. Isaac Babel, the gentle ironist who himself perished in the Terror, began his career as a revolutionary by serving in the Cheka. One of the NKVD agents most useful in running the Cambridge spies was a lapsed priest, a man with a tortured but plainly superior moral nature: the great Hungarian secret agent, Theodore Maly.[5] Diana Trilling reports that she and Lionel Trilling were married by a rabbi for whom Felix Dzerzhinsky represented (with only a touch of irony) a heroic paragon.[6] No leader of the Revolution, not even Lenin himself, was more perfumed with the odor of sanctity than this sardonic and self-exalted Polish aristocrat, a Savonarola who reached his apotheosis in that totalitarian power of which he was a prime inventor.[7] Ascetic, ravaged by revolution, bleak in his unforgiving certainties, radiant with hatred, Dzerzhinsky was Saint Terror.

Dzerzhinsky's protégé Radek, on the other hand, was the jeering cynic of the revolution's rationale. Just as Dzerzhinsky thought any death was justified if it served the Revolution, so Radek thought that any lie was vindicated in the glow of its truth. The union between them is only apparently improbable. Dzerzhinsky's sanctity and Radek's cynicism combined in a fusion of belief and disbelief, faith and scorn, bound together from their earliest days in Warsaw. It is one of the exemplary moral alliances of our era. Meanwhile, outside Russia, in the West, the jovial dynamo who organized that alliance and made it into a new system of power, lying for the truth, was Willi Münzenberg.

Münzenberg was unusual within the senior ranks of German communism in having actually sprung from the working class. Very few of the leading lights of German communism were the tough proletarians of the Berlin slums who made up the Party's mass base. Most of the real leaders were intellectuals, daughters and sons of the upper-middle class. But Willi was the real thing: the son of an alcoholic tavern-keeper in Thuringia, who while the boy was still young had killed himself one day cleaning his gun while drunk. In his teens, Willi survived as a barber's apprentice. It is possible that the genuine deprivations of his youth partly explain why Willi, unlike his more privileged peers, never affected the look of poverty once real power came his way. On the contrary: He swept up and down the Kurfürstendamm in an enormous chauffeur-driven Lincoln limousine; he moved through the halls of power protected by a bodyguard. Like a captain of industry or a Chicago gangster, his own barber shaved and manicured him every day. He lived in an upper-class neighborhood of Berlin. His apartment was filled with Biedermeier; his entire manner of life was undimmed by the usual dour communist style.

Yet despite his elegant surroundings, he was a real communist, and a tough one at that. Willi's youthful photographs show a hard but well-dressed young German with a tight compact body about to spring, light on his feet, solid with energy. His head is large for his small body, and squarish; his forehead is high and impressive, crested with short tousled hair. His eyes, though warm, are shrewd. They assess the camera with a sly lethal glint. The line of his mouth could easily turn cruel; his smile seems granted only very conditionally. There is more than a little of the German tough guy about him. Safely behind closed doors, he moved with all the abrupt habits of command, rapping out his orders like a drill sergeant, foul-mouthed and ungrateful, striking the table with stubby strong workman's hands. Commanding, he was obeyed. He was simultaneously a born executive and a born agitator, and he remained both even after Lenin had made him the "red tycoon," wearing tailored suits and riding in that limousine. Arthur Koestler, who knew him well, called him "a fiery, demagogical, and irresistible public speaker." His voice rang to the rafters of the meeting halls of the Weimar Republic. He brought crowds shouting to their feet. He had the incendiary gift. Koestler reports that "he gave the impression that bumping against him would be like colliding with a steam roller.... Willi sauntered into a room with the casualness of a tank bursting through a wall.... His person emanated such authority that I have seen socialist cabinet members, hard-boiled bankers, and Austrian Dukes behave like schoolboys in his presence."[8]

Münzenberg was "married," although in the Bohemian style of radicals between the wars, there never had been a wedding ceremony. His wife was a beautiful woman named Babette Gross, fine-boned, very tall, willowy. She was an intensely intelligent aristocratic Prussian; her father had been a rich brewer in Potsdam. She was highly educated; easily and fluently multilingual, as was her sister, Margarete Buber-Neumann who, after a first marriage to a son of the philosopher Martin Buber, was married a second time to a prominent German communist: Heinz Neumann, a revolutionary intellectual in the upper reaches of the German Party.

Though a fierce radical and committed communist, Babette was very much an upper-class girl. In youth as in age, the habits of her class must have merged with her politics and her style. To Willi, she must have looked not only beautiful, but like the key to a world. Even when I knew Babette Gross, in her great age, the marks of that Prussian father were still stamped on her. She assumed authority in a way that was surely parallel to the way Willi had seized it. They were a pair as man and woman; they must also have been a pair in their feeling for power.

In fact, much in German communism during its grand epoch between the two wars can be traced to a few intensely intellectual, often academic, families of the upper-middle class, people who belonged more to the world of Thomas Mann and his famous brood than Brecht's back streets. One thinks not only of Babette and her distinguished sister, but of two brilliant academic clans, the Eislers and the Kuczynskis, both family friends of the Manns, both filled with radical intellectuals who became spies, agents of influence, and covert operators in both the Second World War and the Cold War: Hanns and Gerhart Eisler, and their sister Ruth Fischer; Jürgen and Ruth Kuczynski, guided by their father, Robert René Kuczynski.[9] Robert René was closely associated with Willi all through the Weimar years and remained a virtual "Münzenberg man" even after Hitler scattered the German left, and Robert René became an influential refugee teaching at the London School of Economics, serving the Revolution covered by the duplicities of Münzenberg's more-or-less legal wing. Kuczynski's children Jürgen and Ruth walked deeper into the shadow zone around Willi; both took the step into true espionage. During the war Jürgen served as a penetration agent inside the OSS, betraying the Americans. Ruth was trained as a spy in Russia, at a school for covert action founded hand in glove with Willi by the Comintern secret service. She worked in espionage first in China, under cover of Willi's illegal operations there, and later, during the war, in England, later famous under her code name "Sonia," spying against the British, hovering around Bletchley Park.[10] Here were people who instinctively understood the war of ideas in that adversary culture to which Münzenberg came as a stranger, but which he learned to manage and master as few people ever have.

When I met her in 1989, Babette Gross was 91 years old and still willowy. Like her sister, she had long since become a lucid and committed anti-communist. Yet her intelligence was still held in the grip of the tremendous events she had lived through. That July, after long consideration, Gross decided to grant me a full week of interviews in her small apartment on the Einsteinstrasse of Munich. I would arrive every day with my tape recorder, and she would guide me through the history of the century as seen from the perspective of her place beside Münzenberg. It was strange to hear her speak of Lenin as a living man: "Münzenberg was always very impressed with Lenin's *political* skill. You know, Lenin never forgot a name." Of Trotsky, whom I gathered she'd known in Mexico: "He always behaved *exactly* like a classical French man-of-letters." Though always very direct and plain, she would sometimes brush near the grand manner: for example, she twice spoke of "my sister, Buber-Neumann."[11]

With Willi, she had known not only most of the senior people in the German Party, but also many of the founding personalities in its secret service apparatus. Among these were Ignace Reiss, the great espionage master who in certain ways founded Soviet secret work in Europe. When I asked her about Richard Sorge, the no less extraordinary German spy who, under cover as a Nazi, penetrated the Japanese high command until his betrayal in the last days of the war, Babette gave me a long look, then a smile. "I knew him," she said gently, "when he was young and beautiful."

She spoke relaxed, idiomatic, excellent English, remarkable in a woman who (at least so far as I can determine) had never lived in an English-speaking country. She was utterly alert, and her self-possession was at once aristocratic and easy. In her many hours of talk with me, her conversation was always exact and searching; her style of political analysis, whether about events unfolding that July in Germany or conspiracies half a century old, was relentless and incisive. No detail escaped her interest. She tolerated no nonsense, and no deviation from the exact truth as she saw it. Listening to Gross talk about current European politics reminded me that this woman had shared a life with a man whose own political briefings, after he broke with Stalin in 1938, used to be held in a private dining room in Paris while senior agents of the intelligence services of several countries gathered round to listen like so many sophomores.[12]

When I knew her in July of 1989, Babette did not have long to live. In the fall and winter of 1989, she was watching the collapse of German communism as it accelerated and burst past every effort to hold it back. In her phone calls with me during this period, she retained her customary comprehensive attention to the inner workings of the scene. Her entire life had been lived either with or against the events now coming to their tremendous conclusion; she had lived at or near the center of the greatest political drama of her century. Now that drama was moving toward its end. As was her life. She became ill, and ill she went to Berlin for treatment. And so she was in the city of her youth as everything came full circle. Babette Gross was in Berlin as the Wall came down, and having seen the last fall, there she died in January 1990.

Karl Radek seems to have been Münzenberg's patron in Lenin's inner circle and was the means of his rise, though at the ripe age of 30 Radek wasn't all that much Münzenberg's senior. Before the Revolution, Radek's position among Lenin's men was rather like that of a press agent. In fact, when he was in favor and before Stalin had him killed, he served—to use the jargon of a later era—as chief *spinmeister* for the Regime. The Bolsheviks were newspaper addicts, every one of them. It was one of their most characteristic obsessions. The sealed train that carried Lenin to the Finland Station was stacked to the ceiling with every paper in every language. The revolutionary passengers behind the drawn curtains of the cars passed the rocking hours reading every report. Radek's great gift was that of a press agent, albeit a remarkably cynical and conspiratorial one. He was in his element inventing the right news angle; planting the right story at the right time; heading off this or that opponent with this or that burst of bad news. Chewing on his pipe-stem, sneering at the journalists he conned and flattered, the youth was already an adept in the uses of information and disinformation. Radek and Münzenberg together escorted Lenin to the crowded platform in Zurich and the train into which the Bolsheviks were sealed ("like a bacillus in a tube," as Churchill said) for their trip north through Germany, en route to their revolution. Radek was placed in the compartment beside the future dictator, while Münzenberg stayed behind, apparently because of a problem over his German nationality. Just before the train pulled out, it was to Münzenberg that either Radek or Lenin himself turned and shrugged off the famous line: "Six months from now we either will be in power or hanging from the gallows."[13] So it was. After Lenin captured the Revolution, he was able to make his protégés two of the most powerful people in the world.

Münzenberg found himself in power. He was a man of action who was deprived of life when deprived of the resources of command. Unlike his allies Radek, Bukharin, and of course Lenin himself, he was in no way an intellectual. He had none of an intellectual's feeling for how to mine isolation, how to make even powerlessness a kind of opportunity. He was also a provincial. Though he orchestrated the voice of the International, he never spoke anything but his native German, and it was rather rough German at that, with a thick country accent from Thuringia. He had no particular literary skills. Hundreds of books were written to order for him, some memorable, and some even of lasting importance. He himself could barely bang together a more or less four-square paragraph. Virtually everything published under his own name was ghost-written.[14]

The type of personality required to organize life in the shadowland of secret services is less that of the buccaneer than the executive. So it was with William Donovan of the OSS; so it was with Sir William Stephenson, Churchill's "Intrepid." So it was with Münzenberg. The Central Party Archives show conclusively that Willi's front organizations and networks of fellow travelers and propagandists were thoroughly intertwined with the secret services of the Comintern, and with the Soviet's other covert agencies as well.[15] But Willi was not the man in the trench coat; that he left to others, people who reported to him, or to his men. Still less was he some shuffling bureaucrat from le Carré. He thought like a tycoon. Had he not been a revolutionary, he would have made a brilliant self-made millionaire, and communist though he was, many of his enterprises made large amounts of money. His saluting staff, his Biedermeier, his hovering barber and his limousine, all make one think less of le Carré's Karla than of Henry Luce.

Here is Gustav Regler's picture of Willi once he had fled from Nazi Germany and taken charge of the Soviet propaganda response to Hitler's seizure of power: "He now passed his days in a small room at the back of a house on the Boulevard Montparnasse, seated at a desk piled high with papers.... The telephone was scarcely more than a token of his isolation. When it rang his secretary would dash in and answer it while Münzenberg waited impatiently and finally solved the problem with a single sentence. He had the calm and intensity of a chess master walking from board to board, playing twenty games at once."[16]

Both before Hitler and after, Münzenberg's true role in the world was a closely guarded secret, though in keeping with his particular talent, it was concealed in conspicuousness. His talent was for propaganda, albeit of a special kind. For Willi Münzenberg was the first grand master of two quite new kinds of secret service work, essential to this century, and to the Soviets: the covertly controlled propaganda front, and the secretly manipulated fellow traveler. His goal was to create for the right-thinking non-communist West the dominating political prejudice of the era: the belief that any opinion that happened to serve the foreign policy of the Soviet Union was derived from the most essential elements of human decency. He wanted to instill the feeling, like a truth of nature, that seriously to criticize or challenge Soviet policy was the unfailing mark of a bad, bigoted, and probably stupid person, while support was equally infallible proof of a forward-looking mind committed to all that was best for humanity and marked by an uplifting refinement of sensibility.

Willi's first move in any situation was to capture—to co-opt—liberal opinion for communist ends: his second, was to deny that any such sleight of hand had taken place. To create his networks of fronts and fellow travelers Münzenberg used every resource of propaganda, from highbrow cultural opinion to funny hats and balloons. But his two prime tools were co-option and denial: Co-option of liberal democratic opinion; denial of Communist motives. He organized in all the media: newspapers, film, radio, books, magazines, the theater. Every kind of "opinion maker" was involved: writers, artists, actors, commentators, priests, ministers, professors, "business leaders," scientists, psychologists, anyone at all whose opinion the public was likely to respect.

Münzenberg's own public life was very visible. Before his flight from Germany after the Reichstag Fire in 1933, he was a German publisher, and in fact a big-time publisher, controlling an impressive network of left-wing publications. He was also a politician. As a Leninist he naturally despised representative democracy and intended to destroy it. But he found it useful to serve in the Reichstag, holding down an exceptionally safe seat provided by the Party. The

15

gloomy Sessions Chamber of the Reichstag, the hall where German democracy gathered, was a stuffy place, lined with dry wood paneling and hung with musty brocaded curtains. On February 27, 1933, that wood and brocade would kindle into a bonfire momentous enough to grant Hitler totalitarian power and give shape to the ideological clash that led to the Second World War. But until then, the Reichstag regularly rang with the voice of Münzenberg's radical anger. He flourished there, striding past his rival and secret admirer Goebbels, whitened by glaring flashbulbs, ready to tangle yet again in the checkmated politics of a Weimar Republic that it seemed nobody important had the smallest wish to save. Certainly not Goebbels. And certainly not Münzenberg.

Lastly, Münzenberg was nominally in charge of a communist relief organization known as Workers International Relief, or the WIR. To invoke only a few of the organizations that were its clones, it was also known by its Russian acronym, MRP, the organization had affiliates in every country: in America, it was called the International Labor Defense, or ILD. Closely affiliated with the MRP, and founded as part of the Comintern out of similar motives, was the Red Aid, or to use the acronym of its Russian name, MOPR. This propaganda organization was originally founded to counter early Western alarm arising from stories about the gulag—concentration camps—leaking out of Russia. Reports of Bolshevik forced labor camps where non-communist socialists and were incarcerated and abused were getting out of Russia and being featured in the non-communist left-wing press. This had to be countered: MOPR's job was to distract press attention, by accusing the accusers, deflecting attention onto various kinds of "political prisoners," some real, some mere figments of propagandistic imagination, in capitalist countries.[17] Though it became rivalrous with his apparatus, the Red Aid worked closely with Münzenberg in the propaganda campaign of 1933 and 1934, defending Georgi Dimitrov against the Nazi charge that he had led a communist conspiracy to burn the Reichstag. Earlier, MOPR had been active in the Sacco-Vanzetti propaganda campaign. The grandees of power in Europe did not take WIR very seriously. Münzenberg's organization could so easily be portrayed as a merely idealistic, or at least unexceptionable, institution, a sort of Red Cross for the Revolution, sponsoring good deeds for the hard left: cultural events to awaken the world's conscience; fundraisers for the persecuted; mobile soup kitchens for strikers in bleak factory yards.

Soup kitchens were the least of it.

Willi Münzenberg's true, and secret, job in the political world, the job insiders *did* take seriously, was to manage the unseen ties between this propaganda and great power.

His heyday lasted for a little less than fifteen years, from the 1921 Volga Famine in Russia and the Sacco-Vanzetti case in America to the Spanish Civil War. During that time, he was amazingly successful at co-opting and mobilizing the intelligentsia of the West on behalf of a moralistic set of political attitudes responsive to Soviet needs. In the process, he organized and defined the "enlightened" moral agenda of his era. In a sense, Münzenberg's apparatus was as instrumental as any other single factor in giving direction to the political attitudes we now call The Thirties. Hundreds of groups and committees and publications operated under his auspices, or those of his agents. The writers, artists, journalists, scientists, educators, clerics, columnists, film-makers, and publishers, either under his influence or regularly manipulated by his "Münzenberg men," present a startling list of notables from that era, from Ernest Hemingway to John Dos Passos to Lillian Hellman to Georg Grosz to Erwin Piscator to André Malraux to André Gide to Bertolt Brecht to Dorothy Parker ... to Kim Philby and Laurence Duggan, Guy Burgess and Alger Hiss, and Anthony Blunt and Whittaker Chambers. Indeed, the entire cultural and intellectual apparatus of "idealistic" Stalinism outside Russia, and much of its secret *apparat,* operated within a system Münzenberg had guided into place.

Within the apparat, Willi's people were known as *"die Münzenberg menschen"*—the "Münzenberg men." We are used to thinking of Soviet agents as spies and agents of influence. And so were the "Münzenberg men" occasionally also spies and agents of influence. But it is important to understand that they were first and foremost professional propaganda agents, the secret agents of opinion.

17

To organize such people, Münzenberg's senior associates in Berlin and Paris maintained networks of agents working with creative artists, with actors and the film world, with writers and journalists. "Münzenberg men" of every nationality were at work around the world.[18] Many shadowy figures in what I call "the secret world"—the realm of covert government operations—can be traced to their ranks. Consider an American: Harold Ware. In the fifties, "Hal" Ware was posthumously dragged into his fifteen minutes of fame when Whittaker Chambers revealed the work in Soviet espionage of a sometime State Department official named Alger Hiss, and in the process set off a furious sequence of charges and counter-charges that lasted half a century. Back in the twenties, Ware had been a young American radical when Lenin put Münzenberg in charge of the international propaganda relief for the disaster of the Volga Famine of 1922. Determined to help save the socialist motherland, "Hal" Ware "hand-picked nine husky 'sod-busters,' lefties from the North Dakota steppe, whom he took to Russia, along with 'twenty carloads of the latest type American farm machinery, a supply of Canadian rye seed, two passenger automobiles, tents and equipment.'" Sam Tanenhaus, Chambers' biographer, evokes Ware as "a socialist Lawrence of Arabia," leading "this caravan into the rugged country near Perm."[19]

If "Hal" Ware supplied Perm with the North Dakota "sod-busters," it was Willi who supplied those twenty carloads of machinery. Ware was working for WIR; he was soon Willi's favorite American, commended by Lenin himself. And when he returned to America, it was as a "Münzenberg-man" that young "Hal" went to Washington, got himself a job in the Department of Agriculture, and embarked on a career in espionage, using a "study group" of covert Washington communists to shape the apparatus that Chambers eventually exposed.

Or consider a Spanish "Münzenberg-man," Julio Alvarez del Vayo. For decades, historians of the Spanish Civil War have debated precisely what inks bound this notorious Stalinist to the *apparat*. Whatever the links were, they were well concealed, and they were important: during the Spanish Civil War, Del Vayo twice served as the Republics foreign minister. Once the Spanish War had been lost, Del Vayo found refuge in New York, where he became "foreign editor" of the _Nation_—and a ubiquitous player in Soviet propaganda operations in America. Del Vayo's actions and opinions were invariably indistinguishable from those of a Soviet agent. Yet Del Vayo always insisted that he was no communist but a "socialist," claiming, _ad nauseam_, that his tireless service to Stalin resulted from nothing more than the sweet coincidence of his sincere unforced agreement with the dictator's views.

I myself know of no "smoking gun" that indisputably proves that this tiresome evasion is false. Yet a small arsenal of "smoking guns" proves that Del Vayo's closest associates were "Münzenberg-men." All through the Spanish War, Münzenberg's prime lieutenant, Otto Katz, stood at Del Vayo's right hand. Later, in New York, Del Vayo worked in various covertly directed pro-Soviet propaganda ventures with a former French Government official and active agent of Soviet influence and espionage, Pierre Cot. Cot had entered the _apparat_ through Münzenberg's enterprises in the early thirties. In New York, as earlier in France, his ranking associate in covert political work was a major "Münzenberg-man" named Louis Dolivet. It is therefore not surprising to discover Babette Gross revealing that, beginning in the 1920s, when he was still an obscure reporter for a Latin American newspaper, Del Vayo was already working with Münzenberg in Berlin. By 1934, Del Vayo invited Münzenberg to Spain, where he became Willi's guide on the ground to the rapidly changing political situation in that country and his prime contact among its new class of politicians. Two years later, Del Vayo was the Spanish foreign minister, and Otto Katz was always at his side. The Comintern was a major player in the Spanish tragedy, and Willi was coordinating its work. Coincidence?

Of course most of the fellow travelers who were manipulated by the "Münzenberg-men," and certainly most of the people who poured their idealism into the Münzenberg fronts, had no certain proof that their consciences were being orchestrated by operatives of Stalin's government. Most were true believers, people with no secret agenda but with dewy moral dreams about a radical new Soviet-led, socialist "humanism." With a light sneer, Münzenberg referred to this vast soft horde of the radical devout as "innocents." His own phrase for the fronts he created to guide and direct their earnest but politically naive commitments was "Innocents' Clubs."[20] The phrase is revealing. On the one hand, it points to all those thousands who were not, in the jargon of the secret trades, "witting." This was virtually everyone. In any covertly run front organization the number of people who know, *really* know, the agenda, and the true identity of its shapers, must be very, very few. The fewer the better.

But the word "innocence" also suggests a motive. I refer to the need for righteousness, righteousness in the Biblical sense. The thirst for moral justification for one's life in the world is one of the deepest needs we have, one of our most powerful and essentially human drives, ignored at our cost and peril. In his "Innocents' Clubs," Münzenberg provided two generations of people on the left with what we might call the forum of righteousness. More perhaps than any other person of his era, he developed what may well be the leading moral illusion of the twentieth century: the notion that in the modern age the principal arena of the moral life, the true realm of good and evil, is politics. Willi was the unseen organizer of that variety of politics, indispensable to the adversary culture, which we might call Righteousness Politics. "Innocents' Clubs": The very phrase suggests how the political issues Münzenberg manipulated came for many to serve as a substitute for religious belief. He offered everyone, anyone, a role in the search for justice in our century. By defining what was guilty in society, Willi offered "innocence" to anyone who "opposed" it. People hungering for righteousness seized upon the new illusion by the millions.

Their innocence was of course naïve. In sufficiently skilful hands, their faith could easily be put into the service of profoundly sinister events. Münzenberg served Stalinism with every known resource of propaganda, always inventing more, from the protest march to the mock-trial to the politicized writers' congress to the politicized arts festival to the celebrity letterhead to the ad hoc committee for causes numberless. As Koestler said, Münzenberg "produced

Committees as a conjurer produces rabbits out of his hat."[21] And his models for molding progressive opinion endured, outlasting him, running on their own moral momentum. Plainly, a phenomenon such as the Bertrand Russell War Crimes Tribunal, held in Stockholm during the Vietnam War, was set up in conscious or unconscious emulation of Münzenberg's paradigm. In fact, much of the Peace Movement of the Vietnam Era, with its marches and interlocking committees, worked in the same way. Early in this century, Willi had uncovered the tremendous power available to those who know how to set the agenda of the Good. But he also knew, as his fate demonstrates, that this is a form of power that can be used for evil ends.

The instrument through which Münzenberg organized this cultural power was the Communist International, or as it was almost always known, the Comintern. The Comintern was in many ways the quintessential Leninist institution, shaped from its inception by the two leading passions of Lenin's political personality: his obsession with secrecy, and his preoccupation with absolute power. Its aims were never even remotely democratic, never even remotely meliorist, and never were intended to provide any real assistance, however minute, to any branch of the left not entirely under Soviet control.

Lenin created the Comintern in 1919 as a means of spreading the Russian Revolution and of consolidating Marxism-Leninism's dominance over the worldwide left. The new dictator's purpose was to gather the world's radicals into one grand network of communist parties under the control of *the* Revolution, *his* Revolution. In his fantasy, Lenin saw the Comintern laying a kind of long fuse that would snake from Russia into Europe, and above all to that grand, glorious, but unexploded bomb that weighed most on his mind: Germany. *The powder keg of Europe:* It was one of Lenin's favorite clichés. *Iskra,* so one of the most important early revolutionary journals was named: "The Spark." Lenin proposed to make the keg blow with a spark set by him and sent sizzling through the Comintern's invisible incendiary network, a vitalizing fire that would burn from his office straight in to the great German ammunition dump. Luckily for the Europe of the twenties, the fuse fizzled. Even so, the Comintern's network had been well and truly laid down, and by the time Stalin came along it was still in place, ready for the new dictator to use. Europe, meanwhile, had run out of luck.[22]

So the "First Congress" of the Comintern in 1919 was a meeting supposed to initiate the transformation of the world. Despite this ambitious aim, it was not a very impressive convocation. It was neither representative nor particularly international. Lenin slouched on the podium of a crowded little hall near the Moscow Courts of Justice and presided over thirty-five scrappy "delegates"—mainly foreign socialists who happened to be in town. Few had any real connection to their national politics. One English "delegate" was merely Cicherin's secretary, a Russian émigré who'd once been a tailor in England. The Japanese were "represented" by a man with the un-Nipponese name of Rutgers, who'd chanced once to spend some months in Japan. At one point Lenin slipped a note to Angelica Balabanoff ordering her to take the platform and "announce the affiliation of the Italian Socialist Party." She stared back. There was no such group in the room, nor had she been in contact with them. "There was," wrote one English witness, "a make-believe side to the whole affair."

The Congress was make-believe because Lenin did not want it otherwise. On the contrary. The last thing he wanted would have been some dreary posse of international socialists weakening his grip with the babble of their little ideas, their niggling opinions, their trifling—a favorite word, "trifling"—reservations. The "congress" was a facade, held to give the look of a broad base for what Lenin always intended to be a compact, secret, strictly obedient weapon under the control of his government. Once the browbeaten delegates dispersed, he simply dashed off an article in *Pravda* blandly announcing that "the Soviets have conquered throughout the whole world."[23]

That was the imaginary Comintern. The real Comintern was a corps of disciplined professional revolutionaries, put in place to enforce Leninist hegemony throughout the socialist movement worldwide. To this end it ran its own propaganda network and had its own secret service, with both branches intimately linked to one another and to the other Soviet secret services. Their work was at once legal and illegal, and in Münzenberg's case, the two often mingled in special ingenuity. The Comintern's secret service was known as the OMS, and Münzenberg worked in steady collaboration with it; the Central Party Archives show Münzenberg's enterprises intermingled and surrounded by elaborate secret service work. Münzenberg worked in close collaboration with the director of the OMS, V.A. Mirov-Abramov. In addition, substantial evidence strongly indicates that his principal lieutenants were covertly linked to branches of the Soviet services outside the Comintern. One of Münzenberg's tasks was to invent ways to blur the distinction between legal and illegal work and, trailing clouds of deniability, install his men in the resulting never-never land.

While the cultural network had a very public face, it worked in tandem with deep-cover espionage networks. The evidence is strong that two of Münzenberg's principal lieutenants, Louis Gibarti and Otto Katz, were not only "Münzenberg-men," and so agents of the Comintern, but (probably without Willi knowing for sure) agents of the NKVD as well.[24] Gibarti and Katz: an extraordinary team. They *did* know something about trench coats, and careful tracking of their artful dodging through the first half of the twentieth century will turn up surprise after surprise. Gibarti was an elegant but slightly seedy Hungarian, affable, multilingual, and outspoken. He looked, said Babette, like "an opera cavalier." Gibarti ranks as a founding father of the modern mingling of propaganda with espionage and covert action. Though his modus operandi made him seem like a "legal"—in contrast to illegal—Comintern agent, Gibarti's "perfectly legal" organizations were pioneers in the art of doing secret service business in the open. It was probably Gibarti who in 1934 guided a young recruit named Kim Philby through a "perfectly legal" front in Paris and on to Vienna, where Philby took up his first steps as a secret agent.[25]

"Legal" operations, meanwhile, might pursue their propaganda ends while supplying illegal operations with cover. Consider, for example, those honey-hives of the intellectuals, bookstores. In the early days, the Comintern often used bookstores simultaneously as propaganda outlets *and* as fronts for transmitting information for the espionage *apparat*. In Shanghai, Richard Sorge made use of such an establishment within the network; its wonderful name, the "Zeitgeist Bookshop." In New York during the thirties, a then-communist bookseller named Walter Goldwater was approached by Whittaker Chambers, using the name "Hugh Jones," and asked to establish a bookstore near Columbia University, the back room of which was to be used by the apparatus for espionage. Similarly, Münzenberg was a pioneer in the creation of a "Press Agency" which on the one hand might place perfectly legitimate journalism from independent writers and sources in legitimate journals, *and* at the same time place fabricated stories which the *apparat* wanted placed for propaganda, *and* serve as cover for working agents, *and* serve as cover for the flow of information obtained in espionage. Münzenberg's man Gibarti seems to have helped invent this sort of front.[26]

But Münzenberg's information network controlled newspapers and radio stations, ran film companies, created book clubs, ran magazines, sponsored publicity tours, dispatched journalists, and commissioned books. It planted articles and created organizations to give direction to the "innocent." It was a media combine. Yet it differed in a number of ways from the BBC, Time, Inc., or even from an explicit instrument of political propaganda like Radio Liberty. For example, many people working for it did not publicly acknowledge the connection. Many operated under aliases. Many led classic double lives, sometimes totally changing their identities, concealing their true mission from their friends, even their spouses, and certainly from employers, who often included unsuspecting editors, publishers, and producers whose ideas were very remote from the real agenda.[27] The "Münzenberg-men" were, in short, secret agents, people who lived and worked, however publicly, in the secret world: the realm of intelligence gathering, covert action, undercover penetration, clandestine influence, quiet sabotage, discreet blackmail—what the American counter-spy, James Jesus Angleton, quoting T. S. Eliot, called "a wilderness of mirrors." Nor did the work stop with the media. Münzenberg also courted business people who could be used in industrial espionage, both in Europe and the United States. Given Lenin's obsession with electrification, for example, an early target was General Electric.[28] And back when the revolution was still young, it was Münzenberg's task to create for much of this vast unseen enterprise a persuasive public face.

Fulfilling this mission, Münzenberg clearly understood that the Revolution required something more than winning over "the masses." Speaking to a Comintern packed with intellectuals, he pounded at his point: *"We must organize the intellectuals."* The revolution *needed* middle-class opinion makers—artists, journalists, "people of good will," novelists, actors, playwrights ... *humanists,* people whose innocent sensitivities weren't yet cauterized to numbness by the genuine white-hot radical steel. Lenin himself recoiled at this idea. Here were the people he loathed most—he who loathed so many people. The non-communist left? Middle-class do-gooders? Bourgeois intellectuals clutching their precious "freedom of conscience"? Lenin would kill and imprison them by the thousands. It took him a while—until 1921—to consent to use them, too. "We must avoid being a purely communist organization," Münzenberg explained to his men. "We must bring in other names, other groups, to make persecution more difficult." Middle-class opinion makers, liberal sympathizers, however much the Bolsheviks despised them, must be used. Co-option may have struck hard-line Leninists as soft, but as Münzenberg pointed out, the powder keg was not blowing despite all kinds of sparks. However reluctantly, the International would have to resort to *his* weapons: co-option and denial. Leninists protested, while Münzenberg dismissed these impatient purists and the fanaticism of absolutes with sardonic weariness. "I too," he drawled, "prefer the red hundreds."[29]

Lenin came to see what Stalin never doubted: that to achieve its end, the Revolution outside Russia would need to exploit non-communist sympathizers, especially leaders in culture, sympathizers capable of setting the agenda of the Good. Western opinion could never be marshaled strictly from a Bolshevik platform. The world's idealists would never trust a leadership so obviously defined by fanaticism, so plainly committed to pure post-legal *force majeure*, so manifestly bound to hatred. The image of the "human face" needed to be created by "spokesmen" who attracted sympathy, not fear; famous, prestigious, and "independent" spokesmen, the more so the better, who would reassure the non-communist world that despite appearances all was well, Utopia really was a-building; that they had been over to see the future, and the socialist future was sweet and good.

These spokesmen would have to be organized, promoted, and made reliable. It was essential that closely controlled fellow travelers such as Romain Rolland and Henri Barbusse, Lincoln Steffens and Heinrich Mann, be made to believe in their own "independence," an "independence" they would of course rarely if ever exercise. Every resource of manipulation, from rudimentary group psychology to plain bribery, was used to keep these ranks of the famous and influential left safely Stalinist in everything *except* name. As for the name, *that* had to be avoided at all costs. That would destroy the most useful thing about them, which was the deceptive but indispensable look of their "independence."

Managing these "independent spokesmen," keeping them saying the right things to support the cumbersome Big Lie they served—all this could be a very tricky business, and Willi devoted all his ingenuity to it. "[Münzenberg] left nothing to chance," Babette Gross writes, "particularly not the manipulation of fellow travelers."[30] From the tightly interlocked sets of fellow travelers in the Hollywood film colony to the systems of Parisian left-wing cultural chic, he arranged the celebrities into guided and controlled networks, assigning agents to their management, focusing on given communities in the arts, in journalism, in the academy. Here again, non-paranoiac Westerners may have some difficulty grasping that an elaborate secret service network was set up to keep this large number of celebrity sympathizers appearing in the right places and reading the right lines. It is quite true that once a fashionable opinion was properly launched, it would quite spontaneously develop and grow among the ranks of enlightened people. Gibarti is said to have called this ripple effect in cultural politics "rabbit breeding."[31]

Of course, this entire system of co-option and manipulation had to be kept secret and denied. Besides the public charade, there was the deeper matter of managing what we might call the denial within. Every device of vanity and venality, misused trust and intellectual obfuscation was employed. But there was something more. The fellow travelers needed to believe too that their Stalinism was an indispensable part of their integrity, their intelligence, and their independence. They needed to *believe*. In order to co-opt conscientious people into its service, the apparatus had to seize on the most salient moral claims of the adversary culture where they were found. If the American adversary culture rightly saw the oppression of blacks as the society's great institutionalized crime, Stalinism would take the highest of high ground on the "Negro question." No matter that Stalin ruled a country where a significant part of the population languished in what amounted to slave labor camps— where indeed a significant part of the economy was based on the forced labor of millions. If the English adversary culture saw philistinism and middle-class sexual repression as the enemy, Stalinism would embrace iconoclastic taste and sexual liberty as nobody else did; the Bohemianism and flamboyant homosexuality of Guy Burgess were an indispensable part of his slick Stalinism and central to his place in Bloomsbury. No matter that Soviet sexual policy and taste were intolerant to a degree that made Colonel Blimp look liberated.

The net effect of these facades was to bind Stalinism to the self-evident moral views of a given adversary culture, and use that bond to make the local brand of Stalinism feel indispensable to an enlightened life. The role of this in the "denial within" could be very potent. It could be addictive.

But direct management was also required. Agents were often specifically trained to enter the life of this or that "independent thinker"—assuming the independent thinker was famous or influential enough. The idea was to influence, and monitor the fellow traveler's life, and, if possible, run it. With the more important cultural grandees, intimate friends, sexual partners, and even wives could be assigned: political operatives put in place to manipulate the great man in question, while remaining in regular contact with Münzenberg's people.[32]

Many of the "Münzenberg-men" were women. The Russian writer and historian Nina Berberova writes with astringent authority about a cohort of agents or near-agents, the women whom she calls the "Ladies of the Kremlin."[33] These were women who became influential figures in European and American intellectual life partly on their own, but above all through the men in their lives. The men, most often, were famous writers, "spokesmen for the West." Meanwhile, the consorts whom they most trusted were guided by the Soviet services.

Leading this list were two members of the minor Russian aristocracy: the Baroness Moura Budberg, who was mistress to both Maxim Gorky and H. G. Wells, and the Princess Maria Pavlova Koudachova. Moura Budberg's links to the Soviets were shadowy, and remained secret for decades, until they were at last exposed by the Russian historian Arkady Vaksberg in his 1997 book, *The Gorky Secret*. We have more certain knowledge about the Princess Koudachova, who first became secretary, later mistress, wife, and at last widow to the once enormously celebrated pacifist novelist Romain Rolland.

Maria Pavlova Koudachova was an agent directly under Soviet secret service control. There is some questionable evidence to suggest that she was trained and assigned to Rolland's life even before she left Russia after the Revolution. In any case, after Koudachova was permitted to leave Soviet Russia, she sought out the novelist in Switzerland and there began what was her entire life's work: insinuating herself into every corner of his existence and managing it for the *apparat*. It was a remarkably successful effort. The Central Party Archives in Moscow contain innumerable files documenting activities in which Rolland's prominence and wishful principles were exploited, used, and reused, while he danced the dance of "innocence."[34] By the time she married Rolland, the Princess had come to dominate the author's every public move, and she continued to do so until the day he died, whereupon she became the manager of his legend and archives. Throughout, Koudachova worked in close and regular collaboration with, among others, Münzenberg's agents.[35]

Romain Rolland's vanity required that he see himself as possessed of an almost uniquely self-directed and courageous mind. In truth, he was a quite self-infatuated person, easily led and easily frightened. As Koudachova steadily pulled him more and more deeply into his life as a Stalinist apologist, she was in turn supervised by Gibarti, and no doubt many other agents as well. Through all the years of manipulation, Rolland kept himself complacent with half-ignorance, the deniability within. True, by 1932, he clearly understood that Gibarti was a Comintern operative: There exists a letter to Henri Barbusse from Rolland, expressing sudden panic that his own reputation might be sullied by exposure of Gibarti's real role.[36] But could he ever let himself grasp the real role of his own wife? After meeting Maxim Gorky in 1934, Rolland confided to Koudachova how shocked and saddened he was to see Gorky surrounded by political spies in his own household. What the Princess replied is not on record.

That she was a secret service operative, however, and one expressly planted in Rolland's life, cannot be doubted. Babette Gross put it to me plainly in the summer of 1989. "She was an *apparatchik*," she said flatly. "And she ran him."

Berberova proposed a number of other candidates for inclusion among the "Kremlin Ladies": The wives of both Paul Eluard and Ferdinand Leger were among them. Perhaps. Certainly one of the most important was Elsa Triolet, sister of Mayakovsky's great love Lily Brik, who in Louis Aragon found her very own "great poet." With Aragon, Triolet presided over the high chic of European Stalinism for thirty years, knave to Aragon's fool, intimate with the most repellent figures in the Stalinist apparatus.[37] In America one might add Ella Winter to the list, who began her career in politics being introduced by Felix Frankfurter to Lincoln Steffens in the midst of the Versailles Conference. Steffens fell in love with her, and their relation lasted the rest of his life.

Throughout the twenties Winter guided the famous muckraker into the paths of her Stalinism, and by the time of his death, it must be said that Lincoln Steffens had become a creature, an intellectual abject.[38]

After Steffens's death, Winter proceeded to another marriage that was exceptionally useful from the *apparat*'s point of view; this one put her in a leading position managing the networks of Stalinist fellow travelers in Hollywood, a long-standing special concern of the apparatus, with much attention from Gibarti, Katz, and many others. Winter met and married a very successful Hollywood screenwriter, Donald Ogden Stewart—a companion of Ernest Hemingway and John Dos Passos; a runner with the bulls at Pamplona in the company of the circle immortalized in *The Sun Also Rises*.[39] Stalinism and Hemingway aside, Stewart was an attractive but malleable guilt-ridden lightweight, who was wonderfully well connected in Hollywood. At his side, Ella Winter was ideally placed for an active life among networks of Stalinist opinion in the film colony.

Like Koudachova, Ella Winter worked closely with Münzenberg's men, especially those who were active in Hollywood. She knew Otto Katz well, and Gibarti referred to Ella Winter as "one of the most trusted party agents for the West Coast."[40]

***

The Comintern was the apple of Lenin's eye. Stalin, on the other hand, despised the institution, as he despised so many things, and so deeply. To be sure, he used the Comintern apparatus with ruthless virtuosity and raised it to previously unknown heights of activity. Even so he had contempt for its furtive intriguing intellectuals, its internationalist palaver, its big dreams. He took control of it early, and finding its obedience insufficiently abject, he penetrated it from top to bottom with his other services. Eventually he dissolved it. He used to call its Moscow headquarters, in passing, *lavotchka*: the "grocer's hut," "the gyp-joint."[41] Yet he also made it one of the most efficient and pervasive secret institutions in history.

Münzenberg was Stalin's tool. This must be said. A certain kind of revolutionary sentimentality might wish to preserve Münzenberg's memory—first smeared, then all but obliterated by Stalin—for the Leninist paradise lost of the Zimmerwald left and the glory days in Zurich. And much in Münzenberg is very sympathetic, even politically. He may have co-opted the European antifascism that Stalin betrayed, but it *was* antifascism, and he *did* make it a force in the politics of the era. He could also be personally appealing: dynamic, larger than life. Even after they had become passionate anti-communists, Koestler and Regler retained a certain affection for their days with Willi. And it is true that toward the end of his life Münzenberg did, slowly, with the caution of a man dismantling a bomb, try to disengage himself step by meticulous step from the apparatus. He had seen that apparatus turn upon his closest associates and murder them, and he knew perfectly well that eventually it would destroy him too, unless he did something, something very shrewd, to save himself. In Paris during the phony war, he guarded himself using all his skill. Stalin's band of elite assassins, the Bureau of Special Tasks, watched him. The Gestapo watched him. British intelligence, riddled with Soviet agents, watched him. Willi watched them watch, keeping himself covered until June 1940, when things fell apart, and he was fleeing south through France, heading toward the valley of the Isère, and his last day.

Chapter 2

THE PATH TO HITLER:

THE EARLY CAMPAIGNS

W illi was not a Russian. He did not even speak Russian. No matter: In Lenin's entourage the language of the revolution was German. Stalin was rare among the Bolsheviks in not knowing it. As one of the most important non-Russians in Lenin's Zurich entourage, Münzenberg was quite naturally a founding father of the Comintern, and in foreign operations he was so dynamic that by 1921 the Comintern's head, Gregori Zinoviev, had begun to feel threatened. At the Comintern's 1921 Congress, Zinoviev maneuvered Münzenberg out of his main party position of the time, running the Young Communist League. The setback turned out to be a fortunate fall: It left Willi free for his new and great political role as a propagandist.[1]

He found that role in catastrophe.

The Volga Famine

One event above all others at last forced Lenin to assign Münzenberg the task of manipulating opinion in the bourgeois west: the Volga famine of the early twenties.

In 1921 and 1922, a combination of drought, the aftermath of the civil war, and the disasters of agricultural collectivization brought down upon the Soviet Union a famine horrific beyond anything previously known in modern European history. Before the Revolution, Russia had been, time out of mind, one of the principal agricultural exporters on the planet. Under the Soviets, it would never be so again.[2] In 1921, famine descended; around the Volga and in the Tatar Republic, mass starvation proceeded to kill, according to the surely underestimated official toll, not less than two million people. Nicholas Werth, using more modern figures, puts the death toll at more than twice that. "When the famine was at its worst in the summer of 1922, and nearly 30 million people were starving.... Despite the massive international relief effort, at least 5 million of the 29 million Russians affected died of hunger in 1921 and 1922."[3]

In hordes, the starving lined the banks of the Volga, vast numbers of them infected with the typhus that had been all but pandemic in Russia since 1919. They moved toward the river, bowed with Russian patience, or perhaps it was the numb inertia of agony, clustering on the banks by the tens of thousands, "singing and dying," huddled in their masses, waiting for the boats they fondly imagined must *surely* be being sent to feed them, save them. As people within the crowd died, the corpses were passed, hand over hand, out to the rim of the throng, and piled by the hundreds in the spring grass along the muddy banks. It was not uncommon to break into peasant houses and find an entire family seated around a table, the Bible open before them, dead in their chairs.[4]

Lenin's attitude toward the famine was "curiously remote, cold and disinterested. He seemed to regard the famine as only one more of the obstacles that blocked his path."[5] He was also afraid. The

Kronstadt Rebellion had just been crushed with particularly merciless violence. With it was crushed the last plausible claim to a "democratic" Soviet. The rebellion itself been fomented largely in response to the unrest and mass hunger—often starvation—resulting from the Bolsheviks' brutal and disastrous policies toward the peasantry. Though the civil war had been won, hopeless little rebellions kept cropping up everywhere. And now—famine, disastrous famine, gaping at the whole world. In private, Lenin conceded: "We are barely holding on."[6]

At this moment Radek intervened with Lenin, insisting that some international propaganda response was needed and promoting Münzenberg for the job.[7] Willi was summoned to Lenin's study in the Kremlin. He sat in one of the leather armchairs across from his leader's desk. It was a room remote from the old Tsarist apartments, and without regal pretensions. The only hint of omnipotence was technological: an array of telephones, the best in Russia, over which the dictator of the proletariat governed, shouting.

The dictator pointed his beard at him, outlined the situation, and analyzed the options with systematic inaccuracy. No help whatever, he told Münzenberg, could be expected from the West. Only the "international proletariat" could conceivably be expected to give aid. "His plan," Münzenberg later recalled, "was to organize an extensive international relief action, and charge me with its organization."[8]

Lenin was wrong about the response of the West. When (perhaps at Münzenberg's behest) Maxim Gorky was permitted to make a public appeal for help, relief was committed in vast amounts within ten days.[9] The success of Gorky's appeal left Lenin angry and chagrined. For years afterward, its existence was officially denied. Two weeks later, Münzenberg's new enterprise had been established.

By far the major share, however, came from the American Relief Administration run by the future President of the United States, Herbert Hoover. The U.S. Congress promptly appropriated twenty million dollars. Millions more were contributed by individuals. By August 20, supplies had started rolling into Russia. At the peak of the disaster, the ARA was feeding more than ten million Russians every day: Alexander Werth puts the number at "almost 11 million."[10] The Europeans likewise responded, with a program run by the Norwegian explorer and humanitarian Fridtjof Nansen. In terms of material aid, the relief Münzenberg organized through the Comintern trailed far behind. Had Lenin's analysis been correct, the Volga catastrophe would have been almost unmitigated.

An appeal for relief was also set up within Russia. An "All Russian Relief Committee to Aid the Starving" was assembled in Gorky's name, including fifty or so non-Bolshevik intellectuals summoned back from oblivion and insult to help rescue the country. The committee launched its appeals. When they approached the Patriarch of the Orthodox Church, the prelate promptly sent a letter to every church authorizing the sale of all "non-sacramental" church treasures to help the hungry.[11] Response swelled from every side, and became so successful that Lenin and Kamenev thought it menaced Bolshevik hegemony. Non-Bolsheviks, *priests*, mobilizing opinion? The men in the Kremlin panicked and immediately moved to destroy what they had created. When the committee assembled for its third meeting, Kamenev made sure that his own plants within its ranks, and Gorky himself, were absent; he then surrounded the building with black marias and ordered the Cheka to charge the committee room, weapons drawn. According to Bertram Wolfe, every non-Bolshevik in the place was arrested and taken to the Lubyanka. Some, among them the novelist Bulgakov and Tolstoy's daughter Alexandra, were at first threatened with death sentences. They were not in fact killed, but Werth quotes Lenin's order requiring that all the Committee members be "exiled from Moscow immediately, sent to the chief cities of different regions, cut off it possible from all means of communication, including railways, and kept under close surveillance..... Begin insulting these people," Lenin ordered, "and heap opprobrium on them, accusing them of being closet White Guard supporters and bourgeois do-gooders.... Make them look ridiculous and mock them...."[12] Of course, even by Bolshevik standards, these people had committed no crime. Lenin himself conceded the point. "We know perfectly well the loyalty of the committee," he said. "It was necessary for us—for political reasons—to destroy it."[13]

When Gorky presumed to ask why so many of his non-communist literary friends were in prison or exiled, an aide to Dzerzhinsky answered with an interesting image.[14] The committee resembled, he said, a willow twig in water. The twig had begun to sprout. "It had become a center of attention for the so-called Russian 'public.' This we could not permit." The sprouting willow twig had to be smashed.

Gorky responded with humiliation and rage: "You have made me into an *agent provocateur!*"

The truth is that as Lenin contemplated starving Russians dying by the millions, their agony was not more important to him than its implications for propaganda. The bourgeoisie must not be seen to be accomplishing what the Bolsheviks were failing to accomplish. So they must be thwarted. Lenin ordered Litvinov to hamstring foreign agencies with every possible bureaucratic obstacle. When the famine was past, about half the Russians who'd worked alongside the foreign relief people came to their reward: summary arrest by the Cheka and the gulag, an institution already entrenched. It was assumed that any Russian who had worked with these do-gooding bourgeois Americans and Norwegians must be tainted with "counter-revolution." Lenin even ordered that adults, though they were starving, be forbidden access to the ideologically incorrect foreign food. Only children were "immune to capitalist contagion." Thus, parents would starve while their children ate. This insane regulation stood on the books for a full year, though of course the Americans and Scandinavians quietly disobeyed it wherever possible. At last Lenin came to see that feeding children while starving their parents to death was not, after all, an ideologically sound device for cementing socialist loyalty.[15]

But Lenin's response to the famine was uniformly perverse, all in the name of "purity." After Patriarch Tikhon's appeal to the faithful to use church property to help the starving, and in direct response to its generosity, Lenin fiercely intensified Soviet persecution of the Church. One of his friends would recall that as a young man, he'd *welcomed* an earlier—though much milder—famine in 1891. The Young Lenin did not think starvation was such a terrible fate for the reactionary peasantry. "Famine," Lenin explained, "would destroy faith not only in the Tsar but in God too." Thirty years later, Lenin was enraged that the Church had resources of any sort to offer for relief, and proposed to put a prompt end to that. The Prelate's appeal moved him to new, ever more Draconian confiscations and persecutions. Church records indicate that the Soviet government killed 2,691 priests, 1,962 monks, and 3,447 nuns in 1922 alone. The Patriarch's offer had been a costly one.

Secular intellectuals and writers fared a little better than the church, but they did not fare well. After they were mobilized by the famine, Lenin stepped up the regime's persecution of them as well, insisting upon surveillance and deportation, if not forced labor, not just for the actual participants, but on the social classes to which they belonged—writers, journalists, economists, university lecturers: whoever lived by any language other than the language of propaganda, were the new targets. The Word, and those who lived by it, were being criminalized.[16]

Yet the WIR did produce real help, and Münzenberg brought all his managerial brilliance to the task. Tumultuous rallies and heart-rending appeals were organized around the world. Shiploads of grain pulled toward Petrograd. Fisheries were spawned in the Caspian Sea. Fleets were launched. Münzenberg's entrepreneurial genius transformed relief and propaganda into a kind of communist multinational, with himself as its clandestine CEO.[17]

The leading concern, however, was to generate propaganda. I asked Babette Gross when propaganda, rather than relief, became the dominating purpose of the WIR. "At the first moment," she replied, with her typical simplicity.

THE MÜNZENBERG TRUST

When the famine abated, the new propaganda combine did begin to expand in new directions. Münzenberg's fisheries and farms soon gave way to newspapers, magazines, and firm production companies, as well as press agencies. The combine had offices around the world, with branches in Moscow (staffed mainly by Germans), and its headquarters in Berlin. What had begun as a network for relief became a network for molding opinion and (not least), for secret political action. Münzenberg had assembled what amounted to a huge, secretly co-ordinated media consortium. It came to be known, with cheerless Bolshevik irony, as "The Münzenberg Trust."

The story of the Münzenberg Trust has rarely been told. Arthur Koestler only hints at its complexity in his autobiographical book, *The Invisible Writing:*

> Out of the pamphlets issued in support of the relief campaign grew the Trust's own publishing firms, its book clubs, its multitudes of magazines and newspapers. By 1926, Willi owned two daily newspapers in Germany with mass circulations, *Berlin am Morgen* and *Welt am Abend;* the *Arbeiter Illustrierte Zeitung,* a weekly with a circulation of one million, the communist counterpart of *Life;* a series of other magazines including technical magazines for photographers, radio amateurs, etc., all with an indirect communist slant. In Japan, to quote a remote country as an example, the Trust directly or indirectly controlled nineteen magazines and newspapers.[18]

Though Sean McMeekin shows that Münzenberg's *apparat* "hemorrhaged red ink," it was lavishly financed by the Comintern, and extended from Moscow to Berlin to Paris to London to New York to Hollywood to Shanghai to Delhi. It was not limited to print. From George Grosz to Erwin Piscator, Münzenberg funded much of vanguard Weimar culture. His impact on film was profound. At a very early stage of its existence Münzenberg used one of his many dummy corporations—Aufbau, Industrie & Handels, A.G.— quietly to buy up distribution rights in the USSR to almost all

German films then on the market.[19] The revenues from this shrewd investment soon engendered the capital needed for a German-based distribution company called Prometheus Films, the instrument through which Soviet cinema of its grand epoch was released and promoted in the West. Prometheus's first release was Eisenstein's *Battleship Potemkin*, with a score commissioned by Münzenberg's in house composer, Edmund Meisel. Eisenstein's great prestige in the democracies was very much a creation of the Münzenberg machine. Prometheus was soon producing German films as well, and in 1927 Willi added yet another subsidiary, Welt Film, for the equivalent of 16-millimeter non-theatrical distribution. Through this company, the Trust encouraged the creation of college film societies in England and American, all featuring Soviet cinema. For a generation, the notion of a cinematic avant-garde was fused with Leninism.

In 1924, a complete production company was established in Moscow itself, capitalized, staffed, and controlled by Münzenberg: that is, by the Comintern. Following the Russian acronym for WIR, which is MRP, the company was called Mezhropohmfilm Russ and it became the prime production house of Soviet Cinema fir the next decade, the home studio for Vertov, Dovzhenko, Pudovkin. Mezhropohmfilm made real moves, including a number of great ones, for real audiences. Meanwhile its networks provided legal cover for many secret agents with quite different missions, and with the addition of this third pillar to his tripod, Münzenberg's ascendancy in Soviet cinema was close to complete.

THE SACCO-VANZETTI CAMPAIGN

Like Lenin, like Stalin, Münzenberg knew next to nothing about the United States. He visited it only once in his life, in 1934. "Our experiences in America genuinely amazed us," Babette Gross wrote. "The authorities of this 'country of capitalism' put not the slightest obstacle in the way of Münzenberg, the communist."[20] Yet around 1925, the Comintern had entrusted Münzenberg and his propaganda machine with a little-known but meaningful role in giving new shape and political function to the Communist party of the United States. At that time, the American Party, that congregation of the militant naive, the home and battleground for John Reed and Louise Bryant, was in need of rescue. It had been left in a shattered state by its late-Leninist internal struggles combined with devastating police action inflicted on it by what later became the FBI.[21]

Stalin had no serious interest or belief in a mass-based American "revolution." He never attempted to create an American Party or communist movement capable of even remotely challenging the constitutional power, as he would do in Germany, Italy, France, Greece, and the Balkans. That was not to be the American Party's job. The apparatus of American communism would be directed instead toward discrediting American politics and culture and assisting the growth of Soviet power elsewhere. It sought not the outright destruction of the American democracy, however much that might be desired, but practical influence on its culture, the placement of agents who would over the long term seek to smooth and promote the advance of Soviet influence and assist the apparatus in its work of espionage. The American right may have given itself nightmares about the red flag flying over the Capitol and commissars storming the East Room, but I know of no evidence showing that such a thing was ever really part of Stalin's dream; his 1927 remark, made to gullible visitors, that the Sacco-Vanzetti scandal showed America in pre-revolutionary turmoil, was surely a matter of atmospherics. Lenin's mind had been centered upon Germany; Stalin's was on Russia and its vast sphere of power. America lay beyond a very distant albeit important place, a mystery, an annoyance, and a myth. And it was in the arena of myth, not that of the seizure of power, that America had the Soviets' full and frightened attention.

For the world proletariat of 1925, the leading counter-myth to the myth of revolution was, by far, the myth of America. That vision—the notion of the melting pot, the Golden Door, the Land of Opportunity—this is what held the real political attention of the International. To the Bolsheviks, this was the true American menace. And in 1925, the task of the American Party was to counteract it.

Their approach was to create and sustain a worldwide anti-American campaign that would focus its appeal upon the mythology of its immigration. The purpose of such a campaign would be to instill a reflexive loathing of the United States and its people as a prime tropism of left-wing enlightenment. To undermine the myth of the Land of Opportunity, the United States had to be depicted as an almost insanely xenophobic place, murderously hostile to foreigners.

In search of a cause that would disgrace America in the eyes of the proletarian foreign-born, the Comintern found it in the obscure, dying case of two anarchist immigrants who had got themselves into some very bad trouble: Niccola Sacco and Bartolomeo Vanzetti.

Every so often, talking with me in Munich, Babette Gross would drop a remark that made the foundations of the world seem to shift a little. One of these was over Sacco and Vanzetti. The Communist role in the Sacco-Vanzetti case? "It was," she said with a dry shrug, "Münzenberg's idea."

Münzenberg's idea! Is that *possible?* With the Dreyfus case, this is perhaps the most famous legal struggle in the whole history of modern propaganda and injustice. And indeed the origins and communist co-option of the Sacco-Vanzetti case are far more complex than that. It may have been at Münzenberg's instigation that communist propaganda networks worldwide took up the plight of the two Boston immigrants and made it the centerpiece of a vast new anti-American operation—just as a little later Willi's executive decision helped turn the Scottsboro Boys into prime martyrs for the International. But it was other arms of the *apparat* that transformed a case of troubled local injustice into a worldwide *cause célèbre*.[22]

In that effort the communists latched onto the Sacco-Vanzetti case as latecomers and opportunists. Sacco and Vanzetti were not themselves communists, and theirs was not, at first, a communist struggle. The two Italians were anarchists, and so anarchists shaped the political myth of the famous pair during the early 1920s, guided especially by that doyen of Italo-American radicalism, Carlo Tresca. Yet by 1928, Willi was coolly, if disingenuously, claiming credit for the Sacco-Vanzetti campaign, understood as a worldwide political moral mania, and among the highest triumphs of his *apparat*.[23]

Way back in 1920, two Italian immigrants, both militant anarchists, were arrested and charged with stealing the payroll of a Braintree, Massachusetts, shoe factory and murdering its paymaster and his guard. In 1921, they were tried, convicted, and sentenced to death.

At first, the plight of these two ill-fated men seemed to interest nobody. A socialist newsman sent up from New York reported back to his editor, "there's no story in it. ... Just a couple of wops in a jam."[24]

The two men belonged to a small anarchist cell of Italian immigrants like themselves. When the pair was arrested, this group immediately formed a defense committee. Naively convinced that the two would probably get off, they proposed creating "great publicity for the anarchist movement."[25]

But Sacco and Vanzetti did not get off. Nor did their case advance the anarchist cause; its later co-option by the communists was used to betray and undermine American anarchism. The Defense Committee was right about one thing: These two men's condemnation offered the basis for a political vision.

That vision in its anarchist incarnation was the creation of one man above all: an eccentric Westerner, one of the grand lawyers of the American left, a brilliant but more flaky Clarence Darrow named Fred Moore, recommended to the Defense Committee by Carlo Tresca. Moore was, in the words of his assistant, Eugene Lyons, an "artist handicapped by a genius for non-conformity."[26] He was a heavy-using cocaine addict (the Defense Committee more than once used their less idealistic Italian connections to keep him supplied), a drawling Westerner with his revolver often slung in his back pocket, given to affronting judicial dignity by padding around courtrooms in his stocking feet.

Moore invented the case. He set out to rescue his clients with any and every maneuver a fertile legal mind could conceive, convinced they were lost without the pressure of outraged world opinion. To this end, long before Münzenberg knew anything about the case, he single-handedly created the *political* argument of Sacco and Vanzetti: that they were powerless, despised, radical immigrants being subjected to judicial murder by a smug, chauvinist, puritanical, nativist, Red-scared New England establishment.[27] In promoting this defense, Moore was unscrupulous, ingenious, indefatigable, driven. Of his passion and sincerity there can be no doubt. He was a man obsessed. And his belief in his clients' innocence was quite genuine. At first.

Except unfortunately their innocence *wasn't* quite genuine. Best evidence shows beyond all reasonable doubt that Sacco was in fact one of the Braintree gunmen and the murderer of the guard, whom he shot to death after the man had fallen to his hands and knees, begging for his life while struggling to reach his own revolver. Vanzetti may have been innocent of the Braintree holdup, though he probably knew or guessed Sacco's guilt. He certainly had guilty knowledge of Sacco's participation in an earlier robbery where no blood had been spilled.

In a way, the facts make the two men's political solidarity all the more compelling. One word of the truth from either man—Sacco in ordinary decency; Vanzetti in ordinary self-protection—would have saved Vanzetti's life. But it also would have demolished their cause in *disgrazia*. Bartolomeo Vanzetti laid down his life on the bloody altar not of justice but of propaganda. He died lying for the truth.

The murky integrity of this self-sacrifice gives Vanzetti—he was in every way the more interesting of the pair—a tremendously affecting dignity. It also sustained his stumbling, broken, justly famous eloquence. "If it had not been for this thing, I might have lived out my life talking on street corners to scorning men. I might have died unknown, unmarked, a failure. Now we are not a failure. This is our career and our triumph."[28]

The little coterie of anarchists on the Defense Committee also knew the truth, and they too maintained the vow of silence for *la causa*. The last survivor, a man named Ideale Gambera, wrote a full account of the affair for disclosure by his son after his death. Gambera died in 1982, and his son released the documents to Francis Russell, a principal scholar of the case. It was the last word.

Somewhere along the way, Fred Moore seems to have stumbled onto the truth as well. There is no evidence that this in any way modified Moore's passion for his clients' defense, but in 1923, in the midst of a paranoid psychotic episode (he'd attempted suicide and was hospitalized), Sacco dismissed Moore in a violent incoherent rage.[29] Taking his dismissal with dignity, Moore packed up, got into his car, and drove back west, selling knickknacks as he went to pay for his gasoline.

The case now began to die. The appeals dragged on, but the headline makers of the world had dropped the Massachusetts fishmonger and shoemaker. Then, in 1925, on orders of Münzenberg and the Comintern, an American branch of the Red Aid called the International Labor Defense, created in Chicago with James Cannon as its director, was set up to be the focus of organization for the new American communism. Its first mission was to make the Sacco-Vanzetti case into a worldwide myth.[30]

The campaign became a juggernaut, tenaciously co-ordinated from Berlin, vast and unrelenting. Now, once again, protest meetings gathered to shout and sob in the great squares. From all its outlets, organs of the Trust produced an unstoppable stream of attacks on the assassin viciousness of American justice, defending the innocence and holiness of the immigrant martyrs in Braintree. Around the world, heartrending appeals for cash were staged to provide for Sacco and Vanzetti's defense and "protection." Children gave their pennies, workers donated wages, and philanthropists opened their checkbooks.

The *apparat*'s fund-raising was, incidentally, an almost complete fraud. Sacco and Vanzetti and their Defense Committee saw next to none of the money raised in their names. Of the approximately half-million dollars raised in the United States, the Defense Committee received something like $6,000. Of large sums collected in mass protest meetings around the world, the Defense Committee saw precisely nothing.[31]

Since Cannon seems to have understood that Sacco was guilty, it is possible that senior people in the Comintern also knew the truth.[32] Not that anybody cared. The communist goal was never to save the lives of Sacco and Vanzetti. Acquittal would have dissolved the whole political point. Katherine Anne Porter, like any number of writers and artists of the time, participated in the Boston death-watch. She reports an exchange with her Communist group leader, Rosa Baron, "a dry, fanatical little woman who wore thick-lensed spectacles over her accusing eyes, a born whip-hand, who talked an almost impenetrable jargon of party dogma. ... I remarked . . . that even then, at that late time, I still hoped the lives of Sacco and Vanzetti could be saved. ... 'Saved,' she said, ringing a change on her favorite answer to political illiteracy, 'who wants them saved? What earthly good would they do us alive?'"[33] The whole point was that "justice" in the world's leading liberal democracy was a murderous lie. The men *had* to die.

Russell describes the European demonstrations:

> Demonstrations took place that autumn in France and Italy, with lesser demonstrations in Switzerland, Belgium, Spain, Portugal, Scandinavia, and South America. A bomb exploded in the American embassy in Paris. Another was intercepted in the Lisbon consulate. Reds in Brest stoned the consulate there. American consuls in Mexico were threatened with death if Sacco and Vanzetti were executed. In Rome, thousands of workers marched on the American embassy demanding justice for their compatriots.
>
> Some of this agitation was anarchist inspired, some actually spontaneous, but most of it was directed by communist leaders in Paris.[34]

The Communist campaign for Sacco and Vanzetti was aimed at two enemies, and it attacked them both ferociously. The first attack was on America for killing the two men. The second attack was on the anarchists and liberals who had failed to save them. According to Murray Kempton, the *apparat*'s "chief theme was that, since the defense was in the hands of a committee of liberals and anarchists rather than Communists, Sacco and Vanzetti were being betrayed from within," and that the people on the Defense Committee "were as much their murders" as the judge and prosecutor. The "treason of the defense committee" remained a Communist theme for years.

Yet the strategy was also to co-opt the same Committee they sought to destroy. A leading liberal on the Defense Committee, and one of its most effective leaders, was Gardner "Pat" Jackson, whose father's first wife had been the novelist Helen Hunt Jackson, a once world-famous fighter for Native American rights. In his later years, Jackson became a forthrightly anti-communist leftist. For a long time before, however—too long—Jackson had been the perfect "innocent," repeatedly manipulated by the Communists, including by Münzenberg's senior lieutenant Louis Gibarti, who knew him and used him often.[35] Up until the Nazi-Soviet Pact, Jackson's liberalism was repeatedly jolted into bewildered dismay as he was exploited by such hardened Stalinist ideologues as Lee Pressman, a member of the Ware Group. Yet Jackson was always a much-loved man, and the decency of his values, if sometimes baffled by the company he kept, seems never to have faltered. But he was almost comically useable. After Sacco and Vanzetti had been executed, a Communist official turned to him before a memorial meeting and said, "I just wanted you to know that tonight I'm going to call you one of the murderers of Sacco and Vanzetti. I hope you understand that I don't really mean it."[36]

As the case unfolded, Gardner Jackson was developing his influence over Marion Frankfurter, the wife of Felix Frankfurter, then a leading professor of law at Harvard, and later one of the twentieth century's great justices of the United States Supreme Court. Frankfurter was drawn into the affair by the dual force of his passion for justice and his concern for his wife. Marion Frankfurter had a frightening history of mental instability. Her delicate psychiatric state preoccupied her husband and of course tangled his otherwise steadfast loyalty and courage with inevitable emotions of guilt, fear, and the wish to escape.

During the Sacco-Vanzetti campaign, Gardner Jackson placed the cultivation of a thoroughly ingratiating relationship with the Frankfurters high among his prime concerns. His point of focus was Marion. Jackson was a famously seductive man; though his attentions to Marion Frankfurter were surely platonic, they were also incessant. He lucidly saw and exploited her insecurity, her need to anchor herself in a cause, her problem balancing her own sense of inadequacy against the brilliance of her incandescent and intensely ambitious husband.

Marion Frankfurter became preoccupied with Gardner, and through him, with the case. Gardner in turn flattered Marion continually. He arranged to have her join him as co-editor of Sacco and Vanzetti's letters. He involved her at every public level.[37]

It seems plain that the real purpose of this tactic was to reach Felix. Gardner seems to have guessed that Frankfurter's wish to support his wife's cause would lead him into the fold as well. He was correct. The couple became mutually obsessed, egged on at every step by Jackson, who became their constant companion, a daily intimate of the house. When the condemned men's last appeal was denied, the outraged Felix proceeded to write one of the most powerful polemics of his career, a denunciation of the case's legal history, and a brilliant exercise in controlled vituperation. The piece appeared in the *Atlantic*. It was more influential than any other factor in marshalling American non-radical opinion behind the pair, and it was even more influential in Europe. Münzenberg's Berlin office arranged for it to be reprinted throughout the world, while in London H. G. Wells produced a flamboyant summary which promptly became the received British view.[38]

What followed was orchestrated multinational mass hysteria.

August 22 was the night of the executions, and around them the *apparat,* poising itself for the outpouring of international grief, organized a vast international deathwatch. Francis Russell describes the event:

> After the news flashed from Charleston that Sacco and Vanzetti had at last been executed, the reverberations were international. Demonstrations in American cities were duplicated and in many places exceeded all over Europe. In Paris the Communist daily *Humanité* printed an extra sheet on which was splashed the single block word *"Assassinés!"* Crowds surged down the Boulevard Sebastopol, ripping up lampposts and tossing them through plate glass windows. Protective tanks ringed the American embassy, and sixty policemen were injured when a mob tried to set up barricades there. Five thousand militants roamed the streets of Geneva the evening before the executions, overturning American cars, sacking shops selling American goods, gutting theaters showing American films. One of the greatest demonstrations in the history of the Weimar republic took place in Berlin; there were tumultuous demonstrations in Bremen and Wilhehnshaven and Hamburg, and a two-hour torchlight parade in Stuttgart. During that turbulent week, half a dozen German demonstrators were killed. No one was killed in England, but on the night of the executions, a crowd gathered in front of Buckingham Palace and sang "The Red Flag."[39]

The night of the executions was marked by a vigil at Charleston Prison. Before this dour building an enormous crowd gathered in the dark. "I was never in that place before," Porter wrote, "but I seem to remember that it was a great open space with the crowd massed back from a center the police worked constantly to keep clear. They were all mounted on fine horses and loaded with pistols and hand grenades and tear gas bombs." The law in its generosity provides that the condemned are entitled to every minute of their last day. After having been granted this largess, Sacco and Vanzetti were led to the death chamber at midnight exactly. Sacco entered it first, at 12:11. Vanzetti followed at 12:20. By 12:27 both had been pronounced dead. Both men met their end with indescribable dignity.

THE WHITE SEA CANAL

If he was a master at manipulating the "innocents," Münzenberg was certainly no innocent himself. Willi may have sincerely believed that he was lying for the truth, but he *did* understand that he *was* lying. While I know of no evidence that Münzenberg had a clear conception of the Gulag in its full horror, it is certain that Willi did understand that the "proletarian state"—in the teeth of all its fine talk about workers and peasants—was exploiting the forced labor of whole classes of people, arresting countless numbers *en masse* not for their "crimes" but on pure pretext, using their involuntary servitude as a crude, ruthless economic expedient. Willi knew that these people were imprisoned in massive, indescribably abusive concentration camps; he knew where at least some of these camps were, and why. This was a man who had become a socialist to save workers from exploitation, and now the workers' paradise was becoming a slave state.

Prime evidence for this is Münzenberg's public relations work for the White Sea Canal. In September 1931, Stalin ordered work to begin on the creation of a vast canal, supposedly large enough to carry modern shipping, running 141 miles from the White Sea on the Arctic Circle south to Leningrad, its path laid down mainly through a bitterly cold, subarctic wasteland that was forbidding country even by Russian standards. The idea for some such thing had been a fantasy since the nineteenth century: a canal linking the White Sea with the Baltic would permit ships to reach Leningrad from the far north without having to sail around Scandinavia. Yet the dream had always been left in the realm of dreams. Many thought properly. Shipping on the White Sea was very light, and it seemed likely to stay that way. Such a project would never justify its crushing cost.

That did not deter Stalin. In any case, the cost would be less crushing if the state did not have to pay—or even properly feed—the workers involved. Work began on the canal right around the same time that, in America, the Hoover Dam began to be built on the Arizona-Nevada border. The two projects were perhaps similar in ambition: after that, the parallels disappear. The Hoover Dam transformed a vast region in the arid American Southwest. The White Sea Canal served almost no useful purpose at all. The real interest of the canal is not its place in the history of engineering but its place in the history of tyranny.

Stalin ordained that the White Sea Canal was to be built in twenty months: miraculously, it was completed in twenty-one. He further ordained that like a parallel project further south—the Moscow-Volga Canal—the White Sea Canal was to be built entirely by forced labor: the canal's inability to justify its cost would be solved by building it so it cost nothing—except in human lives. The canal was built, without any sort of serious technology whatever, by swarming thousands of forced laborers, scrabbling in the frozen ground, often with their bare hands, working till they dropped. 170,000 forced laborers, dressed in rags, and on near starvation rations, were kept at their tasks by the secret police. The twenty-one months needed to dig it are all the more astonishing because the canal was built with tools and equipment so primitive that even today the story makes one rub one's eyes in disbelief. Anne Applebaum describes the working conditions. The workers used "wooden spades, crude handsaws, pickaxes, and wheelbarrows to dig the canal and to build its great dams and locks… Everything, from the wheelbarrows to the scaffolding, was handmade. One inmate remembered 'there was no technology whatsoever. Even ordinary automobiles were a rarity. Everything was done by hand, sometimes with the help of horses. We dug earth by hand, and carried it in wheelbarrows, we dug through the hills by hand as well, and carried away the stones….' As work progressed, new campsites had to be built along the course of the canal. At every one of these new sites, the prisoners arrived—and found nothing. Before starting work they had to build their own barracks and organize their food supply. In the meantime, it sometimes happened that the freezing cold of the Karelian winter killed them before they finished their tasks."[40]

The cost in life was huge. Applebaum says, "according to some estimates, more than 25,000 prisoners died, although this number does not include those who were released due to illness or accident, and who died soon afterward."[41] Solzhenitzyn puts the number of people who perished much higher, but using even Anne Applebaum's smaller count, simple arithmetic indicates that work on the canal killed well over a thousand workers per month. That would mean that on average around forty people died every day of work, and that, in turn, means that two or more people were done to death every single *hour* that this horrendous project was underway.

Stalin was determined to use the "triumph" of the White Sea Canal as a propaganda coup countering negative accounts of the Gulag that were increasingly finding their way into the Western press, often written by non-communist leftists appalled by the imprisonment and persecution of their socialist or Social Democratic comrades in Russia. Somehow the Gulag had to be made to look good. To this end, the vast engineering fraud of the canal was compounded by an equally egregious propaganda fraud. The canal, the world was told, was a triumph of humane penology, a model of socialist rehabilitation. In later years, the Gulag would be kept hidden, a shameful secret. But during this brief interlude, it was promoted. As Applebaum says, "the White Sea Canal was the first, last, and only Gulag project ever exposed to the full light of Soviet propaganda." In the USSR the leader of this propaganda effort was Maxim Gorky. Outside Russia, the man in charge was Münzenberg.

And remarkably, the campaign had some success. When the Canal was opened, Gorky presided over a corps of Soviet literati who slapped together a celebratory volume that was distributed everywhere in Russia. Meanwhile, Münzenberg's fellow travelers pulled out the stops in the west. Sidney and Beatrice Webb, and Amabel Williams-Ellis (sister of John Strachey, a leading figure in Münzenberg's English fronts) gushed at length about the canal as a uniquely uplifting example of socialist compassion. Skeptics were vilified as enemies of the workingman. The main claim was that prisoners, inspired by the Bolshevik dream, had redeemed themselves by creating an engineering miracle. Their work was an inspiring example of what a really creative and humane police force could accomplish. Today it may seem astonishing that such lies were widely believed. But these were respected people; their standards of truth were believed to be higher than most people's. Today the few who still care sneer at people like the Webbs and Ms. Williams-Ellis. They earned their disgrace. Yet surely some measure of responsibility rests with the man behind the scenes.[42]

And what were Münzenberg's own views? Babette Gross recounts how in 1933, it was decided to take Münzenberg on a personal tour of one such "triumph of human engineering" during on one of his periodic trips to Moscow. Since the White Sea Canal lay far to the north, it was more convenient to tour nearer by, at the Moscow-Volga Canal—yet another example of a humane police force at work. The GPU agent who acted as their guide was proud of the spectacle he was showing. "The entire building site," Babette recalled, "was surrounded by a high barbed wire fence, dwarfed at intervals by guard towers... There were no technical appliances, no crane, no ledger, no lorry." Babette the revolutionary froze with shock witnessing prisoners literally "bowing low" when the secret policeman approached them. She and Willi were led to the edge of the huge pit and stared into it. Below, the new slaves in their ragged stumbling thousands. For some time Willi stood mute. Even the German tough guy seems to have been shaken. Babette heard him mutter under his breath that it was like watching slaves crawling over the pyramids of ancient Egypt.[43]

"PEACE"

Pacifism is hardly a Communist cause. Revolution is, after all, a variety of war: to the Revolutionary it is a war to the death. Class war allows no limit on the use of force. Yet ironically, Münzenberg originally concocted the propaganda institutions he later used as the backbone of his antifascist movement in the West to promote "peace" and pacifism in the West. Or to be more precise, to promote the disarmament of the liberal democracies.[44]

52

Stalin was, after all, a Marxist-Leninist and his thinking in all its cynical paranoiac brutality was guided by Marxist-Leninist assumptions. He saw himself as the absolute enemy of the liberal democracies and he assumed that the democracies were the ultimate enemies of the Communist revolution. The dictator feared above all a counterrevolutionary invasion from the West, and it seemed him certain to come. How could it not, given capitalism? Yet because of a broad constellation of reasons, Stalin was not at all sure he either wanted or could make the Red Army into a force capable of deterring such an invasion. That anxiety was behind his interest in a plan presented to him sometime in 1928 calling for a great, broadly based propaganda campaign promoting pacifism in the democracies.

Insiders came to call this plan the "Peace Conspiracy." It was put before Stalin right after the Sacco-Vanzetti campaign. It is said that the prime author of the peace plan was a French Münzenbergman named Guy Jerram. Wherever the idea originated, the peace conspiracy found favor in the Stalin's eyes. By the middle of 1928, the propaganda apparatus on all its fronts had seized upon pacifism as the principal issue of the hour, and it continued to promote "peace" with all its sententious fervor for the next four years. Louis Gibarti's various fronts, especially an organization active on college campuses called the League Against Imperialism, took up the cry. College campuses were in fact a prime locus for the whole campaign: The "Oxford Oath," adopted in 1934 by the Oxford Union, categorically resolving "under no circumstances to fight for King and Country," is a belated echo of all this agitation. At the League Against Imperialism's first Congress in Brussels in late 1928, the touchstone of talk about the colonial struggle was for this reason not "armed struggle" as one might expect to hear among those seeking to throw off the imperialist yoke. No: "Peace."

The campaign for "peace" culminated in 1932 at a huge congress, also organized under the covert direction of Münzenberg and Gibarti, known as the Amsterdam Congress Against War. It must be said that the kaleidoscope of political sentiment generated by these successive congresses really all variants on the same enterprise. Precisely the same secretariat and cast of characters were behind the Amsterdam Congress as the Brussels Anti-War Congress, and the Archives of the Central Party in Moscow likewise show that these, in turn, were central to the founding events of the antifascist movement after the Reichstag Fire.[45] Because the Congress later held its Paris meetings in the Salle Pleyel, Amsterdam later became known as the Amsterdam-Pleyel World Congress Against War, and when the Nazis assumed power its secretariat was moved to a suburb of Paris—in Aumont. It finally reached its last incarnation under a new name, the largest and most broadly based of all Münzenberg's organizations: the League Against War and Fascism.

Nobody seemed to notice the inherent oddity of a bunch of revolutionaries and their fellow travelers espousing "pacifism" and hiding behind the mask of humanist sentiment. The distinction between pacifism and revolution proved remarkably easy to elide. "War" in this Soviet-sponsored rhetoric of righteousness, and in fact generally on the left thereafter, was never taken to mean *class* war. Meanwhile, because the pacifist propaganda was linked to the League Against Imperialism, the inherent ideological incongruity would be played out in events to come, especially in India, where nonviolence (to the considerable albeit concealed irritation of the Communists) really did come to the fore as a meaningful tactic of political action, initiating an interplay between pacifism and anti-imperialism that was part of a long process. Nehru himself (like the Nicaraguan insurrectionary Sandino, a Gibarti discovery) was a delegate to the Brussels congress in 1932, and when it was over Nehru was spirited across the German border and taken to Berlin to meet with Münzenberg personally. Münzenberg had a profound effect on Nehru. Many years later, in his keynote address to the Bandung Conference of 1955, the Indian leader paid tribute to Willi. It was one of the few times Münzenberg's actual place in modern politics has ever been publicly acknowledged.[46]

Of course Stalin had no *real* interest in pacifism as a means of anti-imperialist struggle. Neither did Münzenberg or Gibarti. The sole concern was Soviet power.

Here we confront yet another major mystery in the history of communist thought. Why were Münzenberg and his propagandists wasting their energies on a campaign against a largely imaginary threat from the liberal democracies while Stalin remained systematically unresponsive to gathering Nazi menace? The year 1932, with its many frantic electoral campaigns in Germany, its banning and then legalization of the SA, its interminable demonstrations and wild provocations and street violence, made it plain to most informed observers that events were leading to Hitler's seizure of power. It was equally plain that that result was not inevitable. During the course of the year, the Nazis repeatedly swung from exulting confidence to despair. Clearly, Hitler's rise might have been stopped by a resolute but flexibly united center and left. Such a course, however, would have required communist participation and leadership, and therefore Stalin's consent. That consent he would not give. At a number of junctures Stalin might easily have ordered the German communists to enter some sort of coalition with the Social Democrats. Such a coalition, made in the first months on thirties, might have put a permanent cap on the National Socialists' hopes. The Russian dictator understood the stakes; he did not fail to grasp the forces at work. It did not matter. He refused to act.

But Stalin was not alone. Communist opinion around the world, blinded by its fantasies of "revolution," was fixated on the "bourgeois" enemy. "Fascism"—a word the Comintern used in a notably vague way—was not the true enemy: it was merely a "late" phase of capitalism. In some ways it was almost to be welcomed, a symptom of the old system's death agony. Certainly to unite with the detested liberals to oppose "fascism" was a contradiction in terms. Liberals *were* fascists. "Social fascists."

To the communists, the Social Democrats were not a left-wing party at all. They were the archenemy, and they had been since the earliest days of Lenin's diatribes against them. Alliance with these "social fascists" was forbidden. Münzenberg and his men might diddle the liberals with cant about "peace": Real revolutionaries knew that 'Hitler was only a puppet whose installation in power was only bringing the victory of communism closer.'[47] Today this nonsense seems suicidal. But was Stalin perhaps right? Did the Communists really have something to fear from a genuine coalition with Hitler's opponents? Who knows whether the Bolshevik dedication to the total destruction of the bourgeoisie could have survived a genuine working alliance with a meliorist left? Much in later history makes one wonder. For the Communists to have entered a bona fide anti-Nazi coalition in this moment of moments in German history might well have meant communism's eventual absorption into a stabilized liberal democracy. The thought is wistful, and perhaps improbable. But it is not necessarily absurd.

***

The fact is that "revolutionary" fervor and a successful response to the rising National Socialist threat in Germany were incompatible. At one point in our conversations about these events, Babette Gross turned to me and said, in a voice that was cold with bitterness: "We wanted a revolution, and we got one. Germany will never recover." It was her most penetrating insight.

The radical challenge of Nazism could not be met by radical means. Only some sort of coalition of the left and center might have worked. Many of the most troubling pages of Babette's book on Münzenberg consist of her harsh summary of the German party's failure to forge the alliances needed to meet the Nazi menace. Münzenberg's specialty, after all, was co-opting liberals. If the goal was really to stop Hitler, that goal never softened the *apparat*'s murderous hostility to the liberals it sought to use. But now? Did the communists want the death agony of Weimar to go forward? Yes. Even if the killer was Hitler. Their only question was what would foment revolution. And so they made their fatal choice.

Babette Gross would recall standing with Münzenberg and other German leaders on a street corner just weeks before the Amsterdam Congress of 1932. It was the day of the internal quasi-legal shake-up of the German conservatives known as the "Papen coup." The situation was so fluid that revolutionary outbreaks were expected at any moment: Münzenberg and his people stood with Babette as if in a metaphoric flinch waiting for the explosion they expected the Papen coup to provoke. It never came. Instead, the Nazis, assisted by communist restraint, rolled on toward their victory unhindered by a united left.

As the year progressed, Willi grew increasingly agitated, torn, and insomniac: At night he paced the rooms of his apartment, feeling anxiety and panic he otherwise could never let show, hoping for revolution, and fearing it. Was this somehow a phase of the German revolution he had spent his lifetime trying to create? Few understood better than he the interpenetration of Nazi and communist constituencies. "Brown on the outside," he used to quip about the urban tough guys in the SA, "red on the inside." Münzenberg had moreover significant links, most of them secret, with the left wing of the SA, especially as run by Gregor and Otto Strasser.[48] At least to this degree, and probably deeper, his own apparatus reached into the Nazi party. But now things were rushing forward, out of his control.

"We wanted a revolution. And we got one."

***

All this is the more striking when we consider that through 1932, as Nazi power was gathering force, Münzenberg was organizing in the Amsterdam Congress the largest assembly of the world-wide right-thinking left ever brought together in one place. It took place in August 1932; it would have been an ideal—if belated—occasion to engage in true anti-Nazi coalition, both in and out of Germany. While Amsterdam was certainly a communist-controlled congress, it was anything but a congress of communists.[49] Amsterdam was genuinely diverse. While Stalin kept the German left fragmented, his propagandists managed to gather under one banner every branch of enlightened progressive opinion from around the world. It was precisely what Stalin had prohibited in practical fact. Enjoying the charade of unity, the delegates gave themselves over to the gratifications of spectacle. It is said that Goebbels adopted much of Amsterdam's *son et lumière* for his own later totalitarian liturgies in Potsdam and Nuremberg. There were well over 2,000 delegates. They represented every imaginable stripe of left-wing opinion, from real pacifists to trade unionists. Even liberals were there. The whole was covertly financed and run by the International; the cash flow, along with its secret accounts, was managed through couriers from Moscow meeting regularly with Münzenberg's confidential secretary.[50] But the congress generated the illusion of a vast diffuse goodwill, a wide united front.[51]

It was nothing of the kind. The Nazis were barely mentioned in this congress against "fascism." Instead, England and France were viewed as the threat. In *The Passing of an Illusion*, François Furet aptly summarizes this glittering exercise in irrelevance:

> The International Congress Against Fascism and War, which met in Amsterdam in the summer of 1932 and was largely the product of [Münzenberg's] ceaseless activity, deviated not one iota from the Comintern's line. It was not an "anti-Fascist: meeting of the sort that would be mobilized a year or two later in opposition to Hitler. Its goal remained "the fight for peace" that had been at the forefront of Soviet policy since 1929; in this context, "Fascism" was understood in a very general, vague sense as something related to the militarization of capitalist countries. Of those capitalist countries, Great Britain and, to a lesser extent, France were considered the most threatening, since they were the triumphant imperialism of 1918. The more peace loving they pretended to be, the more dangerous they were. One of the great themes of Amsterdam was denunciation of "Geneva pacifism"—in other words, the League of Nations... [T]he Congress declared that an anti-Soviet War was imminent.[52]

The essential fact about this astonishing and delusive gathering was its almost breathtaking insistence upon addressing and attacking anything, anything at all, except the *real* fascist threat. A cynical witness might plausibly claim that Amsterdam functioned more to distract attention from the Nazi menace than to confront it. The Congress took place during the very same days and hours, literally, that the National Socialists were most noxiously consolidating their strength. And yet much, *much* more time at Amsterdam was devoted to condemning the United States, to martyrizing Sacco and Vanzetti and the Scottsboro Boys, than was expended on the "brown" threat. A German newsreel made a mere two days after the Amsterdam Congress concluded shows Willi striding into the Reichstag just steps away from Goebbels as the next round in the Nazi's "legal" advance took place. The disaster was taking place. And Amsterdam, claiming everything, did nothing.

In retrospect, by generating a grandiose but politically empty fantasy of *seeming* unanimity and strength, the Amsterdam Congress did indeed distract attention from Stalin's decision to let Hitler divide and conquer Germany. The truth is that Stalin was co-opting the left's glowing antifascism in such a way as to have the curious result of *not* hampering Hitler in any practical terms. It would not be the last time. It happened again in Austria, and later in Spain. Rather than attack the Nazis directly, Stalin promoted "antifascism" in countries where Hitler himself had mixed feelings about the "fascists" under attack. When it came really to confronting the true Nazi menace head-on, from first to last, the Comintern's "antifascist" operation resorted to sound and fury. And refrained.

And so, beneath all this sinister bravura lies a terrible and tragic lost opportunity. In 1932, antifascism co-opted turned out to be antifascism misled. Antifascism misled was antifascism disarmed. Amsterdam gathered the most enlightened figures in the worldwide political left and focused their attention on irrelevancies, resolutely attacking any evil except the Nazi evil. Amsterdam was a Congress of the right people, and God knows it gathered at the right moment. But did it confront the right enemy? The crisis of legality in Weimar was unfolding by the hour. The invisible Soviet hand held the weapon of enlightened opinion in the West quite firmly in its grip. And blinded by "revolution," it waved that weapon pointlessly, and any and every enemy except the Nazi threat.

It was the last time that would be possible. Pacifism, anti-Imperialism, anti-Americanism, denunciations of the English and French—these standard leftist tunes would soon change. Münzenberg's apparatus was about to be totally transformed by precisely what it had contrived to permit.

It was about to be transformed by Hitler.

Chapter 3

Antifascism and Fire

Berlin: February 27, 1933. The night was moonlit and freezing. Adolf Hitler had been Chancellor of Germany for one month. The streets of the central city were almost deserted. At 9:40 a theological student, hurrying home hunched against the cold, was crossing the empty plaza in front of the somber granite pile of the Reichstag—a monument to Kaiser Wilhelm's taste in architecture—when he glanced up and caught inside the glass and steel dome the small, soundless orange flicker of what looked oddly like fire. And fire it was. Within a short time the orange flicker was filling the entire dome with what were obviously roiling flames, and not long after that the inferno pent within burst up through the melting and shattering glass and roared high into the night sky, while whatever was left of Weimar democracy sank into its final and fatal convulsion.[1]

In the weeks before, Münzenberg had been officially prepared for Hitler's assumption of office, which seems to have been quite clearly foreseen by the Soviets. Three months after the Amsterdam Congress, in early January 1933, several weeks before Hitler became Chancellor on January 30, Münzenberg was summoned to

Moscow for consultations on the German situation. There, plans were laid for him to move his headquarters to Paris in the event the situation "deteriorated further."[2]

And when the "situation" did indeed "deteriorate," Münzenberg for one knew perfectly well that he was in grave danger and appropriate precautions had been taken. The night Hitler took office, not long after his return from the Moscow consultations, Münzenberg left his lavish apartment on the Tiergarten, never to return. Berlin on that night of January 30, 1933, was streaming with the SA's celebratory torchlight parades, and though he was still a public man, still a member of the Reichstag, it was obvious that Münzenberg should no longer be spending his nights in a place where he could easily be found. A safe apartment had been prepared for him in an obscure new building in a worker's quarter of West Berlin, and there he was driven, crawling through the fascist celebrations.[3] Legality was unraveling fast; the impending terror storm must have been palpable. The chanting of the mindless minions as they waved their torches was only the ceremonial manifestation of the organized SA sadism which now riddled German life, and which was about to become a new state.

Münzenberg's chauffeur and bodyguard was a young man named Emil, a tough young son of the Berlin working class. That night Emil drove the boss in the Lincoln through the besotted city they would have passed near the Chancellery. There, lit by the blazing windows, bobbing and prancing in delight, Hitler looked down as his followers filed past in fascist ecstasy. In a separate window, von Hindenburg stood near, stolidly thumping his cane to the beat of the rising martial chants.

And then, a month later, came the Reichstag Fire, and with it the actual execution of the death sentence on Weimar that had been passed when Hitler took power. The fire took Münzenberg by surprise; for that matter it seems to have taken Hitler by surprise as well. The burning of the German legislature took place on the second-to-last night of February 1933, thirty days after *Reichspräsident* von Hindenburg had appointed Adolf Hitler the Republic's last legal Chancellor. Who set the Reichstag Fire, and why, remains one of the enduring mysteries in the history of totalitarianism. Its circumstances are wrapped, perhaps permanently, in multiple clouds of disinformation and lies. Yet the Reichstag Fire blazons a very clear mark on the landscape of modern history; it was one of those occasional moments after which the whole of political life is unmistakably changed.

This spectacular catastrophe was the pretext by which German totalitarianism was brought into being. In response to the arson, the newly and legally appointed Chancellor seized the police powers which he knew were essential to his plan to strangle Weimar democracy and establish absolute Nazi power in Germany. With it, Hitler embarked upon his war of state-sponsored terror against his "enemies": the Jews and the democratic Allies who had imposed the Versailles treaty.

But his first target was the German Communists, and it was on the communists that Hitler blamed the fire. The Soviet Union naturally responded, returning assault for assault, or at least propaganda for propaganda, and for the first time, the Soviets moved into what seemed a genuinely confrontational collision course with the emerging Nazi government. Even more urgently than Hitler's accession to power, the Reichstag Fire catalyzed what François Furet calls the "antifascist shift" in Soviet propaganda. Beginning in 1933, the Comintern began to turn away from its old "anti-bourgeois" obsession with "class war," replacing it—and "social fascism" too—with the very different "anti-Fascist Communism" that it brought to fruition two years later in the worldwide propaganda movement known as Popular Front.[4] Hitler ordered a great show trial to be held in Leipzig, condemning the Communists he had rounded up and accused of the fire, showing why the German Communist party had to be wiped out of the Reich. Münzenberg's apparatus, in turn, was ordered to use the machinery of the "Peace" movement to mount a new, worldwide antifascist campaign pinning the fire on the Nazis themselves, and assailing the new regime. It was to be the first great confrontation between the two totalitarian states, and in the obviously gathering crisis, the Soviet state under Stalin was assuming the moral high ground.

Or so it seemed.

The actual Reichstag arson seems to have taken Hitler himself completely off guard. Almost no student of the event believes the dictator himself ordered the fire, and—note well—neither did Münzenberg's propagandists stress Hitler's personal role. Hitler had been dining that evening with Goebbels and his family. Word of the fire came by telephone as the group sat listening to records after dinner. Goebbels at first took the call as a practical joke and slammed down the phone. Only after a second call did the party break up as the Chancellor grasped the truth. *"Now I have them!"* he shouted in astonished delight, and left at once to be rushed to the fire.[5]

Whether he had foreknowledge or not, once on the scene Hitler instantly grasped its rich possibilities for demagogy and just as quickly seized on them in something like a caricature of the Hitlerian frenzy. Led to a balcony overlooking the Sessions Chamber, by then brimful with waves of flame, "Hitler was leaning over the stone parapet, gazing into the red ocean of fire." Suddenly, he swung round. "His face had turned quite scarlet, both from the excitement and also from the heat . . . and he suddenly started screaming at the top of his voice: 'Now we'll show them! Anyone who stands in our way will be mown down. The German people have been soft too long. Every Communist official must be shot. All Communist deputies must be hanged this very night. All the friends of the Communists must be locked up. And that goes for the Social Democrats and the *Reichsbanner* as well.'"[6]

Thus was the Nazi line promulgated on the spot. Hitler decreed that this attack on German political life was a Communist outrage, the first step in a leftist insurrection. The Reds were trying to storm the Berlin citadel with this bonfire; it had been set to rouse every subversive in the country against the re-emergent Reich. They were scared of the fascist power galvanizing around them; they were trying to grab the new Germany for themselves. But they were not going to get away with it.

The Nazis had been looking for a pretext to strike and now they had one. The next day, Hitler promulgated the infamous Emergency Decree of February 28, the juridical cornerstone of Nazi totalitarianism. The idea girding its hysterical rhetoric was simple: The German police were no longer responsible to the judiciary. Thus empowered, the police worked through the night, and before the freezing break of day, the arrest squads were tramping through the streets of Berlin and the other major cities, legally completely unrestrained. Nor were they unprepared. Warrants by the thousands had already been stockpiled in the principal stations, signed and sealed in advance, with the names left blank, ready to be filled in with the name of any Communist, or indeed anyone at all, that Göring and his minions wanted to haul in. They were the blank checks of state terror. The Gestapo-to-be scooped them up in piles.

None of this should have surprised any knowing observer. Hitler had steadily promised to destroy German communism, and now exactly fulfilling his promise, he struck.

Yet despite their own warnings, most German communists, even many senior ones, appeared to be almost totally unprepared for that sudden violence. Münzenberg himself, though he had been through the best briefings in Moscow, was only half-prepared for the threat. From the start, the Comintern had seemed systematically to underestimate the Hitlerian menace.

Much about Hitler was underestimated in 1933, not least his uncanny *speed*. Nobody suspected that he could destroy the Weimar Republic in a single month, or that by the middle of the next year von Hindenburg, that Teutonic grandee who had once deprecated Hitler as the "little corporal," would be on his deathbed addressing his Chancellor in a moribund senile babble as "your Majesty."[7] Among those minimizing the threat were the German communists.[8] After a last meeting with the editors of his daily papers, Münzenberg remarked that the German Party's leadership reminded him of "dancers who had failed to notice that the curtain had come down."[9] Yet shortly before the November 1932 elections, the Communists actually had *joined* with the Nazis fomenting a Berlin transit strike. Ten days before Hitler's accession, Moscow had forbidden any forcible resistance to a huge SA demonstration outside Party headquarters. Ten days before the Reichstag Fire, the cream of the German left gathered for one last divided display of impotence. The Communist left assembled in one hall, the Social Democrats in another. Then came the fire, and the dictator struck.

Willi seems to have escaped arrest himself because of a flukish stroke of good fortune. Münzenberg was certainly among the most senior members of the International on the Nazi hit list, and that morning at first light, an arrest squad was at the door of the Tiergarten apartment. Of course Münzenberg was not there, nor had he been there for over a month. But he was not even in Berlin. Several hundred communist officials had already been arrested in the night, but Münzenberg was away, delivering a speech near Frankfurt-am-Main. He had spent the night with WIR operatives there. When the police came knocking in Berlin, the door was answered by Münzenberg's indispensable confidential secretary, a young man named Hans Schulz. The police glanced at Hans. If only they had known! Schulz, with his plain, pale, deferential looks and gimpy leg carried in his photographic memory, famous throughout the *apparat*, untold and untellable amounts of secret information about covert operations in Germany and around the world. Schulz was Willi Münzenberg's personal contact with the deep-cover apparatus, carefully trained to be the keeper of Willi's secrets. It was Hans's memory that stored the information no one would dream of entrusting to paper. Hans was the keeper of Willi's secrets. Long ago sent to Moscow for his education in covert work, Hans carried in that head more politically sensitive information than any twenty of the other communists rounded up that night. To the police, Hans Schulz looked like a rather washed-out little clerk, who very deferentially showed them from room to room. And of course they did not find their man.[10]

From Berlin the disappointed arrest squad flashed word to Frankfurt. There, Münzenberg's haunts were well enough known for a second squad to be instantly dispatched to his favorite cafe. They were right: At that very moment, the Comintern's propaganda chief was strolling toward his breakfast, carrying a handful of his own newspapers, ready to catch up on the sensational news about last night's fire.

He never reached the cafe door.

I say the police failed to understand who Hans Schulz was. Yet it may be that some in the squad knew more than they admitted. Hitler's move to crush the German Communist party was made possible only by a simultaneous move from partial to absolute control over the German police, and at that moment, contrary to the common myth, the Berlin police were generally leftish.[11] That is one thing that gave Ernst Röhm's brownshirts their menacing importance; the need for a more fully obedient corps would also induce Hitler completely to remake the German police by inventing the Gestapo. The last morning of February 1933 was the precise moment at which Germany was being transformed from a state with police into a police state, and it is notable that for Münzenberg's flight, the decisive move came from a cop. Just as the squad gathered to leave, a tiny event of revelatory interest took place in the foyer. One of the officers, who happened to recognize Hans Schulz's wife, the daughter of a prominent Social Democratic police official, took her aside and whispered: *Run. Warn your friends and run.* He was telling her what he knew and they did not. Overnight, the world had changed.[12]

This transgression in the direction of decency may well have saved Münzenberg.

Only a few minutes after the police had left the Berlin apartment, Babette Gross telephoned from Frankfurt, desperate for news. The cop's warning was repeated. Without it, she, her husband, all of them might have been rounded up with the other German communist leaders. Babette acted immediately. Münzenberg was to meet Emil in the cafe of the Frankfurt train station. The task now was to prevent that rendezvous. She and Emil rushed to the square in front of the station and posted themselves at each entrance. When he hoved into sight, he was springy, full of nerve even in danger, carrying his papers, looking forward to his coffee. Emil ran forward, took his startled boss by the arm, and gently but firmly led him to the car, as Babette jumped in and Emil began to drive.

The old life was over. Emil drove blindly, on the first road out of Frankfurt. It happened to be heading south. Münzenberg was running without a visa or passport; his driver didn't know where he was driving. Suddenly Babette Gross remembered that she had a relation in the neighborhood. Her sister Margarete had been previously married to a son of Martin Buber, and Martin Buber lived nearby, in Darmstadt. To Darmstadt they drove. It would have been far too dangerous for the Bubers to attempt to hide Willi there, but Emil took the car to within a couple of miles from the house, and Babette walked, alone, to her sometime relations' door. The Bubers were aghast seeing the terrified woman on their step and immediately grasped the danger. Buber had one useful suggestion. The Saar was perhaps seventy miles away. Though German, it was—as the result of a bitterly resented provision of the Versailles Treaty—not under German control. It was beyond the reach of the German police. It could be entered without a visa, and Buber had a colleague there, a professor whom he mistakenly believed could be trusted. Entering the Saar *did* require a passport however, and at this moment Münzenberg's passport was as good as an arrest warrant. In any case, he did not have it with him.

A new passport could be found only in Frankfurt. Armed with Buber's letter of introduction, Babette and Emil drove back north and, leaving Münzenberg on a promenade beside the Rhine in the suburb of Mainz, returned to the city. On this day when German totalitarianism was officially born, it was also carnival, and carnival was in full swing. Every office was closed; the streets were filled not only with police, but drunks and revelers. Leaving Emil below, Babette proceeded to the offices of a Trust publishing house, which she found deserted except for one young comrade, who was fourteen years younger than Münzenberg, and looked nothing like him. But some sort of passport was essential, now. The youth promptly turned over his.

The streets below were delirious. The carnival processions swirled around her, but Babette could not find Emil. She ran to a nearby cafe they both knew. A waiter turned her back at the door with the news that the arrest squad had already been there, looking for her husband.

When she found Emil again it had begun to snow, and as they drove back to Mainz night was falling. They found Münzenberg wandering alone by the river.

It was time to move. The Lincoln crawled through the blowing dark, looking for the most deserted country byways heading west.

They felt their way to the border. The Saar would be only a way station on their escape: Visas for entry into France still had to be finagled; Babette Gross would still have to return to Berlin for an essential supply of secret cash deposited with the Soviet ambassador. Nor was the Saar without its own dangers: Buber's colleague, possibly a crypto-Nazi, proved less reliable than supposed. But unless he got out of Germany proper, and quickly, Münzenberg was lost. He had to have an incognito; he had to cross the border; he had to disappear. For this, only the Saar would do.

It was deep in the small hours when the Lincoln pulled into the tiny customs station on the border. The snow was still flying across the almost deserted road. A guard walked out, leaned into the dark car, and waved his flashlight from face to face. Then he paused. Without asking for passports, the guard gave Emil a weary wave-through.

We can only imagine what must have been singing through the young driver's mind as he hit the accelerator and made that long heavy limousine move on out.[13]

***

All at once, an era was coming together.

Hitler was seizing totalitarian power. Within a matter of days after these events in Germany, workmen in distant Washington would hammer together the platform on the steps of the United States Capitol Building where Franklin Roosevelt would take the presidential oath for the first time and then tell Americans that the only thing they had to fear was fear itself.

As for Münzenberg, once he had crossed the German border on that snowy first Walpurgisnacht of the Nazi terror, his path to Paris was reasonably direct. He remained hidden in the Saarland for perhaps a week, waiting for the apparatus to finagle the papers necessary for his entry into France. While he was still there, the Comintern in Moscow was undoubtedly informed of his whereabouts and the Party in France alerted to his imminent arrival. Then in early March, Emil drove the boss across the French border and directly to the City of Light.[14]

It was in Paris that Willi's role in the history of Communism would be swept into its next and greatest phase. And it was in Paris that his role would find a fatal fulfillment. The "anti-Fascist communism" now taking shape would soon sustain one of the dominant moral myths of its era: the notion that Stalin was Hitler's only *true* enemy, that serious opposition to Nazism entailed making peace with the Soviet line. This was a concept that would become steadily more important to Stalin—until he dumped it for an alliance with Hitler. It was also a concept that worked: it was soon accepted as self-evident truth through wide sectors of enlightened western thinking. And it was a concept that could be promoted among non-communists only by the propaganda techniques of which Willi was the inventor and master. He alone knew how to co-opt the rising tide of Western antifascist outrage and put it to work for Soviet ends.

In Moscow, Willi's old ally Karl Radek was becoming Stalin's answer-man on German affairs, and he would act as Willi's ally at the highest level. A vast campaign, having as its first point of focus the Reichstag Fire, was to be organized in Paris, as the founding event of the new antifascism. In that sense it would be the first direct confrontation of the Second World War.[15]

The new Comintern campaign that Willi created with Radek's advice raged. It filled the world press. Every thing about it had the look of complete hostility and total confrontation. The Nazis were using the trial to justify their assumption of totalitarian power. The Communists counterattacked, demonstrating that totalitarian power had been assumed under fraud. Among enlightened and educated Westerners, the communist campaign was of course by far the more plausible of the two; in fact it was persuasive—above all to anyone who needed little persuading about the Nazis. The Münzenberg men hit the Nazis hard, especially the SA, and hit them again and again. And if, in the process, they promoted a number of falsehoods of its own, they were at least plausible falsehoods. Here at last was something like real antifascism. It seemed in essence right, and obviously so. How could it not be?

***

The focus of the Nazi campaign in Germany was Hitler's trial of the people he claimed were responsible for setting the fire and seeking to create a communist insurrection against the National Socialist State. While the Sessions Chamber of the German legislature was still a maelstrom of flames, the Berlin police had rushed into the smoking corridors and nabbed, red-handed, a singed, shirtless, and hysterical young man named Marinus van der Lubbe, who was immediately arrested and led away shouting "Protest! Protest!" in a thick Dutch accent.[16]

Marinus van der Lubbe was indisputably one of the arsonists, and the only indisputable one ever caught. He claimed from the beginning that he had acted alone, and he persisted in saying so until he was beheaded a year later under the Leipzig guillotine.

Van der Lubbe's plain, simple, numb claim to sole responsibility was inconvenient. Nobody on either side wanted an incendiary who really had acted alone. Once Hitler had proclaimed the fire a Communist conspiracy, the Nazis needed Communist conspirators, not this solitary shirtless nitwit. Nonetheless, instead of merely shooting their captive, the Nazis decided to exploit the fact that his seizure in the ruins had instantly made him world-famous. He was at least incontestably guilty. So the Nazis would prop van der Lubbe in the dock surrounded by sundry Communist bigwigs whom they hoped, by hook or crook, to link to the Dutchman in a show trial justifying the anti-Communist terror.

Large-scale arrests of German Communists had been going on since that night. Yet some ten days after the conflagration, by what seemed peculiarly good luck, the Berlin police netted three particularly sensational communist fish. One of the arrested men turned out to be no less than Georgi Dimitrov, a senior Comintern officer and leading Bulgarian associate of Stalin; a famous and practiced conspirator. Two fellow Bulgarians, Simon Popov and Vassili Tanev, accompanied Dimitrov.

The three men were arrested on a tip-off from a waiter in a restaurant where the three of them had gone to dine. This fact is in itself strange. As Margarete Buber-Neumann wrote, "they failed to observe...the most elementary precautions essential in secret service. After the Reichstag Fire, they went calmly went into the 'Bayernhof' restaurant in Berlin, a place infested with Nazis, and sat merrily chatting away in Bulgarian"—a language that to ordinary German ears, such as a waiter's, would sound indistinguishable from Russian.[17] A coded report sent from a Comintern agent to the Moscow center shortly after the Bulgarian's arrest notes in perplexity that Dimitrov had been repeatedly warned of danger at the Bayernhof: the *apparat* knew the place was a high-risk spot. Dimitrov had laughed their warnings away. The agent also reported to the Moscow Center that either Tanev or Popov, explicitly fearing arrest, had earlier complained to several comrades that Dimitrov had insisted upon "pulling" him into a place he knew was dangerous. Several days before his arrest, Dimitrov had another warning: he learned that the Nazis had been alerted to his presence in Berlin, and the agents advising him had "insisted" he leave at once. He had refused.[18] Once in the Bayernhof, with their alien looks and foreign talk, it did not take long for a pro-Nazi waiter, greedy for a cash reward, to head for the telephone.[19] The Nazis soon knew who they had nabbed a very big fish. Dimitrov's companions, Simon Popov and Vassili Tanev, are often described as his "lieutenants." In fact, though technically his subordinates, both were among Dimitrov's factional opponents in the Bulgarian party, and one of them was in Berlin on a separate mission from whatever had brought Dimitrov to town, and was about to leave without him.[20] These men were then arraigned alongside Ernst Torgler, an important Communist deputy in the Reichstag—the only German in the dock—and accused of setting the fire.

Popov and Tanev look like the Rosencrantz and Guildenstern of the piece. After the Leipzig trial, when Dimitrov and the Bulgarians were acquitted and released—for they were, all three, acquitted and released—they were flown "home" to Moscow, where they were greeted with every possible sign of victory and rejoicing. There all three sat for heroic statues. In due course, Stalin rewarded the new antifascist celebrity Dimitrov with promotion to the increasingly hollow position of director of the Comintern.

Popov and Tanev, however, did not fare so well. After their moment in the sun both were dispatched to the gulag. After 1941, Tanev was released from the vast Soviet concentration camp at Kolyma and parachuted into Bulgaria on a very dangerous Comintern mission, where he was apprehended and killed. Popov managed to crawl through all those endless days and endless years in the hell of cold—twenty years in all—until a thaw in 1955 led to his release.

***

Münzenberg was slow to surface publicly in Paris, but within days of his arrival, the city's cultural life and with it the cultural life of the West, had entered a new phase.

On March 21, 1933, days after Münzenberg's arrival, the new dispensation had its debut at an enormously glamorous protest meeting over the Reichstag Fire in which all Paris was present.[21] André Gide, Elsa Triolet, and Louis Aragon, all were there. André and Clara Malraux—sleek, superb, and newly famous—were carefully placed in the very front row. This sort of thing was the basis of a new cultural-political chic, and it would remain so until the end of the Spanish Civil War, the first of hundreds, perhaps thousands of such meetings held around the West. Causes were adopted, celebrities were enlisted. In public and in secret, both legally and illegally, all Münzenberg's skills seemed turned toward a single driven, absolute object: opposition. Opposition and nothing else.

In Paris, Münzenberg settled into his refuge on the Left Bank, and with the help of the Comintern apparatus he was soon installed in a dingy set of offices at the end of a dark, almost unnoticeable alley on the Boulevard Montparnasse.[22] To rally and exploit the rising world sentiment against the Nazis, Münzenberg summoned up a new and refurbished array of fronts. Within weeks the Comintern had procured a publishing house for his use, likewise in the Latin Quarter: Editions du Carrefour on the Boulevard Saint-Germain, a publisher which, before the apparatus bought it, had produced elegant anthologies of poetry and luxurious monographs on modernist painting. One of the people most instrumental in the transfer of Editions du Carrefour to Comintern control was a dandyish young French writer whose two best friends were Raymond Aron and Jean-Paul Sartre. He was Paul Nizan, and the three friends together naturally called themselves the three musketeers.[23]

Inside Paris itself, there was already a fairly well-developed political apparatus waiting for Willi's command, geared both to propaganda and covert action. Willi was able to make use of the French Communist party, which was given a *mandat* by the Comintern—that is, a plenipotentiary command from the Moscow Center—requiring every possible assistance in his operations. Not long after, a similar *mandat,* written incidentally on a piece of silk so it could be sewn into the courier's clothes, was signed by Münzenberg and delivered by Gibarti to Earl Browder, the head of the American Communist party in New York.[24] Münzenberg's prime contact within the French Party was its cultural commissar, with editor-in-chief of *Humanité,* Paul Vaillant-Couturier, over whom Münzenberg would have had authority in matters of management of the antifascist movement.[25] As a result, up through 1935, wherever one sees Vaillant performing some action linked to that campaign, anything from the courtship of André Gide to dispatching Malraux to Germany, it is a reasonable guess that the French propaganda officer had coordinated his actions with Münzenberg.[26]

But the machinery of Amsterdam-Pleyel was already installed in the French capital, bypassing the French Party and directly under Comintern command. Amsterdam-Pleyel had been alerted to the new tactics at Münzenberg's Moscow meeting in early January 1933. The Moscow Archives show a seamless transition between the enterprises of "pacifism" to the new antifascism, organizing the rallies of intellectuals, the public position-taking, the committees of the concerned, the phalanxes of celebrities.[27] Working from head-quarters in the small suburban town of Aumont, Münzenberg's man Louis Gibarti was in charge.

A word about Gibarti.[28] He seems to have joined the Soviet services at the time of Bela Kun's regime in Hungary, serving at various times in Vienna, Moscow, and Berlin. The Far East was one of his earliest propaganda interests, where he must have been an early ally of Borodin. Certainly Gibarti was deep in the Comintern's work in East Asia. In this capacity, Gibarti developed important and long contacts with M. N. Roy, Nehru, and Ho Chi Minh. In a certain sense, Gibarti might be called one of the founders of the Third World movement. His interest in China lingered. During a secret mission to America in the thirties, one of the "innocents" Gibarti first contacted was the famous American China hand Owen Lattimore, who, he claimed, had been presented to him as an American fellow traveler, eager to give assistance to communist needs.[29] It should be added that the League Against Imperialism was always used as an instrument not just for propaganda, but also sabotage and espionage.[30]

Dropping peace was easy. Overnight the World Committee Against War was renamed the World Committee Against War *and* Fascism. Thus was brought into being the largest, if not the most important, of Münzenberg's many contributions to manipulated political innocence.[31]

Under the cover of these public and legal operations, an anti-fascist underground was also established, designed to send agents into Germany both to maintain contact with the German Communists left behind, and to perform other secret work within the Reich. The man who'd been introduced to Lenin as the wunderkind of the underground network was now assigned the task of penetrating Hitler's world. Münzenberg's ingenuity flowered. Once Dimitrov was arrested, for example, it was plain that Münzenberg agents had been placed throughout the prison where the Comintern official was being held. The Münzenberg men in Paris knew that Willi and Dimitrov were in regular and easy contact, right under the Nazis' noses! It was seen as a crowning tribute to their master's skill.[32]

New networks were strung together all through Germany. Sympathetic countesses were dispatched to Germany with documents sewn into their clothes. They "rested" in clinics run by doctors who were also in the underground, linked in turn to inconspicuous ladies in shabby coats, who were contacts for foul-mouthed street-fighters from Berlin's back streets, who in turn took their cue from some nonchalant fellow carrying a violin case. The penniless and the powerful were secretly joined in clandestine action. People who would never even have seen themselves as on the left found themselves joined with hard-core revolutionaries.[33] Journalists were given crash courses in undercover technique and sent into Nazi territory both to prepare their stories and to accomplish various less public tasks.[34] Münzenberg's new networks could spirit people in danger across the border, speed false papers into the right hands. They also maintained a flow of news about the mass arrests of communists, about Nazi rearmament, about the first government persecution of the Jews—and about the construction of a new, large political internment camp located in a little south German town called Dachau.

Paris meanwhile became the Mecca for all the many exiles in flight from the new Reich. They filled Montparnasse, crowded into the cafes. Mingling among them were spies. Ragged and terrified Comintern agents, riding out of the nightmare in third-class railroad cars, would stumble across Münzenberg's threshold, in from the fascist cold.[35] Nothing is more easily understood than how the German exile community, rightly afraid, rightly angry, and apparently without resources, was irresistibly drawn into Münzenberg's Paris ambit. There was hardly a German refugee in Europe whose life was not brushed by Münzenberg's work, and much in the subsequent political history of both Europe and America was founded in the flow of loyalties that came together here. Both Manes Sperber and Arthur Koestler have written with wonderful vividness about those days, working for Willi in the center of the hive. Half the intelligentsia of a great country had been thrown into a grotesque new diaspora. The consequences have rung down the decades.

A quieter and more concentrated instrument of the new policy was an organization called the World Committee for the Relief of the Victims of German Fascism. The World Committee was a smaller and far more fine-tuned front for propaganda and secret work than the League Against War and Fascism. A courier brought specific instructions for its creation from Moscow in early March.[36] Once again, Louis Gibarti was put in charge.

The World Committee did not court thousands of members. That was left to the big soft organizations. Instead, the World Committee sought politically important contacts, and it performed very particular secret tasks. For example, agents of the World Committee for the Relief of the Victims of German Fascism were involved in feeding disinformation to Winston Churchill.[37]

The nominal head and front man for the World Committee for the Relief of the Victims of German Fascism was a politically respectable leftist who despite his independent look was a fully collaborating Münzenberg-man. This was Count Michael Károlyi, a leading politician of the high Hungarian aristocracy, who in the chaos of 1918 had been the first socialist president of Hungary. Because Count Károlyi's social democratic government has been overthrown in the Bolshevik uprising of Bela Kun in 1919, most observers assumed that Count Károlyi must be anti-Stalinist, and hence anti-communist. This was a great mistake. Though they invariably retained grounds for insisting upon their independence, the Count and Countess Károlyi were in virtually all things enthusiastic admirers of and acolytes to the Soviet government throughout the late 1920s and 1930s. Even their occasional distress about the violence of the regime did not deter an essential allegiance. In the mid-thirties, they were among Willi's close friends and advisors, and Willi trusted the Countess sufficiently to send her on a dangerous mission into the Reich, making contacts with the Communist underground there. They continued to be major fellow travelers until the crisis of 1948–52 in Eastern Europe, which culminated in the execution of many of their friends. There can be no doubt that Count Károlyi was witting in his role as head of the World Committee and as a general front man and advisor to

Münzenberg. Meanwhile, the Countess showed great courage on her German missions for Willi.[38]

The World Committee, with Károlyi as its figurehead, functioned like the League Against War and Fascism as a cover and point of entry for agents of influence and covert action. In America, Elizabeth Bentley took her first steps into the NKVD through the League Against War and Fascism.[39] In England, Maurice Dobb, the Cambridge advisor to the League Against Imperialism and an open communist, guided the youthful Kim Philby to Paris, there also to contact the World Committee.[40] From the World Committee Philby was sent on to Vienna, and the start of a momentous career.[41]

Then of course there was the question of Willi's own contact with the unseen world. Once a week, as dusk was gathering over Paris, Willi would leave his offices on the Boulevard Montparnasse for what looked like a stroll around the *quartier*. He would take off in some fresh direction each time, following his whim through the ancient maze of the Latin Quarter. As he walked he would invariably bump into a succession of German exiles, and since he knew them all he would stop and chat. One such little chat took place every week at exactly the same time on the rue de Montparnasse, a small street jutting off the great Boulevard of the same name. Münzenberg would stop and talk to a man who according to Babette looked "like a Jewish doctor." The two would talk, never for long, but without fail. Now and then the personnel would change, and Willi would meet with a taller, considerably younger man. Sometimes it was Willi's secretary Hans Schulz who made the rendezvous: Hans of the phenomenal memory, the one-man secret service secretariat. The big city relaxed. The vesper sparrows circled over the famous rooftops.

This street-corner encounter was a weekly meeting of the Comintern's director of propaganda and his Comintern case officer. It lasted for only a few minutes, rarely more. The chat was concentrated. To the wise, three or four words could define policy and shape high politics. A question. A judgment. A decision. A command. They didn't take long. Even Willi was impressed by the terse economy of the transaction and the instant speed with which his questions and directives moved in absolute secrecy back and forth to Moscow. Ask, and it was answered. But *immediately*. The efficiency of the *apparat*'s web for transmission of information, above all via the so-called "red orchestra" of secret radio operations, had come a very long way since Willi was sending messages in jam jars.[42]

These contacts also met regularly with Louis Gibarti as well.[43] Meanwhile, the famous NKVD resident Ignace Reiss was active in Paris. Babette Gross had been good friends with Reiss's wife Elisabeth in Berlin before Hitler took power. In Paris, however, she was told by Münzenberg that she must feign absolute non-recognition of Reiss or Elisabeth Poretsky whenever their paths crossed.[44]

After 1935, Münzenberg's Paris contact was yet another figure in that Hungarian Mafia of agents to which Gibarti belonged. His real name—at least I know of no other—was Gyula Alpari. Within the *apparat*, he was usually known as "Julius."[45]

According to Babette, Julius was very much a family man, who regularly complained that his job kept him forever on the road. He and Willi Münzenberg went back a long way together, to the Volga Famine at least, and Julius must have known Gibarti for a long time as well, probably since their days together with Bela Kun in 1919. Despite his wish for a sedentary life, Julius had always been near the hot center, always involved in propaganda. In Berlin during the early twenties, he had been editor of *Inprecorr*, a kind of *Congressional Record* for Comintern and the Revolution, and an invaluable document in the history of communism. In 1933–1934, Julius was in Switzerland, editing a Communist journal called the *Rundschau*. In 1935, he went to France and worked at Willi's senior Comintern contact, working closely with Eugen Fried, the Comintern's prime representative in France. By mid-1938, he was beginning to take over some of Willi's work: Dimitrov's diary shows that he had put Julius in charge of the propaganda for a show trial in Spain smearing the non-Stalinist Marxist Party there, the POUM, as Trotskyites and fascist agents. Not long after, Dimitrov notes ominously that the NKVD had let him know they had "certain facts" about Julius in their fatal files.[46]

The later fate of Julius is terrible, and a little mysterious. When the Nazis moved in on Paris in 1940, this major secret agent made no attempt to leave Paris. Why leave? The USSR was deep in its alliance with Hitler. "Antifascism" was a thing of the past. Even so, Babette Gross found his complacency odd. "He must have thought that his papers were exceptionally reliable," she remarked to me, dryly.

If he thought he was safe, Julius was wrong. Thought the pact was still in effect, it would be shattered soon enough, and even before the Nazi invasion of the Soviet Union, at the end of 1940, the Gestapo arrested Gyula Alpari in Paris. In 1944, he was put to death in the Nazi prison camp of Sachsenhausen.[47]

But Julius and his "contacts" were all invisible men. It was Münzenberg's job, on the other hand, to make things conspicuous. An essential part in Parisian influence is chic, and one of Münzenberg's earliest protectors in France was a brilliant and memorable figure in the history of chic named Lucien Vogel.[48] First in Berlin, and later in France, later still in the United States, Lucien Vogel was one of the influential and inventive magazine publishers and tastemakers of this century. Münzenberg had known him since the twenties. As early as 1926, Vogel worked at advancing the avant-garde of post-revolutionary Soviet art and taste. He was among the first to see its possibilities for European high style. He was curator of the Soviet Pavilion of the 1926 International Exposition of Decorative Arts, a dazzling showcase of Soviet constructivism and non-figurative art, the purpose of which was to fuse bolshevism in the mind of the European intelligentsia with the look of everything modern. And of course that was a very welcome project to Willi.

From publishing in Berlin, Vogel proceeded to Paris, where he proceeded to create what became a great glossy magazine of French high style: *Vu*, along with its literary companion publication, *Lu*. Both were vehicles for the Münzenberg Trust; both showcases for Stalinism under its guise of imaginary glamour. Meanwhile, Vogel performed many a service for Willi in exile. For example, almost all offers from the apparatus made to André Gide concerning possible trips to the Soviet Union or a possible film deal with Mezhropohmfilm Russ were conveyed through Vogel.[49] And it was Vogel's daughter, Marie-Claude, who served as Willi's handmaiden as he entered the French world.

In the second week of March, Emil drove Münzenberg in the Lincoln limousine down the budding *allée des arbres* that led to Lucien Vogel's country residence, an irresistibly luxurious retreat and house of spies located a little to the northwest of Paris in the Forêt de Saint-Germain. It was known as La Faisanderie. Built in the sixteenth century, La Faisanderie was a former shooting box of Louis XIV. It was a long, low, inviting house at the end of an impressively extended tree-lined drive, set in the middle of a park. In it, Vogel ran a continuous open house for the very fashionable left, the great good place for the Stalinist upper crust. Vogel knew everybody. He was among the best-placed fellow travelers in Europe, an arbiter of taste, and a host to the manner born. He dressed, according to Count Károlyi, "like a grand *seigneur* of the '90s, with his inseparable pipe, bright checked suits, tight trousers and old-fashioned choker."

There was usually nothing clandestine about a weekend at La Faisanderie. It was merely select—a chaos of political and sexual crossing paths. Guests sometimes complained that it took a week to recover from the fun. The cool stone house was filled with "white Russians, Armenians and Georgians, dark-haired women with jet-black eyes who, lying on cushion-covered low couches would talk Russian loudly to each other, a language neither the host nor his wife nor any of the other guests could understand." Vogel lived "surrounded by Soviet Russians, journalists and officials." There were "smart American women, German spies, and agents and adventurers from all countries."[50]

Another habitué was Pierre Bertaux, a bright young man from a very proper French academic family that was close to André Gide and the Mann family. Pierre Bertaux started haunting La Faisanderie because he was in love with Marie-Claude Vogel, Lucien's daughter.

And for a while this love seemed to be reciprocated, though eventually Marie-Claude unceremoniously dropped Pierre in favor of the doomed and dynamic young Vaillant-Couturier. The personal decision rang with politics. With Willi's arrival in Paris, Vaillant came into his political own, thrust in a way onto the world stage. His photographs of the period show a large, sensual face, sad with the distant gaze of a saturnine romantic. Vaillant seems almost to be considering his own early death. In truth, Vaillant was a brilliant organizer with a profound understanding of his country's cultural habits. The apparatus could not have chosen a better man. And Marie-Claude chose Vaillant.[51]

The rejected Pierre would himself move deep into the secret world, a democrat and anti-communist as well as a leading force in the resistance. Bertaux's father Felix had been the leading French Germanist of his era: A standard French-German dictionary of the period bore his name. Pierre was raised perfectly bilingual; he was completely at ease in unaccented Berlin *Deutsch*. This made him useful. The French government put him in charge of anti-Nazi broadcasts into the Reich and he also became an undercover operative. One of his earliest missions as a secret agent was to go to Germany, pry Thomas Mann's personal fortune loose from German hands, and get it to Switzerland. The mission succeeded.[52]

In an interview with me shortly before he died, Bertaux recalled La Faisanderie as if he'd walked into a magic forest. "It was a world apart," says Bertaux. "There were people everywhere in little informal groups, chatting, lots of canapés, lots of going to the bar, nobody got up when you were introduced, and among those who stayed you never knew who was sleeping with whom. It was all very discreet, and very sympathetic—but a little bizarre." By the time Bertaux first entered the social wonderland, Münzenberg had surfaced. The young man looked across the lounging room and there, he says, was the Red Eminence himself—"a fish in water."[53]

In addition to its delicious food, drink, and those lounging dark-eyed women, La Faisanderie was wall-to-wall spies. Its habitués included many in Münzenberg's entourage, including the ubiquitous novelist Egon Erwin Kisch. There was a sort of pseudo-writer and

Comintern agent named Alfred Kantorowicz, who during the Spanish War became a culture commissar in Spain and whom Münzenberg installed as the man "running the show"—the phrase is Arthur Koestler's—in yet another front organization, the Association of German Writers in Exile.

Also lining up at La Faisanderie's bar was the amazing and ingratiating Mikhail Koltsov. Koltsov is today remembered most often as the model for brilliant Soviet journalist "Karkov" in Ernest Hemingway's *For Whom the Bell Tolls*. But the real Koltsov deserves a book of his own. Hemingway thought him "the most intelligent man he had ever met." Though mainly based in Moscow, and a writer for *Pravda*, Koltsov always worked in close collaboration with Münzenberg's enterprises, especially propaganda among the cultural elite, with whom he was at ease, and whom he invariably impressed. He was a key figure in the *apparat*'s courtship of André Gide and its successful appropriation of Louis Aragon. A good account of how Koltsov's work as a propagandist meshed with Willi's in found in the memoir of his close associate (and an active Münzenberg man), Gustav Regler: *The Owl of Minerva*. Regler shows us Koltsov both in Spain (he probably introduced Hemingway to Koltsov) and in Moscow, where in the mid-thirties, Koltsov served Lev Kamenev as his propagandistic right hand. When Stalin's arrest of Kamenev and Zinoviev initiated the Great Terror, most observers thought Koltsov would be killed along with his patron. But no: Stalin was not yet ready to "liquidate" Koltsov. Instead the writer was sent to Spain, where he met Hemingway, introduced by Regler and another "Münzenberg man," Joris Ivens, who had installed himself at the center of Hemingway's life at this time. In Spain, Koltsov was secretly among the most highly empowered Soviets on the scene: using the code name "Comrade Miguel," he became one of Stalin's prime advisors there. Hemingway was far from alone in his admiration: a man of surpassing intelligence and charm, "Comrade Miguel" made a profound impression on all who met him, including Stalin, who quickly spotted Koltsov's suppleness and intelligence and played with it as a cat plays with its mouse. According to Arkady Vaksberg, who speaks of the journalist's "incredible dynamism," Stalin waited until 1942 to have Koltsov arrested, broken, and put to death.[54]

There was also the question of the French government's connection to Münzenberg, as well as the response of the French Communist party. Münzenberg's presence in Paris created complications to both the upper hierarchy of the French Communist party and the French government itself. The ambivalence of the French government was especially interesting. One might assume the French center and right would have viewed Münzenberg as a dangerous subversive, and indeed this was so in many cases. But it was not altogether so.

The approach to the French government was arranged through a famous writer, Henri Barbusse, whose life, as the Moscow Archives clearly show, was as thoroughly managed by the apparatus as that of Rolland.[55] They were joined by the always well-connected Vogel.[56] It would be necessary to placate the nervous establishment and the nervous communists with a single stroke. To accomplish this act of mediation, Vogel and Barbusse brought in a new and remarkably arcane player, a lawyer and diplomat named Gaston Bergery.

Bergery was an intensely ambitious politician, and an especially shrewd and independent fellow traveler crucially placed between communist and non-communist worlds. He was married to the daughter of none other than Leonid Krassin, Lenin's principal business negotiator in the non-communist world, the object of the famous "Zinoviev Letter," of an earlier Somerset Maugham-like era. Bergery represented an unimportant splinter party in the Assemblée Nationale. Though lack of money and the right party connections doomed his hopes for elective power, Bergery had followed in his father-in-law's path and become a player in the realm of East-West big business. His connections were the best there were. Intimately though discreetly linked to the Soviets, he was also the French legal advisor to General Motors, a broker between two worlds, usable but not controlled by either. He was, according to Bertaux, "one of the most intelligent Frenchmen of his generation."

Bergery had excellent access to the Elysée and the then prime minister of the French republic, Camille Chautemps. Chautemps was a very insightful centrist politician who clearly saw the coming crisis with Germany. Bergery saw what Chautemps saw, and so they cut a deal. They had instantly grasped the desirability of integrating the Münzenberg operations into the French structure. Münzenberg might enjoy French protection so long as he directed his notorious capacities for subversion, disinformation, and trouble against the Germans, not the French. Who knew, they might even from time to time share in the fruits of espionage.[57] In a single stroke, the French would acquire a damaging instrument against the Nazis and co-opt the communists. A secret meeting of the cabinet was convened, and to the astonishment of the uninitiated, Bergery prevailed. Münzenberg *and* members of his apparatus would be supplied with *cartes d'identité* as *réfugiés provenant d'Allemagne*. The condition was that they not interfere in French political affairs. The deal was of course unpublicized, and enforced by the collaborating watchfulness of the Communist party and the French intelligence service. But it *was* a deal, and a triumph. Münzenberg would be more than tolerated in France. He would be protected. From that point onward, one of the surest ways for a German in flight to find the French government's favor was Münzenberg's potent nod.

The *cartes d'identité* were issued. There was nothing to be done about it. The French police, along with the rest of the French right, looked on in impotent rage.

The willingness of the Chautemps government to engage in antifascist activity was vital. At a quite early stage, Pierre Bertaux went to Chautemps with a suggestion that he set up an antifascist German-language radio station to be beamed into the Reich and covertly funded by the French government. Chautemps immediately accepted the idea and Bertaux duly put it into operation, delivering his last broadcast virtually the day the Germans marched into Paris. According to Bertaux, Chautemps did not even need to reflect on this proposal. The moment the young man had finished his presentation, Chautemps simply said, "Fine. Go ahead."[58]

Such was the ambience, secret and public, when Münzenberg arrived in Paris in March 1933. Everything was in place, except for one central detail: He would be needing a manager for the antifascist campaign, a right hand, a lieutenant.

This lieutenant was selected in Moscow in consultation with the two essential people: Münzenberg and Radek. Just as Stalin adopted his new policy with uncharacteristic speed, so the choice of Münzenberg's secret service shadow was made with uncanny swiftness. Fully primed by Radek himself, the chosen shadow boarded the train in Moscow. He carried most secret instructions for Münzenberg with him, and he was empowered in such a way as to be potentially menacing to Willi's power. He came to Paris by the long way, the *apparat* alternate route to the West—that is, not through Germany but north to Leningrad, through Scandinavia, and then south across the Low Countries into France, and on to the Gare du Nord.

This man had been sent from Moscow to serve as Willi's right hand, and in every sense, his spy. However the choice of this secret agent was made, it was a brilliant and daring one. The man who stepped off the Moscow train at the Gare du Nord was perfection composed of every improbability, the highest improbability of all being that with his ravaged face and tender smile, this sometime dilettante, this consort of Dietrich and friend of Kafka, this playboy of the Berlin theater was destined to become one of the most extraordinary figures in the history of espionage.

His name—his real name—was Otto Katz.

Chapter 4

The Lieutenant

O tto Katz, that master of the secret life, was at heart a man of the theater. The secret agent who became Münzenberg's right hand in creating the Soviet's great antifascist campaign of the 1930s loved the world of the stage and film, and he spent much of his life in its precincts. Its people were his friends. From Bertolt Brecht to Lillian Hellman, from Sergei Eisenstein to Fritz Lang, Katz spent his days among the stars, a companion to theater folk, and in the ambience of the international cinema. He claimed, and it is conceivably true, that Marlene Dietrich had been his first great love. It fits perfectly that as he stood in the dock, about to be condemned to death, Otto Katz invoked the name of Noël Coward.[1]

Katz was introduced to both his life in the theater and to his life in the secret world by Münzenberg, who in 1924 had discovered the very young Otto, already a covert communist, already a man with developed feeling for high culture and duplicity, working as a publicist for a liberal magazine, *Das Tagebuch*.[2] By birth Katz was a Sudeten German from Prague, raised in the same Czech-Jewish upper-middle class and generation into which Franz Kafka had been born. It was his lifelong boast that in his youth he had belonged to Kafka's circle, and the claim seems not only plausible but even probable. It is certain that Katz was close to two of Kafka's close friends, Max Brod and (another Münzenberg-man) Egon Erwin Kisch. Kisch was a novelist; his name was one which the Viennese critic and satirist Karl Kraus used to conjure together with Kafka's in varying puns on *Kisch und Kafka*. Kisch was also a committed communist and deep in Comintern affairs. He too came into Willi's sphere of influence quite early. Münzenberg had assigned Kisch as a "cultural worker" engaged in quietly advancing Soviet interests in Berlin literary politics. Otto Katz, in contrast, would find his natural habitat in the theater. Yet, like the CIA's James Jesus Angleton after him, Otto began life as a poet, and like Angleton, he apparently founded a short-lived, highbrow literary magazine when he was a very young man. Nonetheless, Willi soon spotted Otto's possibilities in the more practical area of politics, and began to groom this smooth young dilettante for life as a Münzenberg man, preparing him to be a guardian of the Comintern's interests on the cultural scene in Berlin, with a special focus on the theater. Otto's companionship with Kisch was thus cemented by a common task. In performing that task, Katz came to play a genuine and constructive role within the avant-garde theater of Berlin during its great epoch in the 1920s. During the twenties, he was a classic young radical shaping his identity, finding his path through advanced thought, well on his way toward becoming a typical but superior member of the vanguard intelligentsia of his era. From psychoanalysis to Dada to Constructivism, from Dziga Vertov to the Piscatorbuhne, from Gropius to Walter Benjamin to Kafka, Otto was the very type of Weimar.[3] And it was precisely in sensing the strengths of that type, that Münzenberg also sensed Otto's possibilities as a secret agent.

And it was as a budding "Münzenberg-man" that Katz met his lifelong friend and political contact Bertolt Brecht, that anti-poet of Weimar's ending. In the same capacity, Katz insinuated himself into the theatrical career of the director Erwin Piscator. Brecht and Piscator: It was not bad company for an ambitious young man, and in it, always under Willi's watchful eye, Otto began to emerge as a rather stylish somebody. As a young man he was slender, and he would be slight in middle age; not tall; fineboned; with a high intellectual head and a hairline that began to recede early; along with huge, sad, knowing eyes that made you think, quite mistakenly, that you could see straight into his melancholy thoughts. He had a winning smile; lots of gentle appeal. From the beginning, Otto was possessed of almost legendary charm; he had a great theatrical gift for spinning at will the illusions of unearned intimacy.

Katz's connection to Bertolt Brecht, which was formed in the early days in Berlin, lasted all the way through Brecht's exile in Hollywood. Both figuratively and literally, Katz might be viewed as something like the secret face of Bertolt Brecht, the connection to the Soviet propaganda apparatus that sustained his entire career. Several of the many distasteful aspects of the playwright's personality find a dark reflection in the secret agent. I am thinking especially of their shared response to the grosser cruelties of Stalinism. Both men, whenever they confronted the horrors that the Great Leader regularly perpetrated, tended to respond not with anything so trite as mere denial or distress, but with something closer to sadistic gratification. Cynicism bound both men in a kind of common faith. Each was convinced that the cutting edge of their contempt had sundered the veil of the bourgeois fraud, unmasked the hoax of "humanism."

Disabused of the bourgeois fraud in all its spiritual *kitsch*, Katz and Brecht could welcome the Stalinism that so roundly rebuked all the lesser beings who still clutched the humanist lie, the twaddle of decency and justice.[4] Their shared belief in disbelief makes it only too possible to imagine Katz joining in the saturnine joke of Brecht's post-Nietzschean wisecrack about Stalin's victims in the Great Terror: "The more innocent they are," Brecht sighed, "the more they deserve to be shot."[5]

As a corollary, both Brecht and Katz shared a common talent for lying and a fascination with the Lie as such. Both must rank high in the crowded company of this century's great liars, one in art, one in politics; they seemed to feel a common delight (shared with Radek, incidentally) in the Lie considered as a kind of higher, even the highest, Truth.

But their deepest bond of all, fittingly, was cash, especially cash covertly conveyed. The FOIA dossier on Katz makes it plain that he was one of the Soviet case officers, maybe even the principal one, supplying Brecht with his covert subsidy during his exiled years after 1933, especially in Hollywood. Brecht's conscience was never purchased cheaply. How could it be, given his beliefs?[6]

For the young Otto, the step from being a player in the world of Berlin Theater into the world of the cinema was short. It is not surprising that when the time came for Otto to proceed to Moscow and enter his really serious training as a secret agent, the cover job assigned to him was as an officer of Münzenberg's Moscow film company, Mezhropohmfilm Russ. Otto's link to the world of film persisted almost until the end. Its most important manifestation was probably in Hollywood, where the apparatus sent Katz incognito in 1935 to reorganize the film colony's networks of Stalinist fellow travelers and prepare them for the new tasks of the Popular Front.

For Otto Katz was to become, as well, a prime operative in the *apparat's* penetration of Hollywood. How proud he was of his secret service achievements in Tinseltown! "Columbus discovered America," Katz used to boast, "and I discovered Hollywood."[7] Of course, Otto's work in the theater and in Soviet film, companion of Brecht and Dietrich, Eisenstein and Dziga Vertov, had prepared him for the scene, and as we shall see, Hollywood's Stalinist networks were well established by the time Otto arrived in March 1935, assigned with the task of preparing them for the Popular Front.[8] He appeared incognito, claiming the identity of a fictitious antifascist fighter named "Breda," and it was at this time, using this alias, that Katz personally supervised the establishment of the Hollywood Anti-Nazi League, placing Lillian Hellman's intimate friend Dorothy Parker, along with Donald Ogden Stewart, "in charge," acting as its celebrity window-dressing.[9] The Hollywood Anti-Nazi League became the key communist front around which the work of Stalinist politics was accomplished in Hollywood during the Popular Front.

But Otto's work in Hollywood spread in many directions. From the early days in Berlin, Katz had been associated with Gerhart Eisler, a senior *apparatchik* and one of the more important Soviet agents in America. Both in 1935 and in later years, Katz's work in America was often done in collaboration with Eisler.[10] Meanwhile, Gerhart Eisler's brother Hanns, a musician and communist *apparatchik* active in Hollywood, worked very closely there with Otto as well. Through Hanns Eisler, Otto proceeded to develop relations with the chic German émigré community in Los Angeles, especially affluent innocents, people at the level of the director Fritz Lang.[11] Katz always made it a point to develop connections with any considerable celebrity he could seduce, but especially to deepen his grip on committed Stalinist celebrities like Hellman, Hammett, and Parker. Lillian Hellman for example, who likewise knew and worked with Gerhart Eisler (though she later denied it),[12] was able both in Hollywood and New York to provide Otto with his open sesame to many an influential place.

Beginning with the Hollywood Anti-Nazi League, the networks and fronts Katz helped organize remained active through the Spanish Civil War and right up until the pact. Katz himself visited the film colony repeatedly, usually incognito, until well after the war had begun.[13]

The intention of the Hollywood networks was never, incidentally, particularly to influence the *content* of films. The real purpose was to find lucrative berths for favored people in the German communist diaspora, to generate publicity for the Popular Front, to Stalinize the glamour culture, and to tap Hollywood's great guilty wealth as a cash cow for the apparatus, an abundant provider of untraceable dollars. There are unconfirmed reports that Katz visited Hollywood even after Pearl Harbor, though by then he had been expelled from the United States on perfectly well-founded suspicion of espionage—espionage then being performed, moreover, *during* the Nazi-Soviet Pact, for Hitler's most important ally.[14] So much for the "Anti-Nazi League." Up until the Czech coup in 1947, after Katz had returned to Prague to help set up the Stalinist regime there, quite large amounts of dollars from Hollywood were still being brought, under cover, to the apparatus in Czechoslovakia, through people he knew in Los Angeles.[15]

Though Otto did not remain a poet, he was nonetheless a man of no mean literary skill. He was fluent—he was glib—in five languages: Czech, German, English, French, and Russian, and he wrote with verve, style and enviable if incorrect speed in every one.[16] Under an array of false names, he wrote or edited a number of books, working most often under the name "André Simon." On other occasions he used the name "O.K. Simon"—it was his pseudonym for the Left Book Club in England. Some of these books were quite successful; all are important as documents in this or that propaganda strategy.* They are forgotten now, but if one reconstructs the composition of any one of them, useful insights into the covert needs of the Stalinist apparatus at a given moment will invariably emerge.

Lillian Hellman includes an affectionate and typically mendacious portrait of Katz in her memoirs, recalling the man who "persuaded me that I must go to Spain" as "slight" and "weary-looking," as well as "brave," and "kind."[17] Spinning the myth, Hellman idealizes the man. She traces a path for him through his times which, as no student of Hellman's honesty will be surprised to learn, the facts do not support. First she reports that Katz "stayed in Spain until the very last days of the Franco victory, when, in New York, a few of us found the bail to buy him out and to send him on to Mexico." It must be said that every clause, if not perhaps every word, in this summary is false. Katz was nowhere near Spain at the time of the Republican capitulation. He was never at any time under arrest, or even in jeopardy of arrest, in Spain or anywhere

---

* A detail of literary history: When Paul Nizan wrote his novel, *The Conspiracy*, about young men brushing near the *apparat*, he gave the real spy in the center of the boy's games Katz's pseudonym "André Simon." This is surely some sort of in-joke. Nizan knew Katz well, and was very likely introduced to Comintern work by him. (See Gross, *Münzenberg*, pp. 242–243.) Nizan worked on Katz's project *The Brown Book of the Hitler Terror* (see Pascal Ory's biography of Nizan for passages on Nizan's work on the French edition of *Le Livre brun*).

else—not until his last, cruel incarceration in Prague, that is. Hellman never "raised bail" for him. After fabricating the fantasy that Otto had been liberated from Franco's clutches through her bounty, Hellman carries Katz from Madrid to safety in Mexico. Katz did not go to Mexico until after he spent much of 1939 and all of 1940 in New York, working with, among others, Lillian Hellman herself. During this time, Hellman and Hammett were the instigating spirits in the founding of the fellow-traveling New York daily paper *P.M.*, exactly the kind of Münzenbergian publishing venture in which Otto specialized. That every word Hellman says about Katz is false does not change his important place in her life. From the Hollywood Anti-Nazi League, to the Spanish Civil War, to the founding of *P.M.*, Katz was Hellman's senior mentor for the cultural politics of Stalinism.[18]

Like Hellman, Arthur Koestler knew Katz well—far too well to perpetuate sententious claims about his bravery and kindness. Koestler contrasted Katz with Münzenberg himself: Otto was, he wrote, Willi's "perfect complement . . . [While] Willi was a rugged leader, Otto was a smooth and slick operator . . . dark and handsome, with a somewhat seedy charm. He was the type of person who, after lighting a cigarette, always closed one eye, and this habit became so fixed with him that he often closed his eye while thinking out a problem, even when he was not smoking."[19]

Otto's calculating squint was no less familiar to Claud Cockburn, the Stalinist journalist, British Münzenberg-man, and father to the Cockburn brothers, familiar figures in the left-wing journalism of New York in the seventies and eighties. Cockburn used to invent Soviet disinformation under Otto's supervision, and knew the secret agent perhaps the best of all.[20] There are several mysteries in Katz's relation to Claud, and most, no doubt, are sinister. Cockburn was an active Comintern propagandist, then as always a devoted and very sophisticated apologist for the regime, who seems to have been guided through the more delicate aspects of his work by Otto. While Cockburn's portrait of Katz in his memoir surely leaves much unsaid, much in it rings true. "He was a middle-sized man with a large, slightly cadaverous head in which the skull bones were unusually prominent. He had large, melancholy eyes, a smile of singular sweetness, and an air of mystery—a mystery into which he was prepared to induct you, you alone, because he esteemed you so highly."[21]

Here Cockburn puts his finger on a key to what was by all reports Otto's quite potent charm. Otto used his air of being an insider, his look of a smoky worldliness beyond worldliness, as a means of flattery and seduction. It was an indispensable reflex of his being. He could create the illusion of intimacy with whomever he liked, and using that skill he melted doubtful strangers such as Irving Thalberg and Norma Shearer in the palm of his hand. Katz's seductive power was tremendously enhanced by the allure of conspiracy itself. He *looked* like a spy, and he knew it. He used the glamour of the trench coat to seduce. He had and wore a conspiratorial air; it was not something he played down; it was quite obviously part of his gift for making visibility the best disguise.

Not surprisingly, Otto's seductive power was sexual as well as political. Take the Dietrich story. He insisted that he had been the Blue Angel's first husband, a union joined in their remote youth, when he had been a ticket-taker in a theater in Teplitz, and Dietrich was singing and dancing as a kid in the chorus line. He told the tale of their love to everybody. Cockburn claims that "whereas in every other connection you could call him a liar, hypocrite, and ruffian of every description without his turning a hair, if you appeared to doubt his assertion about Marlene he would fly into a passion, white with rage."[22] We know the spy was at least friendly with Dietrich. During the war, Paul Willert, who was by then a British intelligence and propaganda agent, remembers bumping into Katz and Dietrich together on a Hollywood lot, along with Fritz Lang. (Lang was then and later a complete innocent, incidentally: He was a true antifascist, and all the documents I have seen indicate that Lang admirably and without any second agenda gave his money and energy to fight the Nazi enemy.) It was plain to Willert that Katz and Dietrich were good and old friends.[23] In *An Unfinished Woman,* Lillian Hellman reports (unreliably, of course) that while she was dining with Katz in Paris in 1937, a "famous and beautiful German movie star"—obviously Dietrich—appeared at their table, pausing to kiss him and mutter a confidence. "Please forget what you heard," Hellman quotes Katz as saying after Dietrich left. "We were in love with each other when she was young and I was not so *triste*."[24]

Otto was married to a pretty German wife named Ilse—his "Ilschen." (One report in the FOIA dossiers claims that for reasons unknown he briefly divorced, then remarried "Ilschen.") Koestler remembers from the Paris days running into Katz at the crack of dawn in the open market on the rue de la Convention, "an unshaven and tieless Otto, the collar of his jacket turned up, with a net shopping bag in his hand, bargaining with a fishwife, his left eye shrewdly closed, displaying the same earnest charm I have seen directed on other occasions at Miss Ellen Wilkinson, M.P., or Mlle. Geneviève Tabouis."[25]

Shopping aside, Otto Katz was not a dutiful husband. His affairs were numberless. I remember a moment early in my research, when the wife of a distinguished American academic emeritus, wrapped in an elegant Spanish shawl, leaned toward me and confided: "Young man, you've got to talk to us old ladies. We're the ones who slept with all those spies."[26]

Still, the playboy was serious. The roving eye, the charm, the aliases, the deceptions within deceptions, all served a single-minded focus on the political task. And there was more to him than conspiracy and seduction. The late Czech economist Eugen Löbl, who joined Katz in Prague as a fellow defendant in the Slansky Trials in 1952, knew Katz well in Prague after the war and never, so he told me, guessed that his friend was more than an exceptionally influential journalist. He remembered long exalting evenings of talk with Otto. "He was more than intelligent," Löbl gently recalled. "He was wise."[27]

He was also almost certainly a double agent within the Soviet system, spying on the Comintern he served for higher and hostile powers, closer to Stalin himself, an embodiment of all the intra-agency treachery that must have been at work among Stalin's services by, let's say, 1937. The issue remains controversial for a number of reasons. To begin with, there are many people who still imagine that the Comintern of the 1930s represented a less "Stalinistic" branch of the Soviet government than the NKVD, and that because it was a prime vehicle of Lenin's fantasies, the Comintern has been viewed as somehow more internationalist, more idealistically revolutionary, less bound to the secret police, than the NKVD. A Guy Burgess or Anthony Blunt, recruiting newcomers to the ring, invariably claimed their work was for "the Comintern," though their controls, Theodore Maly and Alexander Orlov, were both high-level agents of the NKVD, or what Babette Gross delicately called in my presence "the other service."[28] It was easier to entice a neophyte to commit himself to serving the International than a secret police.

This moralized distinction between the NKVD and the Comintern is still maintained by a number of students of the subject. It is for example almost universal among apologists for the Popular Front.[29] In reality the supposed difference is close to complete illusion. It is quite true that following 1935 all the Soviet services became more emphatically Russian and anti-intellectual than they had been under Lenin, and that it was an essential part of the Great Terror to shift secret service power away from the foreign intellectuals of the Comintern and toward the Russian policemen of the NKVD. It is also quite true that Stalin despised the Comintern and that the NKVD was the very instrument of his mind. But was the Comintern not Stalinist? It is true that some in the organization may well have silently harbored this or that private criticism of the Kremlin's policy or methods, but the notion that senior leaders of the Comintern after 1928 were ever in any politically concrete way even mildly menacing or hostile to Stalin's power is simply not demonstrable. Most were abject in their devoted obedience to the regime and they gladly performed its work without protest. Nor is there any reason to suppose the Comintern served as a haven for some sort of good "Leninism" that was morally more elevated than the bad "Stalinism" of the NKVD. Many of Lenin's most important appointments had of course been to the Cheka, and many of those Leninists survived and flourished in Stalin's NKVD and Soviet Military Intelligence, the GRU. In fact, when Stalin ordered the NKVD to penetrate, take over, and in effect liquidate the Comintern leadership, it was a Chekist from the earliest days, Mikhail Trilliser, an intimate of Dzerzhinsky and Lenin himself, to whom Stalin entrusted the job. Trilliser was in many ways the complete Leninist. Finally, during the Terror, Stalin freely slaughtered senior officials of both services.

Nonetheless, it is quite true that Stalin's policy was to penetrate the Comintern with the NKVD and GRU, and not the reverse. By 1935 the senior management of the International was entirely in the hands of the other services.[30] It ceased to have any meaningful separate existence. There is every reason to suppose that Otto Katz played some quite real role in this transformation, enacting the charade of a Comintern agent while in fact serving the more powerful agency. When the Comintern fell, Münzenberg also went down. But when Willi fell, Otto Katz, a Comintern "type" if ever there was one, did not fall with him. On the contrary. Katz's emergence as a major figure within the apparatus dates precisely from the moment of Willi's descent from the monster's grace.

The more interesting question concerns Katz's patronage. The senior Bolshevik closest to Katz's career was Karl Radek. This is only natural; as we have seen, Radek was likewise Münzenberg's best friend among the senior Bolsheviks, and any significant Münzenberg-man in Moscow was likely to seek him out.[31] Radek was also the senior Bolshevik most involved in the real and deepest secrets of Stalin's German policy after Hitler took power, the propagandist entrusted with the crucial task of shaping the "antifascist" movement, both in diplomacy and propaganda—a task for which his indispensable European right hand would be his old comrade Münzenberg.[32] In particular, Radek was among the very, very few fully apprised of the true policy of appeasement and collaboration with Hitler for which antifascism was the mask. In fact, he served as Stalin's highest, and most secret, emissary in the discussions that led to these arrangements.[33] This detail is crucial. It was to cover and give coherence to these secret actions that Radek was put in charge of the very same "antifascist" campaign of which

Katz and Münzenberg were the European organizers. With Katz as his protégé, it is easy to understand why Katz was given the Paris assignment and the crucial new job as the secret agent in place for the antifascist agitation of 1933.

Since Katz would necessarily be working with a number of the most delicate and important secrets of the era, it is plain that Radek and Stalin both would have to repose the utmost confidence in their man. The job required a unique combination of talents. The secret agent most entrusted with the covert dimension of the antifascist campaign would need to have a great talent for publicity and the public life, joined to a no less powerful talent for secret action. He would need to inspire idealism and stir moral commitment of a very profound kind, while being involved daily in actions so cynical and duplicitous that the truth is almost ungraspable. He would need to inspire people to make the most profound sacrifices for one of the most momentous and urgent causes of the century, while he would also need to use them in the service of one of its greatest lies. Such an emissary would have to be a combination of contradictions, contradictions bound in a dark linkage of imagination and hardness of heart. That was what they found in Otto, and that was the man who arrived in Paris, bearing the secret agenda for the new movement, in March 1933.

It all began idealistically enough. Münzenberg's first job for Otto, back in 1927, had been to assist him in managing the theatrical career of the director Erwin Piscator, much of whose work was at this time overtly funded by Workers' International Relief.[34] Katz was installed as Piscator's administrative director, and in this capacity Otto found himself managing the egos and fortunes of Bela Belazs and Alfred Döblin, Bertolt Brecht and Walter Mehring, Toller, Tucholsky, and even Marcel Breuer and Walter Gropius. One of his big assignments at this time was to supervise Gropius's preparation of the blueprints for the "Total Theater" to house Piscator's enterprise.[35]

All aspiring warriors of ideas must become expert in the art of provocation. That is, they must learn how to create situations which will force their enemies into self-damaging actions. Katz became a master of this kind of manipulation, and his initiation into its art took place over the Piscatorbühne.

By 1927, Erwin Piscator had formed a flourishing reputation as director for the *Volksbühne*, the Prussian State Theater, an institution funded by the Weimar government, and exactly the kind of Liberal, altruistic operation the *apparat* wished to discredit and destroy. In 1928, Piscator grew tired of being a mere director among directors in this too-anonymous but high-minded place. He wearied of keeping his radical aspirations under liberal wraps. He longed to make a bigger splash in a theater he could call his own.

His problem was leaving the *Volksbühne*. It had always treated Piscator in a reasonably supportive way. He was at perfect liberty to leave it whenever he chose to do so. If and when he came across some preferable outlet for his talents, he only needed to tender his resignation and move on. There were, however, no points in righteousness politics to be gained from so simple and unvictimized a course of action. Piscator needed some way to make his career move look like a saintly act, make his big break look like a rebellion against oppression. Righteousness required that some injustice drive him to the main chance, some social evil was needed to *force* him to make his step up. And if that injustice could simultaneously expose the meaningless sham of German democracy, Piscator's success could serve his friends and sources of funding in the Soviet regime as well.

Unfortunately no appropriate injustice was on hand. So one had to be concocted. This gave Otto his debut in provocation. He enlisted the playwright Ernst Toller, who was also very close to Willi, and together they cooked up a play which Toller was to write, a work intended to pose political and practical problems serious enough to assure that the National Theater would decline to produce it. The play was written expressly in order to be turned down in this way. Thus, when the inevitable rejection came, Katz had only to whip up a hue and cry over this unconscionable act of oppression and "censorship." The Berlin intelligentsia assembled to protest. The press viewed with alarm. Everybody wrung their hands and signed petitions about the highest values of German culture betrayed—those values which Münzenberg, when dictating rhetoric to his staff, used to call "the tradition of Goethe, etcetera, etcetera." Piscator's departure no longer looked like the mere self-interested career move it was, but shone with the saintly glow of victimization. Piscator was not benefiting; he was suffering, and deserved the support of every decent German.

In fact, Piscator's plans to leave the *Volksbühne* were fully formulated long before Toller's play was written and before the "scandal" was invented.[36] Otto had done it all. It was a brilliant debut.

Yet the Piscatorbuhne did not flourish. Within a year there was financial trouble and the enraged director blamed Otto, against whom in later years he would rail as "that nymphomaniacal [*sic*] playboy."[37] Münzenberg discreetly removed Katz and installed him instead in one of the Trust's book clubs, *Universum Bucherei*—which later became a model for Britain's Left Book Club. At *Universum Bucherei*, Otto's arrogance and obsession with fame and glamour drove the drab staff half out of their minds.[38]

Then in 1930, disaster descended. The government found gross tax irregularities in the Piscatorbuhne's books, and held Katz personally responsible. One hundred thousand marks had to be produced, and produced soon, or the foundering agent faced jail. Katz of course turned to Münzenberg. Confronting the boss, all his smooth urbanity was blown aside. Katz staged a weeping, shouting tantrum of despair. He absolutely had to, had to, *had* to have 100,000 marks, or he would kill himself.[39]

Münzenberg knew an opportunity when he saw one. In a small stroke of administrative genius, he decided to save 100,000 marks—*and* introduce his man to another kind of debt. He would remove Katz from the reach of the German government and, at this most vulnerable of moments, promote him. Katz was dispatched to Moscow, there to become a manager in the Trust's Soviet film production house, Mezhropohmfilm Russ, a very big new job, and a new life. Note the psychology: To promote a man at the very moment he has crumbled into abjection, wailing about suicide, shows an unusually subtle instinct for power. "Willi," writes Arthur Koestler, "needed Otto, but he barely bothered to disguise his contempt for him. Once when I asked Willi when he first had met Otto, he said in his cozy Thuringian drawl, 'I fished him out of the Landswehr Canal.' The Landswehr Canal in Berlin is a narrow waterway conveniently located for the dumping of corpses and for committing suicide."[40]

And so Otto took up residence at Mezhropohmfilm in Moscow, head of its German section, at the heart of Soviet cinema in its grand epoch. He brought all his Weimar knowingness to the new job at a moment of German ascendancy throughout the film world. While such German transplants as Lubitsch and F. W. Murnau were sweeping down Sunset Boulevard, Piscator and Lotte Lenya were crossing Red Square.

Yet those who worked at Mezhropohmfilm while Katz was a senior executive say that although Katz's name was on the letterhead, he was rarely around. The real leadership came from another Münzenberg employee, Francesco Misiano, who was at least a genuine filmmaker, something Katz never was—although the Archives show Misiano, like Katz, involved in Münzenberg's more strictly political enterprises as well.[41] Simultaneously Katz became a regular in the community of journalists and writers in Moscow, as always the man who knew everybody in the worlds of journalism, film, literature. As it happened, his old Czech friend Egon Erwin Kisch—Kafka's companion—was also in Moscow around this time. Kisch and Katz, close since Prague, now further solidified an enduring master-sidekick friendship which lasted to the end of their lives. Where Egon Erwin was, Otto was likely to be, Lone Ranger to Kisch's Tonto. And Egon Erwin, a genuinely likable man, was everybody's friend.

When he arrived in Moscow, Katz was little better than a dilettante's dilettante, both in culture and the secret life. He obviously overflowed with talent—with his languages, his speed at the typewriter keyboard, his brilliant connections, his charm, his zest for deception. But he lacked discipline; he needed a firm hand. He had the gift; now it was time to shape the playboy for his destiny as one of the "Great Illegals." The Soviet services now set out to prepare him for the genuine conspiratorial work of the *apparat*, trained in secret technique, and connected to the networks that really mattered. On the outside, Otto would look very much the same, but his gifts would now be anchored to something deep and unseen. He was almost never in his office at Mezhropohmfilm Russ. His work there was obviously a cover.[42] He was elsewhere, in training for his true lifework.

He was doing so at the highest level, almost certainly under the guidance of Karl Radek. In 1927, Radek had made a misstep, supported Trotsky at the wrong moment, and spent some time in banishment while Stalin consolidated his power. But by 1930 Radek had somehow found a way to restore himself to high influence. Stalin reposed special confidence in his views on cultural matters—and on Germany. And it was at this time that Otto Katz, following in the pattern of his mentor in Berlin, became intimate with Radek, his protégé in the new generation.

Otto's personality meanwhile was hardening, changing. "Only in Moscow did I really come to understand the mission and principles of the Communist party," he wrote in a letter to Klement Gottwald just before he was hanged. "As I look back on that period, now, during the last hours of my life, I can truthfully state that in Moscow, in the Soviet environment, I changed."[43]

It was so. In these years, Otto seems to have gone through that rare passage, a genuine transformation of personality. It is not that he became a different man, of course, but some playful, free, and human part of Otto's personality, something that once had rather naturally placed him in the company of Piscator, Kisch, and Kafka, receded and became subordinate to another less attractive part, which had been so strengthened that it took permanent command of his being. Visiting Moscow in the early thirties, Münzenberg and Babette were deeply struck by the change. Babette found the playboy of Weimar "serious, determined and reserved. Whatever he thought about the hardships of daily life in Moscow, about the incipient Byzantinism of the Kremlin, he kept to himself. The current slogans came readily to his lips; he had become a loyal officer of the regime."[44]

By the time he was ready to be sent back to Europe in 1933, Otto Katz was a highly trained secret agent operating at a very high level of awareness. Over the next twenty years, Otto would play out many adventures close to the heart of conspiratorial events. In Paris he would be Stalin's unheroic insider in the antifascist movement, calculating its propaganda, calibrating its networks in Germany, giving his special orders to its couriers in the Reich. In London, Katz would touch the life of politics at all sorts of secret points, from the founding of the Left Book Club to the feeding of disinformation to British Conservatives. In Hollywood, it was Otto who under an alias set up and supervised much in the networking of Stalinist fellow travelers, while back in New York he assisted his friend and comrade Gerhart Eisler in espionage and other secret work. During the Spanish Civil War, Otto would help to import the NKVD terror onto the Iberian peninsula. During the Second World War, while Stalin was in his alliance with Hitler, Otto was busy in New York, until a recalcitrant and almost complacent State Department terminated his visa, something it did only after being repeatedly (and correctly) warned that Otto was a dangerous Soviet agent, and (arrestingly, arguably) "probably a Nazi agent" as well. When this trouble disrupted his New York work, Katz beat a tactical retreat to Mexico City, then a major center of NKVD activity in the Western Hemisphere. He is known to have worked closely there with the longtime NKVD chieftain Umansky, spending the war much involved in Soviet operations within the United States and in the Caribbean, working among other things with Fidel Castro's predecessor, Fulgencio Batista. Batista was at this time much admired and promoted by the left, and Katz was empowered to make Batista grand offers on behalf of the Soviets if Batista would enter Stalin's realm of influence.[45]

At the end of World War II, Katz was summoned from Mexico City back to Prague, accompanied as always by Kisch. Katz became a high-level journalist and government official, and was present at the start of. the coup and the creation of the Czech Stalinist state. By 1949, Otto was forthrightly in authority at last. Apparently he became just as forthrightly insufferable in the arrogance of power.[46] Charm is the most superficial form of intimacy, and even in the old days, when the mask of Otto's charm slipped, the face behind was the ruthless *apparatchik*, the "loyal servant of the Regime." To know Otto really well was often to hate him with lasting venom. The German novelist Gustav Regler, had worked with Otto first during the Reichstag Trial, and then later in Spain: he knew Katz later still in Mexico during the war, after Regler had broken with the *apparat*. Regler's widow told me that Gustav had broken into a little dance of joy when he heard the news that Otto had been hanged.[47]

For hanged he was.

I am tempted to paraphrase the opening sentence of his old friend's novel, *The Trial.* Somebody must have been telling tales about Otto K., because he was arrested one fine morning.

Stalin's gratitude was lethal. Only his indifference let people live. Otto Katz was arrested and put to death in Prague as one of the victims of the Rajk-Slansky purges, the set of show trials that in succession through all the states of Eastern Europe between 1948 and 1952, part of a vast, mad, but meaningful operation through which Stalin consolidated his paranoid power in his newly acquired territories. The Rajk-Slansky purges were an initiating event in the Cold War. In 1948 many people like Otto Katz, leading figures in the old "antifascist" cadres, people who in Europe had laid the groundwork for the expansion of communist power through the thirties and the war, were stepping forward, expecting their rewards in power. The Autocrat saw them as superannuated compromised servants. Many, moreover, were Jews. The moment had come to be rid of them. By the hundreds, even thousands, they were rounded up, charged, and put to death. The politically unusable or invisible were simply executed. More conspicuous figures were disposed of in show trials, charged usually with a list of crimes contrived to advance current propaganda and turn their onetime double lives inside out, transposing decades of secret service into lives with the look of treason, socialist-style. In all the capitals of Eastern Europe, a grotesque theater of confession and death began a five-year run, political terror's traveling road show. Many of the "confessions" produced from city to city were bizarre contortions of precisely the history we will be exploring here; in fact an essential part of the point was the systematic effort to rewrite that history from the dock. Otto Katz had been a principal actor in that theater. Now, in Prague, a defendant in the Slansky trials, he stepped forward for his last long hour in the limelight.

It is seldom pointed out that a central character in this all-but-final wave of Stalin's terror was an American mole, whose name is as obscure as that of his friend and fellow mole Alger Hiss is well-known. Exactly why Hiss is so famous while Noel Field remains obscure is a question well worth exploring. Field was in his way at least as important a secret agent as Anthony Blunt or Hiss, and one way of measuring his importance is the intensity of the Stalinist response to the threat of his exposure. It became an initiating event, or at the very least an incident exactly coincidental with the commencement of the Rajk-Slansky purges, Stalin's great roll-up of the people who had made his "antifascism."

In the summer of 1948, exposure of Noel Field's secret work seemed imminent. The place was Washington; the means the testimony of Elizabeth Bentley and Whittaker Chambers, testimony which exposed Jay Peters as what the Central Party Archives in Moscow now make very plain Jay Peters really was: the Hungarian *mafioso* in charge of sundry espionage networks in Washington— not least among them, a network that included Otto Katz's old colleague in secret work, Field. In other words, exactly the obedient old "antifascist" cadres Stalin was now preparing to discredit and destroy. And Noel Field, emerging from the heart of what was to become the Hiss case, became the instrument, the finger-man through whose charges all those deaths could be assigned. One of his targets was Otto.

At the time Whittaker Chambers made his charges, the alarm running through the apparatus resulted in Noel Field's being summoned to Budapest, where he hoped to be given protection from the deepening secret service cold. But the shelter Field found in the

East became the basis for a new deception. Field was arrested. So were his wife, his brother, and other members of his family. His previous relationship with Allen Dulles, through whom Field had served the Russians and worked against the Americans in the OSS, was now advertised as proof that he was in reality an "American master-spy." The "American master spy" next proceeded to "confess," and through his accusations the old networks could be brought forward and destroyed. Field was not an "American master-spy," of course; he was a devoted communist and *apparatchik*, and would remain so until his death many years later. His true role in 1948 was that of collaborator with the people running the Terror trials. Partly coerced, partly the good soldier, Field played his assigned role as accuser. Through his indictment large numbers of people were condemned to death. But not Noel Field. Field was not shot, not hanged—even though if what he claimed about himself was true, he could have been executed fifty times over. Neither were any of his relatives. Instead he and his wife were imprisoned and released a few years later, on the day—the precise day—Alger Hiss was released from Lewisburg penitentiary. They were "rehabilitated." It had all been, the apparatus explained, a misunderstanding.

Herta and Noel Field never revisited the West. Field became an executive in the Hungarian State Publishing House, and he and Herta remained devout Stalinists of the most chilling kind until the end of their lives.

And so in the hysteria of a classic communist witch-hunt, Otto Katz was arrested. Of course Otto knew with whom he was dealing; he instantly made it clear to the secret police that he would gladly confess at once to anything they wanted him to say: anything, anything at all. This effort to sidestep the thugs in the basement failed. It was not enough simply to agree to what was wanted: It was necessary to be tortured anyway. And so Otto was tortured for months while the fabrications of his "confession" were developed.[48] This "confession" is an exercise in disinformation. It may be viewed as Katz's final service to the regime. It is filled with lies, but they can be revealing lies. Since most were invented to cover something important, they repay study.

The man on trial made his confession then, from the dock, speaking painfully through dentures that didn't fit, and which had been given him only that day. His own had been smashed during his "interrogation." Who would have imagined, back in the old days of smooth talking in Paris and New York and Hollywood, that Otto Katz wore dentures! He stood in the dock struggling to shape his words. Still he managed to get the whole thing out, exactly what he had been ordered to say. At one high point he invoked the name of Noël Coward, whom Otto said had recruited him as a British agent during the war, all to further his treacherous Trotskyite work. He himself, he told the court, was scum, vermin. He was a writer, and yet what kind of engineer of the soul had he turned out to be? A traitor. What kind of model was he to others? A man who did not understand the people. A man who had betrayed everything worth living for. Along the way he smeared a great many other people, both communist and non-communist. Above all he smeared his own life, confessing in special abjection to being a Jew, and a bourgeois; a contemptible human being.

So it ended: the "trial" of Otto Katz. It was only in the last phrases of his speech, the part where he turned to the court and began to beg for death, saying that he was not fit to live even another day, that Otto's voice sank, subsided into a kind of gasping, and he could no longer be heard.

Chapter 5

ANTIFASCISM ON STAGE:
TRIAL AND COUNTER-TRIAL

T hough the Nazis were throwing around claims of Communist responsibility for the Reichstag arson before the flames
were even doused, Hitler seems to have taken his time deciding exactly what to do with Dimitrov. Of course the Nazis accused
the biggest Communist fish in their dragnet of being an arch-conspirator, a ruthless arsonist, a wild-eyed red terrorist. But behind
the bluster, Hitler was probably weighing his options rather carefully. Should Dimitrov be held hostage? Or maybe bartered for something he wanted from Stalin? Perhaps the "arch-conspirator" be
humbled, publicly crushed, maybe even executed? Or maybe some
combination of both choices might be possible.

In any case, Hitler did not decide immediately on his ultimate
course of mounting a show trial that would star Dimitrov. The
Bulgarians had been arrested on March 9. In late March, reasonably
well informed rumors were flying around that there would be no
trial at all, not of van der Lubbe at any rate: word was that the
wretched Dutch youth would simply be publicly beheaded.[1] For

the first many weeks after being arrested in the Bayernhof Cafe, Dimitrov found himself parked in a Berlin prison, handcuffed day and night, fretting over every needling detail of his incarceration, and very much out of touch. Strangely, despite the tremendous amount of information about the Communist underground he carried in his head, Dimitrov does not seem to have been tortured or even very seriously interrogated. At least, no evidence of such an interrogation has ever surfaced. Dimitrov spent his days contending mainly with isolation and boredom. (The eternal handcuffs were an intolerable agony; Popov considered suicide.) In the scrappy diary he immediately began to keep after his arrest, it's the waiting and those handcuffs that make him frantic. As late as May 1933, he is writing "a *day* without *anything!* No letter, no news, no 'prison event'—*nothing!*"[2]

Nor was Stalin in any visible rush to rescue his Bulgarian comrade. Comintern agents on the ground in Berlin even toyed with a physical rescue: they told Moscow they were pretty sure they could break Dimitrov out of the jail. This proposal was met with silence at the top.[3] Slowly, cautiously, in some confusion, a sort of strategy was being born: Stalin would confront the new Nazi threat with what amounted to a dual policy: On the one hand, the world would hear a whole new kind of antifascist propaganda, ferocious and seemingly unrelenting, and emanating mainly from Europe. On the other, Stalin would exercise extreme caution over menacing Hitler in any more serious way. From Stalin's point of view, this "duplicity" was quite understandable. His first concern was to avoid war with Germany. That meant that his desperate German comrades could be defended with the new antifascist propaganda only so long as the Soviet government steered clear of any more dangerous confrontation. There would be no genuine attempt to roll back Hitler's new totalitarianism, no real effort to rescue the German Party. While Willi prepared a new antifascist campaign like nothing ever seen before, Stalin held his peace.[4] In fact, Stalin himself said nothing whatever about the new German situation for almost a year after the Fire, and even then not until *after* Dimitrov and the other communists had been acquitted—

note well: not convicted, *acquitted*—in the strange "show trial" that Hitler eventually staged in Leipzig and Berlin.

This dual policy—using antifascist propaganda to cover what amounted to appeasement of Hitler—drove some fighters on the ground frantic. In 1933, Münzenberg sent the Countess Károlyi into Germany as a courier. Traveling under the cover of her aristocratic maiden name—Andrássy—Catherine Károlyi was to meet contacts in the Comintern underground and spirit away illegal documents they had gathered on the Reichstag Fire and against the SA. After many adventures, the Countess reached Berlin for the main meeting with the most important underground agent of all. This man was a linchpin of the Comintern networks, and he had no shortage of material about Nazi atrocities. But he handed it over to the Countess fuming. What, he wanted to know, was this material going to be used for? To write another *book*? Some more *pamphlets*? Didn't anybody in Paris or Moscow grasp how *desperate* things are here? Do they want these men to *win*? *Forget* pamphlets! *Forget* books! What was needed now was not more chat but a *coup d'état*. These monsters could maybe still be stopped, but only by armed force. *Force*, not propaganda. All the Nazi bigwigs would all be gathering soon in Nuremberg. The *apparat* should send in, through the underground, an airplane fully equipped with the necessary bombs and when the whole gang is together, strike like lightning. Strike suddenly, strike in one blow and kill them all. A *coup*, and *soon*. Nothing else would work.

Countess Károlyi gasped. She couldn't take such a reply back to Paris. "'They are cowards," he retorted, and his eyes were sharp as steel. "They imagine that with pamphlets and chatter in cafes they can undo Hitler and stop war. … We have to declare war on war," he repeated, "and take the risk. Otherwise, Europe as well as Germany will be destroyed. *That* is my last message to Willi!"[5]

But the Countess was not wrong: any call for armed confrontation would be unacceptable at the top. The underground was asking Stalin to risk war with Hitler then and there, and in 1933, Stalin was not going to risk anything of the kind. He would not authorize even the sort of guerilla resistance movement that a decade later would play such a vital role in Nazi-occupied territories outside Germany. Some such resistance could certainly have been mounted in 1933; there would have been plenty of volunteers, but no: The *apparat* would stick to books and pamphlets, and not even the books and pamphlets would be overtly attributed to the Soviets. Münzenberg's budding antifascist campaign would be based on his old methods of co-option and denial: The new campaign would not appear to originate with the Soviet government but with outraged European liberals and sympathizers.

This may seem shocking: some German communists were shocked out of their very lives. The world's foremost Communist was perfectly prepared to let large numbers of his beloved German comrades be trapped in the Nazi round-ups—especially if his secret service could have the proper input into which of them were arrested, and when.[6]

Meanwhile, Hitler seemed almost as eager as Stalin to drop a firewall between the German Party and the Soviet Government. On March 23, 1933, the Chancellor made a speech to the Reichstag, which had dutifully reconvened in new quarters. In it Hitler announced, "He wished to maintain the same friendly relations with the USSR as long as the Communist question remained a purely internal affair."[7] The Soviet government could bargain with Germany so long as it did not interfere with Hitler's assault on the German party. And behold! Stalin did not interfere.

Except on the level of propaganda. Working under orders from the Comintern—that is, from Stalin—Willi was at work on what we might call the new antifascism mere days after arriving in Paris, and only a week after Dimitrov's arrest, he was energetically mapping the fierce founding campaign of the antifascist era. This process would sweep Münzenberg to the high point of his career. The new propaganda was exactly suited to his techniques. God knows that the master of co-option and denial, the "patron saint of the fellow travelers," had the world's growing antifascist outrage to build on. Outside Germany, the new Nazi totalitarianism was being viewed with anger, not *enough* anger, perhaps, but the outrage was real. Nazi charges against the Communists over the fire were greeted with general skepticism, when it was not flat-out mockery and disbelief. Exiled in Switzerland, Thomas Mann—no Communist—watched the Nazi response to the Fire and wrote in his diary about the "grotesque and crude swindle," of "what is universally known to be a brazen and criminal lie."[8] The Nazi line on the Reichstag arson was, to put it mildly, not believed.

This contrast between the propagandists' galvanized hyperactivity and the official Soviet inaction was noticed and resented. In that bewildered, still incoherent resentment, were sown the very first seeds of what would later become a new anti-communism—or more precisely, anti-Stalinism. Many European Communists privately—that is, secretly—held the Soviet dictator responsible for the disaster.[9] The German Communist Party was being wiped out without even a gesture of protest from the Great Leader of the Nations. A senior Comintern personality and one of Stalin's own "closest comrades" was in prison, perhaps about to be tried and executed. More silence. Surely the German catastrophe called for *some* sort of response. Even Willi was disheartened. In late April of that silent spring, Ruth Fischer, an old friend and a controversial but brilliant leader in the German party—the sister of Gerhart and Hanns Eisler—arrived in Paris after narrowly escaping from Hitler's dragnet. She and her lover Arkady Maslow had ridden out of the Reich on a Harley Davidson motorcycle, escaping with nothing but the clothes on their backs. They made their way to Paris via Czechoslovakia. Assuming the disaster had to force some real policy change at the highest levels, Fischer immediately went to see Münzenberg. His first words to her were, "Hopeless. No change. On the contrary things are going to the devil more and more."[10]

Yet if Stalin was silent, the Comintern was not. By summer, something that looked like true antifascism was beginning to appear, and Willi was running it. His campaign may have been reactive, but it snatched the initiative from the Nazis, and Goebbels never really caught up.

***

Hitler eventually decided to stage a huge show trial, mainly in Leipzig, accusing Dimitrov, along with van der Lubbe, Torgler, and the two Bulgarians, of conspiring to burn the Reichstag. It was to this event that Willi decided to respond in first great public antifascist facedown. The Leipzig trail would blame the communists for the fire and for an endless array of other crimes against the German people, arraigning and condemning Marinus van der Lubbe as the arsonist, claiming the Dutch wretch was a mindless tool in the conspiratorial hands of the Communist celebrities in the dock with him, the masterminds behind the fire.

The staging of this judicial charade would be among Hitler's relatively few experiments with the show trial as a form of totalitarian theater. After 1934, he settled instead for pure, plain, post-judicial murder in a pure, plain, post-judicial terror state. In the end the Leipzig trial gave every outward appearance of having been totally and disastrously bungled, above all because it led to the *acquittal* of the defendants. How could such a gross "blunder" as acquittal happen?

It *is* perplexing. The usual explanation—that the court retained some semblance of judicial independence, that it was not yet fully under Hitler's thumb—only begs the question of why Hitler would have entrusted a legal case of overwhelming political importance—and a ludicrously flimsy one at that—to a court that was not under his thumb. On the other hand, if the court was as absolutely subservient to the Nazis as it appeared to be, why on earth did it acquit the "conspirators?"

Seven months passed between the Fire and Dimitrov's March arrest and the beginning of Hitler's tribunal in Leipzig during late September. That left a lot of time for exploring options, plenty of space for negotiation and maneuver. It was not until June 1933—four months after the arrest—that Münzenberg himself went to Moscow for a full strategy session on how to handle Leipzig. He had spent those four months working on a campaign, but it was only in Moscow that Willi hit upon the brilliant idea of responding to the Nazi show trial of Dimitrov with a "counter-trial," an extravaganza to be staged in London, in which major luminaries of Western law and letters would mock and co-opt every move the Nazis made, accusing the accusers, humiliating them at every turn.

Willi's June 1933 trip to Moscow took place in deep secrecy. He traveled with Babette by the circuitous northern route through Scandinavia. His time in Moscow was filled with meetings with the Comintern and its secret service. These meetings happened in a welter of acrimony and new visions, but Münzenberg spent his time at Comintern headquarters in extended consultation with the Comintern director, Piatnitsky, and in meetings on the building's top floor with Mirov-Abramov, the director of the International's secret service. Just as importantly—maybe more importantly—Willi was in steady contact with Radek, his oldest friend and closest ally among the senior Bolsheviks, now also Otto Katz's patron, who had become Stalin's chief advisor on all aspects of German policy, the invisible eminence for the large events leading up to the war: the antifascist movement, the search for the pact, the Terror. Within the Kremlin, he was also the guiding hand in the culture wars of intellectual Stalinism. Catharine Károlyi remembers him at a very grand reception for George Bernard Shaw at the British Embassy in Moscow in 1931, "leaning over the balustrade in a black Russian blouse" deep in conversation with Lady Astor, "very pale with an Abraham Lincoln beard and the aspect of a French *communard.*"[11] Gustav Regler remembers him from 1935, drinking hard at a reception in Maxim Gorky's country villa, ripping open his shirt at the banquet table, fascinating Malraux and the visiting literary celebrities as he plunged forward with ... dangerous talk. His Bolshevik colleagues sat by, frozen with fear.[12] From his revolutionary youth, Radek had been tight with a kind of ferocious eagerness, but there was also something jeering, abrasive, and cynical about him. A rather special weld of cynicism with certitude marked his mind. Like Brecht and his own protégé Katz, like many of the most knowing liars, Radek's rationalizations convinced him that everything important, *really* important, was based in falsehood. As a result, falsehood became for him a kind of truth. To Radek duplicity was the last word. This contradictory but potent point of faith left him arrogant, installed in a perpetual easy victory over the stupid credulity of the innocent. Life, he was sure, was a lie. And that, he believed, made him always right. He was Stalin's ideal intellectual.

For he was an intellectual, a real one. In a circle filled with tenacious boors and clever thugs, Radek was a quite genuine literary-political man in the classic European manner. Polish and Jewish, his manners and outlook were those of a German cultural revolutionary, albeit one with an exceptionally conspiratorial penchant. Conspiracy was Radek's school: He became a hot revolutionary handyman for Felix Dzerzhinsky when he was 18 years old. His connection to the founder of the modern police state was the defining relationship of his youth.[13] Then came Lenin: Even before the Revolution, Radek was not only Lenin's press advisor but also his political fixer in German politics. After the Revolution Radek was among the founders of the Comintern, entrusted with special attention to propaganda and its secret service.

Radek was now at the center and at the top. But then he made a gross false step. Following Lenin's death he supported Trotsky against Stalin in the struggle for power, and this blunder ended his successful first phase. In November 1927 Stalin had him exiled to the little town of Tomsk, cast to the extreme outer edge of Soviet political life. Radek was not made of very stern stuff; exile soon broke his defiance and he began a concentrated search for Stalin's forgiveness, which worked at least to the degree that he managed to worm his way back to Moscow. But it was not a glorious return. He was relegated to a squalid, freezing flat in the basement of a slum. Radek was a man very nearly at the end of his resources. His boyish buoyancy was gone. He grew stooped. His walk shambled, dragged. He was going to die in that basement. Something more was needed.

In 1930 that something was found, and Radek's fortunes absolutely changed. From his basement hole he moved to Dom Pratisetsvo, an apartment building reserved for the most important members of the government. His flat was magnificent. It featured a dazzling view of the Kremlin and the Moskva. It also featured a direct line to Stalin's study.[14]

Precisely how Radek thus transformed his status is not known, but the trick must have been impressive. The strongest rumor is not accepted by all scholars, but asserted by Trotsky and vouched for by his highly reliable secretary van Heijenhoort. It claims that Radek used his basement and his previous bond to Trotsky to act as a decoy for Trotskyites still in Moscow, above all a senior NKVD official named Blumkin, the better to betray them to the firing squads.[15]

However he did it, Radek regained Stalin's favor to a spectacular degree. By 1933 and 1934 it would be hard to find anyone in more intimate confidence with the dictator: mastermind of the antifascist line; ultra-secret emissary to the Nazis; inside advisor in all matters of cultural politics; and his secret right hand in foreign policy. As the senior Bolshevik generally in charge of the antifascist response, and a practiced specialist in German politics, Radek was instructed to craft a new line lavishly admiring the Versailles treaty, which until then had been the object of incessant Communist invective.[16] In fact the Versailles signatories were very alarmed.[17] That the Versailles powers, including the United States, were not sufficiently alarmed to act with preemptive force to remove the Nazis from power in Germany in 1933 or 1934 is of course one of the greatest tragedies in all of human history. Nonetheless, Stalin saw that for the foreseeable future, a fully justified fear of fascism would dominate left wing and even most centrist political morality in the democracies. He wanted the apparatus on the moral high ground. When the going got tough, the USSR would need antifascism's ethical authority, and Radek was charged with capturing it.

But despite a title and a major role at *Isvestia*—his columns set the tone for the new antifascism—Radek mainly stayed in his apartment often reclining on an enormous couch set before his view of the Kremlin towers, doing what he had always done best: reading everything, and calculating every angle. Around him were strewn magazines, newspapers, and manuscripts in five languages. Radek would calculate the line on everything from James Joyce to the

NKVD; from Malraux's relation to Aragon to the latest conspiratorial ripple among the German refugees. Nothing passed him by. He read and calculated. And above all else, he waited for that special phone to ring.

It rang constantly. Radek had become Stalin's private answerman, the most witting insider of them all.

The Moscow Radek surveyed from his grand apartment was pretty grim. It was during that Russian June of 1933 that Münzenberg was taken to inspect the slave-labor camp building the Moscow-Volga Canal; then Willi gazed into the pit and muttered under his breath about the slaves of ancient Egypt. That same month, at the funeral of an old revolutionary friend, Clara Zetkin, Münzenberg spotted Lenin's comrade Zinoviev wandering on the margins of the ceremony. In simple friendliness, Willi beckoned Zinoviev, urging him to come forward and join the rest in the dignitaries' box. Zinoviev stepped forward and broke down, confessing that he was in disgrace, forced to live outside Moscow. Stalin had banished him to a desolate town where he was having difficulty finding enough to eat. Three years later, Zinoviev would be a defendant in the first show trial of the Great Terror. It was a glimpse of things to come.

But Willi did find time for other activity that June. For example, he was taken to see the Comintern's brand new school for training in espionage, set up by Mirov-Abramov to prepare foreign communists for work under the auspices of the new "antifascism," as spies and covert operatives. This dour institution had been set up in the Moscow suburb of Podlipki. The place was patrolled by military guards armed with attack dogs, and was ringed with a double wall. Its "students" had quietly been singled out from the ranks of the foreign parties, talent-spotted and evaluated by among others Hungarian mafiosi like Gibarti, Alpari, and Bela Szantil, amphibians between the worlds of legality and illegality. The new antifascism offered the espionage apparatus wonderful new opportunities for recruiting idealistic youth. On this very first tentative little mission for the apparatus, en route to Vienna, Kim Philby would stand in deep contemplation before the still freshly charred ruins of the

Reichstag. Yet despite its seeming *raison d'etre* in "antifascism," the focus of training at Podlipki was *not* particularly on Germany.

The students at Podlipki were expected to change their names and commit themselves to lifelong secrecy, and the apparatus made it clear that any breach of that secrecy, whenever and wherever in the world it might happen, would be punished by death. Its cover name, behind the barbed wire, was the "Eighth International Sports Base," and it gave training to candidates from Korea to Paraguay. There were many candidates from the United States and Great Britain. Babette Gross names three Germans trained at Podlipki, all of whom, after having been parachuted with radio equipment into the Reich, were found by the Gestapo and shot. One of the German recruits at Podlipki, though not one named by Babette Gross, was Ruth Kuczynski, daughter of Robert René, who later in England, during the War, became the spy connected to events around Bletchley Park and later celebrated under her code name: "Sonia." So far as I am aware, the names of Podlipki's American and British trainees have never been revealed. The discovery of their identities would surely be the beginning of a fascinating tale. Some may have died in the Soviet Union. Once the Great Terror was in full cry— when Radek, Bukharin, and Mirov-Abramov had been arrested and shot, a number of the Podlipki alumni who happened then to be in the USSR were also rounded up and put to death.[18]

In laying down his strategy that June, Münzenberg instinctively understood that his task as a propagandist was to turn the attack on the communists around, to transform Hitler's effort to blame the fire on the communists into just another proof of Nazi criminality. Willi asked, as everybody asked, Who profited from the fire? *Cui bono?* The obvious answer made his method simple: Pin the fire on the Nazis themselves. Accuse the accusers.[19]

This was the response the world was waiting for. Münzenberg was acting on assumptions shared by most alert observers everywhere. The Nazis *looked* guilty. The fire was obviously—dazzlingly— convenient to their seizure of power. The only question in most people's minds was how the Nazi might *not* be the real arsonists. That impression was clinched by the transparent opportunism, violence, haste, and mendacity of the anti-Communist terror of March 1933. Münzenberg did not have to invent these suspicions; everyone shared them. Most people assumed the fire was exactly what it looked like: a Nazi-sponsored conspiracy to destroy the Weimar Republic and the German left.

Though Münzenberg never found any real proof that the fascists had set the fire, his assumption of Nazi culpability, at least at first, may well have been sincere. After all, he *knew* the Communists hadn't done it.[20]

So who else? This buffoon van der Lubbe?

The simple question—who really torched the Reichstag?—remains open to this day. I am strongly inclined to agree with the preponderance of present-day scholarship, which holds that Marinus van der Lubbe did indeed act alone. Yet there does remain some possibility that the Nazis, or some Nazi faction, set the fire. There is no direct proof, and there is a great deal to challenge the assumption of Nazi guilt. Yet the circumstantial evidence cannot be brushed aside. Consider this arresting entry in Goebbels' diary, made on January 31, a mere month before the fire. "In a conference with the Führer we lay down the line for the fight against the Red terror. For the moment we shall abstain from direct countermeasures. The Bolshevik attempt at revolution must first burst into flame. At the proper moment we shall strike."[21] Arthur Koestler, who knew Willi well, insists that in 1933 and 1934, Münzenberg himself assumed the Nazis were genuinely guilty, even while he was fabricating evidence against them. Koestler himself was no less convinced of Nazi guilt. American intelligence people close to the case, people just as impeccably anti-communist as Koestler later became, remained steadfastly convinced of Nazi guilt: among was them Allen Dulles's intimate, Mary Bancroft. (To be sure, Bancroft and Dulles were likely influenced by their prime contact, Hans Bernd Gisevius, one of many German anti-Nazi conservatives who had their own investment in Nazi guilt.) On the other hand, in 1989, Babette Gross, ordinarily so scrupulously exact and unspeculative, astounded me by saying that she thought it at least conceivable that the fire really had been set by the Communist *apparat,* after all.[22]

But the most likely fact is that van der Lubbe acted alone and was exactly what he seemed: a confused insignificant man, desperate for a place, *any* place, in a politics, indeed a world, from which he felt himself forever excluded. He was neurotic, hopeless, placeless, powerless; an early prototype for this century's long, ragged line of lonely fanatics and solitary assassins. He was a creature created by the new politics; he was one of its invisible men, seeking to validate and immolate his life of unseen desperation against the new demagogic visibility of the masses. The type has since become familiar, but in 1933, van der Lubbe was a fresh kind of freak for an emergent age. Nothing is easier than to imagine his wishful, bewildered mind finding its place in the saluting seas of uniforms; he seemed born to sway with the totalitarian throng. He could easily have been a Brown Shirt, except that something, everything, in his make-up was irremediably humiliated, out of it, fatally lonely. "Protest! Protest!" he moaned as they dragged him out of the building he had burned. Protest indeed! In his assassin solitude, poor Marinus van der Lubbe was that new kind of lost, humiliated, solitary soul: the other side of mass man.

The whole case for a larger conspiracy responsible for torching the Reichstag rests on one dubious assumption: That it was a physical impossibility for one person alone to have set so many small fires so quickly in such a very large building. This assumption dominated the claims of both Goebbels and Münzenberg. Tobias refutes it decisively. The boy had stuffed his pockets with cheap phosphorus and paraffin fuses, very easily lit and long-lasting—the kind used every morning by Berlin housewives to start the coal in their kitchen stoves. He had dashed through the empty building tossing one after another of these cheap firestarters at anything that looked like it would burn. Much would burn. The vast Sessions Chamber was lined with tinder-dry wood and dusty curtains, and the snaking fire took only minutes to suck them up into an inferno.

It is *possible*. Van der Lubbe could have set the Reichstag Fire, as he seems to have done everything, all by himself.

Ten days after the fire, a young novelist and literary activist named Gustav Regler called from Germany and presented

Münzenberg with a distant memory and an exceptionally useful bright idea. Until then, Regler had been a talented but marginal left literatus who looked like the young Siegfried and, as a talented Communist writer, was loosely tangled in Münzenberg's networks. Though everyone assumed that it had required many men to set all those fires in that vast building, no witness had actually *seen* anyone enter the building except the lone, loony Marinus as he teetered in through a broken restaurant window. The newspapers were wondering how all accused conspirators could have got in and out without being seen. For Regler, this speculation brought back a distant memory. From his days as a kid on the barricades of the 1918 revolution, Regler clearly recalled that one path into the Reichstag ran underground, through a tunnel. The tunnel housed steam pipes, and it ran from a separate power plant to the building's basement. Here was an obvious and plausible explanation: All those many arsonists must have come tearing in and out through the tunnel. Awakened by this inspired guess, the novelist took it upon himself to locate blueprints of the capital complex in a Stuttgart archive, whereupon he called Münzenberg with the information that for the right bribe he could have the blueprints photographed.

Willi instantly grasped the point. Regler was told at that moment, over the phone, that a book pinning the arson on the Nazis was being planned and he could consider himself hired as a collaborator. "Don't worry about the money," Münzenberg shouted. "Bring me those photographs!"[23]

The bribe was produced and the pictures made. It was only after Regler was safely on the train to Paris that he dared look at what he had. He locked himself in a lavatory. He slipped the pictures from their envelopes. There was the tunnel all right, just where he remembered it. It led straight from the power station to the Reichstag building. But Regler noticed something more. There was a *second* tunnel, branching off the main one, and running to the basement of another, adjacent building. That building was the official residence of the *Reichspräsident*. And who was the *Reichspräsident?* The man who lived in that house was none other than Hermann

Göring. Which meant that there was a direct unseen pathway from Göring's residence into the Reichstag itself.[24]

Regler sank back against the rocking lavatory wall.

Eureka.

Münzenberg set out to prove that through this tunnel a pack of seditious Nazis, mainly from the SA, had streamed into the Reichstag that February night and, after seeing Germany onto the path to state terror, charged out again, back to the safety of Göring's residence.

As their first step, Münzenberg and Otto slapped together and published a sensational "exposé," the book for which Willi had hired Regler over the telephone. This was *The Brown Book of the Hitler Terror,* anonymously orchestrated and partly written by Katz, with the help of many a passionate intellectual drawn into what soon amounted to a Münzenberg propaganda collective in Paris.[25] *The Brown Book* published a few weeks before the Leipzig Trial began, was instantly translated into many languages, and was on display in bookstores everywhere as the event unrolled. Then a second propaganda stroke was designed for the mass media— radio, newspapers, and the newsreels. This was a Counter-Trial, a "judicial inquiry" staged to "prove" Nazi culpability and held in London in early September 1933. The London Counter-Trial handed down its "verdict" the day before the Leipzig Trial began. Simultaneously, the Münzenberg-men set up various investigative commissions and committees of inquiry to keep alive the flow of information and propaganda surrounding the event, while maintaining cover and control over the covert actions that ran alongside it.

There were, in fact, two *Brown Books: The Brown Book of the Hitler Terror,* and a much amplified and corrected companion volume, *The Second Brown Book of the Hitler Terror.* Both make hectic and troubling reading. They are obviously propaganda, but they nonetheless retain some of the honor appropriate to the first systematic effort made anywhere to expose German fascism. They document the rapidly growing catalogue of Nazi crimes, often accurately. The eighth chapter of the *Second Brown Book* deals with anti-Semitic persecutions, and although the entire discussion is discreetly anti-Zionist and canted toward a Marxist reading of anti-Semitism, the exposure and attack are there. *The Brown Books* are a collection of inspired guesses, lies, disinformation, and occasionally rock-solid evidence about the emergent Nazi horrors. Where did this information come from? From any place it could be found. From the Comintern underground. From the *apparat*. From refugees. From documents collected by couriers like Countess Károlyi. From a number of very shadowy conspiratorial figures, especially in Berlin. And from the empty air.

The fervor and relentlessness of *The Brown Books'* antifascism, the novelty and nerve of their exposures, made them two of the most important political tracts of the era. It is quite true that they are trashy, hasty, and dishonest in many ways, including a number of very sinister ways. Yet one need not slip into endorsing Stalinist propaganda to note that their antifascist harangue was, in essence, right. The books had considerable success all over Europe and America. It was impossible to be a politically serious person in the fall of 1933 and not have heard of *The Brown Book*. Here, a mere six months after Hitler's accession, stands a work filled with potent evidence that the Nazis were radically degrading and brutalizing the heart of German politics.

While he was secretly conferring in Moscow during the early summer of 1933, the notion of staging a Counter-Trial suddenly jumped into Münzenberg's mind as a memory from secret revolutionary tribunals conducted in Russia before the Revolution.[26] Since the device was a means for co-opting the Nazis' own propaganda show, it could not of course appear to be controlled by Communists. The Leipzig show trial opened on September 20, 1933. The star communist in the dock was of course Dimitrov, but bringing up the rear was the hapless German communist Ernst Torgler. Torgler was a rather popular communist politician so out of the insiders' loop that after the fire he had turned himself in to the police in a disoriented search for campaign publicity. To put it mildly, the move backfired. Torgler may have been a powerless front man, but he was a very visible politician. Every newspaper reader knew his name.[27]

Not one of the defendants other than van der Lubbe could be shown to have a provable or even plausible connection to the crime. But then the Nazis seemed to mismanage the Leipzig proceedings in all kinds of ways. One would assume that van der Lubbe could at least have been forced to "confess" to the right "conspiracy." But no: van der Lubbe drooled and laughed; his great head lolled and rolled in bewilderment. Yet he never "confessed" to anything except his simple claim of having set his fire. Meanwhile the behavior of the judges was, if not utterly craven, nonetheless disgracefully partial by any standard. The thoroughly propagandistic nature of the whole event was perfectly evident to everyone. Above all, the ludicrous shakiness of the case is important; Goebbels didn't even *try* to make his frame-up look airtight. He acted as if the credibility of the case were almost unimportant.

The trial was understood by everyone as the first battle in the great war of disinformation waged between the right and left wings of the totalitarian age. In it, both the Communist and the Nazi propaganda apparatuses seemed locked in what appeared to be a pitched battle, giving no quarter, sparing no weapon in their absolute confrontation. Of course, ever since the Reichstag Fire itself and the arrival in Paris of Willi and Otto Katz, the propaganda apparatus had been at work organizing the antifascist forces. But now, after Willi's June meetings in Moscow, it seemed for the first time Willi and Otto had permission to hit the Nazis hard, hit them like they meant it, with no holds barred. Their task was to humiliate the Nazis, to make them the laughing stock of civilization, to cover them with guilt and shame. At last the Communist International would confront the new totalitarianism of the right and spare nothing in the new, absolute confrontation.

The London Counter-Trial was an "impartial inquiry" conducted before an assembly of famous lawyers, jurists, and political and literary celebrities, ranging from Stafford Cripps to H. G. Wells, people whose views would be sought by any widely based antifascist movement, and who had been carefully culled for their fame and their appearance of independence. This independence was sometimes even real, though of course everyone was guided with exquisite meticulousness behind the scenes. As usual, there were also "fully witting collaborators." For example, the very same Gaston Bergery who had arranged for Münzenberg's protection and collaboration with the Chautemps government represented the French bar. We may presume Bergery was still a silent partner for his friends in the Elysée and the *Deuxième Bureau*. Others, like the brilliant American civil rights lawyer Arthur Garfield Hays, were imported for their celebrity value and put through their paces as dupes.

This seems to have been the time of Otto Katz's first long sojourn in London, and in it he set out to deepen his contacts with all sorts of noteworthy figures on the left, ranging from Ellen Wilkinson to Victor Gollancz.[28] That aspect of his work was relatively public, and some of it was even publicized. He assumed a role; that of the antifascist idealist, fighting the Nazi juggernaut against all the odds, just one man in a small, fated band of a few decent men and women, who would fight for what they believed, and who might not live long. He began to cultivate the saturnine expression of an almost tragic courage. He began to tell stories of his "missions," going into Germany to save just one life, salvage just one ideal. His listeners were understandably moved.[29] These "missions," however, were almost certainly fictitious. I have found no evidence that Katz was ever in Germany while Hitler was in power.

But the great public event was Münzenberg and Katz's Counter-Trial in London, set up to ridicule the Nazi proceedings, and convened with great fanfare just before the Leipzig Trial commenced. It was generally a great success, though it was not flawlessly run. Blunders and haste let the mask slip more than once, and it made independents like Arthur Garfield Hays and H. G. Wells mighty uncomfortable from time to time. Hays's account in his memoirs of all that happened is quite damning.[30] Still, across the world, *it* was the news. The press was filled not with a Communist conspiracy but a Nazi conspiracy, or more exactly an SA, or "Brown" conspiracy. Goebbels and the Leipzig judges were thrown entirely on the defensive. This extravaganza made headlines, and lots of them, through two expeditious, showman-like, and devastating weeks. During those weeks, some strange manipulations and conspiracies took place, but no matter; before the civilized world reading the press, the Nazis had been humiliated and shown up, and the civilized world properly rejoiced. In Leipzig, Goebbels's trial mauled the judicial process month after yawning month. The world press sank into the muck of its boredom, with the tedium relieved only occasionally, as in the courtroom appearances of Goebbels and Göring themselves. These were buffoonish. Trussed out in one of his most ostentatious get-ups, Göring careened through his appearance ranting about the insults he'd endured in Münzenberg's campaign. He stomped his heels over *The Brown Book.* "It says that I am a senile idiot, that I have escaped from a lunatic asylum, and that my skull is collapsed in several places!" He wheeled on Dimitrov, hollering "wait till I lay my hands on you outside the sanctuary of this court!"[31]

The world snickered. Van der Lubbe hunched in his seat, numb and almost certainly drugged. His raw gawky arms and legs dangled miles out of his striped prison clothes. Sometimes he would moan, sometimes giggle. Torgler on the other hand was presentably dressed, even elegant. He enjoyed the services of an excellent lawyer who mounted a perfectly creditable defense of his client, which was after all "successful." But Torgler's mind seemed elsewhere. Behind his German composure, it seemed to meander in anxiety. There was fright in his eyes.

Meanwhile, Dimitrov seemed fearless. He exuded a confidence noted in every news report, visible in every newsreel. The Bulgarians turned downright jaunty as the days wore on. In the dock, the three of them cracked jokes with their guards; the ruddy-cheeked young German cops in their kepis and Teutonic boots were frequently heard suppressing guffaws. Dimitrov was radiant with confidence and contempt. It seemed nothing could shut him up. Everyone noticed his cocky boldness. Dimitrov baited the court. He hectored the tribunal, jeered at its pompous deliberations. In the final days he outraged it by transforming his own defense into an extremely stirring piece of Communist oratory that electrified the room and was ended only when the guards, laughing no longer, dragged him away.

And then, two days before the Christmas of 1933, the world was astonished to hear that van der Lubbe had been sentenced to death in the guillotine, while all the other Leipzig defendants had been acquitted. *Acquitted?* Göring and the Nazi press raged in bewilderment until a new line appeared, claiming that the acquittal was proof of the autonomy of German justice under Hitler. Torgler promptly vanished into a concentration camp. Dimitrov, Popov, and Tanev were removed from Leipzig and conveyed to Moabit Prison, just outside Berlin itself. There they were held, pending their return to the Soviet Union, for two months longer. Meanwhile, Münzenberg continued his campaign and Hitler refined the plot against Röhm. Then, at the end of February, exactly a year after the fire, they were suddenly released and flown in triumph to Moscow. The work was done.

***

A rather revealing episode about literature makes a fitting ending for this epochal, yet strangely theatrical and rather mysterious founding event of the Second World War. A few days after the acquittal, two Germans associated with the Committee of Inquiry into the Leipzig Trial—in other words, two Münzenberg men— approached André Gide and André Malraux with a proposal for a mission to Berlin. Throughout the Dimitrov campaign Gide and Malraux had been used incessantly in all kinds of capacities, ranging from signing petitions to chairing the more chic protest meetings of the Parisian intelligentsia.[32]

But this new mission seemed more glamorous. Gide and Malraux were to travel to Germany and present themselves (with a mass of petitions) to none other than Hitler himself. Well, if not Hitler, Goebbels—and use their prestige as the most eminent men of letters in Europe to press for Dimitrov's prompt release, for, as it turned out, the Nazis would hold the Bulgarians for two more months, nominally over the status of their citizenship, before returning them to Moscow.

The idea was to make the most, as propaganda, out of this delay. Willi's men appealed to Malraux's sense of himself as a swashbuckler, his vision of himself as the Gallic T. E. Lawrence. A persistent identification with the British secret agent and adventurer was an important fantasy for Malraux.

Within a few days, *L'Humanité* had announced that Malraux and Gide—youth and wisdom together, the embodied conscience of Europe—would travel into the heart of the Hitler terror to save brave Dimitrov from his imprisonment. January 2, the night before their departure, Gide dined at the Malraux' with two friends, both very close to the communist propaganda apparatus, Alix Guillain and Bernard Groethuysen. All the gossip was conveyed to Gide's neighbor and his closest confidante, a woman named Maria van Rhysselberghe, or as Gide affectionately called her, "La Petite Dame." La Petite Dame adored Gide; she acted in many ways as a kind of shadow wife to him, his daily companion, the woman with whom Gide could be himself and not be alone. They lived in the same building, and when Gide was in Paris they saw each other several times a day. Back in her own apartment, however, and without Gide's knowledge, Maria van Rhysselberghe maintained a copious diary filled with all his table talk, the entire inventory of his comings and goings. She was an unannounced Eckermann, who left behind a remarkably absorbing and very reliable record of his life.

All that happened around the visit to Berlin was duly inscribed in La Petite Dame's secret journal. Excitement was high.

Though Malraux and Gide probably did not know it, the mission was a fool's errand and a fraud. Once they had left the Gare de l'Est and crossed into Germany, press coverage came to a complete halt. The disappearance of that attention was an exact correlative of the attention of the *apparat*. Katz does not seem to have felt the smallest interest in what his ambassadors might or might not do in Berlin—least of all what they might or might not say to Hitler or Goebbels. All that mattered was that they be *seen* to go. As Katz may even have foreseen, when the two great men arrived in the German capital, not a single important Nazi was in Berlin. Everyone—Hitler and Goebbels too—had adjourned to Munich for a party conference there. Nor was there anybody from the other side, from the Berlin underground *apparat*, to receive or guide them. They simply got off the train, proceeded to a hotel and thence to the Ministry of Information on the Wilhelmstrasse. It was entirely empty save for its secretaries. The two representatives of the conscience of Europe had no official meeting of any kind with anyone.

Malraux and Gide decided instead to leave a letter addressed to Goebbels. Judging from its style, I would guess (uncertainly) that its author was Gide. It explicitly regrets Goebbels's absence, explaining that throughout Europe the fate of the Bulgarians was causing mounting anxiety, and how much it was to be regretted that they could not return to France bearing the news of the Bulgarians' imminent release. No mention of Torgler in his concentration camp appears at all. This letter was handed to an aide, and the two writers left.[33]

As closely as I can reconstruct it, this is what really happened. It is flatly contradicted, however, by André Malraux's own account of the event thirty-eight years later. In an interview with Jean Lacouture in 1972, Malraux insisted that he and Gide had indeed been ushered into Goebbels's presence, where they made their case. Malraux quoted what he claims was the Reichsminister's response. "What you are seeking is justice," Goebbels is supposed to have said. "What we are interested in is something else—German justice," to which nationalistic, phrase-making Malraux claimed Gide bleated a feeble *"Helas!"*—his sole contribution to the discussion.

So far as I am able to determine, this story is a complete fabrication. That the major Nazis were not in Berlin that day is clear. If for some reason Goebbels' returned unexpectedly or had not yet left, there remains the letter itself, the text of which was widely publicized, the whole gambit of which is to deplore Goebbels's absence. All available Gide scholarship, moreover, is unanimous in reporting that the two men met nobody of any political importance. This includes the eyewitness report of La Petite Dame in her journals, recorded immediately after having herself discussed the event with both Gide and Alix Guillain.

Malraux's account is a fraud.

It is easy to see that a man of Malraux's *amour propre* might have invented his encounter on the heights of evil to cover the stinging recognition, still perhaps felt forty years later, that in his political vanity he had been used; that his aspiration (shared by Gide) to assume the mantle of Victor Hugo and Emile Zola as the *grand homme des lettres,* conscience of Europe, had been made ridiculous.

Yet it was while concocting the story of his meeting with Goebbels that Malraux confided his suspicion, based on what information he does not say, that while he and Gide were enacting the Berlin charade, "Hitler and Stalin were already entering into collusion."[34] By 1972 Malraux, Minister of Culture under de Gaulle, was in a position to have pretty good information on this subject.

In any case, Gide and Malraux were in Berlin with time on their hands. Characteristically, Malraux tried to put together an encounter with a great man: Oswald Spengler, author of *The Decline of the West.* But Spengler was out of town. Well, in that case he might try his in-laws: Clara Malraux's parents were German Jews long resident in France. But the Goldschmidts were also not available. It was just a bad time. For the author of *La Condition Humaine,* the mission to Berlin turned out to be a dead loss.

Gide was at least able to go off and spend the evening in a gay bar.[35] He had always liked that part of Berlin life, and even at that late date, six months before the slaughters of the Blood Purge, it was still possible to find it there, a lingering bit of Weimar, under the lindens.

Chapter 6

BEHIND THE SMOKESCREEN

T he international wave of political sentiment that we now call
"antifascism" was not and could not have been *created* by Willi
Münzenberg. Alarm about Nazi terror was rising through
the West naturally, inevitably, and entirely on its own. Yet in 1933
"antifascism" was still little more than an incoherent, not quite panicked sentiment of distaste and anxiety. It had no focus; it had no
leadership. Willi's Reichstag Fire campaign was the first organized
political effort in the West to define and dramatize a public response
that was growing in strength, if not clarity, with each of Hitler's
successive giant steps into totalitarianism.

The natural antifascism rising in the West needed direction. Sensing that need, Willi captured the issue. Working out of the "witch's
kitchen" of his covert headquarters at 83, Boulevard Montparnasse,
he seized the propagandistic high ground. He defined the new
discourse. He caught the wavering inchoate antifascist wind in his
skilful sails and used its vast and rapidly rising force for his own
purposes. Watching the emergence of perhaps the most noble—
and necessary—political passions of the era, Willi used his old for-
mula of co-option and denial to put it in the service of Stalin.

The occasion was momentous, and the young Communist writers and propagandists working for Willi knew it. Arthur Koestler wrote about it in his autobiography. "The world watched the spectacle with fascination, and with as little understanding of its true meaning as small children have when they watch a complicated thriller on the screen. For the world was not yet accustomed to the stage effects, the fantastic swindle and cloak and dagger methods of totalitarian propaganda. And in this case there was not one producer of the show, as later in the Moscow Trials, but two, who played out their tricks against each other like rival medicine men before the assembled tribe."[1]

Willi's campaign focused the mind of Europe on the Reichstag Fire and defined its meaning. The issue was not the guilt of van der Lubbe, and not even the guilt of the Communist prisoners in Leipzig. The issue of the fire was first, last, and always the guilt of the Nazis and the outrage of their seizure of totalitarian power. It was put together from what Koestler admitted were "isolated scraps of information, deductions, guesswork, and brazen bluff," even though "it ended with a complete defeat for the Nazis—the only defeat which we inflicted on them during the seven years before the war."

Yet from the very beginning, the propaganda battle over the Reichstag Fire made a great many people strangely uneasy. The new certainties generated by what Koestler called Willi's "blind man's bluff" galvanized opinion. They also stirred a vague uncertainty, even among committed antifascists. André Gide himself—who'd thrown all his prestige into the public phase of Willi's campaign— spoke to his closest confidants of this indefinable unease. Exiled in Switzerland, Thomas Mann, who could hardly have been more fiercely antifascist—he is the one who had called the Nazi use of the Fire "a grotesque and crude swindle"—felt something similar. Watching the battle unfold, a notion deeper than outrage—call it a suspicion, or maybe an insight—began to take shape in his mind. It was too tentative, and too troubling, to make public. Yet Mann did confide it to his diary.

"It seems to me," Mann wrote, "that in the final analysis the origin of the fire may itself remain as mysterious and elusive as the intellectual and subjective line dividing National Socialism from communism. As I see it, the unconscious meaning of the trial lies in its exposure of the closeness, the kinship, yes even the identity of National Socialism and communism. Its 'fruit' will be to push to absurdity the hatred between the two camps and their idiotic determination to annihilate each other, when in fact there is no need for such enmity. They are kindred though divergent manifestations of one and the same historical situation, the same political world, and are even less separable than are capitalism and Marxism. Symbolic outbreaks like the Reichstag going up in flames are, we sense, even if we cannot prove it, their joint work."[2]

In November 1933, such a suspicion was not just radical: it was close to incomprehensible. And yet, several generations and a hundred million lost lives later, there is something uncanny in the insight of Mann's November jotting. Not that the notion of the "kinship" between National Socialism and communism would any longer strike astute observers as alien. Many twenty-first century historians would be quick to stipulate the common roots that bound the two totalitarian forms in their insensate war against liberalism. Many would point out the ravages of the two totalitarian forms' "absurd" hatred for one another; their "idiotic" commitment to mutual annihilation, their fanatic drive to define the whole of human life as "political"—and "political in their way, to boot. Plenty of people see all too well the two systems' common devotion to mass murder.

Yet in his tentative, intuitive way, Mann may have sensed something in the situation more specific than the large and now perfectly obvious philosophic parallels between National Socialism and Communism. It is just possible that Mann sensed something in the Reichstag Fire confrontation that was not just symbolically but *literally* the two dictators' "joint work."

***

There is evidence, all of it circumstantial, but far too abundant and compelling to be brushed aside, that certain aspects of the propaganda campaign that Willi used to found the antifascist movement were indeed, as Mann intuited, a collaboration between two dictators. Some such thing was suspected by many insiders for a long time, even at the time of the campaigns, though the mere notion of such a collusion has always been vigorously resisted, if only because to concede that the heroic founding moment of the "antifascist" movement in the West might have been corrupted by collusion with Hitler himself has seemed not only implausible but morally unbearable. Yet the evidence is quite abundant, and it calls for examination.

Let's begin with an almost unnoticed event. Very shortly after Dimitrov was arrested in Berlin, the GPU made a countermove, seizing and imprisoning a certain number of Germans in Moscow, people variously described as "specialists" or "technicians," and sometimes as "spies." Stalin was hardly going to let Dimitrov be held hostage in Berlin without making the obvious countermove. The number of German hostages the GPU seized is sometimes given as twenty; a more accurate count seems to be closer to four, more likely three. We know nothing—well, next to nothing—about these prisoners. Yet clearly they were important to the Nazis in some way.

In 1941, a former officer of the Comintern secret service named Richard J. H. Krebs adopted the pseudonym "Jan Valtin" to publish an account of his lifetime in the Soviet apparatus called *Out of the Night*. At the time of its publication, *Out of the Night* was ubiquitously attacked in the fellow-traveling press as a pack of lies. In the years since, Krebs' revelations have steadily gained in authority. Fridrikh Firsov, for several years the prime advisor on the Soviet Archives for the Yale University Press Annals of Communism series, read the book only after arriving in the West. Firsov reported that in reporting major events, Valtin's uniform accuracy of detail over issues about which Firsov was encyclopedically informed from the original sources had left him "simply stunned."[3]

Krebs was an undercover agent in the high, albeit not highest, ranks of the Comintern secret service. In 1933, shortly before being dispatched on an extremely dangerous tour of duty inside Germany, he was stationed in Copenhagen, monitoring and translating large amounts of secret communications moving between Europe and Moscow via Copenhagen. Some of this material was the secret traffic on the Dimitrov trial.

Here is Krebs' account:

I also translated much confidential material dealing with the arrest of Georgi Dimitrov in Berlin and with the preparations for the Reichstag Fire Trial, which already then promised to develop into an international sensation. The heroism with which the world press has credited the former chief of the Western Secretariat and the present nominal leader of the Comintern in Moscow, because of his bold and clever sallies against the government's "witnesses," Hermann Göring and Joseph Goebbels, was only the result of a carefully and cunningly organized play. The confidential material which passed through my hands in the Vimmelskaftet offices of the Westbureau in Copenhagen contained data as far out of reach of the ordinary newshawk as the complicated codes devised by Piatnitzky's nameless *chiffre* experts.

Months before the Berlin trial began, secret negotiations were already under way between Moscow and Berlin to exchange Dimitrov and his two Bulgarian aides for three German officers who had been caught by the G.P.U. as spies of Soviet soil. Dimitrov had to be saved from being broken down by Gestapo torture, not for his own sake, but for the sake of the Soviet Secret Service and the Comintern, whose inside workings he knew too well.

Under duress, Dimitrov had proved himself less steadfast than many of the comrades under his command. He surrendered to the Gestapo the address of a couple who sheltered him; both man and wife sought escape in suicide when the Gestapo came for them. They cut their own veins, but were rushed in time to a hospital by the Nazi jailers. Dimitrov also surrendered to the Gestapo the name and address of his mistress, Annie Krueger. His wife died suddenly under circumstances that remain mysterious to this day, in May 1933, while Dimitrov was in prison, awaiting trial.

It was at this time that the G.P.U. stepped in with this threat to the Gestapo: "Leave Dimitrov alone. Whatever you do to him, we will do to your spies in Moscow." Negotiations for an exchange of prisoners began through the medium of the Soviet consulate in Copenhagen, and through Dimitrov's sister, to whom the Gestapo, strangely enough, granted free passage in and out of Germany. The deal between Moscow and Berlin was concluded on the eve of the trial. But Dimitrov, for face-saving reasons, was kept in Germany until the end of the great Leipzig show.[4]

Are these claims true? What supports them? What contradicts them? Dimitrov himself seems to have been left dangling for a while. On May 11, 1933—two months after the March 9 arrest—a Comintern agent in Berlin sent Moscow an analysis of Dimitrov's arrest that confirms aspects of Krebs' account, though it seems that Nazis located the safe apartment more through Dimitrov's carelessness than by putting him "under duress." (Again, the question of Dimitrov's interrogation and possible "duress" under the Nazis is key. The documents sustain Krebs' claim that the Comintern was thoroughly alarmed by what Dimitrov might tell the Nazis. Yet there is no indication that the Nazis tried very hard to "break" him.) Dimitrov had been, at best, careless over highly secret matters. He had been carrying a full briefcase when arrested, the agent reports, and its contents were not known. The agent also wonders why there has been no campaign on Dimitrov's behalf, seemingly unaware that *The Brown Book* was already being prepared.[5]

Exactly one day before this report was sent to Moscow, Radek himself had dispatched a telegram to an agent in Berlin named Boris Vinogradov, the senior secret service officer in the Soviet Union's German embassy.[6] "We are thinking here that the life of Comrade Dimitrov and other Bulgarian friends is in direct danger," it begins. "Their friends have asked my advice regarding the arrangement of their defense campaign." Radek points out that the approach ought not to be an effort to prove the innocence of the Bulgarians but to show Nazi guilt, and the entire telegram assumes and alludes to a focus on attaching guilt to Ernst Röhm, the commandant of the S.A. To this end, Vinogradov is directed to begin "discreet talks" with a man named Oskar von Neidermayer; someone named "Grabovski" and "the people from 'Tat Kreuz.'" Radek emphasizes that information in the propaganda campaign being organized should be placed in the *Manchester Guardian* and "American newspapers." He adds, "whether Faigt and Ku are in Berlin or not, you know yourself what you could do in your position, what you are to do using others under your supervision." Radek closes by asking Vinogradov for a prompt reply.

The identities of the people in this telegram are as important as its content. Oskar von Neidermayer was a senior intelligence officer in the German army, a man well known to Radek, with a long history of managing the covert relations between the Soviet Union and the *Reichswehr*. I have been unable to identify "Grabovsky," but the people from "Tat Kreuz" consist of Soviet agents recruited from the German cultural intelligentsia, of whom the most notable was a filmmaker and writer named Adam Kuchkoff, clearly the "Ku" with or without whom Vinogradov is directed to proceed. Adam Kuchkoff was a German-born Soviet agent and a leading figure in the wartime underground, particularly close to his fellow spy, the economist Arvid Harnack and Harnack's Michigan-born wife Mildred, themselves both Soviet agents in Germany, a couple whose heroic story is explored in meticulous detail in Shareen Blair Brysac's absorbing, underrated book, *Resisting Hitler: Mildred Harnack and the Red Orchestra*. Kuchkoff was, in short, a dominant figure in the Soviet's German underground.

The most interesting player in the pack is the telegram's recipient, Boris Vinogradov himself. Vinogradov was the senior member of the Soviet *apparat* in the Berlin embassy, and as such, he was a leading advisor to the Ambassador, a man named Leo Chintschuk, whom in practical terms Vinogradov may even have outranked.[7] As the GPU's main man in Berlin, Vinogradov would of course have been thoroughly briefed about the Soviet strategy over the German regime. Throughout the telegram Radek explicitly assumes that Vinogradov is up to speed: "you yourself know what you could do." He also assumes that Vinogradov is familiar with such "discreet" contacts as Neidermayer and Kuchkoff.

Vinogradov was also a man with a personal life, and his maneuvers in love were linked to his maneuvers in politics. In late 1933, while the Leipzig Trial was in progress, Vinogradov became the lover—and recruiter for Soviet intelligence—of Martha Dodd, the peripatetic daughter of Franklin Roosevelt's ambassador to Germany. On Vinogradov's side, every new phase of his relation with Martha was sedulously reported to his superiors. Martha Dodd, herself a strange blend of naiveté and cynicism, considered Vinogradov the love of her life, and desperately hoped that her work for Soviet intelligence would forever cement their bond. This was not to be. Meanwhile, Martha Dodd had been busy herself with other men as well. (Martha's promiscuity left the German butler of the American embassy breathless: *"Das war nicht ein Haus,"* he later said, *"das war ein Maison."* ["It was not a house, it was a whorehouse."])[8]

Martha and her brother Bill—whom the Soviets also recruited as their agent—had accompanied their father to his Berlin posting in July 1933. The Nazis instantly took her up: Martha so dazzled Nazi matchmakers that she was introduced to that inveterate bachelor, Hitler himself. By the fall of 1933, as the Reichstag Fire Campaigns were unfolding, Martha had become the lover of a key Nazi, Rolf Diels, who in addition to being a founding officer of the Gestapo, had been involved with the Reichstag Fire case from hour one, having been in charge at police headquarters when the half-naked Lubbe was dragged into custody that very night. Hitler had immediately entrusted Diels with prime authority over the management of the Trial, a position he would retain (with one brief hiatus) until the day he personally released Dimitrov from custody. Diels sometimes escorted Martha to the courtroom—even though her German was very poor, barely functional—to prove to her how fair a Nazi court could be.

A specialist in both espionage and relations with the Communists, Diels was on surprisingly friendly terms with his Russian rival, Vinogradov. The Dodds had arrived in Berlin two months after Radek's telegram to Vinogradov, well after any putative collaboration had been put in motion. Yet Martha's love affair with Diels began while the campaigns were being put into place, and it overlapped with her even more passionate affair with Boris.[9]

It is at the least an arresting fact that the Soviet agent in Berlin whom Radek entrusted the management of the Reichstag Fire Trial was on good personal terms with the Nazi agent Hitler had entrusted with precisely the same task, and that these the two experts in covert action were sleeping with the same highly placed girlfriend.

If there was indeed Nazi-Soviet collaboration over the Fire, Radek's telegram of May 10, 1933, establishes a cast of characters, and it is precisely the right cast of characters. First there is Vinogradov himself; and by implication his exact opposite number among the Nazis, Rolf Diels, two men so strangely bound together. There is Oskar von Neidermayer, the German army's prime contact man for Soviet-German exchanges, including covert ones. There are the covert operatives around Adam Kuchkoff, including the Harnacks. (Mildred Harnack, incidentally, later became perhaps Martha Dodd's closest woman friend, as well as colleague in secret work, in Germany.) Finally, Radek's telegram alludes to precisely the spin Willi would give *The Brown Book* and the London Counter-Trial: discrediting Röhm and the SA.

Two or three weeks after Radek dispatched his telegram of May 10, Willi Münzenberg left Paris for the June secret meetings in Moscow determining strategy for the campaign. Here again we confront an arresting coincidence: While Willi's campaign was clearly "antifascist," its prime targets—Ernst Röhm and the SA—happened to targets that Adolf Hitler also had, secretly, in his sights. By the spring of 1933, Hitler also developed a covert but decisive interest in discrediting Ernst Röhm and the SA. Indeed, when Hitler met with Rolf Diels to assign him his role in the Reichstag Fire Trial, the Führer was explicit about the connection, informing Diels that his first, and absolutely confidential order of business would be to gather all he could "on Herr Röhm and his friendships." Hitler let that one sink in for a moment. Röhm was a homosexual. Then he added, "this may be the most important assignment of your career."[10]

This coincidence suggests that this is the moment to look a little more closely at Röhm and his SA, the man and institution that in the spring of 1933, both dictators wanted brought to grief.

The central question facing Hitler during the latter part of 1933 was what armed force, what *kind* of police and army, he should develop in order to put totalitarian muscle into his new power. This decision was even more important than his struggle with the Communists. On it depended the whole basis for his state terror, while internationally the decision would determine the basis for Hitler's pre-war position in the European world.[11]

Hitler's choice lay between the established German army and the SA. On the one hand, as Chancellor he stood at the head of the *Reichswehr*, and it was, albeit mistrustfully, at his disposal. On the other, he owed much to the SA, an untrained gang of paramilitary Brown Shirts, the street army that had been so essential to the Nazi party's rise. The leader of the SA was Hitler's long-term comrade, Ernst Röhm; the two men had been co-conspirators from day one, since 1919. From the start, they had used the SA as their instrument of political intimidation; as the extras in the strutting street theater of Nazism; and as a way of galvanizing the various disaffected, often unemployed working-class German males who formed the basis of the Nazi movement, just as they did of the Communist movement. When Hitler assumed power in 1933, the throngs of Röhm's Brown Shirts were what Nazism *meant*. They were one reason Hitler was so frightening.

Prior to 1933, this manifestly dangerous private army of ideological fanatics had no official standing whatever in the German government. Yet its brutalizing shadow darkened every aspect of political life. One of Weimar's most lamentable errors had been to relinquish any part of its sovereign monopoly on armed force by permitting such an organization to exist at all. By mid-1933, Röhm had a million men paid and in uniform; three and a half million more stood in the SA reserves. This made the SA, the private army of a political party, one of the largest military organizations in the world; certainly far, far larger than the German army itself.[12] That menacing fact was not lost on any foreign minister in Europe. To be sure, the *Reichswehr* was still in place, and Hindenburg was still its patron and senior general. To be sure, the SA was not a true army. Not quite. Not yet.

But Röhm had waited a long time for his empowerment and in March 1933, he was pretty sure that the time for his reward had come round at last.

Homosexual, indiscreet, deluded, Röhm had always assumed and been assured that when the Nazis took power Hitler would dismantle the *Reichswehr* and transform the SA into *the* German army, with Röhm himself as commandant. This aspiration was totalitarian on its face. It assumed that the army ought to be loyal not to that vague multifarious entity called the nation, but to a *party* and its ideology; not to a country as a whole but an idea, or rather pseudo-idea—fascism; not the territorial security of a Germany once notable for its political diversity, but the enforcement within and beyond the German border of one vile dream: *Ein Volk, Ein Reich, Ein Führer.*

The *Reichswehr* for its part despised the SA. Class played a large role in this contempt. In Germany the army was a privileged occupation actively sought out by upper-class men—men precisely like Oskar von Neidermayer, for example, that *Reichswehr* advisor on covert relations with whom Vinogradov was instructed to begin "discreet conversations." *Reichswehr* officers viewed Röhm's cohorts as a pack of dim-witted but dangerous boy scouts and political hopheads scraped up from the under-class. To them it was unthinkable that this sickening posse could claim to stand beside the German army of Frederick the Great, Bismarck, and Hindenburg. The leader of this establishment contempt was the same Hindenburg whom Hitler was so busy manipulating, and the principal object of its contempt was Röhm. As a result, Röhm was thoroughly despised by a number of people whom Hitler viewed as important to his future.

Internationally, the threat of Röhm caused even greater concern and alarm. To Europe, the "German threat" and the SA looked very much the same. Had Hitler fulfilled Röhm's wishes, Germany would have remilitarized in a single stroke, endowed by decree with an immense new army of revanchist fanatics obsessed with conquest, and indebted only to Hitler and Röhm. That such an organization might also prove incompetent would not change much: incompetent armies can be just as dangerous in their way as competent ones. In the late spring of 1933, Stalin, Chautemps, and the British, all three, had an obvious interest in common: to stabilize the *Reichswehr* and prevent the militarizing of the SA. Whatever their other differences, on *that* they agreed.

But the center of the secret is that a militarized SA was a prospect viewed with no less alarm by Adolf Hitler himself. Despite his many promises to Röhm, Hitler did not propose to let them become a reality. The world's most profound political secret of the end of March 1933 was that Hitler had made his own decision: He would go with the *Reichswehr*. And he was therefore in search of a way to rid himself of his old comrade, and be rid of his boy scouts too.[13]

Hitler had a number of reasons. He genuinely feared a preemptive French invasion, and he suspected, probably rightly, that militarizing the SA *would* make Germany too dangerous too fast for Europe's nerves. Hitler wished to reassure the British too. In February 1934, he was placating Anthony Eden with a promise to demobilize two-thirds of the SA and open the rest to international inspection.[14] But his truest motive was his simplest: Would Hitler establish Röhm, overnight and by his own decree, as the most powerful man in Europe? More powerful even than himself? Capable, perhaps, of a coup?

On the contrary.

In late 1933 only a minuscule handful of people knew that in absolute secret Hitler had begun to conspire with his newest henchman, Heinrich Himmler, to consolidate his personal control over the German police and military through an interlocking set of new elite corps. These were to be the SS, the SD, and the Gestapo, and they were to replace the SA as the backbone of Nazi power. Rolf Diels would be an important officer under the new arrangement. And the very first job assigned to this new consortium of militarized police would be to serve as Hitler's weapon in one sudden but gigantic act of gangsterism through which the SA would be demolished and its leadership, beginning with Röhm and all his lieutenants, rounded up and slaughtered in the seventy-two hours of infra-government terror that came to be known as the Night of Long Knives.[15]

It is in this context that Hitler's otherwise incomprehensible order to Diels—that in his management of the Leipzig Trial Diels dig up "information on Herr Röhm and his friendships"—becomes resonant. It is all the more striking when we consider that digging up "information on Herr Röhm and his friendships" was simultaneously a major focus for the Communist campaign. Willi and Otto's whole focus that spring and summer were to destroy the SA's credibility by showing that its leadership was filled with murderous adventurers and that Ernst Röhm was an unstable degenerate not fit for power.

And who could deny that both claims were the simple truth?

Though Röhm was the second most powerful man in Germany, until the Trial he had not been among the more visible Nazis. Before the Leipzig Trial, he had always ceded the spotlight to Hitler, Göring, Goebbels, and others. But now the leader of the SA was suddenly and unwillingly made world-famous when—thanks to the ingenious manipulations of Willi Münzenberg and Otto Katz— the public at large learned that this hero of the new German manhood was a homosexual. It was a simple fact with complex consequences: the leadership of the SA did indeed have the look of a homosexual cult, a fact Hitler did not fail to invoke when he destroyed it. It was a fact known only to relatively few insiders until Willi and Otto made it worldwide news by doing what they did best: black propaganda and forgery.

One of *The Brown Books'* most enduring claims is that Marinus van der Lubbe was a homosexual. The notion survives to this day, one of the few things many people have heard and vaguely suppose they "know" about the arsonist: Lubbe was a homosexual. The notion was very widely believed at the time: Koestler, for example, still it believed in 1951. There is no evidence anywhere for any such thing. It was a pure fabrication of Katz, concocted in

1933 in the Netherlands working under cover and an alias, using various Dutch Münzenberg men and other Comintern contacts in that country.[16]

The lie had only one purpose: To link Röhm to van der Lubbe and the fire, while making the dirty little secret of Röhm's homosexuality front-page news. In 1933 even more than now, serious newspapers would generally not publish information about a person's sexual tastes unless they impinged on hard news. Until then, Röhm's homosexuality had been known to a relatively small number of insiders. But when Katz used the classic techniques of black propaganda to invent a homosexual fling between Röhm and the man who torched the Reichstag, the fact was fair game, and it was plastered across the front page of every newspaper in the world.

The device for staging this fraud was a document that the *apparat* either invented or acquired from some interested party still unknown. It consisted of a list of names, mainly nicknames and the first names of boys, and was produced at the London Counter-Trial by a "Herr W. S."—in fact a Katz operative—who claimed to be a friend of a certain "Dr. Bell." It was claimed that Dr. Bell's special task in life consisted in procuring male lovers for Röhm, but that the physician-pander had prudently kept this secret inventory of their names as his "life insurance."

At the London Counter-Trial, "Herr W. S." testified that Dr. Bell had told him all about picking up van der Lubbe as a hitchhiker in 1931. Finding him "comely," Bell claimed to have supplied young Marinus to *Obergruppenführer* Röhm as a sexual partner. The story was sensational, and it was believed.

"Comely?" To judge by the evidence of his photographs, van der Lubbe was an exceptionally homely, really almost repellent, youth. A simian goofiness was plastered on his squinting features. His flabby body dangled and lurched. He looked comical in his clothes. Here is Koestler's description of him in Leipzig: "a horrifying apparition, half man, half beast. Saliva was dribbling from his mouth, and mucus from his nostrils down onto the floor ... When standing, Lubbe's hands were dangling down and his head bent on his chest like a chimpanzee's. When sitting, his head hung between his knees like a broken puppet's."[17]

Yet *The Brown Book* proceeds with "Herr W. S.'s" tale:

> Dr. Bell fetched a number of papers from a secret cabinet. He pointed to a sheet and said: "This is Röhm's love-list. If I ever publish it, Röhm is a dead man." He showed me the list, which contained some thirty names. I remember very well that one of them was Rinus, followed by a Dutch name beginning with "van der."[18]

The perfectly real dirty secret of the SA had been made international news through pure fraud. And eight months later, when the time came for Hitler to murder Röhm and decimate his corps, that dirty secret would be repeated to the world as the German dictator's prime rationale.

***

If the *Brown Book's* account of the liaison between Röhm and Lubbe was pure fraud, the book's accounts of SA atrocities and outrages were, on the whole, all too accurate. Yet even these first bulletins from the front of Nazi horror were assembled using classic conspiratorial techniques. Most of them were brought to Willi by couriers such as the Countess Károlyi, after the Comintern underground in Berlin had assembled them through a network of covert contacts within the German police force, and even the Nazi establishment: there were people in both organizations who were ready and indeed eager to leak information that would supply the world with proof of the unrestrained and mounting brutality of the SA. One of the prime sources for these leaks was the Berlin Police Headquarters on the Prinz Albrechtstrasse.[19]

The leakers understandably kept a mighty low profile, and clear information about who was pilfering the files in that turbulent place is a little unclear, even now. Several possible sources for the leaks present themselves. One might have been Communists still working for the Berlin police. Under Weimar the Berlin Police had been Social Democratic, or "pink"—sufficiently so that in 1933, there were still many Communists and sympathizers within its ranks. A second likely source might have been the Nazis themselves, insiders tied to the new Gestapo, especially those Nazis who belonged to the faction in favor of dumping the SA in favor of the *Reichswehr*. They may or may not have known that they had a certain kind of support at the very highest level. But one of them we know: Rolf Diels.

A third possible source of leaks were non-Nazi conservatives, true believers outside the Nazi system who still clung to the honor of the *Reichswehr*. Many of them worked for the police, and they were horrified by what they witnessed every day in this loathsome center of police intrigue and violence.

The most famous of these conservatives was a young lawyer named Hans Bernd Gisevius, who during World War II served as a major covert contact for American intelligence and was a crucial conspirator in the von Stauffenberg plot of 1944 to kill Hitler—yet another effort on the part of the *Reichswehr* to reclaim its honor and save the country. In his job on the Prinz Albrechtstrasse, young Gisevius was deep in quiet, angry conspiracy, trying to undermine the SA, working together with his immediate superior, another non-Nazi conservative named Arthur Nebe, who was influential enough regularly to advise Hitler on police matters. We know that the effort included stealing files and supplying them to the anti-Nazi underground: Much of the stolen information surely appeared in Münzenberg's campaigns. The irony is that if Gisevius was the leak, he was probably playing into Hitler's hands.[20]

The parallels between Münzenberg's propaganda campaign and the lethal secret of Hitler's plans for Röhm and the SA may be very suggestive of a motive for the collaboration of which Krebs wrote, but the coincidence is hardly proof. Hitler and Stalin had a common target. The fact is interesting. It provides motivation. But in itself it is far from proof.

Yet the rumors pointing to Nazi-Soviet collaboration, at least in the upper levels of the Communist movement, began early. André Malraux, another writer intimate with Katz and Münzenberg's Paris operation, also pointed out his belief that covert collaboration between Hitler and Stalin began at this time, though Malraux did not provide any details beyond his dark thoughts.[21] In her book *Stalin and German Communism*, Ruth Fischer, asserts that in the Fall of 1933, not long after she and Maslow arrived in Paris, she was told about it directly by Wilhelm Pieck, the senior German communist dealing with the matter in Paris.

> While the trial was running its course, I met two important witnesses in Paris—Wilhelm Pieck, who at this time was eager to speak to Maslow and me, and Maria Reese, a Communist Reichstag deputy and the intimate friend of Torgler. (Later she returned to Germany and became a Nazi sympathizer, but this fact does not impinge on her creditability; she was getting the full details from Torgler's lawyer, with whom she was in almost daily contact.) Independently, both of them told me the same story, that before Dimitrov stood up in the courtroom to make his courageous peroration, he knew of the secret arrangement between the GPU and the Gestapo that he would leave it a free man. The other two Bulgarians were included in the arrangement, but Torgler and van der Lubbe were not. Pieck and Reese were both much concerned with this fact, but from different points of view. Pieck, knowing that Torgler had been abandoned by the Politburo, was fearful that he might see through the combination and make a statement in the courtroom baring the secret deal between the two state police forces. When I saw him, therefore, Pieck was busy arranging for a refugee from underground Germany to arrive in London [that is, at the "Counter-Trial"] with the startling message that Torgler was a traitor to the antifascist cause. Maria Reese's reaction, of course, was quite different; she later wrote a pamphlet breaking with communism, but with only vague allusions to the deal, since she hoped to save Torgler's life and did not want to antagonize the Gestapo. Pieck's courier did go to London and delivered a message in a loud stage whisper, but since Torgler never revealed the arrangement by which Dimitrov was saved, the charge against Torgler was allowed to peter out.[22]

When Arthur Koestler wrote *Invisible Writing, Stalin and German Communism* had just appeared. He wrote: "I myself have no first-hand information regarding the alleged deal. I remember, however, that Münzenberg repeatedly and meaningfully warned us, his staff, 'not to built up Torgler.' The implication was that Torgler might weaken or even turn his coat. But this suspicion need not have been related to the alleged Dimitrov deal.[23]

The files of the Central Party Archives are filled with Willi and Otto's efforts to deal with Torgler's lawyer, Dr. Alfons Sack, a competent, even distinguished, if conservative, attorney whose work consisted mainly of negotiating to his client's advantage in the propaganda storm surrounding the Trial. Torgler was the loose cannon. He had to be intimidated into co-operation with the larger plan, and his anxieties were evident to everyone. In Switzerland, Torgler's mood was obvious to Thomas Mann on the basis of newspaper accounts and photos. On November 1, he noted in his diary: "crazy lies presented to the Leipzig court in the case against Torgler, who looks increasingly small and woebegone."[24]

During the fall of 1933, both Maria Reese and Pieck told Ruth Fischer that Torgler "was not included in the deal" to acquit the Bulgarians, with the likely outcome that Torgler would be found guilty, and executed, with Lubbe. Everyone was maneuvering around this fact. In the end Torgler was acquitted, though the Nazis kept him in "protective custody" until 1936. We can guess that Sack's job consisted in saving his client's life, and while he negotiated for that, Willi kept a watchful if not worried eye on a tricky situation, ordering his staff "not to built up Torgler."

In 1951, Arthur Koestler did not know that after the war, Ruth Fischer established contact with Torgler in Germany. Torgler was by then emerging as a minor, rather bland Social Democratic politician in West Germany. Torgler confirmed Ruth Fischer's information from 1933, and added to other information he had acquired, especially in a revelatory post-war chance meeting with Rolf Diels. Yet Torgler begged Fischer to leave him and his exchange with Diels out of any public use she made of the information. Fischer decided to honor this request, basing the account in *Stalin and German Communism* only on her 1933 conversations. Nonetheless, what Torgler told her in 1947 is now readily available in Ruth Fischer's letters, published in a scholarly edition of 1990.[25] I should add here that Babette Gross, who told me that she had come to believe Ruth Fischer's information about a Nazi Soviet collaboration after she herself met with Torgler at a later date. When I asked her if there was any truth to the claim, frequently made during and after the war, that Torgler had indeed "turned his coat" and served the Nazis, she brushed the story aside. Torgler was, she pointed out, always a leftist: first a Communist, then a Social Democrat.[26] Still, the disinformation about Torgler the traitor, begun when Ruth Fischer first heard it planned in 1933, was widespread, and Torgler lived in fear of it.

Of all the information Torgler gave Ruth Fischer, his account of his meeting with Rolf Diels is probably the most revealing. In a letter to her dated November 27, 1948, Torgler describes a long train to ride he had shared with Diels. "The trip to Nürnberg was thus very worthwhile. Diels told me many very interesting things, especially about our friend Georgi [Dimitrov]. The release of Georgi and his countrymen was the direct result of negotiations between Chintchuk and Hitler. Göring, Diels, etc., were presented with a done deal. ["*vollendete Tatsachen*"] This certainly casts light on things we had already known, so that the versions of Valtin's and our London friend E. [Bob Edwards, a Labour M.P., who had also publicized inside knowledge of such a deal] are thoroughly corroborated."[27]

After his "heroic" performance in Leipzig, and his return to Moscow, Dimitrov became head of the Comintern and in that capacity presided Soviet sponsorship of the "antifascism" that had been given definition through Münzenberg's interventions. Dimitrov was a survivor. He survived his German incarceration; he survived the Great Terror and the Second World War, a remarkable feat for any politician as close as he was to Stalin. He was always very proud of his Leipzig "triumph." He was absolutely subservient to Stalin's whims, and was in the habit of jotting down the dictator's talk word for word in his diary. On November 11, 1937, he recorded a "private conversation with Stalin" about Willi. "Münzenberg," Stalin remarked, "is a Trotskyite. If he comes here, we'll certainly arrest him. Try to lure him here."[28] Dimitrov promptly took the steps that were intended to lure the man who had saved his life to Moscow, and his death.

After the USSR invaded Bulgaria in 1944, Dimitrov was made the head of the new communist government there, and he remained in power until his death in 1949. As we know, both Popov and Tanev had been sent to the gulag soon after their "triumphant" return to Soviet soil, and after his release he wrote a memoir of his experience there. In 1980, Peter Semerdjiev, a former Communist, once a member of the Bulgarian Communist party's Central Committee, and an intimate of Dimitrov during the post-war years when Dimitrov was Communist dictator of Bulgaria, published these memoirs in French. In the preface, Semerdjiev re-asserted the claim that Dimitrov had been released as part of a Nazi-Soviet deal, and greatly elaborated upon it, adding information he had learned while working as Dimitrov's subordinate on the Central Committee in Sofia. According to Semerdjiev, the Dimitrov Conspiracy was quite well known among senior Communists around the Great Bulgarian Leader.

"In this parody [the Leipzig Trial]," Semerdjiev wrote, the main characters are the two dictators, Hitler and Stalin... The script of the trial was prepared by the two dictatorial regimes. On the one hand Moscow, through the Comintern, attempts to raise public opinion and to facilitate Soviet infiltration into the political life of Western Europe. On the other hand Hitler, who had just come to power, desperately needed to attract around him the extreme chauvinistic factions in his country. The trial itself is preceded by a secret agreement between the diplomatic services of Hitler and Stalin in the capital of Denmark. According to this agreement, the three Bulgarians "indicted" will be acquitted and immediately exchanged against "German spies" caught on Soviet territory. This diplomatic act is brought to the knowledge of the Bulgarian "accused" before the trial. This is why, contrary to what happens to the Germans in the same trial, they have the necessary privileges in food, defense lawyer's visits to the family, correspondence, newspapers and a special room where they receive foreign correspondents.[29]

In correspondence and an interview with me in 1992, Semerdjiev admitted that he did not have documentary confirmation of the information he learned while on the Central Committee; in his opinion that material was of such sensitivity that it had all been removed to any archival material relevant to the deal would have been removed to Moscow. Nonetheless, Mr. Semerdjiev was able to add many details to what is known. As he understands it, Stalin's strategy went through some profound modification sometime between March 1, when Hitler issued his emergency decree, and the time of Dimitrov's arrest on March 9. It was a shift toward greatly raising the political and propaganda stakes invested in the trial, and greatly deepening the Soviets' own involvement. It is important to note here that though Münzenberg surely knew about the general outline of the deal, he was probably not one of those who hammered out its precise terms. According to Mr. Semerdjiev, that was left to Wilhelm Pieck, and the Central Party Archives contain copies of telegrams that fully sustain his claim. Mirov-Abramov, however, would have known all about them, and Münzenberg was involved in intricate consultations with Mirov all through June of that year, planning strategy for Leipzig.[30]

Dimitrov himself, from the time of his arrest until the time of his acquittal, was kept constantly informed about events as they unfolded through the thoroughgoing penetration of the prison itself. The apparatus had unseen access all over Leipzig. A copy of *The Brown Book* was smuggled into Dimitrov's quite comfortable cell, and there he read it at his ease.[31] The man in charge of keeping Dimitrov instructed and informed was indeed Wilhelm Pieck, the very man whose behavior had first alerted Ruth Fischer's suspicions in Paris during the London Counter-Trial. Pieck guided Dimitrov through the entire experience of investigation and trial, and it was even Pieck who provided Dimitrov with the substance of his last flamboyant oration before the court, that sudden spontaneous display of courage that had stirred the world.[32]

As Dimitrov deployed his rhetorical fire, denouncing the proceedings as rigged, he had his own private, deep-cover secret: It was that the proceedings were rigged, all right—but in his favor. Say what he might, he was safe; he was delivering his "antifascist" tirades under Hitler's unseen protection; he was the beneficiary of an agreement already reached between the Soviet secret services and the highest-level Nazis, through which he was assured of acquittal and a triumphant return to Russia at the end of what was a propaganda charade played out as a whole high drama of defiance.

Semerdjiev's information is consistent with Valtin's account. According to Semerdjiev, Dimitrov's arrest precipitated a series of secret meetings between the Nazi and the Soviet services. Dimitrov was head of the Western European Division of the Comintern: He knew a great deal about the secret Soviet networks in Germany and its "underground." Although Stalin was relatively indifferent to the downfall of the legal German Party, Stalin was very concerned about compromising these networks. According to Semerdjiev, the two leading items negotiated in the talks between the two services were a degree of safety for the underground networks, and along with it, Dimitrov's release. As we have seen, Dimitrov left Germany, strangely, never interrogated, his secrets still his own.

In an interview with me, Mr. Semerdjiev added to this information. When he was in the Bulgarian Party Central Committee, he said, the assumption that Dimitrov had been released as the result of a deal between the two dictators was widely held and discussed among his colleagues—though none of them would have had the bad form to raise such a thing with Dimitrov himself, who was very vain about his "heroic" performance in Leipzig.

***

Ruth Fischer does not at any point speculate on Hitler's motives in making a deal with Stalin. Torgler accepts Valtin's view—that the three German "technicians" being held in Moscow were sufficiently important to Hitler to trade Dimitrov for them, swallowing a humiliating propaganda defeat into the bargain. Mr. Semerdjiev, like Valtin, accepts the Soviet-held hostages as a full explanation of Hitler's motives.

That argument is plausible, but not quite convincing. Why would these three anonymous people have been so important to Hitler? The record known to me offers no clue about why Hitler would have viewed them—"technicians?" "spies?"—as indispensable. If their safety mattered enough to make Hitler strike what looked like a very bad deal, they must have been very important indeed. In which case, their absolute evaporation in the shadows of history seems a little strange.

Perhaps the three Moscow hostages were not, in themselves, the only factor motivating Hitler. Perhaps, if this story is to make sense, we must enter a final phase of speculation, focusing less on the hostages than on the large political issue that we *know* had a high, albeit secret, priority for Hitler in the spring and fall of 1933. I am speaking of course of his decision to empower the *Reichswehr*, to dissolve the SA, and to rid himself forever of Röhm and his crew.

Any deal must be struck on the basis of some common interest. I submit, as an hypothesis, that it may be more than coincidence that the Nazis and Soviets arranged Dimitrov's release at the very moment both shared a clear common interest—for one absolutely public, for the other absolutely secret: Discrediting Röhm and the SA. The net effect of Willi's propaganda campaign was to depict the SA as a pack of bloodthirsty renegade fanatics, and Röhm himself as an irresponsible degenerate. Surely it is significant that these are precisely the grounds Hitler later used to justify his own assault on both.

The Brown Books know their culprit: It's the SA, the SA, that's to blame. The SA set the fire. The SA is the polluted source of Nazi violence. The SA is brutalizing German politics with its atrocities—and both *Brown Books* present a long, often accurate and fully damning inventory of those atrocities. Most important of all, the Münzenberg campaign never misses a chance to raise the threat of an SA coup against Chancellor Hitler, or even more alarming, a coup against the *Reichswehr*.

By May 1933, Hitler wanted to see Röhm publicly disgraced. He was preparing his old friend for the slaughter. Yet Hitler himself could not be perceived as the source of the propaganda used to ruin the jolly commandant. That would arouse Röhm's suspicions in a very dangerous way. If there was a wish to conceal Hitler's hand in Röhm's bad press, the strategy succeeded. We've long known about Hitler's solemn order to Diels secretly to collect "information of Herr Röhm and his friendships." We've also known about Diel's strange acquiescence, both passive and active, in the leaks about SA outrages making their way into Willi's hands. But to this day, Hitler himself has never been linked, even in suspicion, to the exercise in black propaganda that demolished Ernst Röhm's political hopes. Yet Hitler's desire for precisely that offers a motive that for Hitler may have counted more—much more—than three hostages held in Moscow.

***

Early in the morning of June 30, 1934, about four months after Dimitrov and the other Bulgarians were at last released and returned to the USSR, Hitler flew to Munich. Upon the signal of his plane touching down in that city, the Blood Purge, which Hitler had been planning since the spring before, was set in motion. Hitler's newly empowered elite corps embarked upon its first genuine test as an armed fist. Throughout Germany, the principal leaders of the SA suddenly found themselves face to face with something new, a fresh horror emerged whole from the swamp of Nazi intrigue: the Waffen SS. Arriving at the Ministry of the Interior in Munich, the Chancellor stepped into a reception room to behold the floor piled with corpses; the shot, stabbed, and bludgeoned bodies of sundry SA true believers who'd got up early and donned full uniform to welcome their leader "in state," and who now littered the official parquet in their blood-soaked best. Hitler then proceeded to Wiesee, a Munich suburb, where, in a resort sanitarium, the foremost SA bigwigs had forgathered for a special "conference" ordained by their Führer. Hitler strode into Röhm's bedroom and roughly shook him awake. "Bind him," came the command. Down the hall, Edmund Heines (a central object of Willi and Otto's attack) was found in bed with his own chauffeur. Both men were shot dead as they struggled to scramble free. Up and down the screaming halls the SS went. Hitler then retired to the Brown House, fond venue of so many happy days, while all across Germany the machine guns began to blaze and the co-ordinated wave of peremptory arrests and murders began and went on for the next seventy-two hours.

Back in Paris, this event was viewed with satisfaction, but it was in Moscow that, as we shall see, it was watched with an interest that opened new paths. Stalin was utterly absorbed in the Blood Purge, and he was well informed about it, in advance. Immediately after Röhm had been murdered in the Blood Purge, a third and final book was instantly produced, once again anonymously written by Otto, filled with "documentation" forged by two literary workers in the *apparat:* Bruno Frei and Alfred ("Konny") Norden. This was called *The White Book on the Executions of June 30, 1934*.[33]

Katz's *White Book* functioned to cap the arguments of *The Brown Books* and revise the list of prime SA culprits and arsonists in such a way that the Communist version of SA history was co-ordinated with the actual hit list of Röhm's slaughtered lieutenants—Karl Ernst, Walter von Mohrenschild, and others. *The White Book* has the look of an attempt to square all versions of the event and bring the two disinformation campaigns, Communist and Nazi, into consonance.

It should be noted that Dimitrov meticulously edited the manuscript of *The White Book* in Moscow, and that in those days Dimitrov did very little that was not supervised by Stalin himself.[34]

Another source for links between the Nazi Reich and the Soviets may have been a certain General and intelligence officer named von Bredow, the then director of military intelligence for the *Reichswehr*. Bredow is known to have had elaborate clandestine contacts with yet another "White Russian" organization, this one located, like Katz, in Paris, and known as the "Guchkov circle." Soviet agents penetrated the Guchkov circle from top to bottom. One quite reliable report to the American State Department of 1940 asserts that Otto Katz had acted as a "go-between" for Bredow and the Soviets. This may or may not have been true: It *is*, however, a perfect fit for our available information. The same memorandum asserts, "Katz knows the secrets of the Brown house."[35] As an experienced intelligence officer, not a Nazi, and loyal first to the army, Bredow had every motive to assist Katz. Yet if Bredow believed he was safely on the winning side, he was in error. On the night of the Blood Purge he had helped create, Bredow walked home, apparently perfectly at ease. At his doorstep, he confronted agents of the SS, who drew their revolvers and without one word, shot him dead.[36]

Another fabrication attacking the SA is a now long-forgotten bit of disinformation known as the "Oberfohren Memorandum." The evidence strongly suggests that this extraordinary forgery was concocted by Münzenberg's lieutenant, Gibarti, working through a press front he then ran called the German Information Office.[37] The Archives show that the German Information Office was entirely under Soviet covert control, and also indicate an elaborate role for this "press service" in campaigns to come.[38]

Dr. Ernst Oberfohren was a German professor of political science who in middle age became a rather dour and unspectacular conservative member of the Reichstag. As a conservative, Oberfohren was hostile to communists and fascists alike, though his party, the German Nationalists, was caught in the gravitational field of fascism and had been an uneasy partner in the right-wing coalition of Hitler's first weeks in power. Oberfohren was outraged by this alliance; vocally opposed to those in his party who imagined

Hitler could be brought to heel and "instructed," he seems to have maneuvered rather dishonestly to win his point. He was caught out, resigned his seat, and had a nervous breakdown. As all his worst fears came true, the wretched man either shot himself or was murdered by those thugs on May 6, 1933.

This death in despair of a high insider offered the *apparat* a great opportunity. Safely beyond denial, Oberfohren could be cited as "source" for the inside stories about SA perfidy which Gibarti was then planting in the British press, especially in the *Manchester Guardian*. Karl Radek's secret directives now in The Moscow Archives explicitly order his people to make use of the *Manchester Guardian* as a leading press outlet in the campaign. He was undoubtedly making use of contacts already in place and coordinated by Münzenberg's people.[39] As the high point, the German Information Office released a "memorandum" purporting to have been written by Oberfohren (or a journalist close to him) just before he pulled the trigger in his "suicide." In it he recounts all the horrors he has seen. It made very sensational front-page news everywhere.

It was a pure piece of black propaganda, most likely written by Gibarti himself. Like the rest of the campaign, the Oberfohren Memorandum exempts Hitler personally from current evils. It actively promotes and admires the *Reichswehr,* while seeking to show how Röhm and his men are a menace to German legitimacy. It describes Hitler not as the master of the situation but a front man losing control of the mad dogs in the SA.[40] Hitler's alliance with Hindenburg, Oberfohren said, can never survive the fascist hordes threatening them both. Röhm (assisted by Göring and Goebbels) is forever described contriving to rush headlong into a coup d'état against Hindenburg, the coalition, and the *Reichswehr.* Above all, the *Reichswehr.*[41]

This fantasy, that Hitler was somehow not really in charge, proved peculiarly resilient. The same idea was widely believed inside American Intelligence during the war, including by people close to Allen Dulles—one of whose prime sources was Gisevius. Many German insiders swallowed it whole as well.[42]

On the day of the Blood Purge itself, while the firing squads shattered the calm in Wiesee and Munich, and grandiose eminences were having their brains blown out in their offices, a leading Berlin police official rushed up to Hitler to tell him that Himmler was a dangerous man, he was killing people, and he had too much power.[43]

One wonders that Hitler did not burst into his celebrated insane laughter.

Chapter 7

THE POPULAR FRONT:

PROPAGANDA AND PROPHECY

I f there really was a covert arrangement between Hitler and Stalin over the Dimitrov trial in 1933, the deal fits perfectly in the pattern of duplicity that marked Soviet "antifascism." This is something about which there is no need to speculate. Around the middle of 1934, the public relations apparatus that Münzenberg had created to co-opt the rising wave of Western antifascism rolled on to its ultimate official implementation in the vast propaganda fraud known as the Popular Front. In the summer of 1935, capitalizing on Dimitrov's role as the hero of the new antifascism, Stalin made the Bulgarian conspirator the Secretary General of the Comintern, and had him proclaim as universal Communist Party policy a new "antifascist" alliance between Communist parties and all other antifascists in the democracies. Even socialists. Even liberals. They were no longer "social fascists," no longer Nazis under the skin. Overnight, they were allies, friends. As Babette Gross put it, "No more radical change from the Comintern policies of the past seven years could be imagined."[1] It was a total turnaround, and Willi's apparatus in the West seemed ideal for promoting it.

For innocents in the West, the Popular Front proved that the Communists had risen above ideology in order to stop Hitler. In fact, the Popular Front served Stalin as a human face covering his appeasement of Hitler while he unleashed the Great Terror of 1936–1939. The policies it masked were the reverse of its avowed ideals. In that "contradiction" lies its essence. The Popular Front was always a lie. It never had anything to do with any sort of Stalinist "ideals." It was never intended to "stop Hitler." Its supposed embrace of pluralism coincides exactly with the extermination through mass murder of anything resembling political diversity in the USSR. First, last, and always, it was politically a strategic tactic and morally a fraud. For all its fine sentiments, Stalin used it to cover some of the most brutal and duplicitous maneuvers in the history of politics.

Yet it is difficult to exaggerate the impact of the Popular Front on the moral life of the democracies during the mid and late thirties. The Front was rapturously received by many of the most intelligent and committed people in two generations. The seeming path to peace opened an era of good feeling, and the celebration was ebullient and irresistible. In Paris, New York, Hollywood, and London a new variety of Stalinist righteousness became the dominant ethical chic of the era. It left hardly a single cultural figure untouched. The wishfulness of an age had been tapped.

A myth—a new "enlightened" myth—was taking shape. It held that the Communist state, whatever its missteps on the road to socialism, at least had the virtue of being genuinely, *inherently* opposed to Nazism. As such, Communism represented the only *real* resistance to the horror so obviously taking shape in Germany. The democracies, in their real and supposed inaction, were depicted as bound by capitalism either to the ineffectiveness of liberalism or worse, to a secret sympathy for the Nazis, fascist brothers under the skin, a pack of appeasers. For despite Dimitrov's rhetoric, the Communist assault on liberalism had not been abandoned after all. The Popular Front allowed liberalism to be embraced and condemned at once, while Stalinism was promoted as good, or at least necessary to the good, by virtue of the authenticity of its opposition to Hitler's evil.

It was a powerful argument. Several generations of enlightened people in the West accepted it, or at least muddied their thinking with it. Within the democracies, the Popular Front was if possible more far-reaching, more fashionable, more completely conformist than even the Stalinist fellow-traveling in Paris during Sartre's heyday. Stalin's logic was simple: Let the innocents wring their hands over the slaughters in Moscow. No matter. Decent people couldn't turn their backs on "antifascism." *Any attack on Stalin is an endorsement of Hitler.*

As the senior Bolshevik in charge of the antifascist response, and a practiced specialist in German politics, Karl Radek guided Münzenberg's operations from the top, while crafting a new line lavishly admiring the Versailles treaty, which until then had been the object of incessant Communist invective.[2] The Soviets sought membership in the League of Nations. Meanwhile, the so-called "idealism" of the Front transformed the entire understanding of Communism in the democracies.

Party membership swelled: fellow traveling became *de rigueur*, some sort of revolutionary pose seemed morally—or at least socially—indispensable. The Front soon found a prime focus in the tragedy of the Spanish Civil War, which became simultaneously the Terror's principal European outpost and a prime focus for antifascist moralizing. In Franco-Soviet relations, the propaganda high point of the Popular Front was the June 1936 celebrity tour of Russia by André Gide, which coincided with the installation of the socialist government of Léon Blum in Paris and the death and state funeral of Maxim Gorky in Moscow. Every stop of the War of Ideas was pulled. Meanwhile the dictator was preparing the first act of the Great Terror, the August show trials of Zinoviev, Kamenev, and their fellow "conspirators."

In Europe and America, communist recruitment, not least in espionage, was transformed. This is when the young men and women we might call the "Popular Front spies" entered the apparatus. In England, there was the Cambridge group of Kim Philby, Guy Burgess, Anthony Blunt and their associates; in America, Laurence Duggan, Alger and Priscilla Hiss, and others in the Ware group; in France, the Soviet agents around Pierre Cot, a leading Popular Front politician. In his 1939 book, Walter Krivitsky drew the map of the new recruitment. (1) The British establishment was targeted for espionage recruitment. (2) The Washington bureaucracy of the New Deal was penetrated. (3) The French government of the Popular Front was shot through with Soviet agents. In Great Britain, "antifascist slogans captured a substantial number of students, writers and trade union leaders. During the Spanish tragedy and in the Munich days, many scions of the British aristocracy enlisted both in the International Brigade (the army of the Comintern in Spain) *and in our intelligence services*" (my emphasis).[3] In America bright young people from the Ivy League were the obvious targets. "With the thousands of recruits enlisted under the banner of democracy, the Communist Party OGPU espionage ring in the United States grew much larger and penetrated previously untouched territory. *By carefully concealing their identity, Communists found their way into hundreds of key positions*" (my italics). Finally, there was France, in many ways the most thoroughly penetrated of all:

> The *Front Populaire* was so intimately tied up with the Franco-Soviet alliance that it all but captured the government structure. True, there were those like Léon Blum who tried to keep the military situation from affecting internal politics, but to a large extent such efforts failed. Most of France, from General Gamelin and conservative deputy De Kerillis to trade union leader Jouhaux were so obsessed with the idea that France's security was linked to Moscow that the *Front Populaire* became the dominant fact of French life. On the surface, the Comintern operated through its sugarcoated organizations. Newspapers like *Ce Soir*, book clubs, publicity houses, theaters, motion picture companies—all became instruments of Stalin's "anti-Hitler front." Behind the scenes, the OGPU and the Soviet Military Intelligence were working feverishly for a stranglehold on the state institutions of France.[4]

Espionage is usually sordid and often dull. Yet the stories of these "idealists" seem never to lose their grip the imagination. Blunt, Burgess, Priscilla and Alger Hiss, Whitaker Chambers, Pierre Cot— these fated people personify some aspect of their era and its moral myth. As the new Communism rose on the horizon, they were all brilliant youth poised at the edge of great careers in government. All were destined for power in high places. All were recruited for that reason, and they all betrayed their governments sure that they were serving the greater good. Popular Front "ideals" took root in them all, festering around their individual character flaws and seducing them into living a lie that they saw as their truth. Living that lie in blind self-righteousness, all of them threw their great talents into the service of tyranny and a tyrant's fraud. But it was such a *convincing* fraud! It felt so *necessary!* So *true!* The embers of that fiery conviction still burn; the spies are only particularly memorable examples of the millions who came under the sway of the Front and its moral myth. In the democracies, that myth was composed of all kinds of postures and prejudices that reached well beyond "antifascism" and the celebration of some supposed Soviet leadership in resisting Hitler. Yet its net effect was to invest a "revolutionary" pose, preferably one colored by whatever the current rhetoric of fellow traveling happened to be, with the authority of a moral imperative. The "revolutionary" attitude became the way—for many, the *only* way—to show you were a decent human being.

Perhaps the most remarkable thing about this myth is its durability. The ethic of the Front outlived Hitler and Stalin and persisted beyond the end of the twentieth century. Even after Communism fell, there were still significant corners of opinion in the democracies where any challenge to the honor the Popular Front still provoked spitting outrage. There, if only there, the myth of Soviet antifascism managed to survive, still believed, the last refuge of scoundrels. Decades and generations after Stalin himself dropped the Front for his long-sought alliance with Hitler, the Front's platitudes continued to demand deference, its postures still ingrained habits of the mind.

I suspect that one reason for the durability of the Popular Front's posturing is that despite the mendacity of its cant, the premise of the Popular Front was right on target. Willi's propaganda was prophecy. It was *true*. Events proved it to be true in blood and horror. In 1935, the Nazis *were* the greatest menace that Western civilization had yet faced. And even in 1935, the only militarily practical way to deal with that menace *was* an alliance between the democracies and the USSR. The Popular Front proposed an antifascist alliance that Stalin had no intention of joining. He preferred—he had always preferred—an alliance with Hitler. But what if Stalin *had* been serious about joining the democracies to stop Hitler? What if the democracies had been willing to take him up on it? Imagine that alliance poised against Germany from both East and West, delivering a pre-emptive, deadly serious, ultimatum that they were willing to impose with *force majeure*.

Some such pre-emptive move must have seemed irresistibly alluring to shrewd and serious people in 1935. Stalin's strategic thinking was based on the assumption that Hitler, sandwiched between the democracies to the West and the USSR to the East, could not— and therefore *would* not—fight a two-front war. That was a very intelligent presumption. It *ought* to have been true.

So...what if?

***

It didn't happen of course.

Shortly after dawn on July 3, 1934, three days after the Night of Long Knives had begun the Blood Purge, Hitler's juddering private airplane touched down at Tempelhof airport in Berlin, bearing the Führer back from his hectic days and nights in Munich. On the tarmac stood a tense committee of senior Nazis, assembled to welcome their now absolutely undisputed leader and greet the new age of gangster politics. At the head of the group stood Himmler and Göring, clutching their lists.

The bleak dawn light was an appropriate violence of red on black. Moving past his mute saluting men, Hitler seemed slack, dazed.

He stared into the vacancy. His lips sagged, and as he walked he dragged his feet, as though shuffling through dead leaves, or trash.[5]

No foreign leader had been watching the German events more closely than Stalin. In the middle of the very night of June 30, the night the Blood Purge began, he summoned his men own men to greet the new age. It was after midnight when the Politburo and Soviet intelligence chiefs gathered in the Kremlin for an assessment of the situation. Stalin's demeanor in that small hours meeting was calm, methodical, and entirely unsurprised. His information was remarkably exact, and it had reached his study with amazing speed: As he spoke, Röhm's wailing minions were still being machine-gunned in their beds.[6] Seated near Stalin throughout the meeting was Münzenberg's old comrade and patron Karl Radek.

Stalin opened with some general observations about Nazi politics. Here too he was impressively well informed, doubtless by his excellent networks in the German antifascist underground. Hitler, he said, had chosen this moment to deal with various opponents— dangerous, radical opponents—to his "moderate" policies: disloyal monarchists in the army, for example, as well as Nazi "radicals" like Ernst Röhm. Hitler understood that such people had to be eliminated—purged—because they were unable to supply that unequivocal loyalty the rest of the German army was, as they spoke, so very impressively giving their Führer.

Fortunately, Hitler would definitively terminate these annoyances this very night. As for the Europeans, Stalin predicted (correctly) that their leadership would mistake the change for some sort of weakness on Hitler's part. They were quite wrong. Hitler would emerge from this night not weaker, but the most "mighty" (a favorite word) personage in Europe. The Führer was proving himself. And of course that would have profound consequences for Soviet policy.

Henceforth, Stalin told the meeting, Soviet policy would be bound to Germany. Krivitsky later summarized the dictator's position. "Stalin had always believed in coming to terms early with a strong enemy. The night of June thirtieth convinced him of Hitler's strength." Krivitsky continued: "The course of Soviet policy toward Nazi Germany followed from Stalin's dictum. The Politburo decided at all costs to induce Hitler to make a deal with the Soviet government."[7]

It was—or it seemed—that simple. As the Blood Purge was taking place, Stalin announced that his policy was "to cut a deal with Hitler regardless of setbacks or rebuffs."[8] Five full years before the Nazi-Soviet pact, just as the Comintern's antifascist campaign was about to enter its all-consuming phase in the Popular Front, Stalin's course was set. The room took it in. Krivitsky does not indicate that Karl Radek, the senior wise man of the antifascist movement, showed the faintest flicker of surprise as he listened.

Having made the momentous decision to seek an alliance with Hitler, Stalin soon moved to create the smokescreen for its implementation. This smokescreen was the Popular Front. His true purpose was to create a Second World War in the West that the Soviet Union would sit out, at least in its first phase, during which Stalin would appease the Nazis while diverting their aggression against the democracies. In *Mein Kampf*, Hitler had made it clear that he intended to take on the democracies before he hit the Soviet Union. Stalin's maneuvers were designed to make Hitler keep that promise. In order to assure that Hitler really would turn westward, he needed absolutely secret negotiations arranging for a stabilized division of Eastern Europe, mutual assistance, and eventually a reliable alliance. He never—not even at the height of the Popular Front—was tempted by a true alliance between the Soviets and the democracies. As Robert Tucker puts it, Stalin "earnestly sought to bring about the formation of a strong politico-military anti-German grouping based on France and Britain. But, as we shall see, *it was not a coalition in which he wanted the Soviet Union to participate when the war came.*"[9] (Tucker's italics.)

As to the German Communist Party, as early as March 1933, Stalin had resolved not to risk war over their plight. One might assume that the Comintern's every resource would be consumed by the crisis Hitler was creating for European socialism in Berlin. Wrong.[10] Stalin was convinced that Germany would be his only *after* a war, when the Red Army would be in place to enforce his claims.[11]

On a deeper level, this policy was built on a philosophical recognition of the unseen kinship between the two totalitarian adversaries. As Thomas Mann had grasped early on, the totalitarian systems were ideologically dependent on their mutual hatred. Each was addicted to loathing its opposite monster, and in that loathing, helped to create that monster. The monster fascism, born of the Counter-Enlightenment, fulfilled the rationale of its loathing by directing itself against communism, *its* necessary monster, born of the Enlightenment. Finally, both could join in hating their common enemy: liberal democracy.

Karl Radek had seen and sensed the bond between the two ideologies from the start, and he was Stalin's natural go-between. Arkady Vaksberg claims that during 1933–1934, "Radek carried out a mission, still badly understood, which consisted in 'establishing a bridge' between Hitler and Stalin." Vaksberg suspects that full understanding of that mission would be a "sensational revelation." Moreover, he believes that after profiting from this clandestine contact, Stalin when on the use it to discredit and destroy Radek during the Terror.[12] Radek had favored co-opting the Nazis from the start. He calmly proposed a Soviet deal with Hitler to a meeting of the executive committee of the Comintern in June 1923, right around the time *Mein Kampf* was published. All through the twenties, and until May 1933, both secretly and publicly, Stalin had supplied Germany with a brisk exchange of military assistance—and one of the German officers managing this exchange had been the very same Oskar von Neidermayer with whom Radek, also in May 1933, instructed Vinogradov to have "discreet conversations" about fixing the Dimitrov Trial. Even after Stalin terminated the aid, Radek was authorized to keep alive the prospect of Nazi-Soviet military collaboration. He waxed effusive and sentimental over it. "There are magnificent lads in the SA and the SS," Radek told his German contacts. "You'll see. The day will come when they'll be throwing hand grenades for us."[13]

Radek seemed untroubled by the Nazis' manifest anti-Communism, nationalism, and anti-Semitism. Though he was himself a Jew, he always favored coordinating Soviet policy with the new anti-Semitic Germany. When Maxim Litvinov, Stalin's foreign minister, made antifascist pronouncements—at Stalin's direction, of course—Radek would discreetly reassure the German embassy, which typically attributed Litvinov's hostility to his Jewish ethnicity, ignoring the same thing in Radek.[14] At the very time that Münzenberg was creating the antifascist movement in Paris, Radek was in top-secret meetings with the German ambassador in Moscow (without Litvinov's knowledge) acting as Stalin's emissary in confidential discussions over matters of mutual benefit.[15]

Radek had always claimed that the Nazis were inherently revolutionary, intent upon destabilizing bourgeois democracy. So far— in Radek's opinion—so good: The Nazis would help bring about the crack-up of bourgeois order necessary to world revolution. At the very least, the Nazis could be allies with the USSR against those guardians of established power, England and France. That was Radek's view in 1923; it remained his view in 1933. Stalin agreed. "Hitler," he explained to Molotov and Dimitrov when the pact with Hitler was finally signed, "without understanding it or desiring it, is shaking and undermining the capitalist system... It would be fine if at the hands of Germany the position of the richest capitalist countries (especially England) were shaken."[16]

This justification of the pact with Hitler is a perfect echo of Radek's views. They had always been Radek's views. That Stalin should have been expressing them in September 1939 only indicates how powerful they had been in his strategy all through the smoke and mirrors of Popular Front "antifascism." As Vaksberg points out, Stalin's decision to destroy Radek was not in the least a matter of turning against his advice: it was more probably designed to cover Stalin's own tracks in following it—and to set up a fall guy. Radek had negotiated for the Communists with the Nazis.

In his show trial, Radek was therefore accused of *betraying* Communists to the Nazis.

Meanwhile Radek used his column in *Isvestia* to play the role of antifascism's most eminent Soviet spokesman. He was simultaneously telling his friend and colleague, Krivitsky, that antifascism was "strategic eyewash for fools." Was Hitler decimating German communism? Radek laughed. Only "idiots" imaged that "Soviet Russia should turn against Germany because of Nazi persecution of Communists and Socialists." "Only fools can imagine we would ever break with Germany," Radek confided. "What I am writing here [in *Isvestia*] is one thing. The realities are something else. No one can give us what Germany has given us. For us to break with Germany is simply impossible." The antifascist campaign was a mere maneuver, "a matter of big politics." Stalin "had not the slightest intention of breaking with Germany."[17]

None of this seems to have come as a surprise to Krivitsky, another Polish Jew, who accepted the duplicitous policy without a blink. Krivitsky claims that in 1933–34 nobody in the upper reaches of the apparatus—presumably including Münzenberg—"dreamed" of a genuine break with Germany.[18] To be sure, the antifascist campaign had its strategic purposes. But the strategy was alliance with Hitler.[19]

***

Yet Stalin's interest is the Blood Purge went beyond the way it transformed German politics. He was planning a purge of his own. Throughout the summer of 1934, intelligence reports about the destruction of the SA kept rolling in. Stalin read them all, totally absorbed. He meticulously studied every document. Famous for his *Sitzfleisch*, the schoolboy of terror was doing his homework, page by slow page. No detail was too slight. Every scrap mattered. His diligence would mature in the Kirov murders and the Great Terror, events that would make the Blood Purge seem small.[20]

In that slow rumination lies an important difference between the two monsters. Hitler's tyranny was defined by impatience. He was fast, and speed was his strength. He disarmed his enemies through the theatrical lightning of his violence. Stalin on the other hand was slow—slowness itself. Hitler acted soon, Stalin at last. Stalin's was the soul of the bureaucrat, Hitler's of an actor. Hitler loved the look and feel of risk, while Stalin's terror owed nothing to effect; its whole power lay in immovable certainty, faceless implacability. One is told that it was rare, during the thirties, for Muscovites to pronounce his dreaded name, whereas Hitler's name was spouted in the vile "Heil Hitler!" salute every time people met. For Stalin, patience was murder's highest instrument, and his vengeance, not one whit less cruel than Hitler's, could wait forever. They were the tortoise and the hare of totalitarianism.

And now the tortoise was considering his next slow step.

Stalin did not begin the Great Terror before the "antifascism" of the Popular Front was fully in place. The Terror was in the works long before Dimitrov made his speech. The first large public event used to pave the way for the domestic slaughter to come was significantly modeled on the Night of Long Knives and on the terrorist purge that had that followed it in Germany. In the middle of the night of December 1, 1934, six months after Stalin had buried himself in study of the Blood Purge, wailing sirens and frenzied searchlights raking the sky suddenly roused all of Moscow. On the radio and from loudspeakers in the streets, came the echoing announcement: Stalin's beloved comrade Sergei Mironovich Kirov had just been murdered in Leningrad. The deed was part of a vast conspiracy against the Revolution.

The Leninist world would soon be torn apart in public. Millions would die. In eighteen months, people who had been repeatedly proclaimed the saviors of humanity would soon be groveling before the Soviet courts proclaiming themselves monsters of evil, begging for death. Stalin clearly understood that this bizarre spectacle would need some smoke-screen in the West, some propaganda force to counteract the waves of doubt and revulsion that were sure to come, even among the most devout. This was one of several reasons why the Popular Front "tactic" was proclaimed at this time, promoting the Soviet openness to all people of goodwill fighting fascism. Popular Front was what no decent person could turn against, *in spite of the trials.* Some propagandists wrung their hands. Surely these killings, so public, so extreme, will alienate the innocents? Stalin brushed them aside. "Europe," he snorted, "will swallow it all."[21]

He was right again—but for Europe to swallow it, the Popular Front had to be in place and intoxicating the innocents before the show trails of the Great Terror began. The phrase "Popular Front" seems to have been invented by the French communist Eugen Fried, and a leader of the French party, Maurice Thorez, publicly introduced it in 1934.[22] Not surprisingly, its earliest trial runs as propaganda took place in Paris. In June 1935, just a month before Dimitrov addressed the VIIth Congress of the Comintern and made the Front official policy worldwide, the cultural spectacular of the year was the "Congress in Defense of Culture" at the Salle Mutualité. It seemed to marshal every literary celebrity in the West, from Theodore Dreiser to E. M. Forster to Boris Pasternak to André Malraux. It was perhaps the greatest showcase of the era for the new antifascism in the war of ideas.

The month before—on May 2, 1935—Stalin had signed a pact with the French that at least looked like a mutual assistance pact against the German threat. This treaty was a sham: over the next years, Stalin would use his apparent promise of aid to the French primarily as an inducement for Hitler to sign a counter pact that would allow him to invade the West without worrying about Soviet interference.[23] But the Mutualité Congress set the cultural seal of approval of the Franco-Soviet arrangement. Though everything about it has the *look* of a Münzenberg operation, Babette Gross denied with vehemence that Münzenberg had anything to do with it, and I have found no evidence that he played a decisive role. The secret funding seems to have come through Katz's friend and Stalin's intimate Mikhail Koltsov.[24] Willi may even have been kept on the margins as part of his collaboration with French Intelligence. Certainly, the organizers felt it was crucially important to keep Soviet sponsorship secret, and communist presence minimized, even though the place was packed from wall to wall with all the "usual suspects" from the ranks of the fellow travelers.

Willi was very much present, however, when the VIIth Congress met in Moscow a month later. It is interesting to note that while Stalin himself was also present, he did not speak, probably because he did not want to trouble the Germans by personally associating himself too closely with what Dimitrov was about to announce. He was on the scene however. In fact, the VIIth Congress was the one time in her life Babette Gross actually laid eyes on the dictator. Babette had been standing on the grand staircase of the Palace of Nations, chatting with friends, when suddenly the air became electric, people started to scatter out of the way, a phalanx of guards materialized and then out of nowhere there he was: omnipotence, just a few feet away from her on the stairs, a tiny man with bad skin, descending.

The premise dominating Stalin's strategic thinking about the Nazi menace was the perfectly reasonable assumption that Hitler could not and would not under any circumstances try to wage the two-front war. Stalin—with most other insightful observers—was rightly convinced that Germany could not possibly win such a war, and he therefore assumed Hitler would not attempt it. Yet he fully expected a war, and so long as it was between Germany and the democracies, he like Radek even welcomed what he saw as capitalist fratricide. Stalin had no wish to "stop" Hitler; he would have resisted any effort to quash Nazi aggression against France and England. In 1933, the Polish strongman Pilsudsky quietly sounded out the British and Soviets over joining in a preemptive joint military strike to eliminate the Nazi ascendancy in Germany then and there. Such a strike was Hitler's worst fear. Stalin did not reply.[25]

The war to come would be very much like the 1914–1918 war, bruising, protracted, pointless, and fought at the price of sickening, staggering, loss of life. He intended to foment such a war, and sit it out, safely allied with Hitler, protecting the German's eastern flank and confident that Hitler's evil would be as wary as his own. Of course, despite his considerable admiration for the tyrant in Berlin, Stalin did not want to see Hitler *win*. The idea was to destroy both Hitler *and* the democracies in a Second World War that would end with Stalin moving a fresh Red Army west, into areas prepared for him by his secret services, only after the real fighting was over, when he could stab his battle-weary ally in the back, gangster to gangster.[26]

It was an exceptionally penetrating and far-sighted scenario for the Second World War. Its resemblances to the Second World War that really took place are of course numerous. There was only one great oversight, so typical of the tortoise's about the hare.

Stalin simply did not expect Barbarossa. At least not so *quickly*.

Stalin fumbled his calculations only because he assumed Hitler would be as cautious as he was. As Tzvetan Todorov puts it, "Hitler believed himself to be stronger than he was, simultaneously declaring war against Great Britain, the Soviet Union and the United States. He was motivated by his convictions, not by calculating consequences. Stalin never acted that way. If Hitler had acted as intelligently as Stalin, both would have won... He failed to imagine Hitler's madness."[27]

Yet all of this happened in the context of what seems to us the pure madness of the Great Terror. Despite continuing efforts to contest and obscure the facts, we know a great deal about what happened during this terrible time. The continuing mystery is *why*. The event is a seemingly endless parade of horrors. Its scale alone leaves the mind numb, stupefied. "One death is a tragic event," Stalin is reported to have remarked; "A million deaths are statistics." It was an observation that Stalin transformed into a primary truth of the twentieth century. Even when the mind begins somehow to get some tentative grip on the sheer *scale* of the Terror, the *motives* of its successive waves of mass murder continue to torture thought. *Why?* Sentimentalists often blandly assume that the victims of the Terror must have represented some sort of genuine opposition to Stalin's rule. Doubtless some kind of "opposition" played some role, but it does not seem to have been a central

one. Most of the Terror's prime victims were abject in their obedience. Nor were all those millions killed merely to eliminate Stalin's
potential rivals: very few of the victims had even a flickering hope
of brushing within a million miles of Stalin's supremacy. Even the
exiled Trotsky—a genuine thorn in Stalin's side—had no credible
prospect of regaining power.

In its crude immensity and its murky continuing mystery, the
Terror must remain far beyond our reach here. Still, some meaningful part of its machinations involves Radek's rise and fall, and
these in turn suggest some obscure turn in Stalin's appeasement
of Hitler. Since Radek was Münzenberg's senior political patron,
and the *éminence grise* of the antifascist movement, this aspect of
the story does concern us.

The first wave of Terror began in August 1936 and featured
the show trails of Zinoviev and Kamenev as its prime targets. Once
that was done, there was a second wave of terror in which Radek
himself was arrested, tried, and destroyed. Exactly why Stalin decided publicly to murder his prime advisor on the preeminent policy
issue of the era is unclear. But then everything surrounding Radek's
fall from grace and his destruction is a mystery. We know only that
it happened, and a little about how.

The beginning of the Terror coincided with the outbreak of
the Spanish Civil War, the European event that would sweep the
ideology of the Popular Front onto a dominant position in advanced opinion. While this happened, the first set of show trials
played to great success: Zinoviev and Kamenev read their lines
perfectly. Their "confessions," almost without parallel in the history of abjection, formed the basis for new waves of arrests and
executions. The two had been promised their lives for co-operation, but of course as soon as the show was over, the death squads
were sent to take them to the basement. When the soldiers stepped
into Zinoviev's cell, he instantly grasped the truth. He flung himself on the floor, made a plea for an audience with Stalin, seemingly hysterical. I have seen it reported that Kamenev though
stunned, urged calm on his friend, hoping they might at least face

death with dignity. But the ruckus of Zinoviev's collapse induced one of the young NKVD men to pull his revolver, force Zinoviev into an adjacent cell, and shoot him through the head then and there. Hearing of this scene greatly impressed Stalin. He gave Zinoviev's killer an award for his presence of mind. When the execution squad got Kamenev into the cellar, a first shot failed to kill him, and it was the NKVD lieutenant's turn to become hysterical. He "kicked the executioner with a cry of 'finish him off!'"[28] In later years, Stalin got into the habit of having his valet, a man named Pauker, re-enact the Zinoviev's collapse in caricature during the late-night drinking parties that were his idea of fun. He especially loved to watch Pauker crawling on the floor and clutching at chairs while he mocked the singsong of Zinoviev's Jewish accent, breaking into a parody of Hebrew prayer, "Hear O Israel!" during the begging part.[29]

Then came Radek's turn. Within three weeks of the conclusion of the Zinoviev-Kamenev Trial, Radek himself was abruptly but secretly put under arrest. A few days later, in mid-October 1936, Münzenberg arrived in Moscow expecting his usual round of meetings. When he tried to make his customary appointment with Radek he was told, "under seal of secrecy," that Radek had been arrested and was surely doomed. As Münzenberg listened, a new kind of fear must have dropped into his soul. Any complacency he may have felt by being the foreign right hand of Stalin's key advisor on Germany vanished in an instant: Radek had been arrested with a number of "leading officials who only recently had been among Stalin's keenest supporters and most loyal collaborators."[30]

From that moment forward, Willi's life stood in mortal danger. Henceforth, every move he made would have to begin and end in elementary self-protection. His prime patron, his link to power, had been arrested and had joined the damned. Radek's fall obviously left Willi vulnerable, but where could he turn? To break with Stalin, even in the relative safety of Europe, probably meant death. But there was no safety in obedience, either. Look at Radek and *his* faithful service. A month before he had been Stalin's prime advisor.

Events in Spain were now moving forward rapidly: Willi suspected the apparatus was going to need his services as a propagandist in the months to come. Still, the danger was imminent, even desperate. In their room in the Hotel Metropole, Willi and Babette slept restlessly, expecting the fatal midnight knock on the door. Willi's one thought became how to get out of Moscow alive. Not that he was wholly unprepared: it seems he had acquired what in those days was called "life insurance"—some threat to make the executioner think twice—and as we shall see, he did manage to escape, returning to Paris where, through the Spanish Civil War, he rose to the lifetime apex of his influence over public opinion, spending every day on that summit in clear danger for his life.

Radek knew the treachery of his great patron—knew it in damning detail. That alone was reason enough for Stalin to arrest him. Even before his arrest, Radek seems to have contrived some threat good enough to serve as his own "life insurance" against liquidation. In the Lubyanka, he resolutely resisted his interrogators—at first. When his blackmailed co-defendants asked him to cooperate, he answered that he would only do so with assurance from Stalin himself that he would not die.

At this point Radek sat down in his cell and wrote a long letter. It was for Stalin's eyes only and its contents are unknown, but it was powerful enough to bring Stalin personally to the NKVD building the next day. There Stalin and Radek held a prolonged conversation behind closed doors. What was said is also unknown, but when it was over Radek was a changed man. Radek obviously had convinced himself that Stalin feared him dead more than he feared him alive. Some deal for his life had been cut.[31]

From the moment Stalin left the building that day, Radek became a totally co-operative witness. At his trial three months later, in January 1937, he played the role of abject with special relish, correcting Vyshinsky when the prosecutor fumbled his lines. Insiders, not least the attentive delegation from the German embassy, read his "testimony" as if it was tea leaves.[32] It was Stalin's style to plant the seeds of the next wave of the Terror in the "confessions" given in the preceding trial. Thus, that concealed targets in the trial of Radek and his fellow "conspirators" were the Terror's next victims, namely Nikolai Bukharin and Field Marshal Mikhail Tukhachevsky.

Tukhachevsky concerns us most. Radek had been accused of being a German spy, a device with the special merit of explaining Radek's actual, and fully authorized secret contacts with the Germans, just in case Nazis or anyone else tried to use them in some embarrassing way. But as he testified to this simultaneously real and imaginary crime, Radek planted an ostentatious disclaimer, assuring the court in broad strokes that Marshal Tukhachevsky knew nothing, absolutely nothing, about his own exchange of "certain materials" with the Germans.

Marshal Tukhachevsky was a very remarkable man. Though born to the minor Tsarist aristocracy, he was a dedicated communist. No non-Stalinist information has ever been produced to challenge his loyalty to the Revolution. He was cultivated, multilingual, intellectually playful, with an ironic turn, easily the most intelligent Russian military man of his generation, and so among the most intelligent people in the entire government. He had traveled widely: He knew Germany and its army intimately, and that knowledge had become the strongest single Soviet voice for full preparedness and early confrontation with the Nazi threat. In 1935 and 1936 he was swiftly galvanizing the Red Army. He was tremendously popular in the ranks. He was therefore a man who held views unwelcome to both Hitler and Stalin. That was dangerous.

And Radek wanted the Court to know that he was innocent of treason with the Nazis. The phrase was a plant. To have a traitor, a conspirator, a "mad dog" like Radek, assure the court that Tukhachevsky was innocent was as good as a death warrant. Reading the story in the Western press, months before Tukhachevsky's arrest, Walter Krivitsky turned to his wife and told her flatly that Field Marshal Tukhachevsky was doomed.[33]

When the verdict at the Radek show trial was brought in, everyone on the dock was condemned to death—except Radek. Radek was given ten years' imprisonment. At that moment Radek turned to the courtroom, broke into a shy grin, and with a shrug lifted his hands: "Who knew?"

What *was* Radek's arrangement with Stalin? We know only that that same time that Radek was planting the "evidence" against Field Marshal Tukhachevsky in that Moscow courtroom, documents were being forged in a Gestapo laboratory, papers which "showed" Marshal Tukhachevsky conspiring with the Nazis to storm the Kremlin with a renegade unit of the Red Army, assassinate Stalin, and seize the Soviet government.[34]

The murder of Mikhail Tukhachevsky and the decapitation of the Red Army in the purge of June 1937 was the next wave of the Great Terror, and it is the most obvious and well-documented episode in Stalin's collaboration with the Nazis implementing the Terror. In it, the Nazis, at Stalin's invitation, became direct accomplices in the Terror as it turned on the Army, forging documents "proving" the Field Marshal's treasonous contacts with themselves.

Stalin initiated the plot against Tukhachevsky. Hitler decided to participate sometime near the end of 1936, right around the time Radek cut the deal in his prison cell. Stalin himself had already planned the route of the Tukhachevsky dossier through the channels of disinformation.[35]

In December 1936, Walter Krivitsky met in Paris with the senior NKVD executive then in Europe, a man named Slutsky. They met on the terrace of the Cafe Viel on the Boulevard des Capucines, near the Paris Opera. At this meeting Slutsky ordered Krivitsky to throttle down his anti-German operations. "We have set our course toward an early understanding with Hitler, and have started negotiations," Slutsky said. "They are progressing favorably." As for antifascism, Slutsky added, "there's nothing for us in this rotting corpse of France, with its *Front Populaire.*"[36]

Then came a special part of the assignment. Krivitsky was ordered to select two agents who could successfully impersonate German officers and have them on hand in Paris. Krivitsky was not told that these men would be used to assassinate one of the most well-known NKVD targets of the time, a leader of the White Russian emigration in Paris, who went by the name of General Miller, and that General Miller's death would be used in the Tukhachevsky murders.

The material incriminating Tukhachevsky was provided to Reinhard Heydrich through the Soviets in Paris immediately after Radek's trial. The German forgeries based on them were made under Heydrich's supervision in Germany after Radek's trial was over. Hitler was personally shown the forgeries by May.[37]

These transactions naturally required absolutely reliable secret agents working in deep compartmentalization. In Paris, one center of Soviet-Nazi intrigue was a confederation of the politically lost known as the Union of Tsarist Veterans, a group of old soldiers clinging to the ever more threadbare honor of the army and society the Bolsheviks had destroyed. The Union's leader was named General Miller, who was committed to the sabotage of that irreversible victory and managing of that defeat. In predictable fact, Miller's organization was a playground of European conspiracy, laced through with Soviet agents.[38] Miller's second-in-command was a certain General Skoblin, whose wife was a famous Russian torch singer named Nadezhda Plevitskaya. Both were Soviet agents. Skoblin, moreover, was a Soviet agent whose specialty was contact with the Nazis.

Skoblin's first task was to get into Nazi hands the lie that Tukhachevsky was conspiring with the German general staff. When this bit of information found its way to his office, Heydrich immediately recognized it for the feint it was, but decided to use it as disinformation against some local enemies.

Meanwhile, information damning Tukhachevsky, information even beyond the forged dossier, was concocted. It too seems to have Nazi sources. It was fed into the networks to be passed on to Stalin, and along the way to various people in European politics that might be usefully deceived. It was at this point that somebody—some suspect Katz—put the dossier into the hands of the Czech intelligence service of President Edvard Beneš. We know the route

was Paris; the "source" was portrayed as "German antifascists"—
that is, by some reliable agent or agents based in Paris, known to be
connected to the antifascist underground, operating at a high level
and yet not seen even by the informed as in the NKVD. It would
help if he were already an old hand at this kind of clandestine Nazi-
Communist collaboration, as from Leipzig, and it would not be
surprising if the man were a protégé of Radek trusted by Beneš.[39]
The reputation of Otto Katz has been hounded for decades by
unproved but not implausible rumors that he played some role in
this famous conspiracy. Otto was the right man in the right place at
the right time, connected to the right people. It was at this point
that he was closest to Beneš's foreign minister, Hubert Ripka. In
years to come, Otto would frequently boast of his influence over
Beneš himself.[40]

Beneš was an indiscreet politician who could be relied upon to
talk before he fully considered the facts. A diplomatic joke of the
era held that the three best ways to get information around Europe
were "telephone, telegraph, and tele-Beneš." When his intelligence
service, assisted by his right hand, Hubert Ripka, gave Beneš the
disinformation, the credulous Beneš pounced: What was this? Treason? In the Red Army?

Beneš rushed to inform Stalin, and French intelligence as well.
No matter: Stalin was delighted to have the French think the
Tukhachevsky fraud was authentic. Meanwhile, he listened to Beneš's
warning in solemn wonderment.

Beneš's conviction of Tukhachevsky's guilt was not a minor
force in European politics at that time. According to Sir Isaiah Berlin, even a figure so little trusting of Stalin as Winston Churchill
himself was persuaded that Tukhachevsky really had been a traitor,
and was persuaded on the strength of Beneš's word.[41]

Tukhachevsky was arrested on or about May 28, 1937, and by
May 29 he was "confessing" to espionage and having secret ties to
the Nazis. Meanwhile, a large number of other high level military
men were rounded up—a majority of the senior staff. All "confessed," and the whole group was condemned to death on June 11,

1937. While the Soviet press shrieked about Comrade Stalin's discovery of a military conspiracy to destroy the Revolution, all were shot shortly thereafter, reportedly machine-gunned to death in the courtyard of the Lubyanka, while secret police trucks clustered in front revved their engines to cover the sound of the gunshots and screams. Decades later, when Tukhachevsky's "dossier" was opened for his "rehabilitation," a number of pages in it were found to be literally spattered with blood.

***

Radek's ending passed unnoticed. On January 30, 1937, the day after Stalin's secret emissary in Berlin had had a decisive meeting about the proposed *rapprochement* between the Nazis and Stalin, Radek was led from his Moscow courtroom and never publicly seen again.[42] There are various accounts of what happened next. Solzhenitsyn reports that despite Radek's real or imagined hold over Stalin, he was simply shot. Another report claims Radek was at first set up in relative comfort, so the appearance of a lenient house arrest could be used to persuade Bukharin to cooperate in his own demise. For Bukharin was arrested just as Radek's case was closed.

Another version has it that Radek was removed from that place and dispatched to one of the most bleak and sunless subarctic forced labor camps of all. There he sank into the faceless squalid prisoner's world, freezing, starving, amid the rats, the bugs, in rags. He is said to have survived two years.

Exactly how he died is debated.[43] One story holds he was murdered in a brawl with a prison thug. This version has a suggestive variant. When Lenin and Radek took power, the Bolsheviks embarked on a series of experiments intended to stamp out that bourgeois outrage, the family. As a result of this policy, complicated by the Civil War and disasters like the Volga Famine, Soviet Russia began to fill with packs of pauperized, parentless, sociopathic orphans, desperate marauding packs of children, the *bezprizornii*. They lived by begging and thievery and worse. During the 1920s visitors to the USSR repeatedly spoke of seeing the starving bands of little beggars shoved from station platforms by the rifle butts of Red Army soldiers.

Those who survived grew up. The bands of marauding children became sociopathic packs of adults: brutal, uncontrollable, murderous, real threats. Stalin dealt with them in various ways. Sometimes the NKVD simply rounded them up and mowed them down with machine guns. Sometimes they were sent to the more remote arctic camps to die as forced laborers.

The story has it that sometime in 1939, one such pack of the Great Experiment's monsters cornered Karl Radek in the prison yard. He was far from history now. The killing winter was all around him and he was alone with the Revolution's wretches, nameless. Someone flung him to the ground. Then, following the impulses by which they lived, the *bezprizornii* were all kicking together, smashing out the brains of this brain-proud man against the tundra.

The ancients were sure that Nemesis, the goddess of vengeance, was brutal and fierce. They were also struck by her *ingenuity*.

Chapter 8

THE POPULAR FRONT AND ESPIONAGE

The Courtauld mansion on Portman Square in London housed until 1989 one of the world's great institutions for the study of the history of art. Though the building is very grand—it has eighty rooms—its architectural discretion makes it an ideal example of that restrained aristocratic elegance which the British Empire installed in the heart of its capital during the middle of the eighteenth century. In such a house, the Earl of Chesterfield might have attended upon the graces. Under its neoclassical portico there used to be two doorbells. One was simply for entry to the Courtauld Institute. Another, set apart, was marked DIRECTOR'S FLAT.

On the morning of April 23, 1963, a man named Arthur Martin, an investigator for the British counterintelligence service, stepped up to the door and rang the bell set apart. At that moment the director of the Courtauld was a thin, cold, composed, intellectually very impressive art historian and connoisseur who had been in charge since 1947. He would remain so until he retired, covered with honors, ten years later in 1974. He was named Sir Anthony Blunt.

This was by no means the first of Sir Anthony's decorous chats with British counter-intelligence. Dull encounters like this one had been going on for twelve wearisome years, ever since the disappearance of two men, Guy Burgess and Donald Maclean, whose defection to the Soviet Union in 1951 had instantly become one of the enduring sensations of modern politics.

They were an odd pair, Burgess and Maclean. Both had known each other from their university days at Cambridge, but they had never known each other very well, and in truth they had never much liked each other. At Trinity College, Cambridge, Donald had never been quite fast, flashy, homosexual, or important enough for Burgess. He struck Guy as big and boring, out of it, uncertain, tight with sexual anguish and his Scots-Presbyterian compunction. Yet in his staid, suffering way Maclean had gone on to become the greater success. In 1951, Burgess was a brilliant but increasingly seedy presence in the upper-middle reaches of British literary life, broadcasting, and politics, while in that same year, Maclean was doing better. Until recently Maclean had been serving as a very senior member of the British diplomatic community in Washington, a principal advisor to the ambassador, with access to the most sensitive information in the special relationship between the United States and London.[1] As it happened, during Maclean's tenure Guy Burgess had himself inexplicably been dispatched to the American capital, as if to extricate him from a series of mild-to-intolerable muckings-up in various branches of the London establishment. In Washington, Burgess spent a number of months as a loud, drunk, dirty hanger-on at the middle levels of the British diplomatic community, generating disgust and being impossible wherever he went. He lodged in the basement of yet another Cambridge friend, whose innocent wife Burgess drove straight round the bend with his sickening personal habits. This friend, however, was a man Guy really *did* feel close to. He was Kim Philby.

When Donald was rather ominously recalled to London, Burgess arranged to go back home as well. Maclean knew, but was not supposed to know, that he had been recalled because he was under investigation as a Soviet agent, and Guy Burgess knew it too, since the entire British plan to arrest Maclean was in itself penetrated, very near the top, by the Soviets.

On the night of May 25, 1951, Guy and Donald were together as Guy drove Maclean to a late-night ferry about to cross the Channel from Southampton to Saint-Malo. May 25, as it happened, was Donald Maclean's 38th birthday, but the two men were not in a festive mood. They were running from a warrant for Maclean's arrest. Not the arrest of Burgess—only Maclean. Little was as yet suspected of Burgess. Burgess's task was simply to get Donald to Southampton and set him on the first leg of the rescue.

When Burgess picked up Maclean at his suburban house outside London, Maclean's wife Melinda was preparing a private birthday party for two. She had never before laid eyes on their scruffy, unannounced, and surely none-too-welcome visitor. Here was the man with whom her husband's name was about to be wedded forever. Donald, fearing an MI-5 bug in the room, introduced him as "Mr. Stiles," whom he said was "from the office."

Melinda was on the spot: There was nothing to do but ask "Mr. Stiles" to join the birthday dinner. As the meal neared its end, Melinda stepped out of the room for a moment, and Burgess turned to Maclean, reverting to a harsh, too-familiar tone. He informed him that his hour had struck. They were to leave at once, now, this minute. It was not a suggestion but a command. When his wife of the last twelve years returned to the room, Donald Maclean stood up and excused himself. "Mr. Stiles and I," he said, "have to keep a pressing engagement, but I don't expect to be back very late. I'll take an overnight bag just in case." Then they were gone, leaving Melinda Maclean standing bewildered over the crumbs of the birthday cake.[2]

What those two fated men said to each other on their dark drive south can only be imagined. It was a wild ride: they almost missed the boat. Though their names *are* wed, Burgess and Maclean, after their university coolness, had become more and more bound together in the sick union of their mutual secret and their mutual loathing. Burgess's powers of verbal sadism were legendary, and he had grown more and more blackmailing and abusive toward Maclean as time went on. By now the diplomat had ample reason to fear and hate his old university companion and fellow spy.[3]

When they pulled into the parking lot at the Southampton docks, Burgess more abandoned than parking his rented car and rushed Maclean to a waiting ferry called the *Falaise*. The boat churned in the dark, wide and heavy, about to push off. At this point, Burgess's part in the escape was supposed to end. Back in Washington Philby's instructions had been clear. "Don't you go too, Guy!" Burgess hustled his very tall companion toward the waiting boat. Beside him, Maclean was huge and hunched: tight-lipped with fear. Burgess seemed in charge. He tossed half a crown to the garage attendant, hollered "we'll be back on Monday!" and then as the departure whistle screamed they raced to the gangplank.

The *Falaise* was the night's last ship out. Just as the gangplank was lifting, Burgess acted on an impulse he'd been nurturing for days, his own last-minute addition to the intrigue. Quite unnecessarily Burgess jumped on board too, and as the British coastline began to recede into the dark, history changed a little.[4]

Thirteen years later, the authorities still simply would not let up on Sir Anthony. All that time after Burgess's defection, Blunt was still hearing from boring policemen like Mr. Martin, for no better reason than that Guy and he had once been friends. Intimates, even. They had known each other ever since Cambridge, when Blunt had been a very young don at Trinity College and an even younger Guy Burgess had first come sauntering down the High Street, already a dazzler, equipped with the last word, a lethal condescending smile, and the unstoppable flow of an intellectual patter that would make him "the best of the slick Marxists around London."[5] He was also already a drunk, but while alcohol would at last leave Burgess a sodden, self-pitying wreck, at Cambridge drink only made his undergraduate splendor shine the more. He seemed destined for everything remarkable. The young Anthony Blunt was only one of many to think that Guy Burgess was among the most brilliant and compelling human beings he had ever met.

But that was the past. An innocent association of Sir Anthony's youth. Sir Anthony had gone on to more serious things. How many dull, dreary times over did he have to explain that yes, he'd once found Guy a fine intellectual companion; and yes, Guy's reckless glamour had once appealed, but that he knew nothing about Burgess's secret political commitments. Nothing about his subversions (if subversions they were) at the BBC. Nothing of betrayals or espionage inside British intelligence, though to be sure Sir Anthony himself just happened likewise to have served in British Intelligence during the war. Nothing about Burgess's activity as high-level staff to a member of Clement Atlee's cabinet. Every bit of it was guilt by association. Blunt had denied it all so often that he seemed to batten on denial. With every visit this connoisseur of snobbery grew more amused, more arch, more theatrically patient as the weary old questions grew easier to turn aside. Now Arthur Martin was at the Director's Flat once again, and the tiresome, tolerated little ritual was about to be replayed.

Blunt admitted his guest. Martin sat down, uncomfortably, across from him. Blunt had always intimidated him a little. Between the two he set a tape recorder.

Then Martin moved quickly. The British security services, he said, had recently come into possession of quite unequivocal information proving that Blunt had acted as an agent of Soviet espionage during the Second World War. Blunt answered that no such evidence could possibly exist for the simple reason no such activity had ever taken place. Martin persisted. He had just returned from the United States, he said, where he'd had a protracted interview with Mr. Michael Whitney Straight. Blunt absorbed this information with a level, unflinching gaze and complete silence. He showed no reaction. Martin later recalled the moment: "I think I said something like 'I saw Mr. Straight the other day, and he told me about his relations with you and the Russians.'" He then outlined precisely what Michael Straight had told him those relations were.

Anthony Blunt continued to sit very still, looking at Martin without any sign of fear, except perhaps in the too-tight immobility of his poker face, that narrow shield. One of Anthony Blunt's worst fears had just become real. He was suddenly without his easeful answers. He said not one word. Blunt was thinking as fast as he could, and probably was waiting for Martin's next move. Arthur Martin likewise sat silent. When their silence had gone on so long that Martin was sure Blunt wasn't going to break it, the interrogator leaned forward and said directly into the tape recorder, very slowly and distinctly, "I have been authorized by the Attorney General to give you a formal immunity from prosecution."

Blunt's expression remained one of calculating reserve. With immunity, a prime fear—prison—had been dispelled. Blunt's best rationale against telling the truth—self-protection—was gone. After a few moments he stood up, poured himself a very large drink, and went to a window. There he stood for a rather long time, surveying with his cold expert eye the budding springtime down in Portman Square. It would be interesting to know what options, what fears, what memories of ruined passion may have flashed through his mind as the moments prolonged themselves. The tape-recorder turned in the silence. Behind him, over his fireplace, hung Poussin's *Eliezer and Rebecca at the Well,* which Blunt had discovered misattributed in Paris and bought with money lent by his intimate friend Victor Rothschild.[6] The Poussin was—apart from his secret—his most precious possession. Martin was not going to speak again. At last Anthony Blunt took a long sip from his glass, turned to his accuser, and said simply: "It is true."[7]

The Cambridge Conspiracy is the most voluminously examined penetration of any government known to modern history, and the most famous episode in the history of espionage. In contrast to spy stories in which the motives are money, or revenge, or mere mean nationalism, the power exerted by this set of double lives over the public imagination seems never to be lost. This may have something to do with the fact that their secrets came from so very near the top. Donald Maclean, had he not been uncovered, might very possibly have become British ambassador to the United States, just as his American counterpart, Laurence Duggan, might well have become Secretary of State.

It is often asked, apparently in genuine perplexity, how so many of these privileged Englishmen could have been "traitors to their class." This is to misunderstand both their treason and their class. Münzenberg's apparatus reached into every country of interest to the Bolsheviks: Germany, France, England, the United States, the Low Countries, the Scandinavian democracies, and many more, and in all those places it sought to organize the intellectual elite, particularly wherever that elite was in formation, for example in colleges and universities. Precisely the same people who instituted the Cambridge penetrations supervised parallel operations in New York and Washington, in the Ivy League and at the *École Normale Supérieure*, from Paris and Berlin. The International really *was* international. The obvious yet rarely understood stroke of secret service genius behind all such operations was the simple recognition of an essential bond between the so-called "establishment" (by which is meant little more than the elite of a given society), and what Lionel Trilling called the "adversary culture"—that part of society which, by virtue of its superior education and critical equipment, develops for itself a leveraged position within the middle class, based in ambiguity and the perspectives of criticism and argument, insight and protest. The adversary culture is a branch of the middle class; usually its most vigorous intellectual and artistic wing. It is drawn, albeit ambivalently, to radicalism; radicalism is part of its vision of freedom and truth. The radical solution, it imagines, would tear aside the bourgeois facade; radical insight, it suspects, reaches the deepest truth. In fact the ability really to grasp, if not embrace, radical insight is what the adversary culture believes sets it apart from the vast hypocritical and second-rate middle class to which it belongs but also from which it wishes—understandably—to distinguish itself.

The recruitment of the Cambridge spies and similar agents in all the democracies was based on this simple insight: The adversary culture *is* an elite. That is what the founding operatives of the Cambridge group, Arnold Deutsch and Theodore Maly, understood and exploited. Here was a founding principle of the Popular Front. Elite youth can be best discerned in the *quality* of their protest. They are likely to carry the presumptions of that protest into middle age, and into authority. Catch that protest in its school days. Develop it properly. Deepen it, convince it, frighten it, blackmail it, and network it. Then you will have forged the unseen "revolutionary" bond between Bohemia and power.

If we trace the unseen moral motivations of the Cambridge spies, those engagements emerge as a kind of map, and moreover a remarkably clear map, of advanced British intellectual life in their era. It is a composite portrait, albeit one in shadows, showing the elite of the generation that inherited Bloomsbury culture, that dynamic and difficult group of people whom Noel Annan has given a name that both mocks and manifests a certain smugness: "Our Age." Here were the children of Bloomsbury coming into their maturity, and into power. Theirs was a curiously stereotyped, although very classy, typicality. The Bloomsbury spies manifested many of the best traits of their adversarial time; they made an almost too-natural fit with the generation that preceded them. They were high Bloomsbury's children. The circle emerged especially from that crucible of Lytton Strachey's cultural strategy, the Cambridge discussion club, "the Apostles." Blunt was one of Virginia Woolf's young friends; he also had been the college lover of her nephew, Julian Bell. Guy Burgess steadily exploited his friendship with Harold Nicolson to effect his own rise, and one reason for Burgess's stellar success in that effort was that he was so entirely congenial to the Bloomsbury sensibility. He advanced in the world of the British media in a fashion which Strachey, master manipulator of the Cambridge elite during the previous generation, would have thought to the manner born.

But this very typicality is in itself typical of *apparat* recruitment, and is no less true of American recruitment, from Washington and Hollywood, though in the American capitals the protean elite appeal assumed a Washington or Hollywood face. It was likewise true in France. It was true of Otto Katz himself. I have said that Otto was a classic vanguard intellectual of his time and country, the very type of Weimar, manifesting its presumptions, the moods and modes of Piscator and Dietrich, of Brecht and Feuchtwanger, in all he did and even in all he concealed. Otto began his life wishing to be an artist in Weimar, and he failed. He was at heart not much more than a shrewd dilettante with some extra fire. He lacked what it would have taken to brush anywhere near the greatness of Kafka; even the minor distinction of his friend Kisch was far beyond him. Otto had to settle for being a spy. But he was the perfect spy, and in espionage rather than art, he embodied his age.

It's a standard right-wing riff in the culture wars to condemn the adversary culture wholesale, not least because during the Popular Front a set of fellow travelers, spies, and traitors emerged from it. But the adversary elite is an indispensable source of energy and genius too. We may speak plausibly of the "Bloomsbury spies"; we might likewise speak of the "New Deal spies." The treasons of a handful of players in Bloomsbury and the New Deal can hardly be said to taint those phenomena as such. In a liberal democracy, the adversarial culture includes much that is best in the whole society: most alive, most probing, most inventive, and most conscious. It was so on the Left Bank of André Malraux. It was so in the Bohemia of Greenwich Village. It was so in the rooms of Trinity College, Cambridge.

In saying this I do not in the least intend to invoke some counter-cultural sentimentalism to excuse these wretched men and women. The Cambridge spies were servants of Stalin, and they were Stalinists. So were their fellow spies in France, the United States, and the other liberal democracies. There will be no historical forgiveness for them. Nothing can erase their infamy. Their service to the tyranny and its lie was probably in secret truth even more iniquitous than the damning array of betrayals and acts of cruelty already known to have been performed with their willing assistance. And yet, and yet ... they approached and succumbed to their aspiring evil driven by a set of concerns that were, and remain, admirable and even indispensable: indispensable to the society, and to us. It is very true, they were despicable. Yet they should also be seen in the light of Rebecca West's observation: "There is a case to be made for the traitor. He is a sport from a necessary type." From Prague to Hollywood, it was so.

This juncture of radicalism, cultural elitism, and power had marked Willi's enterprises from the earliest days., motivating his sponsorship of major exhibitions of, say, Dadaist art, and inspiring his sponsorship of Soviet cinema by Eisenstein and Pudovkin in the West. It was also a defining trait of the Popular Front.

In that light, it should not be surprising to know how ubiquitous were the Münzenberg-men in the initiating phases of the great espionage stories. Kim Philby was dispatched straight to Gibarti and Paris carrying a letter of introduction from the Münzenberg-men in charge of the League Against Imperialism at Cambridge. He was inducted into secret work through Gibarti and the World Committee for the Relief of the Victims of German Fascism. Guy Burgess was connected to Münzenberg's Paris operations all through the thirties. The longtime Münzenberg man, Harold Ware, instituted the most famous ring of spies in American history, the one that included Laurence Duggan, the Hisses, and Whittaker Chambers. Otto Katz was a contact for the novelists Josephine Herbst and her husband John Herrmann, busy in the Greenwich Village Bohemia in the year that John Herrmann began as a courier for that network. But the Münzenberg connection was even more potent in France. Perhaps the most important Soviet agent penetrating the French political establishment was Pierre Cot, whom we now know worked, always, in close collaboration with Louis Dolivet, who was not only a Münzenberg man, but who later became to some significant degree Münzenberg's successor in the apparatus—as well as the brother-in-law of Anthony Blunt's most important American recruit, Michael Straight. During the Second World War, when André Malraux met Charles de Gaulle for the first time, he told the general that in the thirties the French tradition of Voltaire had been taken over and run by one Willi Münzenberg. It was a name the general had not heard before.[8]

So despite the British tenor of their treasons, the Cambridge spies were really part of an international phenomenon. They were not just the "Cambridge spies, or even the "Bloomsbury" spies. They were Popular Front spies. When the story of Burgess and Maclean's defection broke, right in the middle of the Hiss case, most observers obscurely felt a similarity between the unmasked

British diplomats and the accused American. Nor was the parallel lost on the principal players themselves. In the last days before his flight, drinking compulsively and at the point of cracking, Donald Maclean slurred a confession to a then uncomprehending Cyril Connolly: "I am the English Hiss."

The covert actions of which we speak began in ideas and in ideals. "You have to remember," Blunt's fellow spy, Leo Long, said after he was exposed, "that we were desperately committed... We didn't trust the British government. It seemed to prefer links with the Nazis... What did we think would happen? I don't think there was much discussion about it. We just assumed there would be a war..." Long's apologia says it all, beginning with the Popular Front's fundamental error: its fatal assumption that as a Marxist Stalin could be trusted about the Nazis, where liberal democrats could not, even while it was Stalin who, while presiding over a blatant and outrageous tyranny, *really* "preferred links with the Nazis," and Stalin, whose systematic appeasement of Hitler makes Munich seem almost mild. Add to that a certain intellectual laziness typical of the Popular Front: "I don't think there was much discussion about it. We just assumed there would be a war." Finally, these failings are trumped—or are they?—by passion: *"we were desperately committed."*[9]

This mingling of high thoughts with shabby deeds is nicely illustrated on the crossing paths of two little-known men. One was an American: Noel Field, a diplomat who was also a Popular Front spy, though he was a spy about whom, in contrast to volumes about Alger Hiss, it seems nobody has two words to say. The other was a Hungarian Mafioso: Theodore Maly, an agent who stands in the first rank of the "great illegals," and probably the man most responsible for conceiving and forging the networks of the Popular Front spies in England, France, and even America.[10]

Both Noel Field and Theodore Maly were gentle, highly intelligent men, driven by exceptional moral energy. Their fates are linked.

The Ariadne whose thread binds Cambridge and America, "antifascism" and "espionage," and leads from Maly to Noel Field was a German communist close to Babette Gross and Willi Münzenberg named Hede Massing. She knew Babette and Willi from the earliest days: The friendship with Babette antedated Hede's work as a spy and also outlasted it, persisting right up to the end of Hede's life. As a young woman, Hede was an actress. Also a flirt, a woman with a roving eye. She married three times, and each of her husbands turned out to be somebody in or near the apparatus. The first was none other than Gerhart Eisler, the brother of Ruth Fischer, and a first-tier *apparatchik* who (especially in America) would work in close collaboration with Otto Katz. Her second husband, a man named Julian Gumperz, was a left-wing publisher linked to the Münzenberg Trust. Hede's third husband was a scholar and writer named Paul Massing, who became part of Willi and Otto's antifascist enterprise in Paris.[11]

While she was living with Paul Massing in Paris, Hede made the transition of which we are speaking: The transition from propaganda to fully covert work, operating under the cover of Willi and Otto's "antifascism" and directed by one of the great illegals and an intimate associate of Theodore Maly: the great master-spy whose code name was "Ludwik," whose true name was Erwin Poretsky, but who is best known as "Ignace Reiss."

During the summer of 1933, everything was coming together. The Leipzig Trial, and the London Counter-Trial were about to take place. Willi and Otto were consolidating their new task. "Antifascism" was taking shape. In England, Maly and his colleagues were successfully perfecting the networks spun from Cambridge. And in America the New Deal of Franklin Roosevelt was in its first hundred days.

Such was the context within which Ludwik summoned Hede to him one summer day with instructions for a new assignment. She was to prepare for a meeting with a "most important comrade." "Try to look your best," Ludwik told her. "Don't be as flippant as you usually are... Show more respect for important people."[12]

Ludwik escorted Hede to a cafe near the Opera called the Cafe Scribe. Hede and Ludwik took a table, ordered an *aperitif,* and made small talk, waiting. A few minutes later, there materialized at their table "a tall, lank, elegant man of about forty-two. His face was tanned, strangely ascetic, his eyes deep and sad. His hands were the long, narrow, aristocratic kind."

It was Maly. Hede did not know it was Maly. She may never have known. She certainly did not know it when she wrote her memoirs. But Maly it was.

The elegant agent sat down and without introduction addressed Hede by her first name. He told her he was known among "our people" in the apparatus as *"der Lange,"* the Tall Man. So why didn't Hede call him that, too: the Tall Man.

At this point, Ludwik slipped away.

Maly had arranged this meeting to preside over a radical change in Hede's life as a spy. Though Massing knew nothing of Maly's work in England, the Tall Man was proud, even a little vain, about his British connections, and Massing sensed they were important. "I gathered," she later wrote, "that he was the head of some apparatus, probably the GPU in England, *and that he was slated to go to America in a similar post.*" (My emphasis.) "'Felik' [Ludwik's assistant] had probably mentioned the fact that I was a genuine American citizen with a genuine American passport; that I was on my way to the United States; that I had been working for Ludwik and might be worthwhile looking over."

So what brought this secret eminence of the Cambridge Conspiracy to the Cafe Scribe were *American* concerns.

Der Lange leaned back in his chair and suggested they have a night on the town. "He was suave, worldly, spoke fluent English. 'It takes an Englishman like me,' he said, pointing to his exquisitely tailored clothes with a wink of his eye, 'to know Paris.'"

The rest of the night was like some wistful little date, less like a rendezvous for spies than a scene from Ernst Lubitsch's film comedy of romance and revolution, *Ninotchka,* recast in a chronically melancholy key. Hede and the Tall Man had dinner in a Norman restaurant, and ended up at 4 a.m. in the Melodic Bar, listening to a black jazz band while, over their sad brandies, *der Lange* grew confidential with her. He confessed that he was a man in love that he was trying to be transferred to America so he could rejoin a woman in Ludwik's network named Gerda Frankfurter. The Tall Man loved Gerda, but she was lost to him. The apparatus had ordered her into the American operation. He did not know if he would ever see her again. The gloom thickened as the evening ended and he lapsed, as he would again, into "depression fits of self-accusation."

Hede was being sent to New York, using that precious *real* American passport of hers, there to engage in an important new phase of secret work. In fact, in America Hede would get to know Gerda Frankfurter well and would work with her often. Maly took out a cigarette box—"it was a rather primitive method, I thought"— tore its top in half and told her that she would know her American contact when she was handed the other half.

A few weeks after Hede Massing arrived in America, a man came to the door of the apartment she'd found in New York. He was stout, vulgarly dressed, self-important, stupid. He announced that he should have the torn top half of the cigarette box, but he had lost it. Here was a prime example of the NKVD's new breed, and he blustered in with his orders.

Working under her new cover as an "antifascist" journalist, Hede began to frequent left-wing circles in New York and Washington, a witting agent making contact among the "innocents." One of the people for whom Hede became a link to what was called the "anti-fascist underground," and was in fact the *apparat*, was Josephine Herbst, a novelist and journalist from the circle of Ernest Hemingway. It appears to have been through her contact with Hede (and very possibly a meeting with both Münzenberg and Gibarti) that Josephine Herbst was sent to Germany on what has every appearance of a mission for the Münzenberg underground, the first of what would be a number of covert actions she and her husband would perform for the *apparat*.[13] Meanwhile, Herbst's husband was being prepared for serious work in Washington. John Herrmann, a not-very-successful novelist who had served as Hemingway's drinking pal from Paris to Key West, would soon be helping to manage the network of Popular Front spies created by Harold Ware, a network exactly parallel in conception to the Cambridge group. As he did so, Hede Massing was cultivating a rising young star in the Department of State named Noel Field. Her task was to guide him, oh so gently, through the secret door.[14]

Hede Massing does not seem to have known that in 1934 Noel Field was already very much in Moscow's eye, and had been for some time. Noel's mother, a devout Quaker woman, was often in Europe and had repeatedly worked as a courier for Ludwik. Mother Field was passionately opposed to Hitler; her frank American face and her precious American passport protected the missions she ran for Ludwik in Germany. I have never seen the claim made that Noel Field's mother was anything other than a sincere but naive antifascist. Nonetheless, she seems to have preceded her son into secret work, and it was secret work for Ludwik. Couriers— note well—are often selected precisely for their innocence. The reason is simple: The ignorant, if caught, will have nothing to say. We might add that it seems that Madame Field senior's brisk rectitude and purity of righteous passion, albeit useful, rather got on Ludwik's nerves.[15]

Whether the apparatus found Noel through his mother or the reverse is an unanswered question. But back in America, Noel Field was already secretly involved in communist activity, and probably had been so since 1926 or 1927, though there is no reason to suppose that this included espionage.[16]

Hede's account of guiding the seemingly innocent Noel Field into espionage is one of the most complete reports of these seductions we have. Her first assigned task was to become the Fields' friend. Accomplishing that proved easy. Hede genuinely liked Noel; she also liked his wife Herta. Massing was lonely in America; she found the couple comforting, "almost European." In fact Herta Field was German-born; and Noel, born in London, came from an American background that was "cosmopolitan." Noel Field and his family seemed to walk straight out of a novel by Henry James. He and his brother might have played in Isabel Archer's garden. Hede found Noel dreamy, idealistic, impulsive. He was also destined for great things at State. In the not-too-distant future, Field would be offered a job in charge of State's German desk, no less.

Thirty years later, Noel Field's publishing colleagues in communist Hungary would fall silent when Noel Field approached them in the halls; they were afraid of being reported to the Committee as the horror-hardened Stalinist passed them by. What a different story it was during that Washington springtime in Roosevelt's first term! As a youth, Field seems to have been, if not exactly charming, at least a likable type. Somewhere there exists a snapshot of the young Noel taken by Herta in a woodland spot a mere ten minutes outside central Washington. Field is beaming at the camera, and buck naked. The picture was taken to prove how swiftly the young diplomat could get from the Seat of Government to the State of Nature.

On another occasion, walking late at night on the Mall, high on wine, Noel paused before the Lincoln Memorial, spread his endless gangling arms wide, and began to serenade the great Daniel Chester French statue with the *Internationale*. Honest Abe looked down on the chanting Quaker.

Hede's task was to coax and set the steel in this rather winning and seemingly romantic soul. Her job was to watch and report every tiny surge that rippled across the hidden surface of Field's good but ingenuous mind. She was to probe and toughen his idealism, win his trust, and locate his capacity for betrayal. Hede had to think with Herta and Noel, feel with Herta and Noel, breathe as they breathed.

Field loved Wagner, and he assumed that his German antifascist friend Hede must love Wagner too. Hede detested Wagner. Night after night, once Noel was home from another day on the rise at State, Hede would join the Fields in their apartment for some of Herta's *gemutlich* cookery. After supper, it never failed: Wagner. Hede would sink back on the couch, feigning joy as the curly-haired Quaker's son stretched out and rolled his eyes over *Lohengrin*. On and on and *on* it went. At last silence let Hede prod things back to earth with some serious talk about antifascism; about the awful struggle going on in Europe; about the Revolution. Above all, Hede would harp on the troubling question of what a merely bourgeois administration like Roosevelt's could really do against the threat. After all, Roosevelt was part and parcel of the capitalist system that had spawned fascism. He was part of the problem, as good revolutionaries like themselves knew. Good intentions were not enough. It really was to the Soviet Union, to Marxism-Leninism, that one must look for the way out. But how? With what help?

It isn't clear exactly how long it took Noel Field to become a true Soviet agent. I myself do not entirely discount the possibility that Field may already have been fully witting and inside the apparatus by the time Hede entered his life. Field may have been more knowing about Hede's maneuvers than he let on. After all, he had been a secret member of the Party for years. Massing reports that Field originally hesitated to steal documents directly from State. She says that her recruit at first preferred to write summaries of important documents, summaries he would bring home and then read aloud to Hede, who would take them down in shorthand. Massing suggests this caution was born in Field's moral compunction— as if shorthand took him only halfway to betrayal. The argument is not persuasive. Field's caution seems far more likely to have been an elementary but shrewd self-protective measure, a way of assuring that the Soviets would get their material without any traceable written link to him. If Alger Hiss had insisted that Whittaker Chambers take shorthand notes, rather than let Priscilla type *his* summaries on the family typewriter, the Hisses might never have been exposed. Who then was the naif? Hede or Noel?

But then all the accounts of Noel Field's espionage work, without exception, are peculiarly contradictory, even though his lifelong work in the *apparat* is made clear by documents in the Archives of the Ministry of the Interior in Budapest. By the mid-1930s Noel Field was an active witting source for Soviet espionage in the Roosevelt State Department. He remained an active agent when he went to Europe to join the League of Nations. He was still an agent when his senior officer in Europe, Walter Krivitsky, defected in 1937. Karl Kaplan, the Czech defector who was the Dubcek government's investigator into the Slansky Trials, reliably told me that the records he had seen in Prague indicated that after 1938, Noel Field was "mistrusted" by the apparatus because he had been too close to Krivitsky, even though Field seems to have boasted that after the defection of Krivitsky's friend, Ludwik, he himself had assisted the NKVD in tracking the old spy to his hiding place in Lausanne, where Ludwik was machine-gunned to death.[17] Mistrust or no, did Krivitsky's own defection end Field's career? Not at all. Field remained a covert *apparatchik* throughout the war, acting as a double agent with American intelligence, and he remained under Soviet discipline after the war, until the moment of his arrest in Budapest in August 1949, when Whittaker Chambers exposed his colleague in Popular Front espionage, Alger Hiss, in Washington.

Stalin had ordered Noel Field's arrest in Hungary as the "master-spy" who had seduced the antifascists into treason. As was often the case with these changes, this bizarre lie had a kind of upside-down grounding in truth. In Switzerland during the war, Field had indeed approached his acquaintance Allen Dulles, an old friend from his early days at State. He did so on Soviet orders. Dulles was now in charge of the OSS station in Geneva. Field had an offer for Dulles. He had worked for years with the American Friends Service Committee and similar organizations; he had first-rate contacts with important antifascist groups across Europe who otherwise "mistrusted" the Americans. As a loyal American, and a thoroughly Europeanized old friend of Dulles, Field offered himself as a liaison to these groups. He would quietly watch out for American interests, keeping Dulles fully informed about how things were going, keeping all the right people in touch.

Allen Dulles, in what some see as a typical lapse of judgment, fell for this "offer" like the proverbial load of bricks, and as a result a Soviet agent became on of Dulles's principle advisors on antifascist politics in Europe.[18] The Americans were about to have a great deal to say about who held power in post-war Europe, and

above

The original spy who knew too much. Walter Krivitsky explains the Nazi-Soviet Alliance a few months before his sudden demise. *(UPI/Bettmann)*

left

Karl Radek, cynicism's sage, just before his arrest. *(UPI/Bettmann)*

above
Willi Münzenberg in Moscow
(far left), about to be empowered, 1921. *(Photo ABZ: Berlin)*

right
Maxim Gorky and H.G. Wells
with Moura Budberg, the spy
they both loved. *(University of
Illinois Libraries)*

below
The Princess Maria Pavlova
Koudachova, Soviet agent,
around the time she began to
manage the life of Romain
Rolland.

above
Willi and Babette. *(Literary Estate of Margarete Buber-Neuman)*

right
Gorky returns to Russia. *(UPI/Bettmann)*

left
Münzenberg in Berlin, after
Lenin gave him his mission.
(Atlantic; Berlin)

below
Otto Katz. The lieutenant—and
one of the most complex secret
agents of his era. *(National
Archives)*

The death of Weimar: the Reichstag burns on February 27, 1933.

Marinus van der Lubbe in the dock.

Dimitrov, Popov, and Tanev confidently await trial.

above
Babette Gross with Arthur
Koestler in 1955. *(Courtesy
of Peter Gross)*

right
Josephine Herbst and John
Herrmann en route to Russia.
(The Beinecke Library)

below
André Gide and André
Malraux prepare for their
delusive "Mission to Berlin"—
the occasion that led Malraux
to suspect a conspiracy.
(Giselle Freund)

right

Ella Winter, whom Gibarti called a prime Party agent on the West Coast, with Lincoln Steffens and Sinclair Lewis.

below

Dorothy Thompson in Red Square. *(Dorothy Thompson Papers: Syracuse University Library)*

below right

Harold Ware—American Münzenberg man turned American spy.

Liston Oak (second figure from left), propaganda agent in Madrid, with literati; Ernest Hemingway, oddly clean-shaven, stands beside Oak. *(Joan Worthington)*

above

Hede Massing, Noel Field's guide into secret work and sometime wife of Gerhart Eisler, testifying in Washington after her break. *(UPI/Bettmann)*

left

Alger and Priscilla Hiss at the time of his trial in New York. *(UPI/Bettmann)*

Field was there to make sure that what they said would be to Stalin's liking.

So it was until the dark day in 1948, just as the crypto-Stalinist cadres Noel Field so sedulously advanced with Allen Dulles were taking or consolidated power in Eastern Europe, Whittaker Chambers came forward and exposed the Ware group, including Field's longtime friend and fellow mole, Alger Hiss. The moment Field read this headline in Paris, Field understood his old life was over. With Chambers exposing Hiss and his fellow agents, Field knew it was only a matter of time before he too was exposed. An American subpoena, even one summoning him as a witness rather than as a target, had to be avoided at all costs.*

Field naturally turned for help from the Soviets. And, of course, the NKVD chief Beria and the *apparat* quite agreed with him: Field must not fall into American hands. But the Soviets decided to remove Field from the Americans' grip in a very different way than they had saved Burgess and Maclean. There would be no apartment, no dacha. Not *yet*. First, Noel Field was to be arrested, as were his wife, his brother, his "adopted daughter" (in fact, his girlfriend), and beyond his wretched family a very large number of other people—most of them leading Stalinists in the antifascist cadres which he had promoted during the war. For now that Stalin was in power in Eastern Europe, he had decided to rid himself of the cadres that had put him there. It was time for a little of Stalin's gratitude, and another wave of purges.

Noel Field became the propaganda centerpiece of this new wave of terror. When he turned to the Soviets for help after Hiss was exposed, the *apparat* directed him to Prague. Field went to Prague. And at that point Noel Field was arrested, and he vanished from the face of the earth.[19] He had been taken to a safe house outside Budapest, where he was held prisoner under elaborate surveillance.

---

* Of course, if (as is sometimes claimed) Field really had been a double agent working for the Americans, he would have needed only to contact his control, Allen Dulles, to be granted ironclad protection from the events unrolling in Washington. But American protection is precisely what Field did not seek.

There he would be held, accused in every paper in the Communist world of being the American "master spy," who had penetrated the antifascist cadres on behalf of Allen Dulles and enticed otherwise good Communists into treason. The people Field had once promoted were now going to be arrested and killed—in his name. He was the man whose "testimony" would be used to purge and hang the leading lights of Soviet antifascism in Europe, in a new wave of mass arrests and purges that began in Budapest and eventually ran through every country in Eastern Europe, culminating in the 1952 Slansky Trials in Prague.[20] As an American who had been ubiquitously active among these antifascist cadres from 1936 onward, Field was the ideal for the role. Since he had known everybody, everybody could be killed in his name.

Thousands died. One of those thousands was Otto Katz.

Exactly how personally cooperative Noel Field was in the vast wave of murder conducted in his name is somewhat unclear. Throughout the purge and its aftermath he was held prisoner in Budapest, and so was his family. He was relentlessly interrogated, as was Herta. He seems to have been tortured—though the records of Field's debriefing show him a fully, even enthusiastically, cooperative collaborator with the secret police.[21] The new Eastern European Terror lasted from 1948 to 1952. During it, Noel Field was never publicly produced. He was never tried, even *in camera*. Nor was he executed, though untold numbers of people in his so-called "ring" were hanged or shot or died in torture, doomed by his "confessions." He and Herta were held in prison until November 1954, a total of six years. They were then released.

Every detail here is mysterious. I do not claim fully to understand the bizarre course of events. Yet whatever Field's role, one fact stands out: *Field was not executed.* Countless others—"antifascist" Stalinist officials, mainly—were put to death in his name, while the "master spy," the ringleader of all treason, came out alive. Why? And why was Field released from prison after a relatively short imprisonment, and moreover released on the *very day* in 1954 that Alger Hiss was released from Lewisburg penitentiary, after Hiss had served his sentence for perjury? Later, Field was among the first in Eastern Europe to be "rehabilitated" from the "excesses" of the purge. Again, why? Surely his "rehabilitation" challenged the "convictions" of a great many people, all judicially murdered on the basis of "evidence" purporting to come from him. Besides, what if he talked? One might suppose that such an experience might have left an "idealist" like Field with second thoughts about Stalin's justice. Wasn't there some danger that he might make some sort of public comment about the many antifascist friends put to death in his name? Field had been the central figure in a very big lie. What if he exposed it?

But Noel Field did not expose the lie. Ever. He was provided with protection and advancement by the Hungarian Communists for the rest of his life, and for the rest of his life, this "innocent," so famous for his compunction and ambivalence, served them with a devotion unmarred by the smallest expression of doubt. He maintained absolute and lifelong silence about the vast crime committed in his name. On the day of their release, he and Herta were told for the first time that Stalin had died while they were in prison, an event that so overwhelmed them both with grief that they fell into each other's arms and "heaved with sobs."

When his grief had passed, the large lanky American never looked back. While Hungary slowly de-Stalinized, Noel lived on in Budapest, more loyal than the regime. He never returned to the West, even briefly, even after it would have been perfectly safe for him to do so. He never gave any historian or journalist an interview about his life. He never made the minutest effort to explain or even clarify his role. The steadfast tin soldier of Stalinism worked for the rest of his life as a middle-level executive in Hungarian publishing. Until the end his co-workers feared him. And with what reason!

Clearly, America's entry into the Cold War had precipitated a crisis in the secret world of the Popular Front spies and the antifascist cadres. This is still not clearly understood, at least not in the West. We know a great deal about what happened in America in those days of Hiss and HUAC and McCarthy. We know next to nothing about how all of that was linked to what was simultaneously happening in Eastern Europe. Put as simply as possible, the antifascists murdered by Stalin while the Hiss case raged in America—and those purges were exactly coextensive with the American furor—had been highly instrumental in the Stalinist seizure of power in Eastern Europe. Clearly, Stalin owed his antifascist cadres a debt. And Stalin did not like debts.

***

Herta Field outlived Noel: She died only in the 1980s, near the time that Hungary at last began to emerge from its decades of oppression. The repressed by that time had begun to return. By the time Herta expired, it was not easy to scare up many Marxist-Leninist true believers left in Budapest, but Herta was one of them. Gathering before her coffin, the people who came to Herta's funeral were told that as the occasion ended they would be asked to rise and sing the *Internationale*. Herta would have wanted it that way. People glanced at each other in embarrassment. They shuffled to their feet, and in *a capella* voices, quavered through the old anthem, stanza by stanza, to the bitter end.

***

But we have almost forgotten Theodore Maly, Hede Massing's date in the Melodie Bar, the secret service genius who first conceived and organized Popular Front espionage, father of the Cambridge group, the true "perfect spy." Who *was* he? Anthony Blunt many times told Arthur Martin that he and his friend would never have entered the *apparat* without seeing the special qualities of Maly and his close associate Arnold Deutsch.[22] Maly, they sensed, was a man of high intelligence and great moral feeling. Maly was grounded in the true high serious.

And so he was. Theodore Maly was a Hungarian *par excellence*; smooth, multi-lingual, cultivated, and knowing, a man with a multiple and nuanced mind. He had many names: lots of people called him "Teddy," others called him "Theo"; depending on which country he was passing through, he used many other aliases as well. He often went under the name "Mr. Peters." Another of Maly's aliases was "Paul Hardt." Finally, there was the nickname Hede Massing heard: *der Lange*, "the Tall Man."[23]

The Cambridge operation in England was crossed from the start with the cadres of Popular Front spies in the American government. It was to America that Maly sent Hede Massing—there to recruit Noel Field—and it was at the suggestion either of Maly or his close associate Arnold Deutsch that Anthony Blunt recruited the American Michael Straight in Cambridge and sent him back to America. From the beginning, Blunt made it plain that he intended Straight to enter the *American*, not the British, apparatus.

Here is how Straight himself tells the tale.[24] One day in 1937, shortly after his closest friend John Cornford had been killed in Spain, Michael Straight was asked to drop by the rooms of the brilliant young don Anthony Blunt "in the loveliest court in Trinity."

In 1937 Straight, who was already a committed student communist, was in the midst of his grief. Part of his conversation with Blunt that day was over what Straight might do in John's memory. As they talked, Blunt asked what Michael planned to do when he left Cambridge. Well, Michael had been vacillating; he did not know. In any event, he thought he would become a British subject.

At this point, Blunt adopted the cool controlling tone of which he was lifelong master. "Some of your friends," Blunt told Michael Straight, "have other ideas for you."

"Other ideas?"

Blunt maintained that same tone of incisive authority.

"Your father worked on Wall Street," Anthony continued. "He was a partner in J. P. Morgan. With these connections, and with your training as an economist, you could make a brilliant career for yourself in international banking."

"I don't want a brilliant career in international banking," I said. "I have no interest whatever in becoming a banker."

"Our friends have given a great deal of thought to it," Anthony insisted. "They have instructed me to tell you that is what you must do."

"What I must do? ... What friends have instructed you to tell me?"

"Our friends in the International. The Communist International. ... My instructions are to inform you of your assignment, and to assist you in every way that I can."[25]

Straight protested that he could not tolerate a life on Wall Street. Blunt agreed to convey Michael Straight's *cri de cœur* to "our friends." In due course, Maly informed Blunt that while it was still essential that Straight go underground in America, his family connections in Washington would serve as well as those on Wall Street.

For one thing, Michael's family owned the *New Republic* magazine. Did it not?

It did. Maly was very well informed about Straight's opportunities in Washington. And indeed Michael Straight would return to America and become the editor of that journal. While he was editor, Straight's sister Beatrice Straight would marry a man named Louis Dolivet, who in turn had been a Comintern agent, and one of the most important Münzenberg men of all.[26]

Maly had made a very deft placement. Within days after his arrival in Washington, before he'd even made contact with his Soviet control, Michael Straight was in the second-floor sitting room of the White House, having tea with the Roosevelts.[27]

Theodore Maly began his life as a servant of God and ended it as a servant of Stalin. That trajectory defines much in him. He was present at the founding of the NKVD—then called the Cheka; a close associate, friend, and protégé of both Mikhail Trilliser, the founder of the foreign wing of the NKVD, and Dzerzhinsky himself. Maly's life followed a path that instructively describes the ethical consequences of Dzerzhinsky and Lenin's vision. Maly was a man whose nature was by every account exceptionally pure, gentle, cultivated, and kind. No reporter fails to note these qualities. Yet this gentle being was present at the creation of totalitarian-

ism, and his life is a demonstration of the union between radicalism and terror.

He was best remembered by his friends for his intelligence, his
blue eyes, the shy sweetness of his smile, and his shrewd kindness.
Back in Budapest, the Tall Man had begun his career in the priesthood, and he made the crucial transition from religion to revolution, from faith to terror, only after being tried in the crucible of
the First World War. When that war broke out, Father Maly had
enrolled as an army chaplain, and worked among the troops on the
Eastern Front of the Carpathians. There he was taken prisoner,
and spent the rest of the war huddled in prisoner-of-war camps,
witnessing horror after horror, watching soldiers dying *en masse* from
typhus and frostbite, trying to bring them the final consolation of
the faith while their bodies crawled with vermin.

Given the experience through which this young priest found
his initiation into hell, it would seem grossly presumptuous, an act
of pride, to suggest that for all his gentle brilliance, Maly was a
weak man. Who would dare call anyone weak in the face of such
things? Yet there *are* people whose faith and humanity are strengthened by horrors no less awful.

They broke Maly.

"I lost my faith in God, and when the revolution broke out, I
joined the Bolsheviks. I broke with my past completely. I was no
longer a Hungarian, a priest, a Christian, even anyone's son. I was
just a soldier, 'missing in action.'"

This path to anonymity, the choice of despairing dissociation,
is one of the most important moral byways of the modern experience. His wish to be good led Maly down the path to dehumaniza-
tion, though it was a path he saw as redemptive. Wrapped in the
facelessness of his annihilated faith, the newly atheistic Maly joined
that "guardian of the revolution," the Cheka, the first incarnation
of the NKVD. His new sacramental task was to remake the world.
One of his early assignments was to move with the squadrons of
the Cheka through the terrain of the Civil War.

Strange to say, this gentle person discovered himself yet once
again in an arena of indescribable brutality.

"We would pass burning villages which had changed hands several times a day. .... Our Red detachments would 'clean up' villages exactly the way the Whites did. What was left of the inhabitants, old men, women, children, were machine-gunned for having given assistance to the enemy. I could not stand the wailing of the women. I simply could not."

When that wailing of the women began, Maly would pretend to have diarrhea—and then, as if in confirmation, he developed a case of quite genuine dysentery. While the Cheka's machine gunners stood in the squares mowing the people down, Maly, favorite protégé of Saint Terror, would run to hide behind a truck. There he would double over in an agony at once intestinal and ethical, hands not over his gut but his ears.

The Terror worked. The Civil War ended, and the Cheka had made the Revolution safe. Except that its cruelties were soon followed by the collectivization of the Russian peasantry, with *its* murders *en masse*. And strange to say, the gentle Maly was once again on the scene.

"I knew what we were doing to the peasants, how many were deported, how many were shot. And still I stayed on. I still hoped the chance would come for me to atone for what I had done."

Atone? Atone while remaining in this secret police? It is an arresting misuse of the notion of atonement, all the more so coming from a former priest. It takes no very advanced theology to grasp that before any sinner can hope to atone he first must cease to commit his sin. The person who wishes to atone for murder must first stop murdering, stop being party to murder, and stop absolutely, without equivocation. In the absence of that turning back, there can be no atonement. Nor can there be forgiveness.

But Maly was lost to forgiveness. When he entered Dzerzhinsky's world, when Maly chose to become an instrument of the Revolution's annealing Terror, he enlisted his soul in a political system which bound the Good to Terror. *"Evil, be thou my good."* For all his sweetness, *in* his sweetness, Maly had become a protégé of that Faustian vision for which the great collective expression in this century has been the revolutionary ethic. Noel Field too, was a sweet man, notable above all for his gentleness. And like Maly, Field too had a recurrent way of finding himself smack in the middle of cruel brutalities.

In his book *Witness,* Whittaker Chambers speaks of the man who served the Revolution faithfully, until one night in Moscow, he heard screams. Just that: *He heard screams.* And he broke. Father Maly also heard those screams, but he could not see the way to turn back or anywhere to turn.[28]

Why? It seems a fair guess that the sadistic conflicts of this gentle human being were inscribed in his commitment to Dzerzhinsky's vision of sanctity. Yet "atonement" filled Maly's mind, and in his search for it, he embarked on a strange, secret, private campaign.

One day there appeared before him a peasant woman pleading for the life of her husband, a man who had been sentenced to be shot for stealing some potatoes to keep his family from starving. This was the collectivization: hundreds of thousands were being killed. In the eyes of the Cheka, this doomed son of mother Russia stood no chance whatever. He was a "class enemy"; his life was meaningless and worthless. The Cheka was not protecting potatoes: It was ridding the regime of an unsubdued, therefore "enemy," *class.* The *idea* was to kill men like this man. The poor man's wife was appealing to the old set of values, as if the theft of the potatoes was a "wrong," and its punishment might be mitigated by mercy. She stood before Maly making her peasant plea for an old thing called the Right.

As a good Marxist-Leninist, Maly of course understood that "right" or "wrong" were moralistic trifling in the large plan of the Revolution's purge of capitalism's evil. Besides, Maly wasn't sure he even had the authority to save the wretch.

Yet then and there Maly decided that—as his "atonement"—he would act. Somehow or other, he would rescue just this one lost little human life. He would gather together all his power, all his persuasiveness, all his pull, everything he had all to save this one utterly innocent potato thief.

He went to his NKVD superior, another member of the Hungarian Mafia, and marshaled his best. Miraculously, it worked. The chief listened, had compassion, and agreed. Together the two men commuted the man's sentence to imprisonment. Just like that. It was done: an act of mercy, a personal intervention, actually performed. And so simply!

At this point Maly happened to be called away, dispatched somewhere else on a two-week assignment.

"When I got back, the first thing I did was look for my case. I could not find the file. I ran to my chief. He did not know what had happened, and both of us started to hunt for the file. We finally found it. Scribbled across it was one word: 'Executed.'"

"This time," Maly said, "I did not get a bellyache."

Instead, he walked in a blank daze to his quarters. When he stepped into the room, Maly discovered that it was his cat that had suffered from a cramp and done the soiling while he was away, leaving its mound right there on his bed. Very quietly, the former priest picked up the offending animal and on the spot strangled it with his bare hands. Then he flung his pet's corpse out the window.

By the next morning, Maly knew that he could no longer live in Soviet Russia. Once again, rather than turn back, he turned—outward. He proceeded instead to headquarters and requested a foreign assignment he had often turned down many times before, even though work in European espionage was a much less bloody business than the NKVD's heavy daily task at home. His superiors were delighted. They had always thought Maly's talents were wasted on the crude slaughters of collectivization.

Trilliser's successor directing the NKVD foreign wing, a man named Slutsky, had always admired Maly for his smoothness, his easy command of many languages, his good looks, his tact and social skill.[29] He promptly gave Theo a foreign job worthy of his gifts. It would lead to his subtle work in England.

When Maly sent Hede to America, he was a man in love, though he was never able to arrange his own assignment to America so he could rejoin his beloved Gerda Frankfurter.

In 1938, at the height of the Terror, he was recalled to Moscow. He was commanded to leave his work with the Cambridge group; that was turned over to a new control, the sinister assassin Alexander Orlov.[30] Everyone knew this recall meant the end, and Maly knew it best of all. He proceeded to Paris and there, en route to the slaughterhouse, he paused. His friends in the *apparat* warned him again. Returning to Moscow was suicide. Find some other way. The man of atonement demurred. Come, come. What were his chances of outwitting the assassination squads if he tried somehow to hide in Europe? Even America? Maly considered his choices.

There was also discredit. If he fled, Maly knew Yezhov's men would use his years in holy orders to create his final portrait as a traitor—and nobody would ever be able to untangle the lie. His agent's honor, his seriousness as a revolutionary, would be smeared beyond repair, forever. To save that honor, Maly wanted whoever in the future might know or care to know that he had died obedient to the Revolution.

Maly went to the Gare de l'Est and boarded the train.

In Moscow, he was assigned a desk job for a few dull months. He sat at the desk and shuffled papers. He read *Isvestia*. He stared out the window into Dzerzhinsky Square, out onto the colossal statue that had been erected there of his old friend and mentor— the same statue which in the great days of August 1991 would be torn down at last by the jubilant crowd, followed by talk of erecting on that spot some appropriate monument, perhaps a huge cross, to serve as a sentinel to the millions dead.

Gazing out on Iron Felix's statue, the Father Theodore Maly that was sat waiting to join those dead. He did not wait long. One fine morning his desk was empty. He was never seen again.[31]

Chapter 9

THE BLOOMSBURY SPIES

Theodore Maly and the Hungarian Mafia's great achievement in Europe and America was to find a wedge into power within the elite of the adversary culture, and especially of the modernism that was at its center. Of course this is a much wider matter than the meaning of treason. To a very remarkable degree, the elites of the twentieth-century democracies chose to define their taste and language through the language of revolution and the dissociation of sensibility. Picasso would hang on bankers' walls. And it is through that attraction to the mythology of revolution that the Popular Front was able to tie espionage to culture.

The Cambridge spies were really a British outpost in a much larger international recruitment of what might more accurately be called the "Popular Front" spies—elite youth in all the democracies, snagged in a net cast by operatives like Theodore Maly and Arnold Deustch, and empowered by the moral energy of Popular Front antifascism. But the Cambridge group was also defined, of course, by local British influences. The Cambridge spies might also be called the "Bloomsbury spies"—not to tar all of Bloomsbury with their crimes, but to point out how powerfully the Popular Front swept through the elite intellectual culture from which these brilliant young people emerged.

They were, as we have seen, Bloomsbury's children. One of Anthony Blunt's early lovers was Virginia Woolf's nephew, Julian Bell; who later volunteered and was killed in the Spanish Civil War. Blunt's best biographer, Miranda Carter, insists that Blunt had nothing to do with Bell's decision to go to Spain: another British writer, Richard Deacon, maintains that Burgess was instrumental in the young man's decision. Whatever the truth, Bell was totally swept up in Popular Front politics, and died for them. Blunt's early work for the *apparat*—before he joined British intelligence—was as a recruiter. In this capacity Blunt recruited Michael Straight in the midst of Straight's grief over the death in the Spanish war of his closest friend, John Cornford, the son of two leading academic members of the coterie, Frances and Francis Cornford. Capping all this was Burgess's elaborate intimacy with Harold Nicolson, the husband of Virginia Woolf's intimate, Vita Sackville-West. The Cambridge spies were Bloomsbury's heirs.

Our understanding of Bloomsbury has become so dominated by the presence and genius of Virginia Woolf that it is sometimes forgotten that the coterie was less her creation than that of her intimate (and one-time fiancé), Lytton Strachey. Strachey always saw himself as a man with a mission. Seizing on the question of taste, Strachey proposed to redefine the ethic and nature of the British elite. While he was still an undergraduate at Cambridge, and later, in and around the First World War, Strachey set his essentially Oedipal task: To use the most shining offspring of the eminent Victorians to attack the philistinism, hypocrisy, and repression which, he claimed, defined the loathed and loved Victorian world of their parents, and thereby define a new era of elite British opinion.

The idea was to put the offspring of the British establishment at the center of the British adversary culture without sacrificing the elite status into which they had been born. The Bloomsberries correctly understood the modernist revolution to be the greatest cultural force of their time. They also believed it was a challenge to everything their parents had thought important. Strachey showed his followers how to enhance rather than sacrifice their position by joining the rebels. His purpose was to reinforce rather than undermine the aristocratic status into which the coterie's members had been born. Plebeian or non-U types, no matter how impressive, had no place in the network. The need to knock his parents off their pedestal was not exactly D. H. Lawrence's problem. Bloomsbury therefore treated Lawrence as a parvenu, and rejected the "underbred" James Joyce, until the genius of both had become so successful they could only make themselves ridiculous by denying it. Bloomsbury was an in-house operation of the British elite.[1] Strachey's real aim was to invest anti-establishment contempt with elite standing. First, last, and always, the real politics of Bloomsbury was a search for cultural power in England.

Strachey himself was a rather nasty item. Julian Bell's brother Quentin describes him as "a creature torturing and self-tortured, slipping from one agony to another, a wretched sighing hand-wringing misfit, a quite impossible person."[2] Though time has partly justified Strachey with Bloomsbury's many triumphs of taste and influence, one must note that apart from Virginia Woolf Bloomsbury produced almost no artists able to hold their own in the true first rank. Bloomsbury succeeded in defining highbrow taste in England. But taste, however elevated—even "perfect" taste—is a shabby substitute for greatness. The coterie constantly confused the two.

For the coterie's rationale Strachey borrowed a cult of "friendship" from the Cambridge philosopher George Moore, so that to this day E. M. Forster's silly pseudo-thought (it was borrowed from Moore: The business about having the guts to betray one's country before betraying one's friend) is almost invariably raised in any discussion of the Cambridge spies. And when your "friends" are collaborating in repression of whole peoples, and in the death of thousands? What then?

For all his talk about the sanctity of "friendship," there was nothing so wonderfully amiable in Bloomsbury conduct, as we know from the incredibly voluminous documentation of every shiver and sigh of every single member of the coterie. Even by the ungentle standards of most literary cliques, Bloomsbury was exceptionally malicious within its own ranks, and with outsiders cruel to the point of systematic sadism.

Paul Johnson describes it well: "Not for nothing was Strachey the son of a general. He had a genius for narcissistic elitism and ran the coterie with an iron, though seemingly languid hand. From the Apostles he grasped the principles of group power: The ability not merely to exclude but to be seen to exclude. He perfected the art of unapproachability and rejection: A Bloomsbury mandarin could wither with a glance or a tone of voice. Within his magic circle exclusiveness became a kind of mutual life-support system. He and [Leonard] Woolf called it 'the Method.'"[3]

In the first generation, few members of the Bloomsbury coterie were fellow travelers and fewer still were true Stalinists. Leonard Woolf's soft-left writing on Imperial policy is more like it, though the Woolfs' political mentors, Sidney and Beatrice Webb, became more or less abject Stalinist propagandists. But Strachey's legacy, which placed the new mandarins throughout British publishing, broadcasting, academia, and intellectual life was, to say the least, fertile ground.

Which is where Burgess and Blunt came in.

On the public level, the Popular Front propaganda apparatus, using its British fronts such as the Left Book Club and its many appendages, led the move to Stalinize Bloomsbury taste, silently sustained by the talent-spotters throughout the universities and in the Münzenberg-Gibarti propaganda network, and tied to the Soviets through a dual NKVD-Comintern network running through Amsterdam, Berlin, and Paris. The process had been in motion since at least 1927, when Ludwik set up shop in Amsterdam. Hitler had nothing to do with its founding, but it reached its apex in the Popular Front, and it culminated in Spain, where certain observers such as George Orwell began to dare to dissent.

Back at Strachey's Cambridge, the obvious heir to all this was Blunt, and a prime venue was the "Cambridge Conversation Club," the Apostles, a long-established campus secret society for aristocratic young intellectuals. Tennyson and Hallam had been members. Strachey and Leonard Woolf had taken over the Apostles before the war, and a generation later Blunt and Burgess remade it for theirs.[4]

Once exposed, Blunt did not defect to the USSR, and when he was offered refuge there at the time of Burgess's defection, he disdainfully refused. He despised the mere thought of life in the Utopia he served. But then, what did Blunt not despise? Blunt's Communism did, however, give him the Archimedean point needed to leverage all this contempt. It served his snobbery. Blunt invariably put himself in a position to despise those he served. He despised the sleek and fluting members of the establishment, whom he viewed as history's fools, doomed to be swept away. He likewise despised the Soviets who ran him, and whom he brushed aside even as he obeyed. Bumblers, clods, boors. In the void between servility and loathing, Blunt found power.

His fellow spy, Leo Long, thought that Blunt had no interest in real politics at all. So what was his motive in serving the Soviets? Long thought Blunt "perhaps" liked the conspiratorial side of spying. I myself think espionage served Blunt's egotism, his habit of arrogance and contempt. His chosen role was to be the most sublimely placed insider of all, the perfect Prufrock of the British establishment. "Deferential, glad to be of use/Politic, cautious, and meticulous," Blunt was invariably to be found just a step behind and a shade to the left of power, the associate and even ultimate of principal figures throughout British life, from the royal establishment, to the Rothschilds, to the highest levels of the intelligence services. Most intellectuals are involved in what might be called powerless power. Blunt wanted more than that: He sought quiet but real command, power he could exercise *without seeming to*. He was made for duplicity.

His relation to women—some women at least—seems to have been that of a needy penitent. As exposure drew near, he became genuinely fearful at the prospect of losing the good opinion of Queen Elizabeth, the Queen Mother. Once, quietly drunk in a taxi with Rosamund Lehmann, he suddenly burst into tears, and incomprehensibly began to beg her forgiveness—though to be sure this bizarre display may actually have been a charade used to test what Rosamund's lover, Goronwy Rees, as someone who knew about Blunt's ring, may have confided in their pillow talk. Toward men, on the other hand, Blunt's attitude was one of hard, suppressed, manipulation, and a silent but relentless search for the point of vulnerability.[5]

Strachey's cult of "friendship" was in practice a cult of homosexuality, and he genuinely believed homosexuals were an erotic elite, moving in a realm of finer feeling that transcended the grossness of heterosexual manhood. In a letter to Keynes he wrote, "it's madness for us to dream of making dowagers understand that feelings are good, when we say in the same breath that the best ones are sodomitical...our time will come about a hundred years hence."[6]

Theodore Maly and Arnold Deutsch were especially shrewd on this score, quite consciously exploiting the group's coterie pride and resentment. Communist morality and Marxism-Leninism in general have been relentlessly hostile to any variety of homosexual freedom, but young radicals of the early thirties clutched the fantasy that communism meant sexual freedom. This was of course quite untrue. At the same time that Amabel Williams-Ellis, Lytton Strachey's cousin once removed and sister of John Strachey, was singing the praises of the White Sea Canal, Stalin had dispatched three thousand homosexuals to the agonies of forced labor and early death in that project.[7] Countess Károlyi records with what whoops of laughter the *apparat* heard of Gide's plan to plead for homosexual liberty during his ludicrous (and, for Gide's honor, mercifully never held) audience with Stalin.[8]

From the start, Münzenberg had made the universities a center of his interest in order to touch the adversary culture in the place where it was shaped. In Cambridge, he and Gibarti were represented by the League Against Imperialism and by the two dons closest to it: Roy Pascal and Maurice Dobb. These two teachers had a profound effect on all the Cambridge conspirators.[9]

After 1932, Otto Katz also made England one of the bases of his power. He had arrived at a moment of special richness in the history of totalitarianism. Theodore Maly was by then well established in England. Maly had come to England well after Ludwik had placed his recruit in the upper track of British intelligence, back in 1927. Maly and Ludwik worked together, from London to Amsterdam. Maly remained in England through most of the thirties, operating now and then from an office next door to the one used by Gibarti's propagandists in London, an outfit known as the Anti-War International, which was in fact the British office of Amsterdam-Pleyel. The front man for the Anti-War International was a Münzenberg-man recruited from the Bloomsbury elect, Lytton's cousin once removed, John Strachey. As usual, propaganda and espionage were functioning hand in hand.

As his train pulled into London, Otto had many friends already waiting for him. Friends *and* the British secret service—for Otto was under the surveillance of SIS "watchers," probably from the moment of his arrival.[10] In later years Otto made it plain that he was fully aware of this surveillance from the moment it began. One wonders exactly who or what made him aware of it.

Katz's immediate task was to stage the show of the Reichstag Fire Counter-Trial, assisted by an unstoppable ball of English political fire, none other than "Red Ellen" Wilkinson. Ellen Wilkinson was a driving force in Labour's left wing; she had also been a hard-left collaborator with Willi and Otto in many a radical effort gone by. To some not quite discernible degree, this founding personality in the British Labour party must have been conscious of Otto's true role. Only a fool in her position would have failed to guess that Otto was a Soviet propaganda agent, and Ellen Wilkinson was nobody's fool. Or rather she was *almost* nobody's fool. She had been, for a while, Stalin's fool, though she later became a staunch anti-Stalinist, and Otto fooled her sufficiently to exploit her antifascism. Ellen Wilkinson remained under Katz's spell through Munich. It has been suspected that he had an affair with her. Certainly they were close. He guided her through Spain. Even the summer of the pact, Ellen quite contentedly paid a visit to Otto on the Riviera.[11]

Another contact waiting with Otto in England was the lifelong Stalinist propagandist, Claud Cockburn. Cockburn had first encountered Otto at least the year before at Amsterdam-Pleyel. In years to come, Cockburn and Otto would work together in many an adventure—in London, in Spain, and doubtless in America as well. Their link would reach a grotesque climax in 1952, when Otto stood wavering in the dock in Prague, mouthing his "confession." Recounting his "crimes," Otto told how he had betrayed the Revolution by serving Trotsky and Lord Beaverbrook in conspiracy with (among others) that ruthless agent of the Imperialists, Claud Cockburn.[12]

What was their real connection? By a curious coincidence, sometime between Amsterdam-Pleyel and the day Otto arrived in London for the Counter-Trial, Claud Cockburn had summoned up a London rumor sheet, an insider's political rag known as the *Week*. The idea behind the *Week* was to publish for the select few a weekly paper filled with the very best political gossip, all carefully but ingeniously arranged to serve the hard left and Stalinist position at any given moment. It was plain that the *Week* could and should not have a mass or even a large circulation. The gratifying sense of being in the select number of those truly on the inside does not flow from reports in *Time* and *Newsweek*. The *Week* has been called a "conspiracy theory bulletin." Its targets were precisely the insiders it was designed to reach: a splendid strategy.

But where on earth did Cockburn pick up this stuff? There were plenty of lies in the paper, but much of its information was dead-on accurate, and often *very* much from the inside. From which desks were these sizzling tales lifted? Cockburn always shrugged off the question. He got his stuff from pals, he said; he had all kinds of pals. Nothing much more than the babble of the boys in the pubs of Fleet Street, where to be sure Cockburn was an inveterate habitué. That and certain . . . well, let's call them "correspondents" in Germany. Certain "friends" in Paris. You know. People. Here and there.[13]

Perhaps. But the *Week* was founded very shortly after Cockburn had a high-level meeting in Berlin with Willi and Otto. Its appearance in London political life coincides precisely with the period of Cockburn's most significant intimacy with Katz. Is it mere coincidence that Otto was a witting agent of both the Comintern and the

NKVD, trained by Willi and Radek for precisely this kind of information and disinformation? Can that fact really have no relevance? More likely, some significant part of the rumors Cockburn spread in the *Week* originated with the *apparat* and was supplied by Claud's best guide through that wilderness of mirrors, Katz.

A suggestive ripple among the shadows that cover Otto's relation to the *Week* is a vague rumor of the time that there be a New York edition of the *Week* financed by Ralph Ingersoll. Ralph Ingersoll was an influential friend and colleague of Henry Luce, who in the 1930s became the lover of Otto's devoted political protégé and dear friend, Lillian Hellman. Not only was Ingersoll besotted with Hellman, but under Hellman's guidance the political life of this senior executive in the Luce organization assumed a decidedly Stalinist cast. He soon became a sponsor and moneyman of pro-Soviet publishing in New York.[14]

Ingersoll became publisher of the Stalinoid newspaper *P.M.*— a classic Münzenberg-style daily. Here too, Otto may well have had his unseen place. Lillian Hellman and Dashiell Hammett guided Ingersoll through every step of this enterprise, practically every paragraph. Hammett regularly interviewed prospective editors in his room at the Plaza Hotel, and in the paper's first months, Hammett or Hellman, either in New York or at Hellman's farm in Westchester County had approved in advance every word that appeared in *P.M.*[15]

P.M. was slated for large circulation, a close American cousin to the Parisian Stalinist daily *Ce Soir*, a paper for which Otto was certainly a covert control, run through Otto's protégé Paul Nizan, and fronted by yet another literary celebrity close to him, the Stalinist poet, novelist, and abject, Louis Aragon.[16]

Did Otto play some similar role at *P.M.*? Was *he* at the Westchester County farm too? It is perfectly possible, even probable, but must rest unproved. Certainly it is true that high-level agents of the apparatus, from Katz to Louis Dolivet, could be found hovering near *P.M.* throughout its existence.[17] Whatever the game, it would have been scrupulously clandestine.

It's frequently been suggested, by Peter Wright among others, that Cockburn may well have been a colleague of Otto Katz in the secret service of the International.[18] It seems likely. By the time the Spanish Civil War rolled round, it is certain that Cockburn was quite consciously fabricating disinformation for Otto, and Cockburn was clearly a Münzenberg-man of some sort, connected in some ways to the clandestine wing of the propaganda apparatus.[19]

At the same time, Cockburn spent his adult life a forthright Stalinist, the most visible and best connected in England. He embodied the new Stalinist snobbery. His was the perfect incarnation of a certain glib sneering condescension—the Cockburn tone was Bloomsbury vulgarized. Guy Burgess talked very much the way Cockburn wrote.

In the fall of 1933, the Counter-Trial had made its headlines and served its purpose. Antifascism was becoming the central issue that the age demanded, and London was following Paris as its capital. But there was more to be done in England than to stage the Counter-Trial.

Among the means used to promote the Stalinist chic was the Left Book Club, in which Katz played a large role. It will be remembered that Münzenberg was one of the inventors of the book club in its modern form—and that a year and a half before he dispatched Otto to Moscow in 1929, Willi assigned his man to be administrator and agent-in-place at *Universum Bucherei*, his book club in Berlin. The Left Book Club was more or less a cookie-cutter version of *Universum Bucherei*.[20]

The front men, of course, were English: John Strachey, Harold Laski, and Victor Gollancz. Of this trio, Strachey was a witting agent; Victor Gollancz almost certainly so, and Laski a sophisticated innocent.[21] With Sidney and Beatrice Webb, the intensely ambitious Strachey became the leading publicist for Stalinist intellectual chic of England and front man for the Anti-War International.

Strachey's biographer says Strachey invariably consulted with Harry Pollitt and "the British communist party" before making his selections for the LBC.[22] No doubt, but Harry Pollitt was a notoriously rough diamond. He knew nothing about the rarified literary and intellectual politics in which the Left Book Club trafficked. The man who really understood these matters was Katz, and from its very first listing the Left Book Club's agenda was a direct reflection of the current concerns of Münzenberg's Paris office, which Katz ran: a book by Rudolf Olden—a longtime Münzenberg collaborator—and a British translation of Malraux's *Days of Contempt*, written under Münzenberg's influence with the "assistance" of two Otto Katz confreres, Manes Sperber and Willi Bredel.[23] Besides this, under a number of pseudonyms ("O.K. Simon") Otto also wrote a number of the club's featured, though long-forgotten, selections.[24]

The name—Left *Book* Club—misleads a little: Like *Universum Bucherei*, it was much more than British communism's bookshop by mail. It was how Stalinist opinion was "networked" in England. The Club offered Münzenberg's familiar array of camps and conferences and propaganda tours of the USSR, and it organized the usual cadres for directing opinion in every area from the theater and art to sports. Whenever propaganda required, the rabbits of protest would leap from the clandestine cap. There were clubs to celebrate Soviet cinema, Soviet art, Soviet anything—joined to the usual untiring search for intellectual legitimacy. This craving for the prestige of cultural big names amounted to an institutional neurosis for the *apparat*,[25] Nor was the church forgotten: Gibarti was particularly proud of how effectively he dominated the political attitudes of the Right Reverend Hewlett Johnson, Dean of Canterbury Cathedral.[26] (Johnson was never the Archbishop of Canterbury, incidentally, though credulous Continentals often jumped to that conclusion.) Johnson could be relied upon to rain blessings on any act of cruelty or tyranny that Louis Gibarti told him to bless, while denouncing as un-Christian any question about the dictator's power.[27]

The link between the Popular Front propaganda *apparat* and espionage is nicely illustrated by a story from the youth of Rosamund Lehmann's brother, the publisher and poet John Lehmann.

In 1933 John Lehmann was a promising and glamorously well-connected young man of letters who had just stubbed his toe against the ego of Virginia Woolf. The result was a painful but brief hiatus in what would become one of the most distinguished careers in modern British publishing.

John Lehmann came straight down from Cambridge at the turn of the decade, and was introduced to his trade by taking on the slightly dangerous job of assisting Leonard and Virginia Woolf at the Hogarth Press, to which he had been sent for the interview by his great friend, the Woolfs' nephew and Anthony Blunt's lover, Julian Bell.[28]

Leonard and Virginia were delighted with Lehmann, and he got the job. He served his apprenticeship with such success that by 1932 or so a certain inevitable friction began to emerge. John Lehmann was much more than merely a bright young man. He soon showed a very genuine and specific aptitude for publishing. Leonard and Virginia were able to leave everything in his hands; for the first time in years, a holiday was possible—days, whole weeks of freedom. Lehmann was no mere gofer. Not only did he have taste and intellect of his own; he was beginning to put the stamp of a new generation on something that had always been absolutely and uniquely theirs.

Despite her quite unfeigned fondness for this golden boy, and she *was* very taken with him, Virginia especially disliked the new note. A fresh generation of anti-poetic realists was emerging, a generation for whom Virginia Woolf was an institution but not a model. The writers of the thirties were assuming their identity: John Lehmann was their man at Hogarth. Virginia watched this move away from her influence through eyes narrowed in mistrust. As the inevitable confrontation drew nearer, things grew rather tense at the Hogarth Press.

At this point, Lehmann decided that the better part of valor was to slip away from Tavistock Square for a while, and join his friends—friends he'd been bringing to Hogarth: Christopher Isherwood, Stephen Spender, W. H. Auden—in German-speaking Europe. *The* place to be. Yet though he does not say so in his beautiful memoir *The Whispering Gallery*—he makes only one passing remark about "the swirl of ... underground ... anti-war and antifascist activities"[29]—John Lehmann did not go to Vienna spontaneously. He was sent.

Who sent him? As things grew sticky at Hogarth, Lehmann had gone for advice to John Strachey. Strachey listened and understood perfectly. He quite agreed: the situation with the Woolfs was becoming strained. Why not take some time away, let things cool down. Visit the Continent. How about Vienna? After all, many of Lehmann's friends—Isherwood, Auden, all sorts of fascinating people—were heading there that summer. And Strachey knew just the way to make the trip worthwhile. Why not travel under the auspices of a splendid radical organization which Strachey ran; surely John had heard of it? The Anti-War International? The Anti-War International was more than merely idealistic. It was in the thick of the *real* antifascist fight. And Strachey could tell him, confidentially, that the real antifascist fight was about to be in Vienna. Vienna would be *the* place to be this summer. The young man's blood raced a little when Strachey suggested that Lehmann travel to Austria as a "secret correspondent."

Well, was Vienna the place where the "real" antifascist fight took place? In fact, Vienna is where the *illusion* of the antifascist fight was played out, in a typical "antifascist" strategy that was quick to confront any "fascist" except Hitler. In 1934, the apparatus selected Vienna as the scene of an important Soviet campaign mixed with covert action. Gibarti was almost certainly a principal actor in the propaganda effort, while the chief of "underground" action, working on espionage and subversion, was Alexander Orlov. After Vienna Orlov moved on to England, where he took over directing the Cambridge group, and after London he moved on to larger things in Spain.[30]

The aim of the Viennese antifascist campaign of 1934 was not, at any point, to oppose Adolf Hitler. On the contrary. Its function was to undermine both leading parties of Austria in preparation for totalitarian change. One of these was on the far right, the "clerico-fascists." The other, on the left, was a Marxist but non-Stalinist Social Democratic party. Stalin and Hitler alike detested both of these parties. And the two dictators' shared motive in Austria was to use the "antifascist" campaign to provoke them both into mutual destruction.

In Vienna, the anti-Stalinist Marxists, socialist city-dwellers mainly, were led by Otto Bauer. The archconservative country-side of the "clerico-fascists" was led by the Austrian premier, Engelbert Dollfuss. Note well: "clerico-fascist" though he was, Dollfuss was every bit as roundly detested by Hitler as the Marx-ist Bauer was hated by Stalin. That is the crucial point. Both dicta-tors wanted both parties destroyed. Neither Dollfuss nor Bauer had ever done his act of submission to his respective totalitarian leader, and the aim of the campaign in Austria was simultaneously to serve both the Nazis and the Soviets by destroying them both.[31] They only seemed to take sides with their" apparent ideological allies. A year later Dollfuss would be assassinated not by commu-nists but by the Nazis, while Stalinist "help" tore Bauer's non-Stalinist party to shreds.

By the time Gibarti and Orlov's effort was over, the combined brutalities of the *apparat* and the Austrian clerico-fascists left Austria's entire non-Stalinist left dispersed, converted to Stalinism, or in jail. Many of Bauer's naive young supporters ran for their lives to their "friends" in Russia: The Soviets gave them a parade, then sent them to the gulag.[32] Simultaneously, and to the Nazis' delight, Dollfuss was destabilized and discredited as well, and by the end of the year the Nazis had assassinated him. A bewildered, weak, utterly intimi-dated government of the anti-Nazi right replaced him, cowering in an effective squeeze between the two dictators. And when Hitler at last moved into Austria in the Anschluss of 1938, Stalin's protests were strictly perfunctory.[33]

And so "antifascism" in Vienna during 1934 required a lot of smoke and mirrors. Bookstore windows groaned with titles on Viennese outrages; the press was drenched in Austria's agony. Vic-tor Gollancz dispatched Naomi Mitchison to Vienna with a "gen-erous" advance to write what became her *Vienna Diary*. Mitchison, an inveterate fellow traveler, was greatly flattered by being made a courier. "I was carrying papers," she proudly wrote, "from socialist friends to their British comrades in my thick woolen knickers."[34]

From Stephen Spender and W. H. Auden to Hugh Gaitskell, the fellow travelers were made to converge *en masse*. Strachey was right. Vienna was *the* place to be.

Meanwhile, John Lehmann took up his job as a "secret correspondent," typing up innocent but fervid "antifascist" articles. Presently he was approached by a "swarthy" comrade, casually introduced, who insisted upon getting together privately with Lehmann. And what did he want to talk about? Politics. Serious politics.

The chat at this sort of recruitment rendezvous was notable for being at once very probing and distinctly evasive. At last the stranger had a suggestion. Up until now Lehmann had merely been writing articles—wisely suggested by the International—and placing them in various publications back home. Wonderful, brave work. But there was other work to do for antifascism. Even more important, more serious work. Special work.

Like?

Well, it dealt with ... "other political information."

Other information?

Precisely what "other information" remained unclear, but the swarthy visitor was persistent, "refusing to take 'no' for an answer."[35]

"My 'recruiting sergeant' was very pressing, but extremely vague about what he exactly wanted me to do."

Lehmann became uneasy. "I smelt a rat ... that is, I decided he would finally reveal that he wanted me to become a Soviet agent." At this point, still deep in his "secret correspondent's" innocence and a little scared, Lehmann turned for advice to John Strachey. What passed between Strachey and Lehmann is not recorded. Lehmann releases only the information that their talk "convinced me I was treading on too dangerous ground." After his conversation with Strachey, "the mysterious gentleman" who had been so very persistent "vanished from my life."

Lehmann ends his mini-confession with a sigh: "Of course I see now that I was peculiarly vulnerable, and perhaps lucky to swim past the lobster-pot as easily as I did."[36]

This heir to Bloomsbury has been standing at the precise point of intersection between propaganda and espionage. Münzenberg's

Anti-War International was a recruiting station for the Soviet espionage apparatus, and Lehmann had just failed his entry examination. Someone who passed the same test—same place, same time—was Kim Philby.

But the mingling of propaganda and espionage among the Bloomsbury spies is best illustrated in the relation between Blunt and Burgess. Poor Burgess seems to have been guided at the deepest level by the cruel muse of failure. He is one of the great and instructive human wrecks. Such people are often enough found in secret services. The life of achievement in art and the intellect is not a very forgiving one. What begins as brilliant youth can very easily sink into some awful region between the second and third ranks, the anonymous place where so often even the best of the quite good sinks and drifts forever. In 1931, it was generally assumed that Guy would become one of the great academics of his era. Given how Burgess ended—bleary, sentimental, slobbering—it is difficult to grasp how many serious people thought Guy Burgess the youth one of the most brilliant, compelling, promising human beings they had ever met.

In preparing this book, I have met many agents of influence who worked for various governments within the Münzenberg tradition. More than one has left me with a troubling, nameless afterimage, the sense of some shadow hovering over our talk. I'm tempted to call that lingering shade the ghost of Guy Burgess. Repeatedly, it comes cropping up again: the same glib charm. The same startling but too-glancing erudition and intellectual range. The same enthralling capacity for gossip; the same breezy knowing of everybody and everything. Often, the same elegance—though often a failed elegance, grown a tad seedy, a little dirty, or sloppy, or out of date, or somehow off. Often the same sexual gamesmanship—whether heterosexual or homosexual is incidental. Often, a similar river of alcohol flowing nearby. These men (the ones I've met have all been men) who began life dazzling everyone with their promise. Like Guy, they set out with the very grandest connections in the world of politics, the intellect, and the arts. And then—

We might call it the Burgess curse. The same desolation, often accompanied by alcoholism. The same deepening obscurity covered by one lurching move from one doubtful option to another, and the same shabbiness of promises worn down, then worn thin, and at last worn out. They strike one as men whose double lives were born in a fatal disjunction between their great expectations and their true secret selves. For them, failure began virtually at the moment of early success, back when splashy debuts looked like achievement. Their failure would be failure felt before it was seen as promise and loss mingled in bafflement.

For many such people, work in the secret world can be wonderfully restorative. It places them in the realm of power. It is almost like the old days of promise. Once again, their hand is on the pulse. Secretly, they can feel it, there again. Except that by that time, the work of ruin is very nearly complete. Those whom the gods have wrecked with promise, they next make spies.

But if Guy Burgess was failure's tragic creature, Blunt was spiritually tied, and absolutely so, to success. He could not, would not, and did not fail: ever. Success defined Blunt's life as firmly as failure defined Burgess's. It may well be that the secret of his prolonged shadowy love for Burgess can be located in this odd coupling of shabby ruin with the impeccably achieved.

In a BBC dramatization of the defection made in the 1980s, the screenwriter has Burgess warn Blunt that he is going to run to Russia with Maclean by mailing Blunt a note containing nothing more than some numbers. The numbers are page references to some lines of poetry, a stanza from Robert Browning, a ballad entitled "Waring," about a once-exciting youth turned failure, who finds he can no longer endure being what he has become. As the poem begins, Waring has decided at last to leave London without so much as a goodbye. He is running, and he will run to ... Russia.

In the film, Blunt gets the note, opens it, and sees the reference. Browning? "Waring?" Perplexed, he takes down his copy of the poems, leafs through the book until he finds the place, then reads, *sotto voce:*

What's become of Waring
Since he gave us all the slip?
Chose land-travel or seafaring,
Boats and chest or staff and scrip,
Rather than pace up and down
Any longer London town?

In a moment, Blunt takes it in. We see him absorbing the shock of recognition. Guy? "Giving us all the slip?" *Guy is defecting too.* Then—at once betrayed, bereft, and very much endangered—Blunt flings the book across the room. I've not seen any evidence that this incident really occurred, but it is a brilliant, genuinely moving screenwriter's touch, and *ben trovato.*

At the height of his adventures in London, Guy Burgess lived in two successive flats there. The first, from the thirties, consisted in the top floor of a place in Chester Square. The second, where he lived during the war, was a large, pleasant place leased through Victor Rothschild on Bentinck Street. The two places seem likely to linger in the iconography of espionage as two *maisons de rendez-vous.* Both have been vividly described several times, notably by Goronwy Rees and Malcolm Muggeridge. In Bentinck Street especially, the muse of history seems to have decided to play one of her periodic pranks: Outside number 9 Bentinck Street is affixed a blue-and-white plaque indicating that here once lived Edward Gibbon, author of *The Decline and Fall of the Roman Empire.*

In Chester Square, Burgess held court, usually in bed like a squalid Louis Quatorze, receiving visitors in rooms filled with the "indescribable debris and confusion from the party that had taken place the night before."[37] Beside the bed were piles of books—Burgess seems to have read and re-read *Middlemarch* almost continually through his adult life—and many liquor bottles, variously knocked back. Also near at hand was a frying pan brimming with the nauseating slop of a kind of homemade stew which Burgess concocted each week-end as a somewhat less liquid fortification for all the alcohol, and in order not to waste any tiresome time at a stove. "An evening at Guy's flat," writes Goronwy Rees, "was rather like watching a French farce which has been injected with all the elements of political drama. Bedroom doors opened and shut; strange faces appeared and disappeared down the stairs where they passed some new visitor on his way up; civil servants, politicians, visitors to London, friends and colleagues of Guy's popped in and out of bed and then continued some absorbing discussion of political intrigue . . ."[38]

The Bentinck Street flat was Guy Burgess's home during the war. As the Allies' capital, London was the capital where all the conspirators came to roost. Many roosted, at least now and then, at Bentinck Street. It was fancy, even luxurious, very much a step up, testimony to Blunt and Guy Burgess's increasing influence over their good friend Lord Victor Rothschild, who had sublet it to Burgess for a song.

If one could capture who, and what, passed through Bentinck Street during those years it would be possible to reconstruct some grotesque but remarkably full secret history of the Second World War. It would be political Proust belated by a quarter century, the cataclysm of the age as viewed by Jupien. Bentinck Street became a kind of salon, in which Burgess gathered the homosexual underworld of London together with some of the most devious and despicable political operatives then at work. I'm thinking for example of the Baron Wolfgang von und zu Putlitz, along with a distasteful creature from the upper anonymity of French politics named Edouard Pfeiffer. The Bloomsbury elite crowned it all.

Malcolm Muggeridge describes a visit there even more memorably than does Rees. Muggeridge was a middle-class boy. In this passage one can hear his own bitter, anomalous protest against Bloomsbury and its snobbery:

> There we found another gathering of displaced intellectuals, but more prosperous, more socially secure than the *Horizon* ones—John Strachey, J. D. Bernal, Anthony Blunt, Guy Burgess, a whole revolutionary *Who's Who*. It was the only time I ever met Burgess, and he gave me the feeling, such as I have never had from anyone else, of being morally afflicted in some way. His very physical presence was,

to me, malodorous and sinister; as though he had some consuming illness—like the galloping consumption. . . . The impression fitted in well enough with his subsequent adventures; as did this millionaire's nest altogether, so well set up, providing, among other amenities, special rubber bones to bite on if the stress of the Blitz became too much to bear. Sheltering so distinguished a company— Cabinet Minister-to-be [John Strachey], honored Guru of the extreme left-to-be [J. D. Bernal], Connoisseur Extraordinary-to-be [Blunt], and other notabilities, all in a sense grouped around Burgess; Etonian mudlark and sick toast of a sick society.[39]

One of the Bloomsbury grandees well known to Burgess was Harold Nicolson. Nicolson met Guy Burgess in the early thirties, and Nicolson's biographer cites Burgess as one of the young men who held some grip on the feelings of Nicolson all through this period, and it was through Nicolson's influence that Burgess joined the staff of the BBC in 1936; in fact, much of Burgess's rise through the British establishment took place under Nicolson's sponsorship. Nicolson shared none of Guy's political values; they were bonded by Bloomsbury assumptions.[40]

Burgess was guided into broadcasting, obviously, by his "friends" in the *apparat*, but only after a year or two first posing as fascist fellow traveler. The Soviet ordered Burgess, along with Kim Philby, to begin posing as a fascist fellow travelers. Burgess dutifully began working in the office and bed of a fascist fellow traveler in Parliament, Captain Jack McNamara. Burgess then took a job directing public relations for a Nazi fellow-traveling front, the Anglo-German Fellowship, a group Philby likewise joined, likewise under orders. Both men were active members of this all-but seditious operation for two years, spouting the fascist-front line.

That this fact alone did not automatically disqualify them both for any place whatever in war-time British intelligence has never been satisfactorily explained. Yet it is difficult to know what, short of a brass band, could have more clearly announced a gross risk to British security. Membership in the Anglo-German Fellowship *proclaimed* Nazi sympathies. No matter. Both men, both recently fascist fellow travelers, were shoehorned into the most sensitive areas of the British services by their untiring admirer, a major figure in the history of British intelligence, Guy Liddell.

On the long list of compromising truths known about Liddell is that he too was a regular habitué at Bentinck Street. How a senior official in British counter-intelligence would have chosen this reckless haunt of all places to let his hair down beggars inquiry. Liddell was also directly responsible for placing both Kim Philby and Guy Burgess into their first jobs in the British intelligence services. By 1936 Philby and Burgess had dropped their fascist pose. What of it? The gross security risk remained, staring right at everyone. Either Liddell didn't know about their old commitment. In which case he was failing in his job. Or he knew they had been posing. In which case he knew they had been Soviet agents. Or he knew the truth and thought it didn't matter. In which case he was an idiot and an incompetent. And nobody thinks Liddell was that. Though everything in this story seems to compromise Liddell, his highly reliable colleague in the British services, Sir Dick White, defended him to the end, and the preponderance of current opinion joins White in seeing Liddell as somehow innocent. Liddell's career was destroyed by the defections.

Harold Nicolson, on the other hand, was a major broadcaster,[41] a power in the BBC: during the war he became the BBC's political head, with full access to Churchill, as well as parliamentary secretary to the Ministry of Information, which ran the secret services. And of course he was a legendary personage in the Bloomsbury group, bound Virginia Woolf through his wife Vita, and a very notable diarist, diplomat, and arbiter of taste.

Nicolson's numerous published diary entries on Burgess are anything but complete or candid. After 1952, Nicolson plainly did his best to cover this ill-favored and credulous union with the spy. The full story in its emotional and political dimensions has never been seriously explored, though an exceptionally meticulous historian of broadcasting, Mr. W. J. West, has studied its consequences for the BBC.[42]

Under Nicolson's patronage, Burgess advanced spectacularly through the Bloomsbury networks; he was soon the most influential political producer in the entire BBC, where he introduced Soviet propagandists and fellow travelers wholesale. These naturally included Anthony Blunt, whose many appearances at the BBC were most useful in his rise.

Meanwhile, Burgess exploited his role at the BBC with subtlety and dexterity.[43] But there was more to it than that. As Nicolson's biographer laconically notes, "there can be little doubt that Guy Burgess extracted from Harold inside information which he passed on to his masters in Moscow."[44]

When Guy Burgess defected, Nicolson as usual wrote in his diary, and what he wrote is revealing. The entry is filled with anguish. "If I thought Guy a brave man, I should have thought he had gone over to join the communists. As I know him to be a coward"—one wonders how Nicolson knows this, exactly—"I suppose that he was suspect of passing things to the Bolshies and realizing his guilt, did a bunk."

There is something a little repellent in this notation. Anguish— yes: But one also is struck by the schoolboy tone; by the weak-minded, evasive thought about "courage" made in a remark that reveals ignorance of both Burgess's actual courage and his actual communism; by the unidiomatic use of the word "realizing" and finally by the kid's talk about "passing things to the Bolshies," and "doing a bunk." Here was an "Apostle," the very incarnation of Lytton Strachey's ideal, who had spent a friendship with one of the foremost of the Bloomsbury group lying to him in every meeting and using him at every opportunity not for mere crude personal gain—heaven forbid!—but in the service of tyranny. Nicolson had been jerked around and kissed up to and deceived not to make a few pounds or pull off admission to some club. Burgess had stooped to all this in order to betray his country and to serve the enslavement of nations. Speaking of it, Nicolson forgets that he was something more than a friend with Guy Burgess. He was a minister in Winston Churchill's cabinet, a man upon whom the fate of whole peoples, strangers to him, to some measurable degree depended. He seems incapable of addressing any of this. He cannot face a scrap of it; he would not even really face it in the years to come. In his correspondence to Moscow, Nicolson continued to treat Burgess as if he were merely an exceptionally errant friend with whom he happened to disagree. He never could see that this "friend" had used him, his position, his confidence, that unmentionable thing called his political power *and* his political trust to betray his friend *and* his country, along with a number of other countries—most wretched of all—into the bargain. It was all E. M. Forster in reverse, but with a relentless vengeance. Rather than acknowledge such a thing, Nicolson's voice reverts to childish babble. "Did a bunk?" He speaks as if Burgess were a ten-year-old classmate caught cheating at some game, albeit a game on the playing fields of Eton.

Yet it would be very wrong to end on a note of mere condemnation of this used and deluded man. Nicolson's diary entry ends on a note of great personal pain. He *is* in agony; he *is* ashamed. "During my dreams," Nicolson concludes, "his absurd face stares at me with drunken unseeing eyes."[45]

Some rough beast, born in Bloomsbury, had slouched all the way home.

Chapter 10

IN AMERICA

The Popular Front had transatlantic reach, built upon work begun during the twenties, not just in mass culture but also among the elite. The range was wide. In America, the *apparat* monitored the marriage of Sinclair Lewis and nurtured the myths of manhood and Bohemia spun by Ernest Hemingway. It influenced the glamour culture of Hollywood. It ran networks of influence in Washington. It reached into the Spanish Civil War.

We might begin with Sinclair Lewis in Austria. In years just after Lenin gave Münzenberg his mandate, Sinclair Lewis was the most famous *serious* American writer alive. His international standing in the mid-twenties is hard to overstate. *Main Street* had appeared in 1920; *Babbitt* in 1922; *Arrowsmith* in 1925. His satiric portrait of American philistinism triumphant, so very angry and so very persuasive had made him seem *the* truth-teller about our large flat land. It was a worldwide reputation was just waiting for Willi, and in 1926, Willi launched a carefully orchestrated effort to entice Sinclair Lewis into the fellow-traveling network. Its focus became his marriage.

The story begins that year in Vienna, where Dorothy Thompson, a compelling young preacher's daughter from upstate New York, was installed as the most rapidly rising star in American international journalism. There was something quite irresistible about Dorothy Thompson in 1926.[1] She was a very nervy young woman, brisk with a certain old-fashioned girl-reporter eagerness, lots of pizzazz. She had a drive to get to the bottom of every story, an urgent insistence upon *really* understanding events. But there was more. For one thing, Dorothy Thompson was quite exceptionally intelligent. She wrote with an innately worldly sense of style, far beyond the common run of journalism. The preacher's daughter was also a penetrating analyst of power, politics, and events.

On the night of Dorothy Thompson's thirty-third birthday, July 9, 1927, a number of influential friends arranged a festive dinner featuring some of the most interesting political society in Vienna. One important guest was Münzenberg's favorite aristocrat, Count Károlyi. The evening was to be capped by the presence of that tremendous celebrity, Mr. Sinclair Lewis.[2]

The occasion turned out to be only a so-so success. Sinclair Lewis did not especially shine that night, but neither did he turn drunk and abusive, as he often did. He seemed preoccupied, ruminating; he was even charming, though in a rather subdued way. At one point he took pen and paper to sketch a crude floor plan for his dream house, an as-yet undiscovered farmhouse on some as-yet unseen hill in Vermont. The sketch was passed around. People sighed, smiled. It was handed to Dorothy. She took it in. After dinner, Lewis maneuvered Dorothy into a quiet corner. In that moment alone, he leaned toward her and very quietly asked her to marry him.

Dorothy Thompson broke out laughing. "Why Mr. Lewis, I barely know you!"

Then she leaned back and gazed for a short silent time into the face of her future.

Dorothy Thompson and Sinclair Lewis came from roughly the same place in their culture and their era; seen from the outside, their marriage was a brilliant and irresistible natural fit. Lewis was, she wrote, "of my own blood, and in many ways of my own nature." Dorothy felt for Lewis that mixed admiration that journalists often feel for imaginative artists, and in her case that admiration helped carry her to love. She might not be awed by counselors and kings, but she was a little in awe of Lewis, by his tortured inwardness and somber power. She found him "stimulating to weariness," and the preacher's daughter added: "He is a very curious and demonic person, hard-drinking, blasphemous, possessed, I often think, of a devil."[3] Lewis meanwhile loved Thompson's fresh, forceful openness and her competence: he felt his depression lift a little in the presence of this wonderfully worldly country girl. He loved her energy; loved her mind; loved her love. It was not enough. Lewis was also an intractable alcoholic, one who felt a wide margin of loathing for anyone who could be so despicable as to love him.

Their liaison was the grand testing passion of both their lives. It was commanding and cruel. Its unhappiness was its heartbeat. It was abandoned only after years rendered numb and hopeless by Lewis's addiction. It was a tragic union.

In the eyes of Willi Münzenberg, the romance between these two shining lights was an incomparable opportunity for influence over American opinion. Münzenberg gave it top priority. Even before their marriage, in the first days of the romance, Willi personally traveled to Vienna to consult with his people and arrange a discreet meeting with the happy pair. Not that they grasped whom they'd met, of course.[4]

A propaganda tour of the USSR was promptly laid out for the lovers, a high-profile honeymoon before the fact. At exactly the same time, a winning and rather talented young American journalist named Vincent Sheean somehow materialized in their lives. Sheean was a fellow traveler mixed up in the Münzenberg operation. He was certainly an instrument of its manipulations of Lewis and Thompson, though the precise state of his innocence then or later is hard to gauge.[5] In any case both partners soon grew fond of Vincent, and Vincent became an eager acolyte to their love—

and a companion on their trip. He ended as a lifelong friend. After they both had died, he said goodbye with a rather good book about their marriage: *Dorothy and Red*.

Sheean may have been more or less innocent. Not so his girlfriend, who was a witting Comintern agent, and in deep. Her name was Rayna Prohme, and Rayna serves as another example of the link between the propaganda apparatus and the espionage system. She was a hot communist from Chicago, a real fire-eater, the recently divorced wife of the playwright Samson Raphaelson, the author of *The Jazz Singer,* and a man who would later play his own considerable role among the Hollywood fellow travelers.[6]

Rayna had worked for Willi and Gibarti as a propaganda agent in both Europe and China, sometimes with the love-struck Vincent at her side. What did Vincent know about Rayna's "special work"? That is not clear, but he certainly knew a fair amount. In 1927, at the same time that Vincent was shepherding Dorothy and Red through the USSR, Rayna was called "home" to Moscow in preparation for a very big new secret service assignment, slated to enter Comintern's school for covert action, there to be trained as a deep-cover penetration agent, a mole who would be dispatched back in the States. Rayna's step into the next circle of secrecy threw Vincent into despair. She was about to be supplied with a cover *life*. She would be assigned possibly a new name, a new existence. Who she was, what she said she believed, whom she said she loved—all these would be assigned lies. Where was intimacy, where was love, in the life of a deep-cover agent? How is one husband to a woman whose life is a lie?[7] It is plain that Rayna was in the process of rejecting Vincent and replacing life with him with her secret work.

Rayna did not live to complete her task. While Dorothy Thompson and Vincent were together in Moscow, Rayna was suddenly struck down by a cerebral hemorrhage and died after a few days of agony. Dorothy nursed the young woman through her passage to death; Vincent was at her side. The young man's despair became grief.

The *apparat* buried Rayna in Moscow with Dorothy Thompson walking beside Vincent in the little funeral procession. The hearse crawled through streets piled with snow while Vincent and Dorothy slowly walked behind. Walking with them was none other than Soong Chin'ling, or Madame Sun Yat-Sen, widow of the Chinese revolutionary. Madame Sun Yat-Sen was a Münzenberg and Comintern operative, one of their most important in the Far East.[8] She worked under full apparatus control. She was the prime patron behind Rayna's rise in the Soviet services.[9] Behind the freezing little cortege of walkers, Madame's vast limousine crept along, attentive and ready in its post-imperial grandeur.

Did Dorothy Thompson grasp the role of the Comintern in visit to Russia? Did she plumb the real nature of Rayna Prohme's career? Did she have any accurate sense of Vincent's role? Sheean reports that he told Dorothy the whole truth about Rayna as the girl lay dying in Moscow. I am skeptical about this claim. Dorothy wrote a long letter to Lewis at the time, describing Rayna's death and alluding to her talk with Vincent. The letter gets the real story quite wrong—so wrong that my guess is that Vincent's confession was to deliberately mislead her.[10]

There were a number of other ways in which the Moscow trip of 1927 did not go well. Dorothy Thompson only nibbled at the bait. The next year she produced a brisk, direct, remarkably well-written book called *The New Russia*. Though written in sympathetic tones, *The New Russia* quite relentlessly identifies the leading deficiencies of the Soviet system, not least of which she defines as a society riddled with a paranoid domestic spy system and the ubiquitous OGPU.[11] Just as Willi had foreseen, Thompson did indeed become the most important American antifascist journalist of her generation, but she also became a strong, well-informed anti-communist at a maddeningly early date.

The apparatus had only a little more success in its courtship of Lewis. He continued to be guided by Sheean, a committed fellow traveler. Yet Lewis never really became a reliable Stalinist after the manner of, let's say, Dashiell Hammett. Lewis dallied as a mere fellow traveler of the fellow travelers—though I fear it was petulance and drink, far more than honor or insight, that spared Sinclair Lewis the disgrace of Romain Rolland.

Lewis balked in his sullen way from the start. At the last minute before the 1927 tour, Lewis announced, typically, that he didn't feel like going. Who the hell needed Russia anyway? He'd come later, when he damn well felt like coming. Dorothy was disappointed, but just as typically she plunged ahead, curious and probing.

In Moscow, Münzenberg had laid on his best—even Theodore Dreiser was summoned from America to provide the visit with the desired literary charisma. Lewis joined the party three weeks late. A lavish great-man reception greeted him. The author of *Main Street* moved through Russia swimming in flattery, banquets, worshipful crowds, and promises of huge editions. Thompson's many letters to him before he arrived are wonderful, not only as records of life on the receiving end of this kind of propaganda operation, but also as love letters. Their tenderness feels fresh as this morning.[12] Thirteen years later the age of innocence was over. The Nazi-Soviet Pact had knocked away many a mask and Dorothy and Red's marriage was all but dead.

Deep in the winter of 1940, at the height of that alliance, Otto Katz arrived in New York in preparation for clandestine work in America. Five days later, Dorothy Thompson picked up the phone, telephoned the FBI, and asked to speak to an agent in charge of espionage. She then provided the Bureau with several of Otto's aliases, told them that she had met him on several occasions, that she knew him to be an agent of the NKVD, and noted especially that he had very close secret links with the Nazis and the German government. Three days after that, the Visa Division of the State Department prepared a memo as close to the detailed truth about Otto as any official American document I have found.[13]

Its final paragraph is particularly impressive. "According to the information given by an unnamed but reliable source, this person was once known in California as Breda. He has been at various times an international spy, agent of the Soviet government, member of the Gapayu [*sic*], acted as a go-between for General von

Bredow, also was in the Reichswehr Intelligence Service and worked at one time for the French Government *as well as for the Nazi Government. He is said to know the inside story of the Brown House"* (my emphasis).[14]

Somebody was on to something very big.

Where on earth did Dorothy Thompson pick up this uncannily accurate information? I cannot say. Wherever she learned her secrets, they were top drawer, and they went straight to the White House, where A. A. Berle, the assistant to Roosevelt who dealt with the matter, ended his analysis of the material before him with an annoyed brush-off Though she was at this moment the foremost antifascist journalist in English, Dorothy Thompson was far from liked in the Roosevelt administration.[15]

So despite Thompson's clear warning, Otto Katz was in New York, moving unhindered through most of the Soviet Pact with Hitler. During this time his close friends Lillian Hellman and Dashiell Hammett were central to creating the Stalinoid daily paper *P.M.*[16] Otto was also in New York when France was invaded, and when Willi Münzenberg met his end, probably at the hands of the NKVD. By that time Willi had broken with Stalin, and was a marked man. Otto has been repeatedly accused of having been involved in Willi's death. That he played some role in Willi's *fall* is clear: Katz himself told Klement Gottwald that he had, in his own delicate phrase, "aided in the struggle against [Münzenberg]."[17] Does that mean he helped organize the murder from that transatlantic distance? It is possible, but Otto Katz's exact role in the death of Willi Münzenberg remains mysterious.

***

But Sinclair Lewis and Dorothy Thompson were far from being the only high profile American targets among writers, journalists, and in Hollywood. It is an instructive exercise in cultural history to make a list of all the people in or near Ernest Hemingway's circle in Paris during the 1920s who later ended either in or very near the Soviet secret services. The roster turns out to be impressively long. There was Dos Passos himself, along with Donald Ogden Stewart, and their great pal, John Howard Lawson. But there were also many more. One of the most interesting of Hemingway's chums from those days of *The Sun Also Rises* was a half-talented but hard-drinking Midwesterner, a would-be writer endowed with much more hope than future, named John Herrmann. And at John Herrmann's side was his more gifted girlfriend and later wife, Josephine Herbst.

Sinclair Lewis may have been famous, but the people around Ernest Hemingway condescended to him as a famous middlebrow. Lewis never became a member in good standing of the modernist Bohemian elite, the rising twenties' generation of John Dos Passos and Ernest Hemingway. Yet they too were soon on Willi's list. The story of their links to the Soviet services makes a more complex tale than the sad story of Dorothy and Red.

It starts among the ambulance drivers in the First World War. During the two years before Woodrow Wilson brought the United States into the war, gung-ho young Americans hungry for real life were obliged, because of American neutrality, to settle for being mere non-combatants in what seemed to them *the* great event of their lives. The European battlefield was the only place that mattered. Yet for young Americans, the only path to the battlefield turned out to be something like driving an ambulance. And so it was that a generation of young men, including young writers, drove ambulances: Dos Passos, Hemingway, E. E. Cummings, and John Howard Lawson all became ambulance drivers, tooling and lurching across the torn fields of France in their Model A or Citröen vans, just so they could *be* there.

The war meant real life, of course, but it also meant Europe—and of course the relation to Europe is a factor in the cultural personality of any American. The war offered these young Americans *their* Europe, and their Europe was not the Europe of Henry James, a culture rendered conscious and beautiful by history, but a Europe of catastrophe and Bohemia, one that was a reprimand to that "civilized" order to which James, as the great expatriate, had consecrated his life.

They made up the generation born around 1895. The ambulance drivers emerged, almost every one of them, from the ample American middle and upper-middle class, with its etiquette books; its mahogany banisters, its Persian carpets; its potted palms and urns of polished brass; its libraries with uniform editions of Tennyson and Henry Wadsworth Longfellow and ... Henry James. Goodbye to all that.

The new generation went "over there" looking for adventure, for authenticity, for release from provincialism. They left Europe seeing themselves as cynicism's truth-tellers, the bearers of disillusion's mission, the guys who would salvage *real* life, *real* feeling from all the lies—the bourgeois lies—that had been discredited in the trenches.

The ambulance drivers did not create that new modernist life. They discovered it, mainly through other, older Americans in Europe such as Ezra Pound, T. S. Eliot, and Gertrude Stein. The generation of 1895 was a second generation. It arrived in uniform and acquired their modernism glancing in wonder through flickering light at the Picassos and Matisses that hung from floor to ceiling on Gertrude Stein's walls on the rue de Fleurus. Once they got the feel of it, they turned "the modern" into the voice of a new generation, teasing it out of the salons. They made modernism famous.

It is difficult today to recall that their modernism was also once fresh as the morning. It is difficult to recall that the *style* of Ernest Hemingway, now so often and so monotonously denounced, even while it is monotonously imitated, once swept through the mind of a generation like a revelation, proclaiming a new and better way to live, a new and better way to feel, a new and better way to tell the truth. It broke on American ears as an *ethical* voice; it had moral power, a new authenticity. From it Hemingway summoned up the myth of a Bohemian heroism and he made himself the most famous writer in English of the twentieth century. In *Manhattan Transfer* Dos Passos heard the nasal music of American talk and captured it with a dry sharp exactitude, giving voice to the civilization of the streets and rooming houses, the subways and the road, a very different "civilization" to which Henry James tried to advance.

Though they came to Europe at the same time, Hemingway and Dos Passos did not actually meet until 1924. By that time the apparatus was aware of them both, and it was engaged in an effort, metaphorically speaking, to take possession of all that was represented by the *symbolism* of these two men's lives.

They met in Paris, and at first the two young lions hit it off wonderfully. Sons of the same world; they understood each other at once. Pals. Brothers. They drank to it. Another pal was Donald Ogden Stewart, who in 1924 was still a classic twenties' "sophisticate," Cole Porter all the way, master of the high life, toastmaster general. Donald Ogden Stewart really was quite a good friend of Cole Porter, along with the "socialites" Gerald and Sara Murphy, and Dos Passos used to join Stewart and Hemingway for glorious springtimes at the Murphys' villa on the Riviera. Meanwhile Picasso was dropping by to visit every afternoon. It was vanguard heaven. Dos Passos regularly wrote home all about it to his other pal, John Howard Lawson.

With a much less high profile, John Herrmann and Josephine Herbst were likewise part of this circle. They were not in heaven, however. As the glamour faded and time wore them down, Herrmann became a spy, and Herbst a Stalinist propagandist.[18] In the late twenties, Donald Ogden Stewart, who later became a leading Hollywood Stalinist, had not yet met Ella Winter, a key Comintern propagandist, and Lincoln Steffens's wife. But Hemingway had met her. A 1926 note from Hemingway to Ezra Pound mentions meeting Ella Winter. The note is typical, and nasty: "You heard of course of Steffens' marriage to a 19 year old Bloomsbury kike intellectual. Last chapter in the book of revolution."[19]

Everybody was getting acquainted.

***

By 1927, the Sacco-Vanzetti case was making the propaganda operation in New York a vehicle for worldwide attention. Certain other efforts were targeted strictly on elite culture. One example was the vanguard of the New York theater, especially a small organization known as the New Playwrights' Theater.[20]

New Playwrights' Theater was a modernist enterprise organized by John Howard Lawson, and its star author was Lawson's fellow ambulance-driver John Dos Passos. Dos Passos was at first enchanted by the offer of work in the theater; he suffered from the novelist's classically unsatisfied itch for the stage. Besides, the little theater in the Village was to be "radical": That is, it would have the "expressionist" look of Americanized Piscator. And of course its politics would be the politics of the Revolution.

Lawson, Dos Passos, and the others at New Playwrights' Theater were unobtrusively supervised throughout the enterprise by the Mutt and Jeff of the American Communist party, two contriving legmen for the *apparat* named V. J. Jerome and Alexander Trachtenberg.[21] Both of these men were *apparatchiki* who took their cues from whichever of Münzenberg's Hungarian mafiosi happened then to be resident in New York.

In any case, the true purpose of the New Playwrights' Theater appears to have been to help "Stalinize" the New York vanguard while assisting its founders, above all John Howard Lawson and Lawson's political sidekick, Frances Faragoh, make their move to Hollywood. New Playwrights' staged two "expressionist" plays by Dos Passos: *The Moon Is a Gong*, and *Airways, Inc.* The plays had a certain elite critical success, just enough to launch Lawson and Faragoh, in 1928 and 1929, in the film industry, where they would embark upon their *real* life's work, which was neither drama nor film, but organizing Stalinist opinion in the American entertainment industry. It was a big move for which the odd little theater in Greenwich Village played was a stepping stone. And it left behind a little mystery.

A fourth partner at New Playwrights' Theater had been a curious fellow with the no less curious name of Em Jo Basshe. Em Jo Basshe is a cipher in the history of theater, but he is of great interest to us, because through his fate we can read the intensity of international secret service interest focused on the small avant-garde cultural scene in which he lived and moved.

Documents in the National Archives of the United States disclose a very peculiar tale about Em Jo.[22] In 1931, two years after Lawson and Faragoh had gone on to Hollywood, British intelligence informed the Americans that during the time of the New Playwrights' Theater and after it, Em Jo Basshe had been a trained and fully witting Comintern agent in place. The information from the British suggests that Em Jo worked in America under the cover of a false identity. A great deal is made of his close association with Willi Münzenberg and Gibarti. The memos assert that Basshe had worked in New York with Gibarti, and that in 1931 he had gone to Europe, there to meet with Gibarti and Münzenberg, to be given his reward and be promoted to a new secret service assignment by them. The British memos explicitly link Basshe to the Berlin apparatus, as well as to Münzenberg and Gibarti personally. They report on Em Jo's movements, conversations, and plans. All the right names are used. The entire account is exceptionally plausible.

But is it true? When I first came across these documents in Washington, the adrenalin surged. Here it was at last—*the* link between the *apparat* and the early Hollywood networks. I seemed to have stumbled by chance onto a forgotten but once smoking gun. Its burnt powder, though half a century old, was still visible on the chamber. Em Jo Basshe: *the* witting agent in the New York theater! Em Jo Basshe. Once said aloud, the name is hard to forget. So this invisible man was Moscow's eye! And not an obvious Stalinist like John Howard Lawson, as everyone supposed.

It was an exciting find. It sent me on a new wave of research. And this research uncovered ... nothing but difficulties.[23]

I was unable to find anything anywhere else that supported the claims of the British dossier in any way. In fact, everything else *seemed* to contradict them, and contradict them in an oddly suspicious fashion.

The Em Jo Basshe I unearthed elsewhere gave every appearance of having been a classic emigrant. These accounts show an Em Jo brought to America at the unconspiratorial age of 12, part of the vast wave of Eastern European Jewry coming to America from Vilna and the Pale just before the 1914 war. The British information contradicts this story by asserting that Em Jo "gives himself out as the son of David Jochelman," an important hard-left Polish Zionist, who lived and worked in London, a protégé of none other than Maxim Litvinov, Stalin's commissar of foreign affairs, and also serving as an "Official Advisor" to the Bolshevik mission run in London by Leonid Krassin. As Jochelman's son, Em Jo would therefore have been raised in London. His position under the protection of Willi and the Comintern would be traceable to his very elevated Bolshevik connections. He would have come to America not as a child but as an adult, and possibly illegally. In any case the British presented him to State as a ranking agent of a foreign power: "definite information has been received by our friends here" [N.B. "our friends" is a standard euphemism for undercover informants] "that the Central Committee of the Workers' International Relief has recently created an International Cultural Department under the leadership of Em Jo Basshe."[24] Under the leadership of Em Jo Basshe! Nothing less.

Well . . . perhaps. Admittedly, I've found no traces of Em Jo's childhood in New York—though certainly everyone *took* him for an American. A British background is mentioned nowhere. The shadow I find passing through the record is that of a stage-struck emigrant kid beginning his career as an eager but unimpressive hanger-on at Eugene O'Neill's Provincetown Playhouse, both on Cape Cod and later in the Village, where he began to work as a stagehand at the age of 19. Em Jo wanted to be a playwright. He wrote several hard-left expressionist plays, mainly about the oppression of blacks. The critics, I gather, were bored; Alexander Woolcott described one of Em Jo's works as a "tragedy in fourteen intermissions."[25] But at least the plays had politics *à la mode*, and that got Em Jo into New Playwrights'. Not that he was a leading force at New Playwrights'. In fact it seems he was mainly used and pushed around.

Add to this John Dos Passos's version of the story. Dos Passos knew Em Jo well, and left the most complete portrait I know in *Most Likely to Succeed,* a poorly conceived but generally accurate autobiographical novel about these events, written well after Dos Passos had become a committed anti-communist.[26] Dos Passos depicts Basshe as the least hardline of the entire group around John Howard Lawson, an earnest, half-talented *schmoozer,* a hanger-out with the Yiddish theater at the Cafe Royale, and in the end a wipe-out as an artist and as a man, a pitiable ruin.

Very much to our point, Dos Passos asserts (novelistically, of course) that when New Playwrights' disbanded, Em Jo argued and broke with his friends Faragoh and Lawson—broke over the Stalinism of their politics. For this reason, when Faragoh and Lawson graduated to Hollywood, Dos Passos shows Em Jo left behind, iced out of the bonanza that had always been Lawson and Faragoh's actual goal. Bereft of Party support, Em Jo turned into a classic and none-too-beautiful loser, slugging back yet another glass of ever-cheaper booze, muttering about how he'd been done in by his old pals, those bastard Stalinists getting rich and famous in Tinseltown.

Now, could the man described by Dos Passos *also* be the fully trained, monitored, and highly placed secret agent described by the British? Conceivably. Mere drunkenness, failure, and an *apparent* break with Stalinism do not necessarily prove otherwise. Guy Burgess was also a drunk and a failure, and he too claimed (now and then) to have turned his back on Stalin. Perhaps Em Jo was the Guy Burgess of the Stage Delicatessen. And yet ...

The total lack of corroborating evidence is troubling. It is all the more troubling when one reflects that the man who supplied this information to the Americans was almost certainly Guy Liddell.[27]

Here may be a key. Suppose Em Jo was not a Soviet agent and never had been. Suppose his break with Stalinism was the real thing. That would have made Em Jo a potentially dangerous man. He might talk, "blow the gaff," as Blunt put it. He would need to be discredited. And maybe scared a little.

How? Well, since we are supposing, suppose a Soviet agent in British Intelligence were to supply the Americans with sterling information naming Em Jo Basshe as a Soviet agent *and* possibly a deportable alien. *That* would make the Americans treat Em Jo's stories with the contempt they deserved. Let the threat of deportation make him watch his mouth.

This is only a hypothesis, I admit. But it is a hypothesis with the merit of fitting all the known facts. On the other hand, Em Jo may really have been all the British said he was.

In any case, he died an early death, seedy, bypassed, and alone. He did not live to see the war.

Meanwhile, Lawson and Faragoh had gone on to Hollywood, preparing to develop the networks of fellow travelers that would later, during the era of the Hollywood Ten, become the objects of worldwide controversy.[28]

The naive sometimes ask why the apparatus took such elaborate pains to set up the Stalinist networks in Hollywood. If propaganda was the purpose, surely it failed: Metro-Goldwyn-Mayer was manifestly not producing Soviet propaganda in 1938. This is to miss the point. Of course Willi and Otto did not think they could call the shots at Warner Brothers. On the contrary, they would never have *permitted* their Hollywood people to give away the game by seeking influence in such a stupidly obvious way. Half a century later, sitting with me over tea in Munich, Babette Gross's voice went tight repeating the litany. You do *not* endorse Stalin. You do *not* call yourself a Communist. You do *not* declare your love for the regime. You do *not* call on people to support the Soviets. Ever. Under any circumstances.

You claim to be an independent-minded idealist. You don't really understand politics, but you think the little guy is getting a lousy break. You believe in open-mindedness. You are shocked, frightened by what is going on right here in our own country. You are frightened by the racism, by the oppression of the workingman.

You think the Russians are trying a great human experiment, and you hope it works. You believe in peace. You yearn for international understanding. You hate fascism. You think the capitalist system is corrupt.

You say it over and over and over again. And you say nothing, *nothing* more. *"Ja, Ja,"* she ended wearily. "You say all of that."

"Columbus discovered America," Otto Katz used to say. "But I discovered Hollywood." The development of the Hollywood networks was directed at first from Münzenberg's Berlin and Paris offices. In New York, Gibarti's men V. J. Jerome and Alexander Trachtenberg had been present at the creation of Lawson and Faragoh's film careers and worked closely with them on the Coast as well.[29] Otto visited Hollywood for what may or may not have been the first time in March 1935, under an incognito. His mission was to consolidate and redirect the fellow-traveling networks established by the circle around Lawson and Faragoh, retooling them in anticipation of the Popular Front. His alias was "Rudolph Breda,"[30] and he adopted the pose of an antifascist fighter who'd escaped to tell the tale of risking his life against the Gestapo. (In fact, I have found no evidence that Otto himself was in Germany at any time between 1933 and 1939.) Otto had correctly assumed that Hollywood would be a sucker for an aristocrat. Therefore the freedom fighter "Herr Breda" arrived with an aristocrat in tow: One Prince Hubertus zu und von Lowenstein. His real name.

Otto and the Prince moved Hollywood to tears, and to use its own language, "captured its heart." Of course a number of people in town understood quite well that "Herr Breda" was a fraud, and not only Faragoh and Lawson. There were also numerous German refugees such as Salka Viertel who had known the real Otto perfectly well back in Berlin. They kept quiet. "Herr Breda" was lying, but it was a noble lie, an antifascist lie. Wasn't it?[31]

Under Otto's direction, a new front organization known as the Hollywood Anti-Nazi League was created.[32] This became the prime facade for Popular Front activity in the film colony. To kick it off, Hollywood at its most glittering gathered to hear Herr Breda's terrible tale. It offered Otto his great moment as the actor Piscator had never let him be. After first assembling a very grand dinner party for the Hollywood elite in honor of "Breda," a vast fund-raising testimonial dinner was planned, a white-tie, $100-a-plate benefit for German refugees. The guests included the Roman Catholic Archbishop of Los Angeles. The master of ceremonies was Donald Ogden Stewart. Stewart describes "Breda" at these social occasions as "irresistibly intelligent and sincere [*sic*], " adding with a typical flick of his antic self-deprecation, "the champagne was very good, too."[33]

Herr Breda began the big testimonial dinner by genuflecting before the Archbishop of Los Angeles and kissing the Fisherman's Ring. Then he rose to speak.

He spoke about the horror going on in Germany. He recounted his (fictitious) struggles against the Gestapo—the same Gestapo with which Dorothy Thompson believed Otto was really in cooperative contact. He told about the real struggles of his friends, his comrades, against Nazism. He wrapped some terrible truths in some terrible lies.

"It was one of the happiest evenings of my life," Stewart wrote. "Herr Breda gave his moving description of the Nazi Terror, the details of which he had been able to collect only by repeatedly risking his own life. I was proud to be sitting beside him, proud to be on his side in the fight... Here was a man who had devoted his life untiringly and at great risk of death by torture to the principles I in my dress suit was just beginning to fight for."[34]

When Herr Breda sat down, Stewart, moved and touched by that edge of self-contempt that never left him, stepped forward ("I in my dress suit") and in a choked voice first asked, and then answered, the question in everyone's mind: "What can *I* do?"

Out came the checkbooks. Hollywood was going to found, and fund, its Anti-Nazi League. The idea was to consolidate the already well-developed Soviet networks in Hollywood, giving them new impetus in fundraising for the *apparat* and glamorizing the Popular Front. This effort would play its large role in American life and political attitudes for the next forty years.

For many years the Prince continued to act as Katz's man in the celebrity culture of both Hollywood and New York, enticing not only the stars, but leading lights among the German exiles as well. Like the Count and Countess Károlyi, like Wolfgang von und zu Putlitz, and the Princess Koudachova, Lowenstein was one of Stalin's aristocrats. He was a skilled and mendacious political "activist" who it seems right to suppose was very much under Katz's influence and control. Though in later years something about the Prince, perhaps his arrogance and indolence, seems to have palled. But at first grandeur of the Prince's title and the sublimity of his sentiments made a tremendous impression in Hollywood Even Thomas Mann succumbed.

When the pact and the war came at last, the "antifascist" pose of Katz and the Prince was not abandoned, but it became more overtly delicate. A new line had to be invented to promote the alliance with Hitler while protecting the old "antifascist" credentials. This took doing. Stalin, ran the claim, was "buying time," because he'd been betrayed by the democracies, which were the prime bad guys, menaces to "peace," which was suddenly again at the forefront of the antifascist agenda. The democracies were "warmongers," Germany and England were just imperialists tearing each other apart. Americans who wanted to help England during the Battle of Britain were falling for the Imperialist line. As for the countries like Finland and Eastern Poland invaded by Stalin, to notice their plight at all was to be a warmonger. Imperialist England, which was getting what was coming to it.

It was at this point that Thomas Mann woke up with an angry jolt. In the spring of 1940, Lowenstein and Katz were in New York, honing this complex new "antifascist" line. Mann's letter breaking with Lowenstein and cutting himself off from the sundry "leagues" and "committees" the Prince ran as fronts is a memorable and satisfying document in the literature of outrage.

Mann begins by frigidly noting a recent article written by the Prince, attacking British "imperialism" for defending its shipping against the Nazi attacks in the sea war. He next dissociates himself from its sentiments in a few harsh and unmodulated sentences.

The Prince's position is frontally attacked. Then he levels his weapon: "No Nazi—or Stalinist—agent in this country could have sown such evil propaganda against the democracies and the life-and-death struggle they are waging against the German regime, as you do." Next, Mann demands the instantaneous removal of his name from the masthead of an organization run by the Prince—an organization "whose general secretary you are for life, it seems." He then ends: "I regret so harsh an end to relations which for years have been carried on so pleasantly, but we live in a world civil war in which everyone must choose sides, and you have chosen yours."[35]

The harsh flat fire of this letter bears testimony to Mann's political rectitude. It also bears witness to the power of the Popular Front as the Big Lie. What Thomas Mann saw with such clarity in 1940 was something not even Thomas Mann had seen in 1935.

The pact with Hitler leaves ample grounds for doubting the "sincerity" of such pawns in the Hollywood network as Stewart and Parker, Hellman and Hammett.[36] While innocents in the rank and file defected in numbers, not one officer of the League defected. Parker and Stewart and Hellman and Hammett all stayed in place, self-righteous as always, never raising a single word of public criticism or even opting for a decent silence.

With the Pact, the Hollywood Anti-Nazi League immediately changed its name to the "Hollywood League for Democratic Action," defending the pact, applauding the joint Soviet-German invasion of Poland., celebrating the start of the Second World War." In the name of being "anti-war." When Stalin invaded Finland, Lillian Hellman promptly attacked the Finns. "I don't believe in that fine, loveable little Republic of Finland that everybody gets so weepy about. I've been there, and it looks like a pro-Nazi little republic to me." (Incidentally, there is no evidence that Lillian Hellman visited Finland at any point in her lifetime.)[37] Meanwhile, at the height of the Battle of Britain, the Hollywood Stalinists wanted the English to know that the Yanks were *not* coming. In fact, the committee was called The-Yanks-Are-Not-Coming Committee. Dashiell Hammett was its leading light.[38]

Hollywood Stalinism is ideally illustrated in the marriage of Ernest Hemingway's friend Donald Ogden Stewart to Ella Winter.

Very soon after the Hollywood Anti-Nazi League was founded, Dorothy Parker and Donald Ogden Stewart were swept up to San Francisco for a conference sponsored by the League of American Writers, the literary front of the Party.

The San Francisco meeting was held on behalf of Harry Bridges, the Stalinist leader of the San Francisco longshoremen. (Bridges was important to the Soviets because through his control of the San Francisco docks, he was able to choke off, or permit, American response to a Pacific War, whatever Stalin wanted.[39]) Linked both to the Münzenberg operation and the military *apparat;* Bridges was part of contingency plans for sabotaging American action in the Pacific not to Stalin's liking. The Central Party Archives have since shown that Bridges operated under full Soviet control.[40] The San Francisco meeting had nothing to do with writers at all, but it was exciting stuff for the visiting Hollywoodians.[41]

On the platform they were introduced to the crowd by Ella Winter—"our beloved Ella" as she was called. Parker and Stewart were, Ella announced, people who with just a few quips "can help us more than a thousand jargon-filled pamphlets."[42] Then came a revealing moment. Some party drudge, missing the beat of the Popular Front, rose to denounce the Hollywood wits as rich party-givers, dilettantes.

Stewart sat on the platform, blushing with his all-too-familiar shame. "Our beloved Ella," on the other hand, was not going to sit idly by while this dreary little nit from nowhere smeared her Hollywood luminaries. The comrade had spoken out of turn. Winter reeled on him, and Stewart was treated to an on-the-spot display of "our beloved Ella's" legendary powers of verbal sadism. When the tongue-lashing was complete, the errant comrade was mute and quivering. Sitting gaped-mouthed on the platform, Stewart had heard Ella rip up a man who despised him almost as much as he despised himself. The screenwriter felt something turn over in his heart. Stewart and Winter were married soon after.

As Stewart's wife, Ella Winter would direct his more or less guileless footsteps down the byways of the *apparat* until he died in 1980, just as she previously had guided the steps of Lincoln Steffens.

For Ella's first marriage had been to Lincoln Steffens. As mentioned earlier, Ella had met the famous American muckraker and begun her affair with him at the Paris Peace Conference in 1919, where she was serving as secretary to Felix Frankfurter, a position for which her professor at the London School of Economics, Harold Laski, had recommended her. She met Steffens delivering him an invitation to dinner with the future justice of the Supreme Court. It is easy to see why Steffens fell for her. Photographs of the epoch show a smoldering, square-jawed, sexy girl with lots of warmth and intelligence in the "flashing" eyes that made Stewart fall in love. Ella had married Steffens when she became pregnant with their son—Pete Steffens—and as a matter of principle, they were divorced very shortly afterward, though they lived together until Steffens died in August 1936.[43]

That death was wonderfully convenient. It freed Ella for the new Popular Front tactic, shifting away from the dreary muckraking literature of conscience to her new life as a propagandist in the glamour life.[44] She was the Münzenberg-woman. According to Louis Gibarti, Ella Winter was "one of the most trusted party agents for the West Coast."[45] She had worked closely with him and the Münzenberg propaganda apparatus from at least 1933, and probably earlier.[46] She had been a sympathizer since the Revolution, but up until a visit to the USSR in 1930, she had occasionally expressed a vagrant doubt about the Bolsheviks. By 1930, all doubts disappeared. Ella Winter became one of the most ardent and systematic defenders of the Stalinist tyranny in the United States, and she remained so to the end.

As Steffens's biographer rather delicately notes, once Ella Winter became a fellow traveler, she invariably "led" Steffens politically. She was his "instructed agent, his Joshua."[47] By the time Steffens died, Joshua had guided Steffens to a Stalinism no longer modified by any hint of critical thought, residual morality, or contact with reality. It was simply abject. When the Moscow Trials opened in the last weeks of his life, he proceeded mechanically to their defense, too tired and morally cowed to respond to even the most obvious and elementary challenges to their validity.[48]

It was only a few months after "Breda" left Hollywood, and even fewer after Steffens's death that "our beloved Ella" began her romance with Hemingway's companion, and doyen of Hollywood chic, Donald Ogden Stewart.

But not everyone had such a high profile. But let us pick up the second strand from Hemingway's circle, the one left by John Herrmann, and his wife, Otto Katz's hostess, Josephine Herbst. This is the thread that runs from Montparnasse to Washington. Josephine Herbst and John Herrmann were born into that generation of 1905 for which the great literary star was Hemingway, and it was on Hemingway that the mystique of both their lives was to a large degree focused. Like him they were classic Midwesterners, born Protestant and in small towns, educated in the land-grant universities. Like him they responded to the discovery of some special talent within them by being drawn east, east to New York, east above all to Europe, as if to their destiny. They missed the European war, but both went to Germany after the armistice, where they became, separately, classic postwar bohemians and modernists. John dabbled in art history, dabbled in literature. Nietzsche was his god. He took to carrying a copy of Gertrude Stein's *Three Lives* as a kind of badge. He wanted people to know that he was part of the new consciousness. Needless to add, he was writing a novel.

Josie was also part of the new consciousness (she'd had a love affair with Maxwell Anderson), and she too was writing a novel. It was called *The Unmarried*. After Germany, Herrmann and Herbst traveled on separate paths to Paris, where John was introduced to Ernest Hemingway by Ford Madox Ford. Hemingway and Herrmann hit it off right away, another natural fit. John became a hard-drinking member of the circle that would soon be celebrated in *The Sun Also Rises*.[49]

The iconography of *The Sun Also Rises* is likewise what makes John's first meeting with Josie seem to us now picture perfect. They were introduced at the Cafe Dôme, where John sat behind a high stack of saucers, curing a hangover by becoming, once again, interestingly drunk. The two drank together. They soon discovered that they too were a natural fit. They understood each other. They thought alike, and they admired alike. Hemingway's star was rising, and it seemed to them to be their star. Besides, John and Josie really liked each other. Enough to go back to John's apartment together.

John's room seemed to Josie another perfect setting for a kindred spirit. He kept a death mask of Nietzsche, and "like a private shrine" a copy of *Ecce Homo.* Love came quickly. Josie started to call John her "beautiful boy," and John thought he'd at last found the woman who understood. They slept together, drank together, knew everybody together. Soon they left Paris together to set up in a Breton fishing village where they could write together, the ideal advanced young American couple of their time, smack in the middle of their fantasy.[50]

By 1926, they decided the time had come really to begin. Really, seriously begin; take on the big world and conquer what they'd left behind. They made the exile's return, and went back to New York.

The link between modernism and political radicalism which in 1927 felt so natural to the likes of John and Josie has long since grown obscure. Many of the founding American modernists—Eliot, Pound, and Stein—were on the right, if eccentrically so. And by the mid-thirties, Stalinist apologists were having trouble hiding their system's inveterate philistinism and loathing of genuine modernist (or indeed any) esthetics. Finally, the modernist esthetic was promoted postwar above all by the so-called "new critics" in American departments of literature. With some exceptions the "new critics" were not very sympathetic to the hard left. They tended to be "apolitical," with a liberal-to-centrist drift, though their numbers also included a fair number of rightists.

But in 1926, the prevailing tone was very different. Among the generation of kids that included John Herrmann and Josephine Herbst, the link between Bohemian modernism and a general left-ism called "radicalism" seemed to be two versions of one thing, like breathing in and breathing out.

Radek and Willi clearly grasped that to organize the elite meant organizing the assumption that artistic and political radicalism were really the same thing. In the middle-class democracies, this notion had some shaky validity. In actual Stalinist practice, of course, it had none at all. Still, the point of efforts like New Playwrights', and of the general ferment seeking to "politicize" New York and Parisian literary culture, was to make this weak-minded assumption seem valid. Herbst and Herrmann's return to New York coincided precisely with the apparatus deciding to take a direct hand in that cultural life, and they were both soon instruments of the effort, classic literary second-raters put on the map by the propaganda apparatus, letterhead celebrities.

Shortly afterward, the Comintern decided to clinch its hold on the cultural front with a vast writers' congress. It was to be held in Russia itself, and it would serve two political ends. The first goal was European: to co-opt the fashions in modernism then at their height. The second goal was more strictly Soviet: to consolidate Stalin's grip on Russian cultural life. In Europe the thing was surrealism, which was to be Sovietized under the leadership of the surrealist seer Louis Aragon, guided at all times by his wife Elsa Triolet, who like Koudachova and Moura Budberg, was another "lady of the Kremlin."[51]

Aragon and Triolet's assumption of their lifelong appointed place on top of left-wing French cultural life dates from the Kharkov Writers' Conference. They stepped into their roles at these festivities. On the weeklong train crawl from Moscow to Kharkov, Aragon and Triolet were constant companions of Fadeev, who had just taken a giant step in Soviet power by being asked to head the Congress. For decades to come, right up until the time, after Khrushchev's secret speech of 1956, when Fadeev killed himself, the sweet political fortunes of Triolet and Aragon would be tied to Fadeev's power.

Two Americans who were eager delegates to Kharkov were John Herrmann and Josephine Herbst, and at Kharkov, Herrmann and

Herbst were drawn into the company of the German delegation, which was run by one of Münzenberg's close associates, a Teutonic propagandist named Ludwig Renn.[52] The couple's rapid rise in the apparatus following Kharkov may well be attributable to the good impression they made on this very influential member of Münzenberg's operation in Berlin. In any case, Herrmann and Herbst left Kharkov not just committed Stalinists, but Stalinists whose names and hopes were known in the more senior reaches of the apparatus. Back in New York, they were soon admitted to the inner circles of innocence.

This worked wonders for their reputations. The names of Josephine Herbst and John Herrmann were suddenly being mentioned in the same breath with Theodore Dreiser; both were accepted as clients by the literary agent Maxim Lieber, who was also an agent in another sense, and who numbered among his clients none other than Otto Katz.[53]

Simultaneously, Herbst and Herrmann began to be gently primed for covert work. Josie was now regularly used by the Party and its fronts as a journalist. Probably to guard her appearance of independence, she does not seem to have actually joined the Party, though she may have been a secret member. John did join, and became increasingly active as a Party organizer. By 1934 the couple was introduced, in New York, to Münzenberg himself, probably by Gibarti. She was also in regular contact with Hede Massing working under Hede's cover as an "antifascist journalist." It appears it was also around this time, perhaps shortly afterward in Europe, that she made the acquaintance of Otto Katz.[54] Shortly after meeting with Münzenberg and Gibarti, Josie was dispatched to Berlin on a journalistic project which also led her to make covert contacts with the Münzenberg underground, contacts certainly authorized and guided by the Paris office, to which she returned months later. By this time, 1935, they were well known to Otto Katz. It was at this same time that the *apparat* began entrusting John with serious "special work": his work in espionage.[55]

Meanwhile, love and art in all their promise were coming unraveled for John and Josie. Like so many the Cambridge spies,

STEPHEN KOCH

John Herrmann was an alcoholic. He was also rapidly developing
into an obvious failure. He had no meaningful position in the literary world. His entire claim to such a position was one poorly published book and his friendship with Ernest Hemingway. Hemingway,
meanwhile, did not take John seriously. It's true, he liked to fish
and drink with Herrmann: "There are no rummies" Hemingway
wrote, "better than John."[56] But believe in Rummy John as a *writer?*
Come, come.

Meanwhile, the force driving Josephine Herbst seems to have
been a kind of churning ferocity. Personally, Herbst could be quite
a nasty item: domineering, abusive, and foul-mouthed.[57] Yet Herbst's
archives do reveal a woman riddled with a wish for tenderness,
though it was tenderness mingled, lifelong, with anger. She was all
need, and as such she habitually saw herself as cheated: cheated in
feeling, cheated in sex, cheated in life.

In 1932 all this—Josie's angry dilemma, John's failure, the role
of both of the apparatus—came to crisis during a stay at the artist's
colony at Yaddo.

During her residency at the famous colony, Josie met a strong,
solid, beautiful, intensely seductive painter named Marion Greenwood, a woman who seems to have habitually defined her very real
force of personality primarily in sexual terms. Marion immediately
sensed the writer's vulnerability and need; it didn't take her much
longer to discover the probably quite simple combination that un-
locked Herbst's homosexuality. Marion Greenwood introduced Josie
to a level of erotic pleasure and hope that she had not found either
in her promiscuity or her life with John. With Marion, Josie let herself know the full gratification of surrender.

This wave carried Josie to the end of her marriage—and then
to rejection by Marion, too. In rather sweet-sounding reversion to
Utopian type, the threesome, John and Marion and Josie all together,
decided to spend a long idyll, getting to know and love each other
in Mexico. South of the border, they would learn to be free and
equal, and love one another, all three. (Mexico, incidentally, was
rapidly becoming a Great Good Place for American radicals and
for the Comintern *apparat* in general, and the tendency would come

to a political climax during the Second World War.) The three Americans went to a little town called Taxco, and there in Taxco the capacity of the human triangle to stand up under sexual strain was tested for the trillionth time. For the trillionth time, it failed. As the weeks passed, everybody tried hard to *sound* free, *sound* loving. The sound grew more and more hollow. John left first, leaving Josie with Marion. Then a perplexed and pained Josie found that her soulful clinging to Marion was getting more and more on Marion's nerves. Things were growing a little unlovely. Josephine headed north, trying to evade the shrug-off that was plainly not far away as Marion turned icy, then turned her back on Josie. She was going, she said, "back to men."[58]

When he left Mexico, John Herrmann had fled back into what he called "his work." This was no longer his work as a writer. His work as a writer was nowhere. Whom the gods have destroyed with promise, they next make spies. Herrmann was following an American version of Guy Burgess's path.

His new work was what the Party called "special work," required a move to Washington, working with Harold Ware. John had first met Hal Ware before the Mexican interlude, when they worked together organizing farmers in the Midwest. Now he would work for Hal recruiting and running networks for agents of influence and espionage in the Washington establishment, work that would involve Alger Hiss, and in an adjacent apparatus, Noel Field.[59]

It takes time for marriages to end. When she too came home from Mexico, in spite of what had happened, Josephine Herbst's marriage was both over and not over at all. It was finished, and yet the hope and dream persisted, marked everywhere by all the pathos of the death of faith. Josie was not through with John, not through being angry with him, and not through needing him. She was often in Washington, often with him in the sweltering heat and wretchedness in his one-room apartment on New Hampshire Avenue. And there Josie was, generally speaking, perfectly aware of what her John's "work" really was.

It must be added that Josephine Herbst was sufficiently trusted in this situation to be allowed that knowledge, in a way that neither

Melinda MacLean nor Eleanor Philby, for example, ever were. At the very least, Josephine Herbst had guilty knowledge of the Washington espionage operations. She knew about them and she fully approved. How witting was she? Quite. Certainly far more so than she ever publicly allowed.

There is no evidence that she herself was personally active in the Washington apparatus, or for that matter in any espionage apparatus apart from the propaganda assignments she undertook for Otto Katz, working as a "journalist" in Spain, in Berlin, and Latin America. There she was plainly working for the Comintern, and her work was giving satisfaction. Yet while she was trusted with the knowledge of John's work, I have seen no evidence either to prove or refute that Josephine Herbst was an agent in espionage in the same way that Herta Field and Priscilla Hiss were.

And yet, and yet: During the Second World War, a rather curious episode did take place.

After Pearl Harbor, Josie applied for and got a job working at the German desk of the newly formed American intelligence service in Washington. This is not in itself necessarily strange. Certainly Herbst was very well-informed on the subject of propaganda and Germany. It seems pretty clear that Herbst had worked for Münzenberg and Katz's propaganda efforts inside Germany and elsewhere, operating both publicly and using clandestine technique. In fact, Herbst was exceptionally well connected with some of the most important people in the field—Soviet agents whose work in this field she knew to have been of high importance. It was very much the sort of information the United States Intelligence Service might well have used in its own struggle with the Nazis.

Except that, curiously enough, no evidence indicates Josie told anyone about her previous history in this kind of work. There is no evidence that Josephine Herbst breathed a single syllable about her special knowledge; about her undercover propaganda work in Germany; about her acquaintance with some of the best-placed propaganda agents then at work; about her great knowledge of the entire antifascist movement. And nothing about her own former husband's work as an agent for Soviet espionage, in regular contact with senior American officials whom she could confidently assume were at that moment betraying their oath to the Constitution.

Her attitude toward the job was thus remote from candor. It was also short on goodwill. Herbst's main comment on the work in German propaganda by the American service was to jeer at its naiveté. This was no doubt in some ways appropriate: the people involved were surely a bunch of amateurs. Apart from herself, that is. This makes it all the more odd that Herbst did not offer to instruct them. *She* was in a position to bring some sophistication and insight to the work. One might wonder why she did not?

After a year of work handling confidential intelligence documents at the German desk of the fledgling American service, Josephine Herbst was at last spotted as the gross security risk she so manifestly was, and dismissed. The dismissal was based on far less information than I have outlined above, and it was followed by a public mini-scandal over the awful injustice being done to her.

In fact, there was no injustice at all. The silence of Josephine Herbst about her work for the apparatus suggests that she had no intention of being either particularly loyal or particularly useful in her service to American intelligence. Yet since she had no interest in actually being useful in the OCI, since she so vocally despised an effort she had no wish to assist, we may well ask why she was so very eager to work there—there and nowhere else? There is no coherent answer to these questions on record. Certainly, after she was asked to leave the American services, Josephine Herbst never again, in any other capacity whatever, performed a single act or gave a single hour to the American war effort against Hitler.

But of course, Herbst was not honest about her politics because Stalinism does not permit people to be honest about their politics. That flaw makes one resist growing sententious over her dilemma as a person. Yet it is a moving dilemma. Here is a gifted woman of her place and time, struggling, struggling hard, to live a life worthy of its promise; struggling hard to reach a destiny she hoped might be hers, a destiny of exceptional moral commitment and the life of art. And here is the failure of that effort.

She was desperately unhappy. Seven years before, Herbst had been in Washington for the awful endgame of the fated marriage that had begun so glamorously at the Cafe Dôme. Her biographer cites a letter written to John after the Mexican affair with Marion Greenwood, once she had returned to him and his work as a spy. It was written at 3:30 a.m. on a sweltering Washington night, and left for him on their kitchen table. Reading it, one can feel the heat pounding, feel the failure, feel the suffocating small hour, black and silent.

"I've just called up to find out the time after sitting & walking here & crying. You shouldn't have let me come back here to stay here all alone ... If I hadn't been let alone so many times like this ... I wouldn't have got into the state I've been in the last few months, the most unhappy woman alive. . . . You've been good to me these last few weeks and I love you more than anything else in the world. If I hadn't I would suffer all the time. But you've never bothered much for a long time to take pains making love to me or to call any part of me beautiful. You never really did that, until *she* did, and that's what's so painful."[60]

Alone in that Washington desolation, Josie had almost nobody to talk to. Yet there was one man who worked with John in his "special work" and who used to drop by the little apartment. They'd have coffee, and talk. He was a very intelligent literary fellow, though he had a rather mysterious Dostoyevskian manner and an odd, vaguely Germanic accent which many people mistook for foreign. Yet Josie found comfort talking to him. He was extremely well read; he instinctively understood a writer's mind. She confided at least a few of her troubles to him, and he listened gently. He was insightful, careful, good. He was really very decent, very kind.

It was a meeting that would mark the rest of her life, and in it a circle that began with Sinclair Lewis came complete. Josie's visitor called himself Karl, and Karl's real name was Whittaker Chambers.

Chapter 11

AN END TO INNOCENCE

O tto Katz founded the Hollywood Anti-Nazi League in March
1935.[1] A parallel event followed in Paris during the suffocating June of 1935, just before Dimitrov announced the
opening of the Popular Front, a grand parley of intellectual celebrities known as the World Congress in Defense of Culture,
which since it was held in a hall called the Salle Mutualité, has
come to be called the "Mutualité Congress." The Mutualité is one
of the most fmous and frequently written-about culture congresses
of the era, a carefully staged piece of intellectual theater, designed
to prepare the cultural elite for the Popular Front. Though it was
a culminating event in Münzenberg-style cultural politics, the
Mutualité was not Willi's show: he made a point of steering clear of
it. The actual powers organizing the front men on the podium were
Ilya Ehrenberg and Mikhail Koltsov, both Russians, both Soviet
propagandists, both closer to Stalin than Willi ever was, and neither
under Münzenberg's discipline. The Mutualité was also one of the
watershed events in the history of Russian literature. It was on this
occasion that two of Russia's greatest poets, Boris Pasternak and
Marina Tsvetaeva, met again after years of correspondence across

the wall of exile. It was also on this occasion that Isaac Babel made his first and last appearance in Europe. The Frenchmen who served as presiding officers of the Congress were and André Malraux and a very uncomfortable André Gide.[2]

Gide's part in the Mutualité Congress is of special interest. The strategy of the Popular Front required the adherence of the entire left wing of the French elite, which, in the tradition of Voltaire, was then as now especially responsive to the intellectual leadership of whoever happens to be the leading—usually "dissident"—man of letters in Paris. In 1935, that man was André Gide. No matter that Gide was a homosexual; no matter that he was a rich man and delighted to be one—very much the *grand bourgeois*. In 1935 Gide was *the* Frenchman on whose shoulders the mantle of Zola was draped. He was the conscience of Europe, the dean of unacknowledged legislators. And so the propaganda apparatus went after him. Relentlessly.

The story of the cat and mouse between the Kremlin and Gide is long, dodging, and delicate. It came to its mysterious crescendo in 1936, on the very threshold of the Terror, when Gide visited the USSR in the most widely touted great-man tour of them all. It ended with the author of *The Immoralist* on a dais near Stalin, delivering the funeral oration over the body of Maxim Gorky and then going home, where he stirred consternation and hysteria in the propaganda machine by writing an attack—to our eyes, a rather mild attack—attack on Soviet life: *Return to the U.S.S.R.*

One instrument in the apparatus's courtship of Gide was almost certainly a young man named Pierre Herbart. During our interview in Munich, Babette Gross told me that the apparatus had manipulated Gide through "various young men" gathered around the master. The suggestion was that, given Gide's homosexuality, these manipulations were somehow connected to that. But which young men? Babette Gross named no names; perhaps she had never known them. But it seems to me very probable that Pierre Herbart was one of the instruments in the game.

Gide's relation to Herbart long antedated his relation to the apparatus. He had first come upon the young Herbart gracing the entourage of his much-mistrusted archrival Jean Cocteau, the author of *Opium*. Pierre was himself seriously drug-addicted, leading the slack life of a handsome hanger-on in the circle of a rich homosexual celebrity. Meeting him, Gide instantly set out to rescue Pierre from what he viewed as the vacuous debauchery of Cocteau's addicted world. He may well have been (briefly) infatuated with Herbart himself. He once confessed to Maria van Rhysselberghe that Pierre had the body he most wished he might have had as his own.[3]

Whatever their sexual connection, Gide did rescue Herbart from the clutches of Cocteau. He paid for Pierre to get treatment in a detox clinic; he persuaded the youth to leave Cocteau's villa in the South of France and enter the more serious precincts of his own household in Paris.[4]

Inscribed all through the life of Pierre Herbart, one senses an insoluble agony over fatherhood. Pierre was himself very much a son of the bourgeoisie; one of his brothers became no less than a director of the Bank of France. But the Herbart brothers were *abandoned* sons of the bourgeoisie. Their father had deserted the family when Pierre was young. Pierre was later asked to identify the corpse of his father, who had been found dead in a ditch, a vagrant.[5]

So it is not surprising that Pierre's relation to Gide should have been less that of lover than adopted son. But there was more to Pierre's Oedipal task than that. In the 1920s Gide had a sexual encounter, once and once only, with the daughter of Maria van Rhysselberghe, Gide's substitute or shadow-wif in all but sexual and liturgical fact. In a unique experience not with "La Petite Dame" but with her daughter, Gide's biological daughter Madeleine was conceived.

At this juncture, Pierre Herbart made his largest single step into the center of Gide's life. He "legitimized" Gide's daughter by marrying Elisabeth, although Elisabeth was almost twenty years older than he: Old enough to be his mother, in fact. Pierre has became at once pretend father and pretend son, bound in ambiguities.[6]

But the rescue of Pierre Herbart also required Gide to provide his protégé with some presentable line of work. To this end, Gide set out to make Pierre into a writer and intellectual. This had a certain dubious plausibility. Pierre was certanly very intelligent; he had good taste; and he did possess a certain narrow competence as a writer. In the effort, Gide and the propaganda apparatus found common terms. That apparatus soon put Pierre on very much a Party-sponsored literary career track. That meant lots of artices and assignments for various newspapers and magazines of the chic Parisian left, followed by a year in Moscow. Paul Hizan was among them. It was 1934 and 1935, and a number of promising young French intellectuals were in Moscow. Thus, Pierre was provided with a career while Gide had acquired a debt to the French Party, its cultural commissar, Vaillant, and his men. As time went on, the apparatus seems to have grown steadily and more confident that it held Pierre firmly in its grasp, and that Pierre was their key to Gide.[7]

The most ominous political event of the Mutualité Congress was, or ought to have been, the curious absence of Maxim Gorky. On the podium, Gorky had originally been billed as its "honorary chairman." But that announcement had been made before Kirov's murder. Sometime in the events that followed that assassination, the arrangement for Gorky's visit was cancelled. Stalin selected Isaac Babel and Boris Pasternak as his delegates, replacing the grand old man of socialist realism, who was unable to come, the delegates were told, because of his poor health.[8]

The true reason for Gorky's absence in Paris was that Stalin had begun to fear the possibility of Gorky compromising his preparations for the Terror, whih were already well advanced. Specially, Gorky entertained suspicions about Kirov's death, suspicions that it seems Stalin had anticipated. Gorky had been surrounded by NKVD flunkies since the moment of his return to the U.S.S.R. from Italy in 1932. But after Kirov's murder, his surveillance became virtual house arrest, with his palatial residence in the Crimea surrounded by NKVD guards. Gorky seems to have anticipated that Kirov's killing was a first step in a purge: he certainly knew that two of his most trusted friends among the senior Bolsheviks, Kamenev and Zinoviev, had been arrested two weeks after Kirov was killed, and he even wrote an article correctly guessing what would be the line justifying their purge.[9] Gorky had smelled a rat.

Gorky was an old man, and for all his faults a brave one. He was not in good health. He suffered from angina; he had had tuberculosis. He was also the most respected spokesman for the Revolution alive—though for both personal and public reasons, he was moving toward disaffection with Stalin. His suspicions were visibly mounting. So Stalin considered: Should Gorky be given that podium in Paris as planned? Sent out of easy reach to talk with important European intellectuals?

Gorky's traveling days were at an end. The author of *The Lower-Depths* would never return to Europe.[10]

Most of the fellow travelers at the Mutualité accepted the story about Gorky's bad health without a second thought. The event swept ahead without him. What actually was said in the turgid deliberations of Stalin's Congress in Defense of Culture has been described many times, and it would be silly to rehearse the rodomontade again here. The hall sweltered; righteousness rose up; the hash of innocence was hashed and rehashed. The participants dripped with sweat and struggled with their rhetoric, maneuvering in and out of largely fatuous and always imaginary "positions." The Popular Front strategy required that the guiding Soviet grip on the Mutualité be invisible but firm. The dull results had their occasionally comic side. At one point Gustav Regler made such a shining speech in defense of Soviet culture that the crowd could not contain its passions any longer. It leapt to its feet and burst into a rapturous chorus of the *Internationale*. As Regler swept triumphantly into the wings, an NKVD agent named Johannes Becher, later a high official in the DDR, greeted him in a rage, hissing "You've ruined everything! You've given us away!"[11]

The only other event of lingering interest at the Mutualité was the case of Victor Serge.

Victor Serge was a French anarchist and novelist whose revolutionary faith took him to Russia to greet the great dawn of October 1917. There he became an agent of the Comintern, and there he entered the conspiratorial world. He always retained his anarchist passions, but he continued to serve the Comintern and to write, in deepening doubt, until 1933, when he heard the knock at the door, was arrested, and despatched to the gulag.[12]

Serge had seen his downfall coming, and as a kind of life insurance smuggled out of the Soviet Union the manuscript of an anti-Stalinist but still devouly revolutionary book called *Literature and Revolution*, with the request that in the event he disappeared, the book either be published or used as a lever for his release.[13]

Serge then disappeared. His cause was taken up by a number of people, some of them Trotskyists, who co-ordinated their response at the Mutualité. At the end of a long, propagandists day, a distinguished Italian radical with strong anarchist sympathies, Gaetano Salvemini, stood up. Salvemini had been a leftist senator in the Italian Parliament; he was a fierce and unrelenting opponent of Mussolini. He now taught Italian Civilization at Harvard. Taking the floor, Salvemini demanded that the Congress denounce the Terror in the USSR as well as Germany, and then asked if the Russian delegation could provide an explanation of "the way Victor Serge was being treated in the Soviet Union."

Trouble. Ehrenberg and Koltsov instantly went into a huddle together, plotting damage control. Too late: Another speaker was on her feet, a Trotskyist named Madeleine Paz. She immediately seconded Salvemini and announced to the Congress that she had reason to believe that the distinguished French writer and revolutionary Victor Serge was being held prisoner in the USSR. She demanded to know his whereabouts.

It is a measure of the tender sensitivities of Stalinist cultural politics that this single request provoked absolute consternation in the hall. *Where was Victor Serge?* With this one challenge to the Lie, the invisible hand trembled palpably. A kind of group hysteria swept the room. The delegates, until now so docile, were suddenly shouting at each other. Fists were being clenched. There was abuse and gnashing of teeth. Folding chairs were being picked up and waved in the air.

Gide and Malraux, up on the podium, looked out on this spectacle, and down came the gavel. The session was unceremoniously ended, and the simple question from Salvemini and Madeleine Paz hung unanswered in the emptying aftermath.[14]

The night of the mini-riot at the Mutualité, Gide found himself badly shaken. The next day, he sought an audience with the Soviet ambassador. The interview was refused. The morning after that, terribly agitated, Gide rose early and prepared the first draft of an exceptionally shrewd letter of protest to the ambassador. Gide was careful not to take Serge's part in anything. The letter was, if anything, too courtly. Gide limited himself merely to pointing out the "feebleness" of the Soviet response to the questions about Serge. That feebleness, he said, had left the partisans of the USSR "fatally disarmed and disabled" before its critics.[15]

That evening, Gide read this draft to assembled friends. Alix Guillain, a high-level Stalinist journalist and the wife of perhaps the most influential left-wing academic in France, attacked Gide's letter with all the angry puritanism of her kind. Couldn't Gide see that Serge's defenders were *poseurs?* Just *think* what the enemies of socialism could do with the talk about friends of the Soviet Union being "disabled and disarmed"; just *think* of how they would twist and distort those words.[16]

Gide listened carefully, said little, and the next day rejected Alix Guillain's advice. Instead, he again rose early and personally delivered the letter to the Soviet embassy.

It is testimony to the importance Stalin assigned to Gide's role in the Popular Front in France that six months later, Victor Serge was released from the gulag. According to Robert Conquest this was "the almost unique occasion on which foreign opinion was able to influence Stalin."[17]

What can be the real reason for this anomaly? The Soviet Union was about to make a really serious move for a large new measure of control in the French government. Covert agents would accomplish some of the move; much would be plain to all. The educated classes in France would need to be convinced that this new communist influence was right and wise; and since the French Revolution, the French educated classes had been used to giving an exceptional moral deference, not to their government leaders, and not to the Church, but to some pre-eminent literary doyen. Stalin of course could never understand this simple truth, but Radek certainly understood it with complete clarity. France was the land of Voltaire. That deference to the doyen was basic to the sociology of the French elite; it was a habit learned in the *lycée*. As that doyen, Gide was essential to the credibility of the new policy. And Gide knew it. Despite all his agitation before unfolding events, he seems to have taken a remarkably accurate measure of the power that he now found in his grasp, clearly understanding that it was power far beyond that of any other literary man of his era.

The next year, Gide would at last consent to make a tour of the Soviet Union. By then, the Popular Front government of Léon Blum, riddled with Soviet agents, was in power, and Gide had been an honored guest at its installation. And by then, the secret service intrigue around the French writer would focus not on Victor Serge, who had been released, but on the mysterious death of Maxim Gorky himself.

Like Gide, Maxim Gorky took his role as an unacknowledged legislator of mankind with ardent seriousness—but unlike Gide, Gorky approached his task not as a fellow traveler but as a genuine revolutionary. Gorky's role in the Revolution dated back as far as Lenin's own. As a writer, Gorky had come to fame early. At the turn of the century, he was one of the most celebrated writers in Russia, and by 1901 his seditious works had got him into fairly serious trouble with the Tsarist regime. By 1905, Gorky had met Lenin and was a committed Bolshevik. When the Revolution came, Gorky was probably the most *famous* Bolshevik in the Party. As a friend of Tolstoy, he made a bridge between Russian high culture and the underground of conspiratorial cells, contributing financially to Lenin's operations, enmeshed in the Party's secret fiscal networks. Meanwhile, his own fame spread.[18] Maxim Gorky was not among those artists made by the Revolution. On the contrary, he helped to make it.[19]

And when the Revolution came, he took up the grand task of creating a new culture for the new Soviet man with a pompous provincial grandiosity that might be touching if one could somehow overlook the damage done in its name. Gorky was most unlike Gide in his grandiosity. He had none of Gide's irony, none of his feeling for the private life, none of his taste for ambiguous things. Gide may have taken up the mantle of Zola, but he had tossed it over his shoulders at a loose rakish angle, and wore it with a smile that showed his sense that the "theater of conscience," though important, also had its absurd side.

On the other hand, the relation of Maxim Gorky to Lenin and the senior leadership of the Bolshevik Revolution is a tragic pantomime of the bond between culture and high politics. When Lenin assumed office, Gorky saw his own place as the voice of the Revolution's humanity, which he proposed to balance against the role of Lenin, whom he saw as the very voice of power. Precisely this fantasy, in my view, led Gorky into moral bankruptcy. It was also the living paradigm for ten thousand tiresome art-and-politics debates to come, along with the culture congresses and symposia that orchestrate them, the patron saint of the countless gatherings devoted to this pseudo-theme. Yet Gorky was a very intelligent man, and not easily deceived. His insight into Lenin's character was sharp. Richard Pipes cites Gorky quoting, without comment, a Frenchman who had called Lenin a "thinking guillotine," and also cites Gorky on the subject of Lenin's misanthropy: "He loved people. He loved them with obligation. His love looked far ahead, through the mists of hatred."[20]

His love looked far ahead, through the mists of hatred. Gorky became the house humanist among the Bolsheviks. In this role, he frequently went to Lenin pleading for the lives of various condemned souls. He later wrote that Lenin seemed always a little perplexed in these meetings, wondering why Gorky cared about these trifling lives and deaths.[21] Lenin, on the other hand, had very limited patience for Gorky's humanistic meddling. Early on, Gorky had been a highly visible personality in Lenin's government. But by 1921, at which time the dictator seems to have grown weary of Gorky's doubts and pleas, Lenin decided to put some distance between himself and the writer. He ordered Gorky to proceed abroad, where his argumentative conscience would help sustain precisely the illusions that Münzenberg was trying to generate. Gorky went, returned to his beloved Italy, and proceeded to have one of the best decades of his life. Abroad, Gorky was sought out by the whole Russian intelligentsia, both communist and non-communist. He knew them, invited them into his household, talked and argued with them at length. His life was filled with the flow of foreign gossip, opinion, and commitment. People who would have feared him in Russia came to like and trust him abroad. They spoke unguardedly. Nonetheless, it was Gorky's habit to make extensive notes of these conversations, strictly for his own purposes, and not the Cheka's. These notes became in effect a high-level archive of Russian opinion abroad. During the mid and late twenties, major Bolsheviks—including Bukharin, prime object of the fourth wave of the Great Terror—confided their doubts about Stalin. So did many important figures in Soviet culture: Isaac Babel, Stanislavsky, and Meyerhold.[22] People turned to him with their confidences, including many politically dangerous confidences.[23]

In 1932, the time came for Gorky to make his return to Russia. Though Stalin and Gorky had not got on well during the twenties, the dictator was now disposed to lavish on Gorky everything the Soviet world could offer any writer. Gorky was to have a central position in the new culture. With his return to Moscow, he became the object of what amounted to a kind of literary "cult of personality," which was in certain ways parallel to Stalin's own. Gorky had always lived with every privilege the regime had to offer. He was now installed in something close to princely grandeur, supplied with a palatial country estate and a magnificent town house in Moscow. His works were published in huge editions and made obligatory reading. The apparatus at home and abroad treated him as one of the leading geniuses in the history of humanity. Cities, streets, and squares began to be named after him in almost mindless profusion. Gorky's original vision of his role reached a kind of grotesque fulfillment. He was the central cultural icon in the Stalinist world.[24] The fate of that icon is captured in the story of his relationship with the Baroness Moura Budberg and Moura's relation to Gorky's suitcase.

Gorky's suitcase! One of the most mysterious objects in the annals of espionage. When Stalin called Gorky back for his triumphant return to Russia, the question arose as to what should be done with the seething records he had made in all his contacts with Russians abroad.

Gorky was very clear that archives of this sort could not, under any circumstances, return with him to Russia. He knew perfectly well how dangerous those documents could be, in the wrong hands. Indeed, his behavior over this archive seems to show that in 1931 he clearly understood that his return to Russia meant that he would be willingly ending the intellectual and artistic freedom he'd enjoyed abroad, and that in future his life would be subject to full totalitarian scrutiny. As Gorky prepared to vacate his villa in Capri, he went through his entire body of papers, culling out every scrap that might compromise himself or others in Soviet eyes. He then packed all the assembled papers into one solidly filled suitcase, which he closed and belted shut.

This suitcase, Gorky determined, would be left behind, in the hands of some reliable custodian whom he trusted completely. He carefully explained to those around him that the suitcase was to remain in the West, and not be returned to the Soviet Union even if he himself asked, demanded, that it be brought back to him. If at any time anyone heard such a request made either by him personally, or in his name, they should totally disregard it, and deem it false on its face.

It is not clear exactly to whom Gorky at first entrusted the suitcase. But we know that by 1933 it was firmly in the custody of Gorky's former consort and companion, the Baroness Moura Budberg.[25]

The allegiances, or lack of them, which motivated the Moura Budberg, are something of a mystery. Whom did Moura really love? Whom did she really serve? There is no simple answer, and in fact the life story of this extraordinary mythomaniac challenges the simplicity of the word "real."

Moura Budberg was raised in the middle regions of Moscow "society" during the reign of the last Tsar. She married very young, and married up—to an untitled member of the aristocratic Benckendorff family, with whom she had two children. Her husband was in the Tsar's foreign service in Berlin and London; at his side, even before 1917, she had fully embarked on her career as the grand cosmopolitan she would remain until the end of her life.

But Moura's principal career was as a survivor, albeit always a survivor at the top. During the Revolution, her husband was murdered by a mob in Latvia; their children barely escaped with their lives, and were separated from her. In Petersburg, the young and terrified widow sought and got the protection of Robert Lockhart, who in 1917 and 1918 was the most important Western diplomat and British secret agent in Russia. She and Lockhart became lovers, and though Moura incidentally married a Baltic Baron in what was strictly a legal charade (though through it she procured her title), the really important man in Moura's life during the Revolution was Lockhart.[26]

At the end of 1917, in the midst of the conspiracies and intrigues surrounding Lenin's maneuvers toward the Treaty of Brest-Litovsk and his response to the allied landings at Arkangelsk, Lockhart was trapped in a provocation exploited by Dzerzhinsky, perhaps abetted by Sidney Reilly, in which Lockhart and Moura were arrested simultaneously on grave, highly inflammatory charges. That they both would be shot, and shot soon, seemed plain.[27]

But they were not shot. They were released.

Why they were released remains a matter of conjecture. We do know that while the couple was being held in the Kremlin itself, the man in charge of their imprisonment was a handsome but murderous and fanatical onetime London tailor named Jakov Peters, and that Peters was deep in the mysterious events that followed.

We know too that while Peters was holding Moura, the Baroness seduced him, and that once her jailer was fully infatuated with her, she manipulated his jealous feelings to negotiate her release. We know that the deal included Lockhart; he was released with Moura, and he promptly returned to London. Moura, on the other hand, was obliged to remain in Russia, proving her continuing usefulness.

It was at this point that the Baroness entered the life of Maxim Gorky. She was sent to live as a "secretary and translator" in his vast apartment in Petersburg. She soon became a central figure in his large and complex household, and Gorky plainly conceived a passion for her.[28]

Was it real love? Like many mythomaniacs, Moura Budberg seems to have believed that she could not afford or even physically survive any too-rigorous distinction between the real and the unreal. There may have been real love between Gorky and the Baroness; at the same time, most witnesses believe she manipulated Gorky's emotions with great calculation. Anthony West, the son of H. G. Wells and Rebecca West, to whom Moura in later years was virtually a stepmother, wrote about her with authority. According to West, Moura turned to Gorky early in their affair and made a "confession," all tears. She had not been sent to him as a simple translator and secretary. She was a police spy. She had saved her own life by submitting to this job, this mission: spying on him. Zinoviev, the unspeakable Zinoviev, controlled her. Zinoviev was trying to discredit Gorky in Lenin's eyes. And now she was caught; she loved Gorky, and yet she was their prisoner.

West claims that Gorky was greatly moved by this confession. He regarded it as proof of Moura's love. Instead of shattering Gorky's trust in her, it confirmed it, and he only loved her more. Moura believed in *him;* it was proof that she had risked the vengeance of the *apparat* by telling him the truth. Meanwhile, his new trust provided Moura with permanent protection against exposure. Nobody could tell Gorky anything about Moura that she herself had not long since confided in him.

In 1920, this sexual story repeated itself with a new man. During that year, H. G. Wells, whom Moura had already met in England through the British Russophile Maurice Baring, arrived as a guest in Gorky's household in Petersburg. During this visit, Moura seduced Wells as easily as she had seduced Peters, and entered into what became a lifelong liaison with him. According to Anthony West, Moura made exactly the same "confession" to Wells that she'd made to Gorky. She had been sent to spy on him, and now she was in love. It had much the same effect on Wells, binding him to her only more deeply.[29] There exists a photograph of the three of them together. In it, Gorky looks in warm camaraderie at Wells, while with rather heavy lids Wells takes in Moura, and for her part Moura tosses the camera a look of undeniable Russian allure.

After she made her "confession" to Wells, Moura claimed to have severed all relations with the Soviets. This was a lie, and years later, Wells unexpectedly discovered the lie. Moura was in frequent, and important, contact with the *apparat*. The Russian historian Arkady Vaksberg is the first writer to plumb what these meetings were really about. Between 1933 and 1936, Moura Budberg made at least six trips to the Soviet Union, each of them covered in complete secrecy. While in Moscow, Moura would hand over to the NKVD some small selection of documents culled from the archive Gorky had left in her care. Then the NKVD would hand over to Moura, without taking any receipt, large sums of cash. Moura would sometimes—perhaps often—meet with Gorky on these trips, though its hardly likely she told him about their purpose. On at least one occasion Stalin himself joined her and Gorky for lunch. Stalin turned out to be well informed about Moura, and she led the lunch table talk with her famous, irresistible charm.

According to Anthony West, when H. G. Wells learned that Moura was still in touch with the Soviets—he does not seem to have known over what—he confronted Moura with her lie. Her response was dismissive, saying, "as a biologist, he had to know that survival was the first law of life." Had she lied? Yes, she had lied: She had wished to live. To stay alive, she had paid "the going price." Did Wells not like it? He would have to take her as she was.[30]

West came to believe that his father's last years were poisoned by his recognition that despite Moura's falsehood and opportunism, he could not bring himself to do without her. Loving Moura in her special dishonesty as he once had loved her in what he thought was her special truth, Wells stayed with her to the end.[31]

In any case, when Gorky returned to Russia in 1931, Moura remained behind in Europe, turning from Gorky to Wells. Between 1931 and 1935, Gorky's relations with Stalin, despite occasional strains, had been warm. For example, Stalin was a quite regular visitor to Gorky's house—as was the head of the NKVD, Yagoda.[32] Publicly Gorky was promoted as "Stalin's closest friend." But by 1934, Gorky had begun to irritate Stalin with his pleas and questions. 1935 deepened the rift, especially with Stalin's awareness of Gorky's suspicions about the Kirov murder.[33]

But there seems to have been another, more private, dimension to Gorky's mistrust of Stalin. Six months before Kirov was shot, Gorky's own son Max had died unexpectedly, and in strange circumstances. In contrast to his father, young Max was a systematic lightweight. Conscience of the Revolution? Voice of humanity? Max loved racing cars and fun. Most of all he loved liquor. He was an alcoholic with a smart, pretty, and very ambitious wife: Timosha Peshkova. Two of Max's favorite drinking pals were his father's physician, a Dr. Levin, and his father's secretary, a man named Kryuchkov. Both these men were agents of the NKVD. Both were under Yagoda's discipline. And Yagoda, the all-powerful director of the NKVD, was ferociously in love with Max's ambitious wife.[34]

And then Max strangely died. The manner of Max's death was that following a bender with his friends the NKVD agents in May 1935, the young man passed out in the springtime snow, and was brought in with pneumonia. Placed under Dr. Levin's care, he did not recover.

In 1938, when the Great Terror was nearing the end of its vast course, Stalin undertook to rid himself of Dr. Levin and Kryuchkov in a show trial that claimed that they had conspired, with their evil master Yagoda, in the murder of both Maxim Gorky and his son Max. They of course confessed, and of course they were convicted and executed.[35]

Did Yagoda have Max killed? There is plenty of reason to be suspicious. For us the issue is that Gorky *thought* Yagoda might have had his son killed. That thought, added to Gorky's doubts about the Kirov killing, may have induced Gorky to reconsider his role as Stalin's house humanist.

In any case, six months after young Max died, the still combative Maxim Gorky publicly came to the defense of Kamenev. This was when Stalin dropped Gorky as honorary chairman of the Mutualité Congress.

It has been claimed with some plausibility that at this same time Gorky had begun writing a manuscript attacking the regime. It is said to have been a phantasmagoric work in which Stalin is cast as a gigantic—mountainous—flea. That sounds like Gorky all right, but if he really did write such a thing, the text has never been found. Gorky is said to have had the manuscript with him in his house outside Moscow. If Gorky managed to keep such a manuscript hidden from the police spies who surrounded him, it would be testimony to his cunning. Spies like Kryuchkov read every letter, received every telephone call, and typed every manuscript page. Perhaps Gorky managed to conceal his new work in some obscure corner of that huge manor house. It is known that the moment Gorky died NKVD moved in on his country house, tearing it apart looking for his "papers."

It does one's heart good to think of this dying peasant genius, his son dead, his dream of the new kingdom reduced to squalor, recovering his power to fight, turning himself into a kind of aged David accumulating a little horde of literary rocks, hidden from Goliath. It may even be true. But a manuscript giving us Stalin in the form of a gigantic flea would not be needed to explain the dense conspiratorial atmosphere that surround the death of Maxim Gorky. The Stalinist police hovered over his every move, his every breath, watching him day by day, hour by hour.

Why? Gorky was a big celebrity, yes. But why this relentless official vigil? The key fact here is a matter of timing—the time Stalin had by then scheduled start date of the Great Terror. It had been fixed for early August 1936. If he had been alive to protest this event, Maxim Gorky would have been the one person in the entire country—there was nobody else—whose voice would be heard in the West. It was therefore essential to Stalin that Gorky be off the scene—one way or the other—by August. As things worked out, Gorky was dead, either murdered or of natural causes, by mid-June—just in time—a mere *six weeks* before the show trial that would condemn as insatiable monsters of treason and conspiracy two men,

Kamenev and Zinoviev, whom Gorky regarded as innocent, as his patrons, and as his close colleagues and friends.

For the Great Terror to begin, *Maxim Gorky* **had** *to be dead by August*. And so he was.

Those who doubt that Stalin had Gorky murdered during his final illness argue that the old man was on his way out anyway, so why take a compromising risk instead of letting nature take its course? Yet Arkady Vaksberg's research—the most thorough and judicious yet done—shows that it is far from clear that Gorky's final illness had to be a fatal. After contracting pneumonia on June 1, Gorky was very sick for about a week, but in the second week pulled into a solid rally. He had excellent physicians—Dr. Levin had to step aside—and he continued to improve steadily for the next full week. He was in the midst of this seeming recovery when he took a sudden, inexplicable turn for the worse on June 17, and become desperately sick in a way no intervention could stop. He died the next day. He was a man of 68, and his health, while far from good, had always been at least resilient. What happened? After examining every scrap of evidence, Vaksberg concludes that Maxim Gorky may have died naturally—and probably did not. Whether his death was natural or murder, from Stalin's perspective the key fact is not medical but political.

There was no story about a gigantic flea in Moura Budberg's suitcase, but there was ample evidence to send any number of people, including some very highly placed people, to their deaths. The suitcase contained letters compromising to Bukharin, to Rykov, to many notable people marked for liquidation. By 1933, the NKVD was sure Moura was in full possession of the documents and knew exactly what was in them. The cat and mouse began. The NKVD was determined to recover them. Moura was determined to use them to maximum advantage. She broke the stash into separate groups and hid them carefully, some in England, some on her property in Latvia. She then began to bargain, piece by piece, enriching and advancing herself, in covert negotiations that went on for years, well into the decades after Gorky's death. This was the meaning of Moura's six secret visits to the USSR before 1936, the ones that so astounded and dismayed H. G. Wells. Moura was selling selected documents for cash on the barrelhead before Gorky's death. Meanwhile, during her secret visits to the U.S.S.R. Moura redeployed all her charms on the clueless Gorky himself, trying finagle the legal rights to possession of the archive—probably through a power of attorney or a clause in his will. These suggestions were anathema to Gorky, and Moura's maneuvers on one occasion provoked in him a shouting rage so violent that Moura was driven from the house. Two quite reliable witnesses claim that she prepared a will for Gorky leaving her the papers outright, and when he refused to sign it, she proceeded to forge Gorky's signature herself, something she long ago learned to do, when she was his "secretary." (If this really happened, the "will" vanished after Gorky's death.) Meanwhile, for reasons that have never been explained, Moura was with Gorky for virtually every minute of his final illness, flown in (via Berlin) at NKVD expense, appearing at his side virtually the day he became ill and staying in or near the sickroom until the end. This was not, as has sometimes been claimed, at Gorky's request, "to say farewell." Gorky had long since ceased to love Moura. There is no evidence that in early June Gorky believed he was dying. Nothing supports the claim that Moura came at his request. Once he was gone, Moura extended her stay. When the NKVD rearranged her return flight, the airline was told Moura was lingering in Russia to "assist in arranging Gorky's literary legacy."

The deathwatch in Maxim Gorky's sickroom coincided almost exactly with André Gide's grand celebrity tour of the Soviet Union.

The story of André Gide's much manipulated journey to the USSR has been told many times, first by Gide himself in the book he published in September 1936, *Retour a l'U.R.S.S.* It was an attack on the entire Soviet system. Pierre Herbart later described the scene in Spain, in the first months of the Civil War, when he took the galleys to Mikhail Koltsov in his bivouac. Koltsov was Stalin's prime confidential agent in Spain, and his most trusted operator among the cultural celebrities of the Popular Front. The agent was handed the proofs of the *Retour.* Koltsov complacently flipped them open and began to read. After a few moments, he started in shock. He began to turn the pages faster, in agitation. Attack! Gide had written an attack! The expression on his face was pulling into one of rage defined by fear.[36]

Despite repeated warnings to Münzenberg by (among others) the Count and Countess Károlyi that Gide would never be a reliable fellow traveler, Gide at last agreed to embark, with a retinue of distinguished French intellectuals, on the grandest propaganda tour of all. The trip was scheduled for June 1936, and the apparatus gave Gide the highest priority. His maximum visibility endorsing the Soviets was key to solidifying the Popular Front in France. Gide was greeted everywhere by rapt officials and huge trumped-up crowds. No excess of ingratiation, no form of flattery was spared.

Traveling with Gide and his retinue was also Pierre Herbart. It is clear that as some point along the way, Gide began secretly to move toward his decision to turn against the apparatus. When did he reach this decision? How did he reach it? In Russia, he gave every appearance of being the perfect dupe. Four months later, he produced an important and even noble anti-communist book. What made him change? We do not know.

It is plain that two months after Gide returned from his Soviet trip, while he was writing the book, the watchful *apparat* was fully convinced that the book would be totally supportive of the Popular Front but also Stalin and the U.S.S.R. They arranged to make it the bestseller of the year, the flagship book of the new phase. And then something went wrong.

Stalin's original plan for aligning the Popular Front with the Terror had included an English replay of the Mutualité Congress to be held almost a year later in London during May. Mikhail Koltsov and Ilya Ehrenberg were once again to be in charge, and almost all of Gide's traveling companions, along with such celebrities as Elsa Triolet and Louis Aragon, were expected to be in attendance. Another honored guest was to have been the celebrated translator, companion of Russian writers, and friend to Russia abroad, Moura Budberg. But when Gorky became really seriously ill on June 1, plans changed.

To promote the Front, the French writers had to be part of the news event. To keep Gorky quiet, they must not actually reach his bedside. Koltsov and Ehrenberg were assigned a job: to preoccupy the great and famous with Gorky's dying, while preventing anyone from reaching his bedside prematurely.[37] Koltsov and Ehrenberg now turned their skills to deathbed politics, the diplomacy of the sickroom corridor, played in the Stalinist key. Who, if anyone, was to stand by Gorky's bedside? And when?

Meanwhile, the effects of the Popular Front on European politics had initiated the intended, and some unintended, havoc. Léon Blum's Popular Front government was installed on June 6, 1936. Within days, strikes were spreading across the country. Gide would leave for Moscow from a Paris all but paralyzed by labor unrest. At the same time a Popular Front government in Spain was careening toward the crisis that in July would break out as the quintessential event of the Popular Front: the Spanish Civil War.

The push-pull of this situation began to be felt in Gide's life. Four days after Blum became premier of France—June 10—Ilya Ehrenberg had dinner with Gide and informed him that Gorky was very ill and about to die. He urged Gide to put aside everything and prepare to leave for Moscow immediately. Forget the London Congress; hurry to Russia to see the old man before he expired. Gide agreed. That night, he began urgent preparations.[38]

The next day Gide's apartment was filled with people helping him prepare to leave that very day. Humorless and intense, Gide was frantically packing, struggling to maintain order as he readied himself to leave within hours. But that same day Gorky took his turn for the better. He had rallied. He no longer seemed moribund. He suddenly seemed to be doing quite well.[39]

The French writer Jean Malaquais, who was present that day, recalled that at around 2 o'clock that afternoon the phone rang in Gide's apartment. The room, filled with all Gide's entourage, fell silent. Something had happened. Perhaps Gorky had died. Malaquais picked up the phone.

"It's the eye of Moscow," Malaquais said, mock sinister, to the listening room. There was mild laughter as Gide took the phone.

The caller was in fact Ilya Ehrenberg, explaining that despite yesterday's urgency, there had been a sudden change. Gorky was better. Much, *much* better. In fact there was now no hurry at all. This precipitate rush to Moscow was really quite unnecessary. In fact it would be far, far more convenient if the visit did not take place right now at all. Gorky would be all right, and in fact a later date was much to be preferred.[40]

Gide listened. When he hung up the phone, the room was waiting. Was Gorky dead?

"C'est remis," Gide answered, dryly. ("It's been postponed.") The room burst into gales of laughter.

Ehrenberg had in fact presented Gide with a new timetable for his arrival in Moscow. Ehrenberg explained that everything had been worked out quite carefully. The ideal date for Gide now to arrive would be, he said, June 18. So the 18th it was.[41] André Gide's plane touched down in Moscow in the late afternoon of June 18 about five hours after Gorky breathed his last.[42]

The same sinister shuffle between urgency and delay over Gorky's deathwatch was danced by Louis Aragon and Elsa Triolet, with Koltsov rather than Ehrenberg as their guide. Little though they liked Gide, Aragon and Triolet had been much involved in planning his trip, and they were among those whom Gorky was asking to see. Earlier that spring, Ehrenberg had warned the obedient Elsa away from any too precipitate visit to the dying master's bedside. In June, when the old man's demise became international news, the French couple thought it best to give at least the appearance of hurrying to his side. They actually visited Elsa's sister Lily Brik, who actively encouraged them to delay in Leningrad as long as possible, apparently consciously detaining them.[43]

When Koltsov at last arranged to drive Aragon and Triolet to the estate, he knew Gorky was about to die, though en route, he flattered them with the information that Gorky himself had demanded they be brought to him "the moment they arrive."[44]

The moment they arrive? Their arrival had quite intentionally been delayed for days. On the afternoon of June 18, as Gide's plane was nearing Moscow, Koltsov pulled up before the gates of Gorky's country mansion. At the gates, they were refused admission by the guards. While their chauffeur argued with the gatekeepers, Dr. Levin appeared. Of course the physician was given immediate entry. The French delegation watched him go in. Then they fretted, until a short while later, Levin re-emerged, and Koltsov approached him. The secret agent and the NKVD physician talked quietly together for a few moments. Then Koltsov turned to Aragon and Triolet in tears to say that Gorky was dead.[45]

The national mourning around Gorky's death included a huge state funeral in Red Square. A speech by Gide was to be featured. It was an important part of Popular Front strategy that the leading representative of European literature be on the podium.

Gide and Pierre Herbart had been installed in the Hotel Metropole, and there he prepared for his prime appearance of the tour. Koltsov was very much the organizer of this aspect of the event, and it was through Koltsov that Herbart was instructed to pass on to Gide what it was thought would be an appropriate approach in his talk. The subject was to be the fate of the adversary culture under the Revolution. Koltsov suggested the approach deal in a theory of what he called "currents" as opposed to "counter-currents." Put simply, this view was that outside the Soviet Union, outside the land of the Revolution, conscious and enlightened people should be prepared always to go "against the current." Inside the Soviet Union however, because of the triumph of the Revolution, opposition ceased to be admirable or even admissible, and the impulses of adversary culture should therefore be suspended. Inside the Soviet Union, the duty of the intelligent was to go *with*, not against, the current. Because the adversary culture had triumphed in Russia, opposition no longer had any place. See? Simple.

Inside his room at the Hotel Metropole, Gide went to work preparing a speech devoted to this theme. At his side was Herbart.

A word about Gide's relation to Herbart. It is plain that Koltsov and Münzenberg viewed Herbart as an obedient servant of Stalinism. Yet when Pierre returned in May 1936 to act as Gide's escort to Moscow, it was no less plain to La Petite Dame that

Pierre was no longer an uncritical admirer of the Stalinist state.[46] Pierre spent considerable amounts of time urgently confiding stories of governmental stupidity and cultural censorship to the master. As Gide's visit was arranged, she also became aware of something almost conspiratorial going on between the older and younger man. La Petite Dame, who prided herself on knowing everything, noted that they were now deep in long confidential conversations on subjects unknown to her. Shortly before the June departure, as she sat with Gide in a car while Pierre darted into a store to buy some cigarettes, Gide turned to Maria and said to her, rather mysteriously, "Pierre and I understand each other." And nothing more.[47]

Were the two of them moving toward a break even before the departure? The day before the funeral, June 19, Gide's work on his speech was suddenly interrupted by a knock on the hotel room door. It was opened, and before them stood, to Pierre's astonishment, none other than Nikolai Bukharin. Though Bukharin was slated to be one of the other speakers at the ceremony, he was already a man marked for destruction, and that destruction did not fail to come. Radek's show trial would lay the groundwork for his demise, which would emerge during the show trial in which agents Kryuchkov and Levin would also be tried and executed for the "medical murders" of Max Peshkov and Maxim Gorky himself. But on June 19, 1936, Bukharin, though stripped of power, was still one of the most important Bolsheviks alive, and Pierre at least knew it.

Gide was still deep in his speech, but Pierre immediately introduced him to this very grand personage, trying to convey his role in his introduction.

Gide made the author's assumption that Bukharin was interested in his speech and insisted on rehearsing some of its ideas for his guest. Using Koltsov's suggestion about the "currents" and "counter-currents," Gide summarized his oration—how Gorky with his genius for protest had been a force against oppression, and that indeed throughout the history of culture, that culture now so endangered by the fascist threat, artists had always played a more or less vigorous, more or less veiled, adversarial role. But with the Revolution, something essential in culture had changed. With its triumph, the artist was no longer the *adversary* of power. He was now a voice of *affirmation*, sustaining the "calm and radiant triumph" made possible by fighters like Gorky.

Gide looked at Bukharin, waiting for approval. Bukharin did not express his opinion. Instead he explained, in French, that he was very desirous of a private conversation with Gide. *Entirely* private.

He thinks I am a police spy, Herbart thought. "No, no," Gide hastily replied. "Pierre is not *de trap*. You may speak freely, Comrade... Bunin."

Bunin? Bunin was a novelist and poet, a sometime friend of Gorky, not a Bolshevik at all. He was an émigré who had left the USSR well over a decade before.

It was a gaffe to cause despair. Bukharin stood in silence before Gide. Awareness and innocence stood staring at each other. A smile began to play over Bukharin's lips, a smile as Herbart later said, of "unspeakable contempt." He then backed out of the room without another word.[48]

The next day, Gide stood in Red Square and delivered his speech proclaiming the end of the adversary culture to a vast assembled crowd, rapt in mourning. On the high dais stood Stalin himself.

Not far from the dictator's side, in what many would have taken as the greatest honor life had to offer, stood the Baroness Moura Budberg.[49]

Chapter 12

THE SPANISH STRATAGEM

The creation of the Popular Front marked the triumph of Münzenberg's methods, and yet for him personally, it also marked the beginning of the end. All through 1935, Willi's suspicions that the monster might turn its lethal wrath in his own direction still lay quiescent. He remained a major foreign communist. He still held great power. To judge by every appearance, he continued to be trusted. It is true that by 1935, his authority had begun to slip a little. For example, he was not put in charge of the Mutualité Congress. But it was not until a year later, in the middle of 1936, that Willi first began clearly to discern the shape of his real future under Stalin, and so to know fear.

The year before, during the summer of 1935, the atmosphere at the VIIth Comintern Congress, like the atmosphere in the whole city of Moscow, was one of forced gaiety. Yet already the disappearances and arrests of various communists known to Babette and Münzenberg were making people talk in whispers. One sunny afternoon, Babette sat at a table on the cafe terrace outside of the Hotel Metropole, with her friends Suzanne Leonhard and Sophie Liebknecht. A more highly placed trio of women among the ranks of foreign communists would have been hard to find. The conversation took a critical turn. First, someone made some wisecrack about Stalin's new policies. Then someone made a little joke about the quality of life in the USSR. Babette broke in quipping, "don't talk that way," she said. "You'll get us all arrested."

Another joke. Except nobody laughed. The three women sat frozen in silence. Something in their lives changed.[1]

Willi's real business of that summer did not take place in the Palace of Nobles at all. Every day Münzenberg was picked up at his hotel and driven to Comintern headquarters, where he began to be shown the true, unseen, and the new dispensation. Even though the VIIth Congress seemed to represent the apogee of Comintern power, and the Popular Front the culmination of Münzenberg's style of cultural politics, in fact the old system was being systematically dismantled from within. The dismantling of Willi's operational power was in the works. It was part of the evisceration of the Comintern itself. The Archives of the Central Party contain correspondence between Münzenberg and Dimitrov months before, in which Münzenberg complains of sabotage of his operations from within the Western European Bureau, and is obviously concerned enough to ask explicitly that he "be permitted to retain my functions."[2] The crisis he'd feared now came. In a series of covert actions and bureaucratic turns, Willi's "antifascist" functions were being usurped and put under the hidden control of the intelligence services and secret police—an exact reflection of antifascism's unseen relation to the Terror.[3]

Workers International Relief? It was no more. Mezhropohmfilm Russ? The great production house of Soviet cinema, the home of Vertov, Eisenstein, Dovzhenko, vanished into the bureaucratic haze. The old fronts and their networks were to exist under new systems of control, with many of the operations displaced. In the new organizations, Willi would function as "liaison," or "advisor." Gibarti's World Committee for the Relief of the Victims of German Fascism would no longer serve. Despite its many achievements in disinformation and espionage, an entirely new front would now be required. It would be known as the *Rassemblement Universel*

Populaire, or "RUP." Willi would not be in charge of RUP. It would be run by an unctuous but rising young Rumanian secret service star named Louis Dolivet, a good friend of Otto Katz, and closely allied with the Popular Front spy and penetration agent Pierre Cot. Dolivet had been trained in Willi's shop, and comfortably on the inside of the new arrangements. Dolivet would take the lead. Willi would "advise."[4]

At these meetings for secretly reshaping the International, two men in particular emerged as the new Moscow powers, perfect emblems of the moment. The first dealt with Willi on cultural politics and propaganda. This was the repellent Andrei Zhdanov. It was that famous man's first really important senior job. Zhdanov will be remembered as the most brutal of the many brutal people who, from this time until the dictator's death, ran Stalinist culture.[5] Zhdanov was the enforcer of the Terror in art, the secret police-man of socialist realism. When one hears about the horrors visited upon Soviet writers and artists during this period, when one thinks of the hell known to Mandelstam and Akhmatova and Meyerhold and all the uncountable others, it should be remembered that the presiding officer of their anguish was Zhdanov. Even Münzenberg, a man not easily startled, was startled by Zhdanov's gross crudity and virtually total ignorance of Europe. This was the man who would now instruct Münzenberg on all new aspects of Soviet cultural and propaganda policy in the heyday of communist cultural idealism.[6]

But a second even more powerful individual governed the meetings; though this man never himself appeared at the meetings. Others conveyed his directives; his name was only invoked: "Comrade Moskfin." It may have seemed odd that "Moskfin" avoided the meetings with Mirov; he somehow seemed never to be personally present. But so it was. His name was a strange one, faintly sinister, and to Münzenberg, new. "Comrade Moskfin?" Yet by "Moskfin's" command, IWR was finished off; by "Moskfin's" order the assets of Mezhropohmfilm Russ were made to disappear.[7]

Willi probably did not know that Moskfin was in fact Mikhail Trilliser, the director and founder of the foreign arm of the NKVD and now a senior figure in the GRU. Trilliser's presence on the scene clearly announces the takeover of Willi's apparatus by the secret police. Trilliser embodied, in fact, the interpenetration of all three services. The NKVD and military intelligence were assuming functional but covert control of the International. Zhdanov and Moskfin-Trilliser: Here was the new age; here was the new cultural brutality; here was the covert but ubiquitous new role of the secret police. This was the power behind the mask.[8]

And so, when he returned to Paris that summer, Willi Münzenberg, though still in the apparatus, had been demoted. His new given tasks were to serve as a Communist front man in the new Popular Front Fusion party of the German left in exile. This tricky job had its real significance, and in it Münzenberg made many of the contacts with non-Stalinists in exile that would serve him three years later, when he himself was edging toward his own break with Stalin. In addition, many of his old networks still worked under new names, and he still ran them. Finally, he served as an advisor to Dolivet and RUP. The old power was slipping away fast.[9]

The *Rassemblement Universel Populaire* was the social and political instrument of the Popular Front in France.[10] It was not really run by the Comintern at all, but was linked to the apparatus by the Soviet trade unions. Münzenberg was to be its quiet eminence, a liaison with the Russians; not more. It had splendid headquarters on the rue de la Paix; the address was selected for its chic and its name: Paix. Here was the new rich look.

For the Popular Front was very much a matter of style—and in Paris RUP embodied that style. In America at the same time a similar shift occurred, in a move away from "intellectual" communism to the new style of the Hollywood fellow travelers. The charmless days of poverty were over. German exiles with their ragged, wearisome moral passions would no longer be the focus. RUP would be social; RUP would be chic; RUP would sport a touch of class. Dolivet was an ideal agent to place among the very rich. For one thing, crypto-communist or not, Dolivet quite unabashedly worshipped and adored anyone and everyone who was what Cole Porter used to call "rich-rich."[11] (After the war, Dolivet—then a confederate of Julio Alvarez del Vayo—married Michael Straight's sister Beatrice.) Dolivet was very suave; many thought "oily" the *mot juste*. The Swedish banker Olof Aschberg, a thoroughly reliable friend of the apparatus, would serve as RUP's master of ceremonies and financial manipulator. In Aschberg's mansion on the Place des Nations, grand receptions would greet the new age. Parisian money would gather. Elsa Triolet would write malicious novels about the goings-on.[12]

It was a look intended to wed high political righteousness to the drape of a sable coat, the Revolution with a perfect crease, confident with the easy aromatic grace that comes with a look of complete success. This was the heyday of Hollywood communism, the glamour left. Revolutionary congresses would no longer gather in grungy labor union auditoria: From now on Stalin's minions would assemble in Carnegie Hall.[13] Lillian Hellman would appear draped in mink to accept checks for Spanish relief.[14] The Hollywood fellow travelers were expected to look on top of the world, strolling on sloping lawns, and settling in for tinkling cocktails. Theirs was a wedding of the moralism of Lincoln Steffens with the chic of Scott Fitzgerald. On the West Coast, the marriage of Donald Ogden Stewart to Ella Winter made the new symbolism literal. The prevailing atmosphere is captured in Mary McCarthy's short story "The Genial Host," which, McCarthy herself pointed out, was based on a real evening in Lillian Hellman's circle, albeit with the genial hostess herself not depicted. The new taste for luxury was brought to absurdity in the array of champagne dinners and Rolls-Royces assembled for a Writers' Congress in Spain at the height of the Civil War.[15] This was the communism of country houses, the antifascism of evening gowns. It was all that sparkled in the eyes of Elsa Triolet.

As this new style was taking shape, so was the Terror. In August 1936, eight weeks after the death of Maxim Gorky, Zinoviev, Kamenev, and Smirnov—founding heroes of Leninism—were given their show trials, taken into the basement of the Lubyanka, and shot. It had begun.

About a month later Münzenberg was in Brussels with Louis Dolivet, doing some work for RUP. They happened to cross on the street an old friend of Willi, a Dutch Bolshevik who had broken with Stalin and become allied with Trotsky in exile. When he saw Münzenberg with Dolivet, knowing well of course that Willi was still deep in the service of the secret power, Sneevliet stepped directly into Münzenberg's path and said very loud, so everyone could hear: *"Cain, where is thy brother Abel-Zinoviev?"*

Münzenberg could not speak.[16]

***

Shortly after his encounter with Sneevliet in October 1936, Willi was recalled to Moscow for further instructions. The archives show a letter from Dimitrov written a month before, proposing a wide array of new operations submitted for approval.[17] Münzenberg was obviously trying to shore up his position, demonstrate his usefulness. He was now asked to come to consider the results. He was asked to come with Babette. Though it was unusual to be asked to bring his wife, it was not unheard of. The couple went together, traveling somewhat uneasily.

Shortly after he arrived in Moscow, Willi was taken aside and told under conditions of the most absolute confidence that Karl Radek had been secretly arrested and was certain to be condemned.[18]

The moment must have made his blood freeze. Radek arrested! Radek was not only Münzenberg's oldest partner in the apparatus, he was his patron at the highest levels of Soviet power. If Radek had fallen, when would it be Willi's turn?

Not long, it seems. In that era, the prime instrument of ideological conformity within the Comintern was a body known as the International Control Commission. The ICC was a kind of star-chamber for the apparatus, used to arbitrate genuine problems, but much more significantly to enforce the line and rein in those who might from time to time become forgetful about obedience.

Incredibly, Münzenberg himself was now called before the International Control Commission.[19]

The charges raised against Münzenberg by the commission were alarming by virtue of their very flimsiness. He was charged with having been lax in vigilance. The Falangist mutiny in Spain had broken out two months before. Willi was accused of having permitted a "Franco spy," a typist named Liane, to infiltrate his office. Münzenberg almost laughed out loud. Liane? A Franco spy? He easily showed the Commission had entirely bollixed its facts about Liane. This, he told the commission, was "flea-killing."

But that of course was the problem. The commission didn't particularly care if its "facts" looked right or wrong. And they didn't retreat before Willi's scorn.

On this trip, Babette and Willi had been put up in a new hotel on Red Square: the Hotel Moskva. There they found themselves very much alone. Fear had descended generally all over Russia. Old Leninists were denouncing each other on every side. People were doing anything, anything to avoid arrest; anything to prove their devotion to the regime. Nobody came to call. "After all," Babette said, "we might be among the damned."[20]

So they might. Unconcerned that Münzenberg had made monkeys of them over Liane, the International Control Commission called him back for a second appearance. And then a third.

Münzenberg now understood that his life was in direct and imminent danger. "They were preparing the noose," Babette wrote. "He now had only one idea. To leave Moscow as quickly as possible."[21]

But how could he leave Moscow? Willi knew he would have to negotiate his exit, and with his powers of negotiation rested his and Babette's single hope for salvation. And negotiate with what? Radek was gone. Willi's protector was as good as damned and his own prestige was turning to poison. Willi would have to buy out the place appointed for him in the impending purge, and he would have to buy it quickly. With what?

Spain. He would save himself with Spain.

At the very time that the ICC was interrogating him, Stalin for the first time ordered the Soviet Communist party to announce its public support for the Spanish communists in the Civil War.[22]

Far more importantly, Stalin signed a secret order increasing the flow of volunteers and covert arms into the conflict.[23] It was the military face of antifascism—though as usual the concrete steps were directed not against Hitler, but against a fascist who was more or less irrelevant to Hitler's plans or about whom he had mixed emotions.

Yet Stalin absolutely insisted that this flow of arms and volunteers not appear to be connected directly to his government. He was particularly adamant in his demand that money for the Republic not come from Soviet banks. There was to be no Soviet credit for the Spanish Republic. The flow of arms and men would have to come from sympathizers in Europe and America: volunteers. This is where Willi saw his opportunity. He understood that the arms and cash and volunteers Stalin needed for his Spanish policy would have to come from the soft, sympathizing networks he had created. The new order could not be implemented without him. He—he and Otto Katz—had been essential to the covert arms supply and propaganda into Spain from the first days of Franco's rebellion.[24] Spain, Babette later wrote, was "the sheet anchor," and they clutched it to keep from being swept away.[25]

But could that anchor hold?

Münzenberg proceeded to Comintern headquarters for a meeting with Palmiro Togliatti, an Italian communist who was the senior man in charge while Dimitrov was away on vacation. Münzenberg used Stalin's new order to make his case. If the secret edict was to be implemented, Togliatti had better call off the ICC and let Münzenberg get back to work in Paris, because Willi alone could arrange the flow of arms and men without a clear link to Russia. If he absolutely had no choice, he would return from Paris to deal with the ICC—but later, later. Spain needed him now. Willi made this argument with all the force that had made him famous, and it seems to have worked. Togliatti appeared to take his point, and he promised to issue the exit order.[26]

Unfortunately orders from the Comintern no longer carried quite the same authority they once did. Willi returned to the Hotel Moskva. He and Babette prepared to leave immediately. Just at the moment of their departure, a knock at the door brought them their sole visitor. It was Heinz Neumann, Babette's brother-in-law, married to her sister Margarete, and a major figure in the German wing of the Comintern. He and Margarete lived in Moscow, at the Comintern's Hotel Lux. The archives show that Neumann's fall was linked to the fate of Münzenberg. Neumann and Münzenberg had sided together in the intra-party arguments of the German communists as far back as 1932 and the Amsterdam Congress. They usually had been opposed by Wilhelm Pieck and Walter Ulbricht, devoted enemies whom the files show systematically seeking Münzenberg's downfall over many years. As early as February 1935, the dossiers show Münzenberg interceding on behalf of his brother-in-law in a dossier labeled, ominously, "the Case of Heinz Neumann."[27] During the VIIth Congress, Neumann had been designated the fall-guy for the discarded "social fascist" policy, as a result of which he had been relieved of his once-exalted duties and was now working as a lowly translator in the German wing.

Heinz Neumann had come to say goodbye. The three of them talked, anxiously. Then the time for departure came, and in that awkward moment the unsaid obvious surfaced at last. They could not speak. Then Neumann broke down and wept. "We knew," Babette later said, "that we would never see each other again."[28]

Not many weeks later, the knock did indeed come in the middle of the night at the Neumanns' room in the Hotel Lux. As Heinz was being taken away, Margarete began to weep. He turned to Margarete in the classic reflex of all husbands before a wife's tears. "Don't cry—," but then he stopped himself. "Cry then," he said. "There's plenty to cry about." These were his last words to her. He was never heard from again.[29]

Margarete was herself arrested soon afterward. She was dispatched to the gulag, and during the war she would doubtless have perished there had Stalin not turned her over to his Nazi ally. Thus Margarete was transferred from the Communist camp at Karaganda to the Nazi camp at Ravens-brick, one of the many whom Stalin thought it would be slightly better to have the Nazis kill or imprison than himself.[30] There she became an intimate friend of

Franz Kafka's great love Milena Jasenska.[31] Margarete managed to survive until the liberation of Ravensbrück in 1945. With the Nazi collapse, certain death threatened Margarete all over again. It appeared she might be "liberated" by the advancing Red Army, and thus fall into Stalin's hands once more. This time she could be sure he would not fail to finish her off. When the gates of the camp opened, she and a friend began to walk, walk, trying to get west. At last, bedraggled and exhausted, she came upon a small band of American soldiers who somehow had commandeered a horse and cart. "Get in," one of the soldiers said. "You've walked enough by the look of you. You're going to ride now." Suddenly it was over.[32]

But in that October of 1936, it was time for Willi himself to escape. Leaving Heinz Neumann behind, he and Babette proceeded to the train station. In those days, visitors to the Soviet Union surrendered their passports to the police upon entering the country and were given them again only when, and if, they were granted permission to leave. They reached the station, but "nobody came to hand us our passports with the exit visas and tickets."

Togliatti's command had never been issued. Or it had been brushed aside.

This seemed truly the end. Babette and Willi could return to the hotel or they could wander through the streets, surely under surveillance. They returned to the hotel. There they sat up in their room through the entire night, waiting for the arrest squad they were sure would come. But when at last the dawn came, the knock had not sounded.

With the dawn, Münzenberg knew that he had at best only one final chance to save himself and Babette. The moment he could, he left for Comintern headquarters and was ushered into Togliatti's office. There, according to Babette, he staged a "tremendous scene," shouting table-pounding encounter that must have been the performance of a lifetime. Arkady Vaksberg reports having been told by Fredrikh Firsov that Willi convinced Togliatti that "without him all the Comintern links to Spain and the list of their hiding places would be lost."[33] We know only that when he was through Togliatti, thoroughly cowed, lifted the phone and issued the order for their exit visas in Münzenberg's presence. This time it worked.

They left that day.

Their journey home was not peaceful. Crossing the Baltic from Finland they were caught in a violent storm; for two days the sea battered their ship. Babette and Willi feared that if the ship took refuge in a port, it might be a Soviet port, and God knew what new dangers that might bring. The couple had begun their new life of peril. They would live it now every moment until the fall of France and Willi's death. For the moment, they at least had their lives, and they were at least on their way back to the West. And they had one thing more: As the Terror raged around them, they still had hold of their sheet anchor, the grappling device to hold them against the overwhelming killing current.[34] It was a strange salvation. Willi never once entered Spain during the entire engagement,[35] and he specifically warned Babette never to go to Spain, at the risk of her life.[36] Yet he was, for the moment, saved by Spain.

The tragedy of the Spanish Civil War, the political event *par excellence* of the Popular Front, has been analyzed and described many times by many able historians.[37] It would be out of place to summarize here the large historical arguments that surround the war. For our purposes, examining the role of secret service work in culture, it seems best to focus on one question and its consequences: Stalin's motives.

Most serious analysts now agree that Stalin's motives in the Spanish Civil War were *not* especially directed toward victory. Apart from antifascist talk, his policy was never calculated to lead to victory for his Spanish allies. On the contrary.[38]

Nor did the Spanish Republic go down to defeat in March 1939 because Stalin was incompetent. The fields of the twentieth century are white with the bones of those who underestimated the intelligence of Josef Stalin. Stalin's Spanish policy retains the appearance of being incompetent and self-defeating only so long as one assumes that the Soviet dictator genuinely wanted to *win* the war, that for some reason he felt a sincere desire for the left-wing Republican government to be the undisputed government of Spain. Yet why would he have wanted that? There are many things that can be won in a war besides victory.

It is only when the dictator's actual interests have been correctly identified that Stalin's course of action suddenly becomes quite coherent. It was a classic Stalinist performance, shrewdly and successfully pursued. His aim, in my view, was not the victory of the Spanish Republic, but to use Spain in a large geopolitical game that entailed organizing the Spanish defeat. Stalin wished to take possession of the Spanish government not to hold on to it, but to trade it away.[39]

Here is a quick summary of the course of political events. Briefly put, in early 1936, a Popular Front government very much along the lines of the ones envisioned at the VIIth Congress of the Comintern took power in Spain, a coalition of the left, under the premiership of a non-Stalinist but *Marxisant* radical named Largo Caballero, a skillful but aging politician with a wide popular following, especially among the Anarchist workers and peasants of northeastern Spain, in Catalonia and its capital Barcelona. Largo Caballero was an honorable man who understood his destiny in the light of the more vague dreams of the revolutionary left. He seems to have faltered into Stalinism, moved and flattered by the vanities of this dream, and he saw the Popular Front as his last chance to become the Mediterranean Lenin he hoped to be. He was certainly not a Stalinist, nor even a Communist in the narrow sense. In 1935 and 1936, the Communists were among the smallest and least-admired parties on the Spanish left. The really large left-wing faction was the anarchist wing, and this was Largo's political base. Of course, despite their small numbers, as Willi had pointed out to Togliatti in their showdown, Stalinist operatives riddled Largo Caballero's government from top to bottom. The *apparat* was ubiquitous in his government. It was happening in London, Paris, and Washington too. But in Spain it was writ large.[40]

Once the new Popular Front government took office in Spain, the next phase of radicalization consisted of provocations and counter-provocations from both the left and the right. These were both spontaneous and covertly controlled. They were appalling in their violence and cruelty, and they now became a standard feature of Spanish political life. Taken in sum, they brought about the total destabilization of Spanish society. The country became increasingly polarized, and was soon almost hysterically so.[41] Vast demonstrations filled the squares of Madrid; placards with Stalin's face became ubiquitous; the government itself became a vehicle for the rhetoric of revolution.[42] Meanwhile, the Spanish intelligentsia seemed entirely to succumb to the systematic blindness of "politicized" thought, drunk on the ideological elixir.

It was in this atmosphere that on July 17, 1936, a young military officer with a large following made a pronouncement in which he rejected the legitimacy of the government and proclaimed himself the leader of a military rebellion.[43] As such, Francisco Franco became the leader of a forthrightly fascistic uprising against the Spanish Republic. It was civil war.

Stalin's first response that summer was to have Willi and the Comintern make a lot of noise but do very little.[44] It was the age of the celebrity volunteer. An early arrival was André Malraux, sent from Otto and Willi's office, and offering, very covertly, to act as a go-between in the purchase of some French airplanes.[45] At the same time the NKVD apparatus was ordered to start arranging for the covert supply of military material and clandestine advisors. Stalin had two prime requirements. The first was that any people traceable to the Soviet government stay out of the line of fire, and second that all military purchases be kept secret and not made on credit.[46] The Spaniards and their allies would pay cash on the barrelhead. Malraux loved his job. It was not really very substantive, though it established him as the French pseudo-hero of the new struggle.

Stalin was waiting to see if Franco would win, and win quickly. Franco did not win quickly. Plainly, the Spanish Republic would and could fight back. As the summer gave way to fall, Franco's rebellion was not succeeding. In the passionate slogan of the hour— *¡No pasaran! (They shall not pass!)*

At this point Stalin decided to take advantage of the situation in a new way. In the early fall of 1936, right around the time that Willi learned of Radek's arrest and felt the Terror brush near, the dictator issued his secret decree ordering new and greater aid to Spain.[47] Meanwhile, the Soviet Party grandly announced its alliance with Spanish communists. This was the moment that Willi appeared in Togliatti's office, making the argument that the Münzenberg offices in Paris were indispensable to the new policy.

In fact, the true substance of Stalin's October 1936 decision was not so much to aid Caballero's struggle as to use his aid as a pretext for seizing total control over the Spanish government, Stalinizing it in its every aspect, and rendering it entirely subservient to his will. That this might undermine the larger war effort against Franco, even doom it to failure, was not really an important consideration in Stalin's eyes. The essential element was that people who were really *nash*—obedient Stalinists—replace the Largo Caballero government. Though Largo Caballero was surrounded by Soviet agents and remained intellectually under the thumb of Julio Alvarez del Vayo, the long-standing Münzenberg agent and close associate of Otto Katz, he still fondly supposed himself to be an independent leftist.[48] That was not enough for Stalin. Largo Caballero would have to be replaced by an entirely obedient puppet. In November, the *apparat* had made its selection: The factotum would be Largo's Minister of Finance, a corrupt professor of economics named Juan Negrin, and the coup that installed him was carefully timed to put him in power in May 1937. At this same time, the Terror would be unleashed in its full violence in Spain.[49]

Why then would Stalin have been more interested in controlling the Spanish government than in defeating Franco? It is important to understand that Stalin did not undertake to replace Largo Caballero and destroy the non-Stalinist Spanish left because of some purely intellectual desire for ideological purity in Spain. That kind of motive would have been much more typical of Lenin than Stalin. Stalin didn't really give a damn about ideological purity in Spain or anywhere else. He wanted control over the Spanish government because he believed Spain would make him a new kind of player in European politics, bargaining between England and France on the one hand, and Germany on the other, and using Spain as his chip. Stalin had no objection to a shooting war to the west of Germany, especially one that might entangle the democracies or at least provide the basis for intense antifascist propaganda. And antifascism in Spain was all the more welcome to Stalin because the fascist in question was *not* Adolf Hitler—whom Stalin was still sedulously courting at exactly this time—and because Spain did not play a particularly significant role in Hitler's plans for Europe. Perhaps the most widely held platitude of Popular Front propaganda was that "fascism" had to be "stopped" in Spain. As a matter of practical politics, this notion was not only wrong, it was absurdly wrong. The fascist who most urgently needed to be "stopped" was Hitler, not Franco, and Hitler ruled *Germany*, not Spain. In fact, "stopping fascism in Spain" had next to nothing to do with "stopping Hitler." Hitler did not greatly care how the Spaniards settled their domestic differences, and Stalin, meanwhile, was certainly not going to let himself get sucked into a really serious Nazi-Soviet military showdown in Spain or anywhere else in Western Europe. Nothing could be more obviously against his interests, and he was rightly convinced that Hitler would also avoid any such imbroglio, simply because Hitler's true focus was on France, northern Europe, and England. For both dictators, Spain was a sideshow. Stalin certainly would not permit a serious Nazi-Soviet showdown in Spain or anywhere else to his West, and he was rightly convinced that Hitler would be sure to avoid it as well. Neither dictator cared much about Spain; it was the ideal scene for a proxy propaganda encounter.

That said, everything in Spain served Stalin. A Communist Spain might menace Hitler just enough to induce the German into concessions to assure that menace would slowly fade away—something Stalin could easily arrange. On the other hand, a fascist Spain placated Hitler and nicely heightened the fascist threat to France and England. Either victory or defeat served Stalin.[50]

***

Stalin's takeover of the Spanish government moved in several phases. First the apparatus had to infiltrate every aspect of the Spanish Republic's base of power, whether political or military. Caballero would have to be removed and replaced with the obedient and corrupt Negrin. At the same time, every possible force for resisting this takeover, any possible opposition in Spanish political life would have to be eliminated by force. Since the communists were a small minority on the Spanish left, this would require a huge, concerted assault against some of the Republic's main leftist constituents. Of course Stalin understood that this would demoralize the war against Franco and that fact did not trouble him at all.

A further piece of evidence suggesting that Stalin was proceeding toward an intentional sacrifice of Spain was his refusal to grant its government financial credit. Hitler and Mussolini liberally granted credit to Franco, thereby assuring that their client would win the war. Stalin was perfectly capable of supplying at least as good material and credit to the Republic as Hitler was sending Franco. But he knew that a government well armed and winning with his excellent equipment might not be entirely under his control, since he did not expect the Republican government to survive long enough to repay any credit he might extend. Therefore he insisted that his intentionally inadequate trickle of arms to Spain had to be paid for in cash on the barrelhead. To promote this policy, Stalin ordered the apparatus to set up an elaborate worldwide network for private financing of the Spanish war effort. To privatize the financing of the Spanish Civil War seems a curious choice for a communist; not that anyone noticed. In the righteousness clubs, the new, ceaselessly promoted test of virtue was giving money "for Spain." "Spain" became the favorite charity of the Popular Front. It was to finance the Republic's betrayal.

But keeping Spain on a short financial leash was not enough. Knowing that he had the Spanish government at his mercy, Stalin now undertook simply to assume control of their national treasury. Not for nothing had he first served the Bolsheviks by robbing banks. In this tremendous act of international grand larceny, Stalin's principal confederate was none other than Caballero's finance minister, Negrin: Indeed it was by assisting the *apparat* in looting the Spanish treasury that Negrin purchased his hour in the sun as premier.

In his 1939 book, Krivitsky described the robbery of the gold in the Spanish treasury, as did Alexander Orlov after his defection. The idea was to loot the country of the gold bullion that was its national treasure and transport it all to the Soviet Union, knowing full well that it would never be returned.[51] How this was accomplished is an incredible tale. Since the days of Philip II, an essential part of the Spanish patrimony had been the accumulation of one of the largest gold reserves in the entire world. Using Negrin and the *apparat*, the Soviets persuaded the Caballero government to transfer huge amounts of this gold to Moscow, partly for "safekeeping" against the menace of a Franco victory, and partly as "collateral" for their "credit" in buying arms. Of course Stalin had no intention of returning anything, ever.[52]

There are moments when a cynical interpreter might view the Civil War itself as more a literary event than a military one, despite the brutality of the war and its casualties. Since the days of Byron at Missolonghi, no military conflict was so richly given over to the rhetoric of the writer-hero as Spain—a direct consequence of its prime focus as propaganda rather than successful warfare. The cultural politics of the moment culminated above all in one painting: Picasso's great *Guernica*. But the mystique also produced many books of lasting power. At least two very good, and arguably great novels were produced by the two leading literary "heroes" of the hour: Malraux's *Man's Hope*, and Hemingway's *For Whom the Bell Tolls*. As an early negotiator with the Spaniards, Malraux was undoubtedly more politically witting than was Hemingway. Nonetheless, Malraux's presence in Spain was primarily propagandistic, as were his later adventures as an aviator, white scarf flying as he buzzed above the Ebro. Malraux's real service to the Soviets in Spain was to set the tone of Byronic glamour that dominated its image from the beginning until almost the end.[53]

But Spain was an irresistible center of all the literati in this period. On September 14, 1936, Stalin ordered a policy meeting on Spain to take place in the Lubyanka, during which the next phase of Soviet presence in the Spanish War was determined.[54] Until then most of the Soviet response had been made through the Comintern efforts, both secret and public. It was now decided that all Comintern operations in Spain would be placed under the direct control of the Soviet secret police, and it was simultaneously decided to use that secret police to take over total command of the Spanish Communist party.[55]

The politics of all this can be interestingly traced through the destinies of two indispensable secret agents then on the scene. Their names were Berzin and Orlov.[56] We have already come across both men. J. K. Berzin was the senior intelligence officer sitting at Radek's side in the Kremlin when Stalin summoned his officers on the Night of Long Knives and told them the new secret policy toward Hitler. Orlov on the other hand was a protégé of Yagoda, and when he left Spain he went on to England to take over running the Cambridge group from Theodore Maly. Berzin was an old-style Leninist, a military man-*cum*-intelligence operative, cynical and witting enough to have sat at Radek's side that night, trusted and unmoved. Orlov was a nastier item: a new-style NKVD thug, a graduate of the torture chambers in the basement of the Lubyanka, moving on up.

Berzin and Orlov: Each operated in Spain in great secrecy; each was given tremendous power. Berzin worked under deep cover. His mere presence in the country was a closely guarded secret, known to only a few officials of the Spanish government.[57] He was secretly in charge of the Loyalist Army in all its forms, including those foreign legions of the Comintern, the International Brigades. Berzin's right hand Vladimir Gorev, a senior general of the Red Army, also in Spain secretly. When the two generals arrived with, the rest of the Soviet team—which incidentally included Mikhail Koltsov—the Republic assigned Gorev a Russian speaking adjutant, who was present at Gorev's side through the man y momentous events that followed, including Gorev and

Berzin's unseen but decisive role in saving Madrid during Franco's assault of November 1936. This adjutant was a radical professor of Spanish from the Johns Hopkins University named José Robles Pazos. And as it happened, Robles was a close friend, back in America, of John Dos Passos.

Orlov was the covert commandant of the secret police in Spain.[58] He was the man Stalin appointed to run the Spanish Terror. Because Stalin was preparing the Red Army purge, he was in the process of shifting power away from his army to his secret police, and so Berzin and Orlov were soon at bureaucratic odds.[59]

Nonetheless, Orlov and the generals worked together to take control of the Spanish government. In October 1936, Stalin plotted his course. Two weeks later, Negrin was selected by Stashevsky to replace Largo Caballero and Orlov began to prepare for anti-anarchist provocations Madrid and Barcelona. By December *Pravda* had proclaimed that violent purges were the only path to victory in Catalonia. These actions were directed from Madrid and Valencia. Berzin and Orlov were of course fully aware of them.[60]

In early April, Stashevsky was in Moscow for meetings with Stalin and Tukhachevsky, whom the senior people still believed was empowered, even though the plan to kill them all was well advanced.

Then came May. It was in May that the *apparat* staged the coup that removed Largo Caballero. The public pretext for this move was a demand made to Largo by the Spanish Communist party that he join the Soviet organs in destroying his Anarchist allies in Catalonia, a demand that in effect would have meant the liquidation or suppression of virtually all non-Stalinist leftists among the government's alliance. In a propaganda move being advanced by Claud Cockburn and Katz, an anti-Stalinist Marxist group called the POUM was lumped with the Anarchists and all were denounced as "fascist collaborators." Largo was perfectly aware that these charges were lies, and of course flatly refused to approve. He was then told that Soviet aid depended on his submission. He still refused. At this point he was removed as a "defeatist" and replaced by the "victory" party of Negrin. The newspeak of Stalinist jargon tells the story. Because he pursued victory, Largo was removed as a defeatist. Negrin, because he was prepared to preside over defeat, led the "Victory" party.

In May, the new Terror promptly descended. The slaughters in Barcelona were shrieking forward in full cry. These were the events brought to light—though not fully understood—by George Orwell in his *Homage to Catalonia*, the first really serious break with the Popular Front by an important literary leftist. The leader of the POUM, a man named Andres Nin, was arrested, tortured, and at length murdered by Orlov and a murder team that worked with him.

At this moment, Stalin was seemingly at the apex of his influence in Spain. The Spanish treasury had been safely removed to Russian territory. Stalin had taken complete control of the Spanish Republican government. The Soviet role in Spain was either lied about or admired to the point of delirium throughout the Popular Front. Nobody seemed to notice that at this point the Axis powers stepped up their aid to Franco while Stalin began to gear his own assistance down.[61] By 1938 Stalin coolly told the Spanish ambassador that his "credit" was "exhausted."[62] In fact the Spaniards had never had any credit. They had paid for their poor bargain with all they had and with that bargain they were assisted to a foreordained defeat, which descended on them just two convenient months before Stalin sealed the alliance with Hitler that had been his object from the beginning.

But what had become of José Robles?

With the creation of the Popular Front, the apparatus set its sights on taking possession of the now unchallenged celebrity of Ernest Hemingway. He was an ideal Popular Front personality: In his way, Hemingway was as important in America as Gide had been in France. The directors of the Popular Front hoped to transform him into the biggest literary fellow traveler of them all.

It is hard to overstate, even today, the *ethical* impact of Hemingway's style on at least two generations of Americans. "He liberated our written language": so wrote his third wife, Martha Gellhorn, and though Martha Gellhorn was a woman with few illusions about Hemingway the man, decades later she could still pay him that just tribute in all admiration.[63] In his American way, Hemingway was performing what we might call the Byronic task: He rejuvenated the literary language and infused it with the promise of a hard, credible heroism. It was irresistible. And it was quickly recognized as the tremendously forceful thing that it was. By 1935, Hemingway's reputation had long since passed far beyond its origins in the modernist vanguard. He was by far the most famous highbrow American writer alive, and one of the most admired and influential literary heroes in the world. He had freed up the language, and that accomplishment, joined to his fame, meant that in the logic of things the Spanish War would be Hemingway's war, *par excellence*. In fact, one might almost say that the *style* of the Popular Front had been created with Hemingway and Malraux explicitly in mind. The new look was much indebted to their influence. For example, all three of the principal leaders in the Hollywood Popular Front—Lillian Hellman, Dashiell Hammett, and Dorothy Parker—were writers whose prose vulgarized Hemingway's style. In English, Hemingway was the most influential moralist of the Word in his era, passing beyond even Eliot. And the propaganda apparatus wanted him as much as they wanted Gide.

We already have seen how many people in or near Hemingway's circle were in or near the apparatus, and with the creation of the Front, some in innocence, some not, all went into a full court press around their hero. By 1936 the effort was fairly well advanced. Hemingway was becoming a fellow traveler, and his kind of style was very much Popular Front style.[64]

The device used to entangle Hemingway in the Münzenberg apparatus was a rather high-class propaganda film designed to be a fundraising vehicle in Hollywood and the more intellectual capitals It was thought indispensable to involve Hemingway as conspicuously as possible with this film.[65] Notice the choice of film as the vehicle, rather than anything written. Since Hemingway knew next to nothing about filmmaking, his actual role would be kept safely marginal, with the *apparat* maintaining full control over the product. Simultaneously, Hemingway had fallen in love with Martha Gellhorn, herself a fellow traveler, and a remarkably well-connected one: For example, she was an intimate friend of Eleanor Roosevelt, and often stayed in the Roosevelt White House.[66] For every possible reason, Hemingway had to be central to *The Spanish Earth*.

Step one was to involve Hemingway in the front committee that sponsored the film while it also concealed and assured *apparat* control. The *apparatchik* really running this committee was the filmmaker himself, a longtime and fully reliable "Münzenberg-man," the Dutch filmmaker Joris Ivens.[67] It was called "Contemporary Historians," and it consisted mainly of crypto-Communist celebrities like Lillian Hellman, Clifford Odets, and Dorothy Parker, along with "innocents" like John Dos Passos, Archibald Macleish, and of course Hemingway himself. Dos Passos had been Ivens' first targeted celebrity in America, and part of the logic in that courtship was to reach Dos Passos's great pal Hemingway. The idea was to concoct a propaganda movie that would entangle Hemingway in a Comintern enterprise, though in fact the real filmmaker would be Ivens, and real control would rest with him. This was the film that came to be called *The Spanish Earth*. The purpose of Contemporary Historians was to deck the picture in celebrity, raise money, and hide the Comintern's ownership of the whole operation.[68]

The year 1936 brought the long friendship of Dos Passos and Hemingway into a decisive phase. While Dos Passos had started his career a little ahead, Hemingway's reputation had now clearly bypassed Dos Passos's, and done so forever. To compound this rivalry, Dos Passos and particularly his wife Kate were very fond of Hemingway's wife Pauline, and they had very little sympathy for Hemingway's increasingly callous infidelity to her with Martha Gellhorn. Finally, Dos Passos, who until then had been by far the *apparat*'s favorite American vanguardist, was being displaced in the hard left's hagiography by the bigger star. Dos Passos's psychology, let us recall, was very much that of the good boy. Being good was as essential to his mentality as being bad was to Hemingway's. This meant that when Dos Passos heard serious arguments raised against his beliefs, he tried to take them in and respond to them. And serious arguments against Stalinism were now being heard, raised especially by Trotskyists in the increasingly harsh intellectual fray of New York. They were the kind of doubts that Hemingway the bad boy dismissed as niggling, intellectual, "chickenshit"—a favorite word. Dos Passos on the other hand listened and was uneasy.[69] From the *apparat*'s point of view, he was getting a little unreliable. If things got out of hand, though the apparatus had sedulously built him up, it might be necessary to discredit him. Nonetheless, Dos Passos remained one of the Contemporary Historians, though Ivens was clearly intent upon sabotaging Dos Passos's role in the film, and his reputation generally, as was the *apparat* itself, concerned with Dos Passos's increasingly "Trotskyite" tinge. It was agreed that Dos and Hemingway and all the happy band of Contemporary Historians would work on *The Spanish Earth* together.[70]

We have now reached the spring of 1937. Stalin's new policy was fully in place. Republican forces, guided by Generals Berzin and Gorev, and dominated by the Comintern's International Brigades, Madrid had withstood the siege of November, though the Republican government had removed itself to Valencia. Hemingway was already in Spain, and on March 3, Dos Passos sailed from New York for a brief stay in France before proceeding to the war. Very soon after, probably on Orlov's orders, and for reasons that may never be fully known, John Dos Passos's good friend José Robles was arrested in Valencia by the NKVD, taken into a basement, and shot to death.[71]

Of course Dos Passos knew none of this. His first stop in Valencia was with his prime contact there: Julio Alvarez del Vayo. Dos Passos presented himself brightly, ready for duty in Spain. They had lunch. The next stop for Dos was to see his friend Robles.

Except that for some reason nobody seemed able to tell him where Robles lived. That seemed odd: Dos Passos had understood that Robles had quite an important job in Valencia, yet nobody seemed to have heard of him. Soon Dos Passos found himself knocking on doors in the streets of the town, following vague leads from place to place. At last he came to a poor apartment in a poor quarter. There he found Robles's wife Margare, alone.

Alone and beside herself. José was gone. He had simply not come home one day, and since then she had not been able to get any information at all about where he was. Nobody would give her any help at all. She had been to the police, to del Vayo's office, to every important Spaniard she could think of, and she had learned nothing. What could they possibly have arrested him for? José was the most passionate Loyalist alive. Margare was terrified.

Dos Passos instantly understood that his duty was to help Margare Robles find and defend her husband. He acted at once.[72] His first step was to return to del Vayo and ask for information. In a flat lie, del Vayo professed ignorance of the entire matter.[73] Either then or a little later in Madrid, Dos Passos also approached another influential acquaintance, José Quintinilla, a secret policeman who did vaguely admit he'd heard there had been an arrest, but that the matter was minor. It would be cleared up soon, soon.

Julio Alvarez del Vayo at this moment had a great deal more to lie about than Robles's disappearance. Given the secret agenda of the Spanish War and his partnership with Katz, del Vayo's propaganda office was a far more conspiratorial place than a mere bureau for guiding and misguiding the press. Its actual task was the search for ideological conformity. A significant number of people working for del Vayo at this time were actually undercover agents involved in keeping the apparatus informed of any possible deviation from a Stalinist loyalty.

In Del Vayo's office there worked two young men. One of them, still only teenager, was Robles's son Francisco, or "Coco" Robles. Another was a bright young American communist propaganda agent, sent from New York via Moscow, named Liston Oak.[74] Oak had begun his secret work in New York, and his assignment in Spain was a promotion. He worked with the American in Del Vayo's office, among other things acting as a gofer and guide for visiting celebrities in Spain. When in Madrid, he spent inordinate amounts of time in the service of Hemingway, scouring the countryside for alcohol in sufficient quantity and quality for the master properly to hold court at the Hotel Florida.[75]

But as an *apparat* insider, he knew that Robles had been killed, though he apparently did not know why. Oak had been submitting reports to Del Vayo on the political reliability of various people involved in the effort, and he may not have grasped at first the purposes to which his reports on political correctness would be put. But Oak was a bright fellow. He soon began to discern the pattern and suspect he was being used as a finger man in a murder machine. And somehow or other, sometime in March, Liston Oak discovered the truth about his Coco Robles father, José.

With this knowledge, Liston Oak made what in retrospect was his first small step out of the Lie. He took aside young Coco Robles and told him that he knew, knew for certain, that his father was dead. The NKVD had shot him. And he asked that the boy and his mother please, *please* stop asking so many questions.

Dos Passos, meanwhile, still believing Quintinilla's line that Robles was being held for some minor infraction, proceeded to Madrid, where he was to join Hemingway and Ivens and the crew of *The Spanish Earth*. Hemingway and Martha Gellhorn were staying at the Hotel Florida, basking in all that came from Hemingway's position as celebrity-in-chief, whether it was the liquor brought by Liston Oak, or the publicity he was enjoying over his role as the new hero in what he called "my second war."[76]

When Dos Passos arrived, he was anything but welcome in Hemingway's eyes. As Hemingway saw it, Dos Passos was more interested in stirring up trouble, whining over this man Robles than he was in making *The Spanish Earth;* in addition, Dos Passos's disapproval of the affair with Martha Gellhorn had become fairly obvious by this time. It may have been sensing this that Gellhorn's own manner with Dos Passos became quite high-handed and arrogant. In any case, the two motives roused all of Hemingway's vengeful anger. What did Dos Passos know about what real men have to do in real wars? If ever there was an armchair radical, Dos Passos was it. Why the hell did he have to keep yammering on about Robles? Move on. We have a victory to win.

It was into this thickening atmosphere that Josephine Herbst also had arrived very shortly before, in mid-April.[77] Herbst was by no means famous enough to be counted among the Contemporary Historians, but she was much more witting politically. My guess is that Herbst was sent to Spain to help monitor and control the American literary celebrities in Madrid. She was inside the apparatus; enough to be trusted with the information that her husband was an agent of Soviet espionage in Washington. She had already done undercover work for the Münzenberg people in Germany, and in all probability had done it elsewhere both at home and abroad. But in truth, Herbst's entire presence in the literary world was essentially a creation of the propaganda apparatus.

Thus, as Herbst arrived in Spain she went immediately to del Vayo and, it is plain that as an insider to the apparatus, the situation was clearly laid out before her. She was forthrightly informed that Robles had been shot, without even a court-martial or any judicial proceeding whatever, as a fascist spy.[78] Herbst was told about the tensions this was causing among the American celebrities. She was consulted on how to handle it. Twenty-five years later, writing about these events in an elegant essay filled with falsehoods and evasions, Herbst admits that the apparatus wanted her to keep Dos Passos in the dark about Robles.[79] Herbst claims that as a matter of her own conscience she disagreed with this approach, and as Dos Passos's friend, proceeded to act independently, insisting that he be told. This claim cannot be proved, and is highly unlikely: In my view the evidence suggests that in Madrid Herbst did precisely the job the apparatus wanted her to do, and did it well. In any case, we certainly know that she left Valencia after a forthright briefing by her colleagues in the secret police *apparat,* and that she carried with her a clear mandate to play some part in the mess in the Hotel Florida.

If we look beyond her moralizing to what Herbst actually did, we see her arranging for the public humiliation and discredit of her dear friend John Dos Passos by surreptitiously spreading the lie that his close friend in Spain was a fascist spy and had been shot for it. This she did in the midst of a highly publicized series of communist provocations about "fascist spies" in the Republican ranks, then filling every paper and all political talk in Madrid. It was creating general hysteria about fascists penetrating the Loyalist effort. Those charges were being taken in all seriousness by the literary folk on the scene.[80] All evidence likewise indicates that the *apparat* lie about Robles as a fascist, spread in secret by Herbst, was likewise taken as the straight stuff by all the Americans at the Florida.[81] Moreover, though she later claimed to have doubted the truth of the story she was quietly disseminating about Robles, at no point did those doubts meaningfully change her actions in Madrid. Certainly she did not allow them to mitigate the public humiliation she now set out to inflict on Dos Passos.

When Herbst checked into the Florida, she was of course promptly drawn into the tensions between Dos Passos and Hemingway, both of whom she knew well. One morning after a terrifying, if slightly comic pre-dawn shelling of the hotel, she soon found herself speaking to Hemingway in complete privacy: It was over brandy—just after breakfast—in his room. Hemingway, like Dos Passos still under the impression that Robles was merely under arrest, embarked on a rant about Dos Passos's meddling. Herbst now made her move, and recalled it later in her own Hemingway-tinted prose. "I put down my drink and said, 'the man is already dead. Quintinilla should have told Dos.'"

Hemingway stared back thunderstruck.[82]

She quickly assured him that she spoke with authority. She had learned the truth reliably in Valencia, but from somebody whose confidence she could not break, someone who in turn had learned it from someone "higher up." Why Herbst could not break this "confidence" is unclear. Why she did not break it thirty years later is likewise unclear. In any case, the lie was safe with her. She told Hemingway that, since she was bound to keep the identity of her informant secret, if Dos was to be told, the story would have to seem to come from somebody other than herself. Using this very curious moral claim, Herbst assured her own anonymity.[83]

Under cover of that anonymity, Herbst next coached Hemingway on how he might handle Dos Passos's dilemma. Dos must be told. Dear friends like themselves could hardly let him remain in the dark. But told how? Where? They contrived not to take the obvious course of simply walking down the hall to Dos Passos's room, knocking on the door, and quietly telling him the truth. They knew perfectly well the story would come to him as a frightening defeat and shock; one might have thought that this was a moment in which the kind gesture called for privacy and discretion. No: Herbst and Hemingway decided to tell Dos Passos the next day, and in quite the opposite context. There was to be a large public gathering of noteworthy Russians and Germans and other foreign VIPs. Everybody would be there, and Hemingway and Dos Passos as the two leading celebrities on the scene would be the center of all eyes. Guided by Herbst, Hemingway decided this would be a far, far better place to tell Dos Passos about the death of his friend. But since Herbst could not be named as the source, who could they claim had told Hemingway the news? They decided to say that a "German correspondent" had broken it to him, right there at the party, on the spot. But what could they do when Dos Passos naturally asked to speak to this German correspondent himself? Well, Hemingway could say that the German correspondent had refused to speak to him.

Such was the strategy Josephine Herbst developed with Hemingway that night. Herbst thought it was a perfectly splendid plan, and she watched with knowing interest as it visibly aroused Hemingway's sadism.[84]

That afternoon Hemingway plunged into the job with the full vigor of that sadism. The occasion was a celebrity luncheon at the castle previously belonging to the Duke of Tovar, in honor of the Soviet-Spanish International Brigade.[85] At this highly political, very public gathering Hemingway swaggered up to Dos Passos in full view of the many people who were gathering round them in circles, and announced as cuttingly as possible that in case Dos Passos was still wringing his hands about his pal Robles, he might want to know that Robles had been found out as a fascist spy and shot.[86]

Dos Passos responded in consternation. Shot? A fascist spy? Where did he learn that? Hemingway instantly produced his and Herbst's lie about the "German correspondent." The "German correspondent" he added was in the room at that moment, but he would not speak to Dos Passos. It seems to me obvious that the plain implication of this lie was that the "German correspondent" saw Hemingway as trustworthy, and Dos Passos as not trustworthy. And so it was surely taken by all the many influential people standing there listening.

Meanwhile, Josephine Herbst stood at a distance, anonymous and safe, watching her handiwork take its cruel effect. Safely apart, peering across the room, she could not hear her two friends' voices, but she could watch Dos Passos's visibly mounting pain as Hemingway cut away at him.[87]

When Hemingway was done, Dos Passos spotted Josephine Herbst and turned to her for help. He approached her "with a little coffee cup in his hand," shaking, manifestly in extreme emotional pain. He explained the situation. Then he wondered again why, if Ernest had spoken to this German correspondent, he himself could not. Fully witting, Herbst calmly told Dos Passos that in her opinion the time had come for him to stop asking questions. She referred him to del Vayo, and with that she left him twisting in the public humiliation she herself had engineered.

Writing about this performance twenty-five years later, Herbst ascribes her motives to the promptings of an exquisitely delicate conscience, invoking claims that do not survive serious moral examination. Herbst's behavior toward Dos Passos was manipulative and dishonest from top to bottom. Its result was, I believe, its intention: to silence and humiliate Dos Passos while floating the lie, widely believed by almost everyone present, that his friend was a traitor. This was done in such a way as to create the very public impression that Hemingway was a politically reliable person while Dos Passos was not. That the Stalinist apparatus had embarked upon a courtship of Ernest Hemingway while simultaneously undertaking to discredit the too-inquisitive Dos Passos likewise strikes me as not incidental but central to the entire event. As to Herbst's later claim to have doubted the *apparat*'s fabrications about Robles, it seems only to make Herbst's performance the more cynical and contemptible. She was silent about those doubts in Madrid. It seems to me that Herbst was doing a job: to spread the lie about Robles

317

in such a way as to cement Hemingway's bond to the apparatus while discrediting Dos Passos as publicly as possible. Moreover, I believe it was almost certainly a job she had been assigned. In any case, it was a very nasty piece of work, and Herbst performed it to perfection.

But there is more. My research has established that a man was staying in the Hotel Florida at this time who, though a political associate of Herbst, is nowhere mentioned in her otherwise quite shamelessly name-dropping account. She can't have missed him; she mentions fraternizing with his party. Yet she never mentions this unseen friend in her talk about Spain, or for that matter anywhere in all her writing. Like her own husband, he was a Soviet agent. Once in Madrid, she almost certainly performed that mission in the literal physical presence and probably the collaboration of the NKVD agent who had for several years been her mentor, guide, and quite possibly, control. This man was Otto Katz. It seems likely, virtually certain, that Katz was himself at the Duke of Tovar's castle for the occasion when Herbst set up Dos Passos's humiliation, in a role that could very plausibly be described as that of a "German correspondent." While Josephine Herbst stood at her safe distance watching Ernest Hemingway perform the cruel task she'd set for him, Otto Katz was almost certainly on the sidelines too, likewise watching.[88]

After the humiliation of John Dos Passos before the assembled cultural grandees in Madrid, Hemingway was free to take the leading American role in the Popular Front. Talk about *The Spanish Earth* continued, and Dos Passos even remained in Madrid long enough to give the filmmakers and Hemingway a number of suggestions that were actually adopted. But everything was ruined. For one thing, stricken though he was, Dos Passos refused to back down. He refused to accept the lie. He still saw his duty with Margare Robles. His next task, as he saw it, was to return to Valencia, comfort Margare, and extract a death certificate for Robles from the Spanish government, since he knew that the widow could never collect on Robles's life insurance from Hopkins without it. He went to del Vayo, and in another lie del Vayo promised to procure such a document. Of course he never did.[89]

Before leaving Madrid, Dos Passos ran into another friend from the Hemingway circle, Evan Shipman—a Hemingway flunky, truth be told—who sneered that now that the "treason" of Dos Passos's dead pal Robles had been exposed, Dos Passos would do himself some good by clearing out of Spain. No place for traitors in pure, pure Spain. In later accounts, Hemingway himself would repeatedly crow over Dos Passos's "cowardly" departure from the country. Without exception, these stories were flat-out fabrications. Dos Passos left Spain exactly when he'd always planned to leave Spain, and from this moment forward, Dos Passos's behavior was notable not only for its rectitude but especially its courage.[90]

We are now very near the end of April. The May provocations are about to begin in Barcelona, and after Valenica it was to Barcelona that Dos went next. The Terror was about to be unleashed in Barcelona without restraint, and the detested Nin, whom Dos Passos was slated to meet and interview, would soon be murdered, along with his cohorts. When he got to Barcelona, Dos Passos was accosted in the lobby of his hotel by a very tall, but manifestly ill, young Englishman who was eager to shake the hand of John Dos Passos. His name was Eric Blair, and he wrote himself, using the pen name George Orwell. He was a big admirer. Dos Passos and Orwell went into a side room off the lobby and had a long and troubling conversation about the direction of events, though neither knew, yet, about the bloodletting about the begin in Catalonia.

But Liston Oak did know about it. The young American was also in Barcelona that late April, and he bumped into a man he's known from the New York docks, a professional party "enforcer," that is a professional murderer and thug, named George Mink, who told him he had been brought by the party to do a few little jobs connected to the big changes that were going to be happening here in May. Nin for example. The Party was going to liquidate Nin. Knowing this, Oak went to Nin's headquarters and warned the man—a wildly reckless action for an *apparatchik* like himself—and of course since the party had Nin under surveillance his "treachery" was instantly known. Oak was immediately called before another party enforcer, and told he had been seen. The Party wanted an explanation.

Late that night, Dos Passos was heard an almost inaudible knocking at the door of his hotel room. When he opened the door, he confronted the frightened face of Liston Oak. Oak had reached his own fear. He was convinced that he would never leave Spain alive unless he left it now. Right now.

And he had come to Dos Passos for help in the escape. They would never let him leave with what he knew. He was being tracked; if he ran, he would never reach the border alive. Oak had come to Spain as an invisible man, and he knew perfectly well that he could and now almost certainly would die in Spain an invisible man, just as Robles had died invisible—invisible, except for the fluke of Dos Passos's loyalty. His very presence in Spain was a secret. If they killed him now, nobody would ever know or credit the truth, except at best a few friends and abused intellectuals back in New York.

But Dos Passos? Dos Passos was a famous man. The apparatus could not liquidate him without an unpayable price in worldwide publicity. Dos Passos's face had been on the cover of *Time*. He carried the shield of visibility, and Liston Oak knew that he was going to die, and die very soon, unless he had some sort of shield.

In that hotel room the young man whispered because he knew the room was bugged, and in a whisper he pleaded for help.

Dos Passos took all this in and once again acted with clarity and dispatch. He told Oak that he was from that moment no longer Liston Oak from del Vayo's propaganda office, but Liston Oak the private secretary of John Dos Passos. They were leaving together for the French border immediately, that very hour. As they made their way north, Liston was not to leave Dos Passos's side, not once, not for a moment.[91]

And so it was that John Dos Passos left Spain and communism, shielding the terrified young defector not with his body but with his fame, keeping him covered on their every step north. It was not until the two had crossed the border at Perpignan that the young man could emerge from the horror into which they had both been lured, and was free.

Chapter 13

MÜNZENBERG'S END

After his escape from Moscow in October 1936, Münzenberg's energies were directed to saving his own life. That did not, however, lead him to anything like a quick or overt break with Stalin. On the contrary. Though Willi knew he had fallen from Stalin's grace, once he returned to Paris clutching the "sheet anchor" of his Spanish operations, he performed some of his most notable services ever to the regime. Yet even as he used Spain to escape from the net of arrests dropping around Radek, Willi understood that henceforth his survival would be a strictly provisional thing, and that the menace of liquidation would become even more dire once his usefulness in the Spanish War came to an end.

Seven months later, during the bloody summer of 1937, that end came at last. The Spanish government was entirely in the hands of the NKVD. The Comintern in Spain, behind its Byronic facade of Popular Front idealism, had become a mere mask for the secret police. Put in personal terms, the process that would separate Otto Katz from Willi was now complete. Put in more general terms, the Comintern, which had always been the base of Münzenberg's power, was being liquidated. For the first months of

1937, Willi retained some measure of influence within the apparatus. He could still protect himself with an uneasy mixture of blackmail, service, and visibility. But in May and June of 1937, it was very clear that he would soon stand in need of a quite new kind of shield.

We have called it "the shield of visibility." For Willi, it took many forms. Around the same time, Whittaker Chambers would call the process of assembling such a defense "creating an identity." But Chambers was a man who had gone underground; he had chosen the invisibility and anonymity of life as a spy, only to discover how easily you could die in that half-light, unseen. During the years after that recognition, Chambers lived in terror, sure he would die as Robles had died, as Liston Oak had feared dying. Safety meant escaping that lethal obscurity. Chambers had to reappear, be seen again. He needed to re-enter the civic life, get a job, a visible job; writing regularly, with a byline for all to see. He had to be known to friends, attend the PTA, live once more in the human sphere rather than in the dank anonymity of conspiratorial hatred.

With Münzenberg, the process was rather different. Münzenberg was in far more direct danger than Chambers ever confronted, but as a leading "antifascist," Willi was already a famous man. His safety now depended upon whether he could use his visibility as a shield, even though he was locked in a secret struggle against his old comrades. Not surprisingly, he found his self-defense behind the facade of the antifascist movement that he had helped create.

Willi's effort to shape a new and better shield out of his antifascism was a perilous course. By 1937, Stalin's search for an alliance with Hitler was already very far advanced, and there was a general understanding among witting agents that the Germans would no longer be the objects of any serious hostile operations. The Popular Front, including the Popular Front's Civil War in Spain, would soon be tossed away.[1] In December 1936, shortly after the Spanish Stratagem was fully conceived and on its way to implementation, Walter Krivitsky had a meeting in Paris with Slutsky, the foreign director of the NKVD. Slutsky's immediate object was to acquire from Krivitsky's networks two young male agents capable of impersonating Nazis over a fairly long period. Krivitsky was not aware of it at the time, but these recruits were to be used in the conspiracy to frame Field Marshal Tukhachevsky and the rest of the Red Army general staff. In his talk with Krivitsky that day, Slutsky forthrightly laid out the state of affairs, some six months before Negrin was installed and the Spanish Terror turned up to full strength.

"We have set our course toward an early understanding with Hitler," Slutsky said, "and we have started negotiations. They are progressing favorably."

Krivitsky was slightly confused. This was the month after Negrin had been selected as the Stalinist premier-to-be of Spain, and five months before he was actually installed. Krivitsky was well aware that Stalin was seeking an accommodation with Hitler, but the secret agent didn't yet really grasp the link between the German deal and events in Spain. How, he asked Slutsky, could the German conversations be proceeding so very well despite the Spanish imbroglio? Slutsky brushed aside the contradiction. "This time," he said, "it's the real thing. It will be only a matter of three or four months before we come to terms with Hitler. . . . There is nothing for us here in this rotting corpse of France with its *Front Populaire*. . . . I can give you Stalin's own view in his own words. He recently said to Yezhov, in the immediate future we shall consummate an agreement with Germany."[2]

This was in 1936; it was not 1939.

Six months later, the Spanish Terror would be fully unleashed. As the Spanish Civil War wound down toward that defeat which Stalin, in my view, had long since chosen for it, the Soviets turned their attention to those spots in Eastern Europe where Stalin expected the largest gains: Romania, Poland, Finland, Austria, Czechoslovakia, away from sideshows like Spain to the places he proposed really to hold and really make submit.

This meant that as 1937 gave way to 1938, Münzenberg's usefulness to the apparatus was ominously dwindling toward nothing.

At the same time, while Otto Katz continued to move between Valencia and Paris, Otto was less and less concerned with Spanish matters; instead, he was more and more steadily involved in Eastern European politics, especially in the Beneš government, managing the covert communists within the Czech foreign ministry. His role there grew increasingly active and conspiratorial. From Spain to Eastern Europe; from the Comintern to the NKVD; here were the new realities of the secret world as it moved toward the Second World War.

During the three and a half months between Radek's arrest in October 1936 and his trial in January 1937 in Moscow, Münzenberg was maneuvering in uncertainty, trying to solidify his position in Spain by building on his role in RUP and in the new German Popular Front. During this tune, it was far from clear what kind of deal Radek would make with the dictator, or what direction the show trial would take. Would Münzenberg be condemned from the dock? It was easily imaginable. Would Radek in his "confession" take Willi down with him? If the deal with Hitler was near consummation, it would be easily imaginable. Could the Terror reach straight into Paris?

When Radek's trial began in January, Münzenberg decided that it would be best for him to become "ill" for the time being, and for purposes of his "health," seek a little seclusion in the country. A cover story was concocted: He was suffering from a "mild cardiac neurosis." There was also a story about a "nervous breakdown."[3] It is plain that there was nothing wrong with him at all. Nonetheless Willi checked into a little-known clinic in the French countryside, secreted on what had once been the country estate of the French romantic poet Chateaubriand. There he submitted himself to the care of a remarkable French physician known as Dr. Le Savoureux.[4]

As best I can determine, the clinic of Dr. Le Savoureux was a perfectly genuine medical establishment. At the same time, it was a safe house in what amounted to an anti-Bolshevik underground. It bore the resonant name "La Clinique de la Vallée aux Loups." There, in Valley of the Wolves, near the little village of Chatenay-Malabry, Münzenberg found haven while the Radek trial ran its course.

Dr. Le Savoureux seems to have been a man of very considerable courage and impressive ideological suppleness. His own nationality, I gather, was French. He was married however to a Russian, a daughter of Plekhanov, a revolutionary and a former companion of Lenin who had become a leader of the Menshevik faction against Lenin in the days just before the Revolution. The doctor and his wife therefore moved along the Russian émigré left—circles famously penetrated by the Soviet services. Nonetheless, the clinic on the estate of the old romantic poet seems to have been safe. At least it was hard to kill people staying there. In it, Dr. Le Savoureux ran a sort of protection service for people in danger.

While Willi was hiding out in the clinic at Chatenay-Malabry, the doctor told him an interesting tale. During the spring of the same year, none other than Nikolai Bukharin, who would succeed Radek in the dock during the next great show trial, had been in Paris during an official mission to the West. This visit to Paris had taken place in the spring, a few months before Maxim Gorky's death.[5] That visit, with the contact Bukharin made with Dr. Le Savoureux, casts an interesting new shaft of light on the old Bolshevik's visit to Gide in his hotel room the day before Gorky's State Funeral, and especially on Bukharin's urgent desire to speak to Gide privately and confidentially. It also casts new light on Bukharin's sudden recognition that Gide was not going to be competent to hear whatever he had to say. That is when Bukharin backed out of the writer's hotel room, mute with what Herbart had called his "smile of unspeakable contempt."

Bukharin's official mission in Paris had been to arrange for the purchase for the Soviet archives of major papers in the archives of the German Social Democrats. They included important papers of both Marx and Engels, and this was to be a perfectly legitimate purchase. The discussions were to take place with the Menshevik curator of the papers, a scholar named Boris Nicholaevsky.[6]

Bukharin's conversations with Nicholaevsky soon passed far beyond mere discussion about the possible purchase of the papers. They became confidential, then secret. Bukharin began to speak with great candor on the political machinations taking place at the highest levels around Stalin.* Nicholaevsky's slightly fictionalized report on these conversations, later published as "A Letter from an Old Bolshevik," is a major document. George Kennan has called it "the most authoritative and important piece of source material we have of the purges."[7]

It appears that during this same visit, perhaps through Nicholaevsky, Bukharin was also introduced to Dr. Le Savoureux. It seems that the possibility was at least raised that Bukharin, for whom the Soviet shadows were lengthening at an alarming rate, might defect to the West and become, presumably, a kind of second Trotsky.

Bukharin, at any rate, was with Dr. Le Savoureux when he received his telegram ordering him to break off his discussions with Nicholaevsky and return at once to Moscow. It was obviously a signal of the end, an invitation to an execution. Bukharin was rigid with fear. His voice shook as he spoke; he was white, in despair. It was plain that his life was at an end.[8]

Dr. Le Savoureux tried to persuade Bukharin to refuse this summons. I can only suppose Bukharin and the Menshevik also spoke about what sort of protection Bukharin the defector could hope for, under the threat of Stalin's vengeance. Trotsky's exile was lived, and lived precariously, inside a nomadic armed camp, under security

---

* A glimpse of Radek in these intrigues can be found in Nicholaevsky, *Power and the Soviet Elite*, p. 37. "The Letter from an Old Bolshevik" (Nicholaevsky's representation of his conversations with Bukharin in 1936), suggests both what a senior figure like Bukharin knew, and what he did not know, as the Terror approached. It's an arresting detail that, according to Nicholaevsky, Bukharin believed that the Popular Front had been set up as a response to a secret propaganda network established in the USSR by none other than Ernst Röhm. He was told that a "network" of agents working for the Nazis had been set up by Röhm, dominated by homosexuals active in Moscow cultural life! This all-but-forgotten "conspiracy" was surely a Stalinist canard, but in it one glimpses again several threads we've already seen. The "homosexual conspiracy" of Moscow has the look of an intrigue parallel to the Reichstag Fire Trial—its Russian branch, as it were. It may well have been part of Stalin and Hitler's joint effort to discredit Röhm by focusing on his homosexuality, and thereby prepare him for his demise.

far more stringent than what was then accorded to most heads of state. And even so, within three years, the ice-axe would be driven into his brain.

Bukharin could not, or would not, make that move. He would not, or could not, turn aside this summons to the slaughterhouse. It makes one wonder all the more what message he wished to confide to Gide in those moments before Gorky's funeral.

Feigning illness in the Valley of the Wolves, sheltered in Dr. Le Savoureux's safe house, Münzenberg waited for Radek's trial to run its course. He watched every twist, every ripple in the flow of the trial's mendacity. As it moved forward, Münzenberg discovered that he was not being denounced in the courtroom, not implicated. Radek was at last convicted, but mysteriously he was not condemned to death. For some reason, Stalin had decided to delay Radek's demise; for the moment, there would be no bullet behind his ear. This must have been, for Willi too, a kind of reprieve. Münzenberg's jeopardy had deepened, but it was not yet absolute.

With reason. In January 1937, Willi's usefulness to the regime still had five or six months to run. He was still busy with his task, organizing the propaganda networks of the last lying Comintern cause in Spain. Willi's "sheet anchor" still held.

But once the Soviet secret police had completed its kidnapping and capture of the Spanish Republic, Münzenberg lost the last protective device he had to bind his life and safety to Stalin's power. Within a month of the Spanish Terror, the machinery of Willi's undoing began to work overtly. In October 1937 the German Party obediently expelled Münzenberg himself. The rationale for his denunciation was typical Stalinist newspeak. Münzenberg was deemed insufficiently devoted to the Popular Front. In other words, the Popular Front was finished, and with its fall Willi was without his shield.

He would therefore need a new approach. Once Spain was past, Willi's strategy now became to take up genuine leadership in the antifascism of the German émigrés, even at a time when the apparatus was withdrawing from that concern. It was the era of what Münzenberg came to call the "Heinrich and Thomas Mann Committees," and Willi's tactic was to manipulate within these righteous-ness groups so as to keep them constantly alive, while keeping the Party slightly off guard. He was trying to outmaneuver the system he himself had created; Münzenberg had become mongoose to his own snake. As a result, these groups often acquired a more authen-tically antifascist tone then they'd had earlier. Willi was sure that his safety required him to stay continuously involved in the propaganda operations that united his friends and his enemies, both real and apparent. He could not break with anyone, nor could he commit himself to anyone. If the dissociations of terror can be called intel-lectual independence, now at last Willi was in possession of that "independence," the illusions of which he had spent the previous two decades organizing. He needed enough distance from Stalin so that he could discreetly disobey; at the same time, he needed to stay close enough to the apparatus so that it could not shoot him with-out shooting its own foot. So it was a very special dance.

In the archives, for example, there is the report of a meeting of a "Heinrich and Thomas Mann Committee." It took place in 1938. Both Willi and Otto were present, though they were both now deep in the hostility of which I speak. The prime "innocent" present was Thomas Mann. Otto's purpose in the gathering was to suborn one of the righteousness committees with some apparatus money from England. Willi was not going to let him get away with it. The battle flew back and forth, past the author of *Death in Venice*, con-ducted in double talk. In the end, Otto's effort failed, Willi was left still crucial to the committee, and Thomas Mann departed, digni-fied but bewildered.[9]

Meanwhile, the NKVD, following Stalin's order to Dimitrov, set out on a systematic effort to lure Münzenberg back to Russia. This was good news; it meant that the shield of visibility was effec-tive enough to prevent simple assassination in Paris. Time and again in communications from Moscow, Willi was asked, ordered, com-manded, lured, cajoled, begged. Messengers ranging from Count Károlyi to Louis Fischer, editor of the *Nation*, came bearing the invitations.[10] Time and again, Willi dodged the call. Dimitrov him-self sent many requests. At one point a senior NKVD agent named

Beletsky, whom Willi knew to be high up in Stalin's political assassination squadron, the sinister Bureau of Special Tasks, personally approached him, all smiles. Come home. Don't be afraid. "Who decides your fate?" Beletsky asked him, in a pertinent question. "Dimitrov or the OGPU? And I know that Yezhov is on your side."[11]

It was a trap, of course, and of course Willi sidestepped it. As late as May 1938, four months before Munich, these efforts still were going forward. That month, Louis Gibarti was recalled from his NKVD work in New York and returned to Europe, assigned instead to new work in Spain and Paris. Before Gibarti left New York, he was taken aside and warned by Earl Browder, the chairman of the American Communist party, that he should have nothing to do with the traitor Münzenberg.[12]

When Gibarti returned to Paris, he instantly sought out Willi. They met in as public a place as they could arrange: the terrace of the Cafe Viel. As they sat together, Münzenberg pulled out of his pocket a recent letter from Dimitrov, renewing the appeal to return to Moscow. Gibarti read it, and tried to make the case that Dimitrov was right; there was nothing to fear; it would be perfectly safe for him to return.

Safe? Willi shrugged. If he returned to Moscow, he said, he would be shot like all the others. Ten years later, he would be rehabilitated. And so, he concluded, it was a trip he'd skip. Then Münzenberg folded the letter, slipped it back in his pocket, and while Gibarti searched for an answer, gazed out into the springtime square.[13]

But Münzenberg was a publisher, and to maintain his visibility he needed some public forum for these new maneuvers. He needed a magazine. In 1938, he founded a new and in many ways groundbreaking journal of politics and ideas, a publication which he named, with what must have seemed then quixotic bravery: *Die Zukunft*, the future. *Die Zukunft* was to be a high-level forum for the arguments and hopes of the menaced German left. But it was also intended as Münzenberg's shield. The magazine was a classic Münzenberg-style mix of innocence, intellectual grandeur, and unseen agendas. Its personnel included rebels and geniuses, sympa-

329

thizers and secret agents. Arthur Koestler and Manes Sperber edited it; the brothers Mann wrote for it; Gibarti worked out of its office, and Otto Katz meddled in it. As the decade now hurried toward its climax in war, almost against its own intentions *Die Zukunft* evolved into something that in retrospect has the look of the first truly anti-totalitarian journal for the senior intelligentsia.

It was a model for publications to come. The manner and even the personnel of *Die Zukunft* suggest Melvin Lasky's postwar publication *Der Monat*, and through that link, the publications of the Congress for Cultural Freedom: *Encounter, Preuves,* and *Tempo Presente.* In the movements of the Popular Front, guided by the life-and-death politics of the Terror, the profile of what would become a post-war anti-communist intelligentsia was taking shape.[14]

Finally, like many people deposed from great power, Münzenberg wrote a book. It was called *Propaganda als Waffe (Propaganda as a Weapon),* a skillful and spectacularly well-informed analysis of Nazi methods in the propaganda war. *Propaganda als Waffe* should be viewed as more or less Willi's own, though the real writing in it was much assisted by a still loyal Münzenberg-man, Kert Kersten. Politically, the book is both flamboyant and careful. Very careful. It is relentless on its attack on Hitler; its tone about Stalin is one of bland deference. It slams no doors.

Meanwhile, switching from tones of seduction to the snarl of menace, the apparatus grew more and more frustrated. The Comintern archives contain extensive dossiers laying out the "Case of WM," with the most concentrated work against Münzenberg being supplied by Wilhelm Pieck, the man who was the intermediary in the Dimitrov Conspiracy, and later the first president of the Stalinist East German Republic. In June 1937, a Comintern functionary, Bohumil Smearl, arrived in Paris attempting to retrieve for the Comintern large deposits held in various European banks in Willi's name.[15] Kurt Sauerland, a young writer loyal to Münzenberg, was being held prisoner hostage to Münzenberg in Moscow. He would surrender the deposits, Willi reportedly told Smearl, only if Sauerland were released. Willi was now bartering with lives. (The tactic was a passing success and long-term failure. Young Sauerland's life was spared until Münzenberg was safely dead. Then he was executed as well.)[16] But Willi was not without some threats of his own. It has also been claimed that Münzenberg threatened to go public with secrets of Soviet covert operations if he were expelled from the German Party.[17] That threat failed: The Party moved to expel him in late 1937, though in yet another cat-and-mouse game his expulsion only became final in the summer of 1938.[18] Still, he was threatening to talk. And how much might he tell? A little? A lot? Would he bargain with his revelations? Münzenberg was becoming a really dangerous man.

Meanwhile, the tortoise had lifted his scaly foot and was considering his next step. The next step was the Second World War. After September 1, 1939, it was no longer possible for Münzenberg to remain protected by his ambiguity. In *Die Zukunft*, for the first time, he denounced Stalin. Yet in retrospect, even this performance seems rather mild, a purely moralistic attack. In truth, Münzenberg's response to the pact and the war was as much a matter of covering his own position as a serious assault. And now he would be needing protection of a new kind.

He may have found some protection with the European services. With the war, the secret services of the democratic allies began to gather in Paris. A sometime Münzenberg-man, Paul Willert, was assigned to be the representative of British intelligence in the British Information Office opened in Paris under Noël Coward. It was at this point that Münzenberg began to hold his little lunches.

Once a week, in the private dining room of a restaurant on the Left Bank, Willi would give a lunch for the assembled young secret service agents of the allied forces. During these meals he would systematically analyze the advances of the new Nazi-Soviet allies from his uniquely well-informed point of view. One of those regularly in attendance was Paul Willert. The assembled agents listened like schoolboys.[19]

It was a very ingenious new political device Münzenberg had created. He now knew that he would need to be turning to the allies for his protection, but he also knew that the French, English, and American governments, and especially their secret services, were penetrated by Stalinist agents and sympathizers, and that he could not entrust himself to them. The restaurant room was a good venue. Speaking there, he knew that his views would be heard every week in the English and French chancelleries. At the same time, while he met with these young men behind closed doors, he met with them in semi-public, entrusting his physical safety to none of them. Yet.

The British especially were interested in his fate, and at the senior reaches of the British government, Ellen Wilkinson, now a passionate anti-Stalinist, became particularly interested in Willi's destiny. It was at this time that Münzenberg warned Ellen that she should use the utmost care in any matter concerning either him or Arthur Koestler when dealing with the British intelligence service, that one of his most dangerous enemies was to be found there.[20] It was likewise at this point that both Ellen Wilkinson and her friend Herbert Morrison became implacable adversaries of Guy Liddell, much to the outrage of Liddell's prime protégé in SOE, Kim Philby.[21] In fact it was Wilkinson who now brought an end to Liddell's previously uninterrupted rise in the British security services. Was Liddell the man Münzenberg feared? The record is unclear, but plainly Willi was not quite prepared to entrust his safety to either the British or the French.[22] He felt it was essential to keep his distance from them, while at the same time remaining steadily within their view.

This combination of conspicuousness and concealment could last only so long. In the spring of 1940, the invasions of Scandinavia and the Benelux, followed by Hitler's attack on France, at last knocked the shield of visibility from Münzenberg's hand.

***

In my opinion, Willi Münzenberg probably met his death at the hands of the NKVD. But the fact is far from certain. As the reader will see, a plausible case can and has been made that Münzenberg committed suicide, hanged himself from a tree on the outskirts of a wood near a tiny town in the Isere valley of the Midi in the early evening of June 21, 1940, the day after the fall of France. And despite improbability, I grant that suicide is at least a possible explanation.

Certain it is that Münzenberg died violently, and by strangulation. I believe the more likely case is political assassination. Most analyses of Münzenberg's death maintain that he was probably killed by an NKVD execution team tracking his flight south during those days of frantic desperation when France was falling. That argument rests upon the certainty that Willi had been an NKVD target for years, and that at this time the Bureau of Special Tasks was regularly exploiting the southward flight of refugees to settle scores.[23] Moreover, in early 1940 Münzenberg had delivered on an old threat to Stalin, publishing in a Belgian paper the names of forty important German communists killed in the Great Terror. This sort of list had never before appeared from such an authoritative source.[24]

But was the end suicide or murder? I am uncertain. The logic of my uncertainty runs something like this. If Willi did not commit suicide, he was certainly murdered. *If* he was murdered, he was almost certainly murdered either by the NKVD, or by the NKVD assisted by the Nazis. Moreover, though there is a plausible case to be made for suicide, that case rests almost entirely upon the unsupported word of a prime suspect in the murder. Add to this that Münzenberg was in no way a melancholic or saturnine personality. Nobody among his close associates has ever been able to accept that he could take his own life. His situation on June 21, 1940, was desperate, but not impossible. With really determined effort, he might well have escaped from France. In truth, every single person who was in flight with him, without exception, did reach safety, and they all reached it fairly soon.

Still, at that moment in 1940, Münzenberg understood that he was peculiarly on his own and that he was a hunted man, living under a particular menace of his own. He knew his escape from France, and his future wherever he went, would be shadowed by the secret services of two lethal dictators, both of whom wanted him dead. Here is where suicide seems possible. A certain kind of very dynamic person, cornered, may refuse even at the last to surrender control, and in that defiance may take things firmly back into his own hands, albeit for the last time.

Suicide or murder? Whether Münzenberg died in defiant despair, or was killed cornered, he died the victim of what he had helped create.

Here is what we know happened, with some speculation.

At the beginning of April 1940, the *blitzkrieg* against Norway and Denmark began: By the beginning of May the panzers were rolling into the Low Countries. The French government ordered all German (and American) men not of draft age and not previously interned to internment camps. As the last issue of *Die Zukunft* appeared, Münzenberg had to make his decision. Would he take flight, seeking a way out of France, running presumably toward English protection, on his own? Or should he submit to the internment system, and to the very uncertain protection of the French? It is important to know that in making this decision Münzenberg turned for assistance to his friends in British intelligence. Very shortly before he made his move, he had a meeting with Paul Willert and Sefton Delmer, both of SOE. And he asked Willert and Delmer what they thought he should do.[25]

One need not raise any questions about the reliability of either Paul Willert or Sefton Delmer to realize in retrospect that this was an insecure conversation. For if Münzenberg's path of escape was relayed back to British intelligence in London, as it certainly would have been, the SOE official receiving it in London might well have been Kim Philby. Moreover, even if Philby did not know Willi's path, serious questions have been raised about the reliability of Sefton Delmer.[26] One way or the other, the conversation was dangerous. In any case, the British agents advised Münzenberg to enter an internment camp, and take that route south.

Thus, on the advice of Delmer and Willert, somewhere around May 13 or 14, 1940, Babette and Münzenberg went to a stadium called the Stade des Colombes, together with throngs of German and American men being gathered to be interned. The German victory grew hourly more palpable. Everyone knew they had to get to the Spanish border, and the path out, probably through Casablanca, or perhaps Marseilles, or conceivably the Swiss border.

Babette and Willi had made exact plans for a rendezvous in the south once they left internment. She was to be interned in a camp for German women near Gurs. But now as the crowd swarmed around them the moment of parting came. They put their arms round each other, and then Münzenberg walked into the throng of evacuees in the babble of German and some American English. They were swept away from each other.

Willert and Delmer had been right: Waves of refugees from the Low Countries clogged every route of escape from Paris to the South. Internment was in a way easier than flight, and everyone expected it to be short. Many saw it not as imprisonment, but as a superior means of escape. The men were separated out into groups of one hundred and sent to various sites. The one chosen for Münzenberg was at Chambarran, south of Lyons. And so Willi departed, part of the anonymous stream.[27]

It has been suggested by some that Münzenberg had a clear destination not in Casablanca but Marseilles, where it is said that he was to meet his old friend Valeriu Marcu, a rich Rumanian émigré, a former communist, and a practiced conspirator and friend of Münzenberg from the earliest days, before the Revolution. Marcu, it is claimed, had a large sum of money for Willi, along with the documentation needed to let him sail out of the port of Marseilles a free man. This rendezvous, if it was ever real, may or may not have been planned in conjunction with the British services. Babette Gross did not believe the story. Moreover, the evidence seems to indicate that in the crisis of June 21, Willi was interested in moving not toward Marseilles but Switzerland, where he and Babette had safe bank accounts. I myself tend to discount—though I don't outright dismiss—the story of Marcu's role in the "rescue."[28]

The camp of Chambarran is an enormous military base near Lyons. The picture we have of Münzenberg once he reached the place is curiously bucolic, given the kind of fear and anguish one would expect the whole company to be feeling. Here is the great tycoon of the secret life, subdued, to be sure, but out in the sun of the fresh springtime, working not unhappily at his assigned job, which was tending the camp commandant's garden. For the first time in his adult life, Willi was out of touch with power. For the first time in his adult life, he was neither more nor less than a man among men, chopping away at the French soil, planting beans. Reports differ slightly, but he does not seem to have been particularly depressed. True, he was—small wonder!—downcast, introspective. He drifted into uncharacteristic silences. His talk was filled with worry about Babette.[29] Yet depression is not the word the witnesses used.

The men interned at Chambarran were mainly middle-aged German exiles, many of them members of that German left which Willi had been so instrumental organizing as the Popular Front. In fact, the company was distinguished. With Münzenberg was Kurt Wolff, the great German, and later American, publisher: Leopold Schwarzschild, the liberal writer and editor. There were many others. These were among the leading lights of that German civilization which Hitler was murdering. It must be added that in all the camps—Chambarran, Le Vernet, Le Cheylard, and others, the apparatus had its cadres well in place.[30]

Typical of such cadres was the person who appeared on the scene next. The newcomer was especially noticeable among all those middle-aged men because he was so young. He appeared among them one fine morning, looking like he was in his early twenties. The fellow had, it was universally recalled, red hair. Let us call him the "Red-Headed Youth." The Red-Headed Youth had a strange tale to tell of having been a communist in a Nazi concentration camp, from which he had managed to be released. Released, he had made his way to France, and now found himself in Chambarran.[31]

This unexpected newcomer, whose name remains completely unknown, was peculiarly interested, even pre-occupied with Münzenberg. He worked hard, and conspicuously, at winning Willi's trust. In her interview with me, Babette remained highly suspicious of anybody who, like the youth, had a communist affiliation which made him so obviously dangerous. Nonetheless, according to all reports, from the start the Red-Headed Youth finagled his way steadily, and finally successfully, into Münzenberg's daily presence. This accomplished, he ingratiated himself with Münzenberg at every opportunity. In early June he began to insist, with tiresome, untiring, and finally successful persistence that he be transferred to the hut where Münzenberg slept. Soon he was in Münzenberg's company all the time, and Willi seemed to accept him. The youth was eager and helpful and always there; a strong young arm.

But the French capitulation drew very near. Münzenberg began to be very much concerned with the next step in his escape. He was in possession of a map of the area between Grenoble and Valence, and after studying it carefully he undertook to convince various acquaintances in the camp to join him on a flight together toward Switzerland—the nearest neutral border. An especially enthusiastic voice behind this idea was the Red-Headed Youth.[32]

There were others, however. Among the older Germans Willi attempted to enlist was a rather well-known Social Democrat trade unionist, a non-communist, even anti-communist, known to Willi from the Popular Front days in Paris. His name was Valentin Hartig.

It must be said at once that Valentin Hartig's behavior on the scene, and above all his subsequent political history, can only be viewed with the most intense mistrust. It is plain that the man who most encouraged Münzenberg in his ill-fated plan to strike out for Switzerland was Hartig.[33] It is equally plain that on June 21, 1940, Valentin Hartig abandoned his fellow refugees, and did so without explanation. He separated from them there and headed—where? When he left Münzenberg and his companions Hartig ran not south but *north*—north to Paris, there to join the conquering Nazis. Where he was welcomed. Though historically very much a man of the left, Hartig there became active in the conquerors' collaborationist trade union movement.[34]

This sinister turn, combined with Hartig's association with the Red-Headed Youth, make me view him with the bleakest suspicion. Babette Gross, after corresponding and meeting with Hartig extensively after the war, was at last convinced that he was entirely innocent in Münzenberg's demise. I do not share that confidence.

Possibly he gave Babette some accounting never made public. If so she did not reveal it in our conversations. Certainly Hartig's behavior has never been satisfactorily explained in any document or report known to me.[35]

By June 18 it was plain that total French capitulation was only days away. On June 21 at 5:00 in the morning, the commandant of Chambarran called the men together in the camp yard. According to one report, the gates of the camps were simply flung open and the men set free. According to Helen Wolff, many of the interns, including Kurt Wolff, were herded onto buses and dispatched to another internment camp further south, deemed more secure.[36] Not so with Münzenberg. It appears that Willi and a large number of other interns were ordered to form a column and begin marching on foot, headed toward a camp to the southwest which they were not serious about reaching: Le Cheylard.[37]

It seems that among those on this march were Hartig, Leopold Schwarzschild, Hans Siemsen, Klement Korth, Paul Westheim, Münzenberg, and crucially, the Red-Headed Youth. It has been claimed that Kurt Wolff was also on the march: Helen Wolff assures me that her late husband's diaries flatly disprove this claim.

Unlike Kurt Wolff and others, who left on buses, Münzenberg and his group set out on foot, following highway D20 south, toward Marseilles. By the afternoon of that day the men had trudged perhaps fifteen, twenty miles. They stopped to rest in the lovely spring-green valley of the Isere River, a place where three tiny hamlets sit clustered together on the verge of a great European forest, the Forest of Caugnet. The three towns live as one: Saint Marcellin, Montagne, and Saint Antoine—tiny hamlets all, with only Saint Marcellin big enough to have a mairie and a post office. They are hamlets built around twelfth-century churches, places where people marry the same people with whom they learned to walk and talk. It is a town where the cemetery is as familiar as the school, where one can speak—without inexactness—about what the whole town knows.

The German refugees stopped in Saint Antoine and there, near its ancient church, decided to spend the night. Everyone was very

tired; no one wanted to go on. Nonetheless, Münzenberg continued to argue for the break toward Switzerland, though he was still
getting no real volunteers for the venture except, it seems, the Red-
Headed Youth. And Hartig. In the process Münzenberg claimed
that he had on his person 2,000 French francs—a huge sum for any
refugee to possess at that moment. As the men were settling in and
resting, Willi announced that he had learned from Hartig that there
was a car for sale over in the next town, and that he proposed to go
there with this money and buy it. He was quite sure there was a car
there: Hartig, honest, honest Hartig, "already had reconnoitered"
the scene, already had been over to the town. And with a car—
think what they could do with a car! There it was, so temptingly,
just a couple of kilometers away.[38] They could easily walk there in
under half an hour. Willi, typically, decided to act at once. He would
walk over to Montagne and try to buy the car Hartig had found. It
was understood that whether this effort succeeded or failed, he
definitely planned to return to the others left behind at their resting
place. Of course the situation was fluid, but there is no evidence
that anyone thought Münzenberg and his friends were embarking
on their flight then and there. Valentin Hartig, everyone agreed,
should go along because Hartig knew where the car was, and because he spoke such good French. In Montagne they either would
or would not buy a car, and then they would return.

Among the others who went with Hartig and Münzenberg was
the Red-Headed Youth. Why? The youth was among those pressing hardest for the Swiss scheme, and buying the car would have
clinched that plan. Perhaps he also knew how to drive: It is not at
all clear that either Willi or Hartig did. (Münzenberg had always
been driven by his chauffeur and bodyguard, Emil.) In any case, he
seems to have been one of those going to Montagne, apparently
along with another of the younger men in the group, though this
latter fact is murky.

So off they went, either three or four together. "I can still see
him," Siemsen later said, "waving his hand as he went off across
the fields."[39]

With this wave, Willi Münzenberg vanishes from history.

***

He never returned. More to the point: *Not one of his companions ever returned.* Not one. Westheim, Siemsen, and the rest sat waiting in Saint Antoine and they waited in vain for any one of them to come back. All four (if they were four) men vanished without trace.* But by nighttime, all four men were gone, gone without a word of explanation or clue as to their reasons for flight.

This simple raw *donnée—not one came back—*is the single indisputable assertion we can make about the whole mystery, the unique point of firm ground in a shifting tale. Münzenberg: vanished and dead. The Red-Headed Youth and possibly another young companion: vanished. Valentin Hartig: A man of the left, vanished, only to reappear in Paris under Nazi auspices, during the alliance between the communists and fascists.

If just one of Münzenberg's companions—*any* one—had returned to Saint Antoine, with or without a car, in whatever state of perplexity, to explain whatever disaster or slip-up, the entire matter would have a very different look. *Somebody* would at least *look* innocent.

We know the four men reached Montagne without incident. The road ran close along the edge of a dense wooded place called the Forest of Thivolet. This they passed and then they were seen and heard in the town, negotiating hard for some deal on a car: To buy or rent made little difference. The first such effort failed, but the men were directed to another person in the town, a Mme. Gorbetier, who had a car she might be willing to sell. Mme. Gorbetier later recalled that a visitor did come, alone. The stranger who approached her, she said, spoke easy fluent French, and there was no deal over the car. Because of the fluent French, it is plain that Mme. Gorbetier's visitor was not Münzenberg. It has to have been Hartig.

---

* According to one report, Hartig did briefly reappear before the group that evening, but he reappeared (if he did) without the others, without the money, and without any explanation of anything, and after this brief contact proceeded to disappear again, this time definitively.

But why was Hartig alone? Was he negotiating for the group, while they rested back at the cafe? Or was he possibly negotiating for himself, for his own escape? Was Hartig himself carrying the 2,000 francs, or had the money been left with Willi? We know only that the elusive Herr Hartig was seen again later that day by Mme. Gorbetier, but this time in the late evening, eight miles away in a third village, Saint Marcellin. Once again, Hartig was quite alone. After this last sighting on the scene, Valentin Hartig also vanishes, en route to Paris and the Nazis. And by this time Münzenberg was probably dead.

But here is the crucial truth. With Hartig away first trying to buy the car, then having disappeared entirely, Münzenberg had been left alone with the Red-Headed Youth—and the second young man. The three sat waiting in the Montagne cafe, and were observed there. It is said that Münzenberg sat so utterly exhausted by the day's exertions that he was reluctant to go on. But at this moment the sequence becomes very murky.[40]

Sometime after Münzenberg and his two or three companions had grasped that there would be no car in Montagne, one of two things happened. Valentin Hartig disappeared from the scene, for reasons unknown. He probably never returned to his companions in Saint Antoine, either to return Willi's 2,000 francs, which he may have had in his possession from the visit to Mme. Gorbetier, or to explain what had happened. He simply departed, glimpsed that night in Saint Marcellin, hurrying back to his soon-to-be protectors, the Nazis.

This left Willi alone with one or two young men. And it is quite possible that an exhausted and despairing Münzenberg then and there may have impetuously taken his decision, dispatched the two young men into the woods, and once he was alone, gone to the edge of the forest himself, found the farmer's baling cord on the ground, and rigged up the noose with which he hanged himself. I do believe this is psychologically possible. I know it is physically possible. Willi knew how to tie a hangman's noose. A family story recalled that when he was a little child, in the midst of a ferocious argument with his abusive and alcoholic father, the boy threatened to kill himself, and climbed up into the attic of the family tavern with a rope. There he tied the noose, and then sat considering the ultimate act. While considering it, he fell asleep. He was later found there, asleep, using the noose as his pillow.[41]

Now in 1940, he may have tied the noose again. And he may have used it.

But there is another scenario, at least as plausible, for murder. When the first effort to acquire a car fell through, Hartig may have departed on his visit trying to buy Mme. Gorbetier's car, possibly even in possession of the 2,000 francs. It is obvious that Münzenberg trusted Hartig. While he was gone, Münzenberg and the young men rested in the cafe, awaiting his return. But Hartig did not return. It is possible that by pre-arrangement everyone supposed Hartig would rejoin them with the other refugees in Saint Antoine. In any case, the three were left alone there. It was getting dark.

At this point Willi and the two youths stood up and left. They were seen to walk away from the cafe together. Quite obviously, they intended to return, without the car, and without Hartig, to their refugee friends just a few kilometers away. That is the direction they took. They would have to hurry to arrive in Saint Antoine before dark. The road ran past a quite small stand of woods.[42] They may well have thought that by cutting through it they would have a short cut. In any case they entered it.

Münzenberg walked into the rustling obscurity only a few hundred yards at most. He was with the two youths. They were now out of sight. And whatever happened next must have happened very quickly.

If Willi Münzenberg was murdered, as I myself believe he was, the method was probably one common among assassins. A firm cord, strong enough to be called a rope and capable of holding the suspended weight of a man's body yet supple enough to be coiled around the killer's hands, is made into a largish loop. The victim is approached from behind, and the loop is suddenly slung around his neck while the killer pulls the crossed strands back and apart with all his force and at the same time drives his knee into the victim's back. That hard forward thrust of the knee, snapping against the violent backward garroting of the rope, breaks the victim's neck in a single looping blow and produces immediate strangulation. The victim cannot fight back. Death, if not instantaneous, is very swift. The killer would have to be a strong, skilled, probably young man, and the result would be all but indistinguishable from death by hanging, except perhaps for a bruise from the knee in the middle of the victim's back. If this is indeed what happened to Willi, it would have been a simple matter for the killers to then tie the rope into a noose, hoist the already dead man onto a tree, and leave him turning there while they disappeared.

Task one in any assassination plan would have been to get Willi alone, to lure him away from his fellow refugees; to get him alone with his killers. It was Hartig who convinced him to leave the group in search of that irresistible car. That done, it was Hartig who arranged to go off and leave Münzenberg alone with the two youths. Whereupon Hartig left the scene, en route to Nazi protection. If Willi was killed, he was surely killed by the two youths, assigned to the job by the NKVD. Babette is right. Münzenberg would never have trusted the young men without Hartig. They were obviously dangerous. But Hartig? He trusted Hartig. He thought Hartig was safe—no communist, a Social Democrat, a reliable man, with no ties beyond what could be seen.

That was the part I think he got wrong.

I concede that Hartig *may* have fled north in simple cowardice, leaving Münzenberg behind with the young men for reasons unconnected to the killing. Babette Gross may well have been right to conclude that he was innocent in the death. Nonetheless, in the absence of other evidence, I continue to find Hartig's behavior suspicious. Certainly if Münzenberg was killed, Hartig's behavior was strangely and sublimely convenient to the killers.

Münzenberg's possibly fatal error was to trust that Hartig was what he claimed to be: a "Social Democrat." He was not; he was a man of the left who felt free to entrust himself to the conquering Nazis in Paris, in exactly the same way that Julius Alpari, Willi's old contact man in espionage, high inside the Soviet apparatus, felt perfectly safe with the arrival of the *Wehrmacht*. I submit that posing as a Social Democrat, Hartig was ideally placed to extend his double life to the services of both dictators. I do not say that he did; we are speculating here. But if Valentin Hartig did collaborate in the killing, then it seems to me possible that Münzenberg's end was itself a collaboration between the Nazi and Soviet services.

It was October by the time the corpse was found. The leaves were falling fast, though they had not covered over Willi's decomposing body when the dogs of some autumn hunters discovered it. The rope that had held him to the oak tree probably broke quite soon: when the corpse was discovered it was in a sitting position, knees up, under the tree. There was no money on his person, but a valuable watch was on his arm. In his pockets was a postcard addressed to Babette, a letter on the letterhead of the Paris PEN Club, and some papers that could not be distinguished. The men who found the body raced to the *mairie* in Saint Marcellin to report their discovery, but before they did, while the hunting dogs yelped and whined around their gruesome find, each man clipped a small piece of the rope from around the corpse's neck. This was peasant wisdom. For some reason, it was thought that a scrap of rope from the noose of a hanged man brings hunters' luck.

Epilogue

Some communist on trial for his life in Prague has suddenly confessed in open court that I gave him written instruction to be a British agent and that I was in a superior position in the British Intelligence Service. His name is André Simon, and I vaguely remember meeting him in Paris in 1940. Wanted to reply to the Press that, owing to recent dental surgery, my lips are sealed.

—*The Diaries of Noël Coward*, November 5, 1952

Ten years after Willi's death, by 1950, America had made its entry into the Cold War, and Otto Katz was back in Czechoslovakia, where he stepped forth from the shadows, out into the dim new totalitarian light, a powerful man. During the war itself, Otto had been kept well away from direct hostilities. Spies tend to step aside as armies advance. He had made his headquarters in Mexico, exiled but far from idle, involved in many political maneuvers.

Yet Otto had changed. After the 1948 Communist coup in Czechoslovakia, the once-subtle charmer now turned coarse with power. There had been a time, on Norma Shearer and Irving Thalberg's terrace, when Katz had made magic happen with the purr of that Sudeten voice. He now grew arrogant and vulgar. His vanity, once so shrewdly deployed, turned clamorous and shrill. An American leftist remembers attending a Paris "Peace Conference" in 1946, when a taxi screeched to a halt beside him on the street. Leering from the open cab window was Otto; he had made the taxi stop merely to drop the name of the big shot he was going to see: Maurice Thorez.[1] Even Otto's "modesty" took on a posturing and boastful tone. After a meeting of East European grandees in Prague, Katz held back, imparting that he did not want to "give the impression of being the power behind the throne."

But there was never any real safety in Utopia, even for the most obedient servant. With the Cold War, Stalin was determined to wash his hands of his old "antifascist" cadres that had played such an important role on the path to the Second World War and the way it had played out. He did not trust them. And with the coming of the Hiss Case in America, Stalin saw a way to liquidate them all, using Noel Field as the finger man accusing all his old colleagues in the "antifascist" cadres of treason. Spectacular show trials using Field's "evidence" were staged in all the Eastern European States—and in the DDR. Large numbers of loyal Stalinists from the antifascist cadres would be summarily tried, and summarily put to death.

And that is how Otto Katz was arrested one fine morning. In November 1951 the Prime Minister, Rudolf Slansky, was arrested along with many other important members of the government, most of them Jewish. Katz was not in the very first round up of victims. Our last glimpse of him as a free man is standing on a streetcar, where he happened to run into the terrified wife of Otto Sling, one of the arrested men. He is said to have tried to comfort her, rather gently.

It was a little after this talk on the streetcar that agents of the apparatus he had served all his life came to take Otto away.

The account of how the confessions of these show trials were extracted from their prisoners comprises one of the many terrible documents of witness in this century. Artur London's *Confession* and Eugen Löbl's *The State of My Mind* are accounts of how every conceivable device of physical agony, gross humiliation, untellable abjection, exhaustion, terror, release from terror, false promise, false camaraderie, and then terror again were brought to bear in systematic and invincible orchestration. Everyone confessed. To anything, everything.

Otto Katz? According to Löbl, he confessed the moment they came for him. He offered no resistance whatsoever. "He confessed," said Löbl, "in the elevator."[2]

And in late November 1952 Otto stood in the dock and read exactly the lines required. His confession does not particularly dwell on Noel Field, but it is interesting instead as a kind of grotesque parody and contortion on his life as a secret agent. Since the Prague Trials were overtly anti-Semitic, Otto dwelt on how as the son of a rich manufacturer he had always been drawn to "Jewish bourgeois elements." He confessed to having been a "Trotskyite" since his days with Piscator. During the pact he had become a Zionist agent, through the evil influence of a Jewish member of Daladier's cabinet, Georges Mandel. He made a point of having conspired with that reactionary, Beneš. In America he conspired with Louis Fischer and the "Jewish nationalist," Felix Frankfurter. In Paris, Noël Coward and Paul Willert recruited him for British intelligence. In America the "agent of capitalist Jewry," David Schoenbrun, had brought him into the American secret service and worked with the Israelis. The monster, Earl Browder, had influenced him. He had worked for the Zionists in Mexico. He had been bagman for Slansky and other "conspirators" among foreign journalists.

Many years later Löbl would recall that Katz's confession had a peculiarly histrionic tone, and recalled Katz speaking of "no tree high enough to hang me from."[3] Löbl wondered whether Katz had perhaps been signaling all his friends in the West through irony, or whether he simply went to his death, rather as he had lived, a *"poseur."*

Without answering this question, the transcripts as published suggest something slightly different. Arthur Koestler was convinced that Otto's confession was a signal to him, from across the lines, and that its language was written in direct imitation of the confession of Koestler's hero, based on Bukharin, in *Darkness at Noon*.[4] As he came to the end of his confession, Katz spoke of his life as a writer. "I am a writer, supposedly an architect of the soul. What sort of architect have I been... Such an architect of the soul belongs to the gallows." Then, like many of the defendants, he embarked upon a plea for the death penalty. "The only service left to me is to warn all who by origin [*sic*] or character, are in danger of following the same path to hell."

Then he proceeded: "The sterner the punishment..." and then, in mid-sentence, something in Otto betrayed him. *The sterner the punishment...* but as he spoke, his voice collapsed. His lips continued to move, but his plea for death fell into an unintelligible whisper around the words, a kind of gasping.

Otto Katz was hanged the next morning.

But before the executioner came for him, before dawn, Otto knelt on the floor of his cell and having been given some paper, he concluded his life, as he had lived it: writing. He first composed a long letter to Klement Gottwald, the president of the country, renouncing his confession and making a case for his own integrity. The letter is a coherent and highly intelligent performance, very remarkable given the circumstances under which it was written. It is filled with lies, to be sure: But it is fluent and even glib; a considerable document, and in some ways a persuasive one.

Next Otto turned to write a final letter to his wife. She had been permitted a final visit to him in his cell earlier that morning. This was to be his written goodbye. After he was led away to be hanged, the guards found a pile of pages left behind, false start after false start to this letter, along the draft he did manage to complete. "My dearest darling Ilschen," Otto begins, and begins, and begins again. He struggles to work in a phrase: "I devoted all the inner forces of goodness I had to our relationship"—but time and again he stumbles over it, and has to take a new sheet of paper. At last he gets it down, and adds: "Remember that, and forget everything else about me." Using the past tense, he speaks of their work as Communists in language that touches religious rhetoric: "I have had enough time to think about the future, and I saw it in all its glory. I saw a place reserved for you..." Did he write believing or disbelieving, for her eyes or for the eyes of the apparatus? He himself may not have known. He repeats the dream, and urges her "forward, ever forward," and then kneeling over that three-legged stool he writes the last plea: Forget me. Forget me. Live and forget me.

Otto's hanged body, like that of Rudolf Slansky and their fellow victims, was burned. The ashes and bones were put in sacks, and a couple of secret police agents were told to take them out of the city and get rid of them where they wouldn't be found. Some appropriate valley of desolation was named, but the drive all the way out there was pointless and dull. The whole chore with these sacks was pointless. Who cared? Who would every care? On a desolate road outside Prague, the agents simply pulled over to a ditch filled with trash. They tossed the sacks onto the rubbish and drove away, leaving them to the oblivion of the blowing winter wind.

BIBLIOGRAPHY

Books

Acheson, Dean. *Present at the Creation: My Years in the State Department.* New York: Norton, 1969.

Alexander, Tania. *A Little of All These: An Estonian Childhood.* London: Cape, 1987.

Allen, Peter. *The Cambridge Apostles.* Cambridge and New York: Cambridge University Press, 1978.

Alpern, Sara. *Freda Kirchway: A Woman of the Nation.* Cambridge, Mass.: Harvard University Press, 1987.

Ambrose, Stephen E., with Richard H. Immerman. *Ike's Spies. Eisenhower and the Espionage Establishment.* New York: Doubleday, 1981.

Andrew, Christopher, and Oleg Gordievsky. *The KGB: The Inside Story of Its Foreign Operations from Lenin to Gorbachev.* New York: HarperCollins, 1990.

Applebaum, Anne. *Gulag: A History.* New York: Doubleday/Random House, 2003.

Arendt, Hannah. *The Origins of Totalitarianism.* Third edition. New York: Harcourt, 1966.

Aron, Raymond. *Memoires: Cinquante ans de reflexion politique.* Paris: Julliard, 1983.

Baigell, Matthew, and Julia Williams, eds. *Artists against War and Fascism: Papers of the First American Artists' Congress.* New Brunswick, N.J.: Rutgers University Press, 1986.

Baker, Leonard. *Brandeis and Frankfurter: A Dual Biography.* New York: Harper and Row, 1984.

Bancroft, Mary. *Autobiography of a Spy.* New York: Morrow, 1983.

Beauvoir, Simone de. *The Prime of Life: The Autobiography of Simone de Beauvoir.* Translated by Peter Green. New York: Paragon House, 1992.

Bell, Quentin. *Virginia Woolf: A Biography.* Vol. 1. New York: Harcourt, 1972.

Beioff, Nora. *Tito's Flawed Legacy.* London: Gollancz, 1985.

Bentley, Elizabeth. *Out of Bandage: The Story of Elizabeth Bentley.* First edition, New York: Adan Devair, 1951. Reissued, New York: Ivy, 1988. Annotated with appendices and an afterword by Haydon Peake.

Bentley, Joanne. *Hallte Flanagan: A Life in the American Theater.* New York: Knopf, 1988.

Berberova, Nina. *Histoire de la baronne Boudberg*. Biography translated from the Russian by Michel Niqueux. Editions Actes Suds, 1988.

Bernhard, H. et al. *Der Reichstags brandprozess und Georgi Dimitroff*. Institut für Marxismus-Leninismus beim ZK der SED, et al. Band 1, Berlin: Dietz Verlag, 1982; Band 2, Berlin, Dietz Verlag, 1989.

Blackstock, Paul W. *The Secret Road to World War II: Soviet Versus Western Intelligence, 1921–1939*. Chicago: Quadruple, 1969.

Bohlen, Charles. *Witness to History*. New York: Norton, 1973.

Bolloten, Burnett. *The Spanish Civil War: Revolution and Counterrevolution*. Chapel Hill and London: University of North Carolina Press, 1992.

Borkenau, Franz. *European Communism*. New York: Harper, 1953.

Boyle, Andrew. *The Climate of Treason*. Revised edition, London: Hutchinson, 1979. Paperback revision, London: Coronet, 1980.

Brissac, Shareen Blair. *Resisting Hitler: Mildred Harnack and the Red Orchestra*. New York: Oxford University Press, 2000.

Buber-Neumann, Margarete. *Kriegsschulplatze der Weltrevolution. Ein Bericht aus der Praxis der Komintern, 1919–1943*. Stuttgart: Seewald Verlag, 1967.

—— *Milena*, translated from the German by Ralph Manheim. New York: Seaver Books, 1978; Holt, 1988.

—— *Under Two Dictators*. Translated from the German by Edward Fitzgerald. New York: Dodd, Mead, n.d.

—— *Von Potsdam nach Moskau*. Stuttgart: Seewald Verlag, 1957.

Budenz, Louis. *Men Without Faces: The Communist Conspiracy in the U.S.A.* New York: Harper, 1950.

Burke, Michael. *Outrageous Good Fortune*. Boston: Little, Brown, 1984.

Carlton, David. *Anthony Eden*. London: Allen Lane, 1981.

Carr, E. H. *Twilight of the Comintern, 1930–1935*. New York: Pantheon, 1982.

Carr, Virginia Spencer. *Dos Passos: A Life*. New York: Doubleday, 1984.

Carter, Miranda. *Anthony Blunt: His Lives*. New York: Farrar Straus and Giroux, 2001.

Caute, David. *The Fellow Travelers*. New York: Macmillan, 1971.

—— *The Great Fear: The Anti-Communist Purge Under Truman and Eisenhower*. New York: Simon and Schuster, 1978.

Chambers, Whittaker. *Cold Friday*. Edited and with an introduction by Duncan Norton-Taylor. New York: Random House, 1964.

—— *Witness*. New York: Random House, 1952. Reprint, Lake Bluff, 111.: Regnery, n.d.

Cockburn, Claud. *A Discord of Trumpets*. New York: Simon and Schuster, 1956.

Cockburn, Patricia. *Figure of Eight*. London: Chatto and Windus, 1985.

—— *The Years of The Week*. London: MacDonald and Co., 1968.

Cohen, Stephen F. *Bukharin and the Bolshevik Revolution: A Political Biography, 1888–1938*. New York: Knopf, 1973. Revised edition, New York: Oxford, 1980.

Connolly, Cyril. *The Missing Diplomats*. London: Queen Anne Press, 1952.

Conquest, Robert. *The Great Terror: A Reassessment*. New York: Oxford, 1990.

—— *Harvest of Sorrow*. New York: Oxford, 1986.

—— *Inside Stalin's Secret Police. NKVD Politics, 1936–1939*. London: Macmillan, 1985.

—— *Stalin and the Kirov Murder*. New York: Oxford, 1989.

Cookridge, E. H. [pen name of Edward Spiro]. *The Net That Covers the World*. New York: Holt, 1955.

Cooper, Duff. *Old Men Forget. The Autobiography of Duff Cooper, Viscount Norwich*. New York: Dutton, 1954.

Costello, John. *Deadly Illusions*. New York: Crown, 1993.

—— *The Mask of Treachery*. New York: Morrow, 1988.

Courtois, Stephane, et al. *The Black Book of Communism: Crimes, Terror, Repression*. Translated into English by Jonathan Murphy and Mark Kramer. Cambridge, MA: Harvard University Press, 1999.

Coward, Noël. *Future Indefinite: An Autobiography*. New York: Doubleday, 1954.

—— *The Noël Coward Diaries*. Edited by Graham Payn and Sheridan Morley. Boston: Little, Brown, 1982.

Dallin, David J. *Soviet Espionage*. New Haven: Yale, 1955.

Davenport, Marcia. *Too Strange for Fantasy*. New York: Scribner's, 1967.

Deacon, F. W., and G. R. Storry. *The Case of Richard Sorge*. New York: Harper and Row, 1966.

Deacon, Richard. *The British Connection*. Unpublished, 1982.

—— *'C': A Biography of Sir Maurice Oldfield, Head of MI6*. London and Sydney: Macdonald, 1985.

—— *The Cambridge Apostles*. New York: Farrar, Straus, 1986.

Desanti, Dominique. *Les Clés d'Elsa: Aragon-Triolet*. Paris: Ramsey, 1983.

Dewar, Hugo. *Assassins at Large*. Boston: The Beacon Press, 1952.

Dimitrov, Georgi. *Das Reichstagsbrandprozess*. Berlin: Neue Wege, 1946.

—— *The Working Classes Against Fascism*. London: Gollancz, 1935.

—— *The Diaries of Georgi Dimitrov 1933–1949.* Ivo Banac, ed. (German passages translated by Jane T. Hedges; Russian by Timothy D. Sergay; and Bulgarian by Irinia Faion.) New Haven and London: Yale University Press, 2003.

Dos Passos, John. *The Best Times: An Informal Memoir. 1896–1970.* New York: New American Library, 1966.

—— *The Fourteenth Chronicle: Letters and Diaries of John Dos Passos.* Edited and with a biographical narrative by Townsend Luddington. Boston: Gambit, 1973.

—— *Most Likely to Succeed* (novel). New York: Prentice Hall, 1954.

—— *The Theme is Freedom.* Freeport, N.Y.: Books for Libraries Press, 1970.

Draper, Theodore. *American Communism and Soviet Russia.* New York: Viking, 1960. Reprint, New York: Vintage, 1986.

Dunlop, Richard. *Donovan: America's Master Spy.* New York: Rand, McNally. 1982.

Dziak, John. *Chekisty: A History of the KGB.* Lexington: Lexington Books, 1988.

Edwards, Ruth Dudley. *Victor Gollancz: A Biography.* London: Gollancz, 1987.

Fest, Joachim. *Hitler.* Berlin: Verlag Ullstein, 1973. English translation by Richard and Clara Winston, New York: Harcourt Brace Jovanovich, 1974.

Fischer, David James. *Romain Rolland and the Politics of Engagement.* Berkeley, CA: California, 1988.

Fischer, Louis. *Men and Politics: An Autobiography.* New York: Duell, Sloan, 1941.

Fischer, Ruth. *Stalin and German Communism.* Cambridge: Harvard, 1948. Reprinted with new material, New Brunswick, NJ: Transaction Books, 1982.

Fischer, Ruth, and Maslow, Arkady. *Abtrünnig wider Wilen: Aus Briefen und Manuscripten des Exils,* Herausgegeben von Peter Lübbe. München. R. Oldenbourg Verlag, 1990.

Furet, François. *The Passing of an Illusion: The Idea of Communism in the Twentieth Century.* Translated into English by Deborah Furet. Chicago: University of Chicago Press, 1999.

Gardiner, Muriel. *Code Name: Mary.* New Haven: Yale University Press, 1983.

Gerhart, Leo. *Frühzug nach Toulouse.* Berlin: Verlag der Nation, 1985.

Gide, André. *Littérature engagée.* Texts assembled and introduced by Yvonne Davet. Paris: Librairie Gallimard, 1950.

—— *Retouches à mon retour de l'U.R.S.S.* Paris: Gallimard, 1937.

—— *Retour de l'U.R.S.S.* Paris: Gallimard, 1936.

Gisevius, Hans Bernd. *To the Bitter End.* Translated by Richard and Clara Winston. Westport, Conn.: Greenwood Press, 1947.

Glees, Anthony. *The Secrets of the Service: A Story of Soviet Subversion of Western Intelligence.* London: Cape, 1987; New York: Carroll and Graf, 1987.

Gnedin, Evgeny. *Iz istorii otnoshenii mezhdu SSSR i fashistskoi Germaniei: Dokumenty i sovremennye kommentarii.* (From the History of Relations between the USSR and Fascist Germany: Documents and Contemporary Commentary.) New York: Isdatel'stvo "Khronika," 1977.

Goldberg, Anatol. *Ilya Ehrenburg; Writing, Politics and the Art of Survival.* London: Weidenfeld and Nicolson, 1984.

Gross, Babette. *Willi Münzenberg: A Political Biography.* Translated from the German by Marian Jackson. East Lansing, Mich.: University of Michigan State, 1974.

Guillbeaux, Henri. *La Fin des Soviets.* Paris: Societe française d'editions litteraires et techniques, Edgar Malfere, directeur, 1937.

Guilloux, Louis. *Carnets: 1921–1944.* Paris: Gallimard, 1978.

Hamilton, Ian. *Koestler: A Biography.* London: Secker and Warburg, 1982.

Hare, Richard. *Maxim Gorky: Romantic Realist and Conservative Revolutionary.* London and New York: Oxford, 1962.

Hayman, Ronald. *Bertolt Brecht.* New York: Oxford, 1983.

Hays, Arthur Garneid. *City Lawyer.* New York: Simon and Schuster, 1942.

Heijenhoort, Jan van. *With Trotsky in Exile: From Prinkipo to Coyoacan.* Cambridge: Harvard, 1978.

Heller, Mikhail, and Aleksandr M. Nekrich. *Utopia in Power: The History of the Soviet Union from 1917 to the Present.* Translated from the Russian by Phyllis B. Carlos. New York: Summit, 1986.

Hellman, Lillian. *An Unfinished Woman.* New York: Little, Brown, 1970.

Hemingway, Ernest. *Selected Letters: 1917–1961.* Edited by Carlos Baker. New York: Scribner's, 1981.

Herbart, Pierre. *À la recherche d'André Gide.* Paris: Gallimard, 1952.

Herbst, Josephine. *The Starched Blue Sky of Spain.* New York: HarperCollins, 1991.

Hilger, Gustav, and Alfred Meyer. *The Incompatible Allies: A Memoir History of German-Soviet Relations, 1918–1941.* New York: Macmillan, 1953.

Hingley, Ronald. *Joseph Stalin: Man and Legend.* New York: McGraw-Hill, 1974.

Hiss, Alger. *Recollections of a Life.* New York: Holt, 1988.

Hodos, George. *Show Trials: Stalinist Purges in Eastern Europe, 1948–1954.* New York and London: Praeger, 1987.

Holroyd, Michael. *Lytton Strachey.* New York: Holt, Rinehart, 1968.

Hook, Sidney. *Out of Step: An Unquiet Life in the 20th Century.* New York: Harper and Row, 1987. Reprint, New York: Carroll and Graf, 1988.

Hoopes, Roy. *Ralph Ingersoll.* New York: Atheneum, 1985.

Humbert-Droz, Jules. *Dix ans dans la lütte antifasciste: Les Mémoires de Jules Humbert-Droz, 1931–1941.* Vol. 3. Neuchâtel: A la Baconniere, 1972.

Isherwood, Christopher. *The Berlin Stories.* New York: New Directions, 1954.

—— *Prater Violet.* New York: Random House, 1945.

Johnson, Chalmers. *An Instance of Treason: Ozaki Hotswni and the Sorge Spy Ring.* Stanford, Calif.: Stanford University Press, 1964. Revised edition, 1990.

Johnson, Diane. *Dashiell Hammett: A Life.* New York: Random House, 1983.

Johnson, Paul. *The Birth of the Modern: World Society 1815–1830.* New York: HarperCollins, 1991.

—— *Intellectuals.* London: Weidenfeld and Nicolson, 1988; New York: Harper and Row, 1988.

—— *Modern Times: The World from the Twenties to the Eighties.* New York: Harper and Row, 1983. Reprint, New York: Harper Colophon, 1985.

Jowitt, the Earl. *The Strange Case of Alger Hiss.* New York: Doubleday, 1953.

Kaplan, Justin. *Lincoln Steffens: A Biography.* New York: Simon and Schuster, 1974.

Kaplan, Karel. *Dans les Archives du Comite Central. Trente ans de secrets du bloc sovietique.* Paris: Albin Michel, 1978.

—— *Report on the Murder of the General Secretary.* Translated from the Czech by Karel Kovanda. Columbus, Ohio: Ohio University Press, 1990.

Károlyi, Count Michael. *The Memoirs of Michael Károlyi: Faith Without Illusion.* Translated from the Hungarian by Catherine Károlyi, with an introduction by A.J.P. Taylor. London: Cape, 1956.

Károlyi, Catherine. *A Life Together: The Memoirs of Catherine Károlyi.* London: Allen and Unwin, 1966.

Katz, Otto. *Der Kampf um ein Buch.* Paris: Carrefour, 1934.

—— *The Nazi Conspiracy in Spain.* By the editor of *The Brown Book of the Hitler Terror.* Translated from the German manuscript by Emile Burns. London: Gollancz, 1937.

Katz, Otto [ed.]. *The Brown Book of the Hitler Terror and the Burning of the Reichstag.* Paris: Carrefour, 1933.

—— *The Second Brown Book of the Hitler Terror.* Paris: Carrefour, 1934.

—— *The White Book on the Executions of June 30, 1934.* Paris: Carrefour, 1934.

Kennan, George. *Memoirs: 1925–1950.* Boston: Little, Brown, 1967.

—— *Memoirs: 1950–1963.* Boston: Little, Brown, 1972.

—— *Russia and the West Under Lenin and Stalin.* Boston: Little, Brown, 1960.

Klehr, Harvey. *The Heyday of American Communism: The Depression Decade.* New York: Basic Books, 1984.

Knightley, Phillip, *The Master Spy: The Story of Kim Philby.* London: Deutsch, 1988; New York: Knopf, 1989.

Koestler, Arthur. *The Age of Longing.* New York: Macmillan, 1951.

—— *Darkness at Noon.* New York: Macmillan, 1941.

—— *The Invisible Writing: The Second Volume of an Autobiography.* New York: Macmillan, 1954; New York: "Danube Edition," Stein and Day, 1969.

Koestler, Arthur, et al. *The God That Failed: Six Studies in Communism.* With an introduction by Richard Crossman, M. P. London: Hamish Hamilton, 1950.

Krivitsky, W. G. *In Stalin's Secret Service.* New York: Harper's, 1939. Reprint, Westport, CT: Hyperion, 1979.

Kurtz, Peter. *American Cassandra: The Life of Dorothy Thompson.* Boston: Little, Brown, 1990.

Kuuriinen, Aino. *The Rings of Destiny: Inside Soviet Russia from Lenin to Brezhnev.* Foreword by Wolfgang Leonhard. Translated from the German by Paul Stevenson. New York: Morrow, 1974.

Lacouture, Jean. *André Malraux.* Paris: Seuil, 1973. Translated from the French by Alan Sheridan, New York: Pantheon, 1975.

Lamphere, Robert J., and Schachtman, Tom. *The FBI-KGB War: A Special Agent's Story.* New York: Random House, 1986.

Langer, Elinor. *Josephine Herbst: The Story She Could Never Tell.* New York: Atlantic-Little, Brown, 1984. Paperback edition, New York: Warner Books, 1985.

Laqueur, Walter. *Stalin: The Glasnost Revelations.* London: Unwin and Heyman, 1990.

Lash, Joseph P. *Eleanor and Franklin.* New York: Norton, 1971. Paperback edition, New York: Signet Books, 1973.

Lawson, John Howard. *Film in the Battle of Ideas.* New York: Garland, 1985.

Lazitch, Branko, and Milorad M. Drachkovitch. *The Biographical Dictionary of the Comintern*. Palo Alto, Calif.: Hoover Institution Press, 1973.

—— *The Comintern: Historical Highlights: Essays, Recollections, Documents*. New York: Praeger, 1966.

—— *Lenin and the Comintern*, Vol. 1. Hoover Institution Publications no. 106. Stanford, Calif.: Hoover Institution Press, 1972.

Leggett, George. *The Cheka: Lenin's Political Police*. Oxford: Clarendon Press, 1981.

Lehmann, John. *The Whispering Gallery*. New York: Harcourt, Brace. 1955.

Leonhard, Wolfgang. *Child of the Revolution*. Translated by C. M. Woodhouse. Chicago: Regnery, 1958.

Lerner, Warren. *Karl Radek: The Last Internationalist*. Stanford, Calif.: Stanford University Press, 1970.

Levine, Isaac Don. *Eyewitness to History*. New York: Hawthorne Books, 1973.

Lewis, Flora. *Red Pawn: The Story of Noel Field*. New York: Doubleday, 1965.

Liang, Hsi-Huey. *The Berlin Police Force in the Weimar Republic*. Berkeley, U. of California Press, 1970.

Lockhart, Bruce. *Secret Agent*. New York and London: Putnam's, 1933.

London, Artur. *The Confession*. Translated by Alistair Hamilton. New York: Morrow, 1970.

Lottman, Herbert. *The Left Bank: Writers, Artists and Politics from the Popular Front to the Cold War*. Boston: Houghton Mifflin, 1982.

Luddington, Townsend. *John Dos Passos: A Twentieth Century Odyssey*. New York: Dutton, 1980.

Lynn, Kenneth. *Hemingway*. New York: Simon and Schuster, 1987.

Lyons, Eugene. *Assignment in Utopia*. New York: Harcourt Brace, 1937; reprint, New Brunswick, N.J.: Transaction Publishers, 1991.

—— *The Red Decade: The Stalinist Penetration of America*. New York and Indianapolis: Bobbs, Merrill, 1941.

MacDonald, C. A. *The United States, Britain, and Appeasement: 1936–1939*. London: Macmillan, in association with Saint Anthony's College, 1981.

Malraux, André. *Anti-Memoirs*. Translated from the French by Terence Kilmartin. New York: Random House, Holt, 1968. *Anti-Mémoires*. Paris: Gallimard, 1967.

Mann, Thomas. *Diaries*. Translated from the German by Richard and Clara Winston. New York: Knopf, 1982.

—— *The Letters of Thomas Mann: 1889–1955*. Selected and translated from the German by Richard and Clara Winston. New York: Knopf, 1971.

Massing, Hede. *This Deception.* New York: Duell, Sloan, 1951. Reprint, New York: Ballantine, 1987.

Mayenburg, Ruth von. *Hotel Lux.* Munich: C. Bertelsman Verlag, 1978.

McMeekin, Sean. *The Red Millionaire: A Political Biography of Willi Münzenberg, Moscow's Secret Propaganda Tsar in the West.* New Haven and London: Yale University Press, 2003.

Meade, Marion. *Dorothy Parker: What Fresh Hell Is This?* New York: Random House, 1987.

Medvedev, Roy. *Let History Judge: The Origins and Consequences of Stalinism.* Revised and expanded edition. Edited and translated by George Shriver. New York: Columbia University Press, 1989.

—— *Nikolai Bukharin: The Last Years.* Translated by A.D.P. Biggs. New York: Norton, 1980.

Meyer, Cord. *Facing Reality: From World Federalism to the CIA.* New York: Harper and Row, 1980.

Milne, James Lee. *Harold Nicolson: A Biography.* London: Chatto and Windus, 1980–1981.

Mitchison, Naomi. *You May Well Ask: A Memoir 1920–1940,* London: Gollancz, 1979.

Morel, Jean-Pierre. *Le Roman insupportable. L'Internationale litteraire et la France (1920–1932).* Paris: Gallimard, 1985.

Muggeridge, Malcolm. *Chronicles of Wasted Time.* Vol. 1, *The Green Stick.* London: Collins, 1972; New York: Morrow, 1973. Vol. 2, *The Infernal Grove.* London: Collins, 1973; New York: Morrow, 1974.

Münzenberg, Willi. *Propaganda als Waffe.* Paris: Carrefour, 1938.

Newton, Verne W. *The Cambridge Spies: The Untold Story of Maclean, Philby, and Burgess in America.* Lanham, Md.: Madison, 1991.

Nicholaevsky, B.I. *Power and the Soviet Elite.* Ann Arbor, Mich.: University of Michigan Press, 1975.

Nicolson, Sir Harold. *Diaries and Letters, 1930–1964.* London: Stanley Olson, ed. London: Collins, 1980.

Orlov, Alexander. *The Secret History of Stalin's Crimes.* New York: Random House, 1954.

Ory, Pascal. *Nizan: Destin d'un revolte.* Paris: Ramsey, 1980.

Pawel, Ernst. *The Nightmare of Reason: A Life of Franz Kafka.* New York: Farrar, Straus, 1984.

Payne, Robert. *The Life and Death of Lenin.* London: W. H. Allen, 1964. Reprint: London: Grafton, 1987.

Penrose, Barry, and Simon Freeman. *Conspiracy of Silence.* London: Grafton, 1986; New York: Farrar, Straus, 1987.

Persico, Joseph. *Piercing the Reich: The Penetration of Nazi Germany by American Secret Agents During World War II.* New York: Random House, 1979.

Perus, Jean. *Romain Rolland et Maxime Gorki.* Paris: Les Editeurs Français Reunis, 1968.

Philby, Kim. *My Silent War.* New York: Grove Press, 1963.

Pincher, Chapman. *Their Trade Is Treachery.* London: Sidgwick and Jackson, 1981.

Pipes, Richard. *The Russian Revolution.* New York: Random House, 1990.

Popov, Blagoj. *Ot Leipzigskogo protsessa v sibirskie lagerya.* Edited, with a preface by Peter Semerdjiev. Second edition. Paris: Movement for the Liberation of Bulgaria, 1984.

Poretsky, Elisabeth K. *Our Own People: A Memoir of "Ignace Reiss" and his Friends.* London and Oxford: Oxford University Press, 1969. Ann Arbor, MI: University of Michigan Press, 1969.

Porter, Katherine Anne. *The Never-Ending Wrong.* Boston: Atlantic, Little, Brown, 1977.

Powers, Thomas. *The Man Who Kept the Secrets: Richard Helms and the CIA.* New York: Simon and Schuster, 1979.

Pritchard, R. John. *The Reichstag Fire: The Ashes of Democracy.* New York: Ballantine Books, 1972.

Radosh, Ronald, and Hobeck, Mary. *Spain Betrayed: The Soviet Union in the Spanish Civil War.* New Haven and London: Yale University Press, 2001.

Rees, Goronwy. *A Chapter of Accidents.* New York: The Library Press, 1972.

Regler, Gustav. *The Great Crusade.* With a preface by Ernest Hemingway. Translated by Whittaker Chambers and Barrows Mussey. New York: Longman's Green, 1940.

—— *The Owl of Minerva. The Autobiography of Gustav Regler.* Translated from the German by Norman Denny. New York: Farrar, Straus and Cudahy, 1960.

Reinhardt, Günther. *Crime Without Punishment.* New York: Hermitage House, 1952.

Rhysselberghe, Maria van. *Les Cahiers de la Petite Dame. Notes pour l'histoire authentique d'André Gide, 1929–1937. Les Cahiers André Gide, #5.* Paris: Gallimard, 1974.

Richardson, R. Dan. *Comintern Army: The International Brigades and the Spanish Civil War.* Lexington, Ky.: University of Kentucky Press, 1982.

Rolland, Romain. *Inde, Journal (1915–1943)*. Paris: Albin Michel, 1960.

Rollyson, Carl. *Lillian Hellman: Her Legend and Her Legacy*. New York: St. Martin's Press, 1988.

Roosevelt, Kermit. *War Report on the O.S.S.* Prepared by the History Project, Strategic Services Unit, Office of the Assistant Secretary of War, War Department, Washington. New York: D. C. Walker, 1976.

Russell, Francis. *Sacco and Vanzetti: The Case Resolved.* New York: Harper and Row, 1986.

Salas, Jesus. *Intervención extrajera en la guerra de Espagna.* Madrid: Mostoles: Madre Tierra, 1990.

Schoots, Hans. *Living Dangerously: A Biography of Joris Ivens.* Translated from the Dutch by David Colmer. Amsterdam: Amsterdam University Press, 2000.

Schwartz, Nancy Lynn. *The Hollywood Writers' Wars.* (Completed by Sheila Schwartz.) New York: Knopf, 1982.

Seale, Patrick, and Maureen McConville. *Philby: The Long Road to Moscow.* New York: Simon and Schuster, 1973.

Sheean, Vincent. *Dorothy and Red.* Boston: Houghton Mifflin, 1963.

––––––– *A Personal Memoir.* New York: Modern Library, 1939.

Shipman, Charles. *It Had to be Revolution: Memoirs of an American Radical.* Ithaca, NY: Cornell University Press, 1993.

Slanska, Josefa. *Report on My Husband.* New York: Atheneum, 1969.

Slonim, Marc. *Soviet Russian Literature: Writers and Problems.* New York: Oxford University Press, 1967.

Solzhenitsyn, Aleksandr I. *The Gulag Archipelago: 1918–1956. An Experiment in Literary Investigation.* Vols. 1–2. Translated from the Russian by Thomas P. Whitney. New York: Harper and Row, 1974.

––––––– *The Gulag Archipelago: 1918–1956. An Experiment in Literary Investigation.* Vols. 3–4. Translated from the Russian by Thomas P. Whitney. New York: Harper and Row, 1974.

Souvarine, Boris. *Souvenirs sur Panait Istrati, Isaac Babel, et Pierre Pascal: suivis de lettre a A. Soljenitsyne.* Paris: Editions Lebovici, 1985.

Spender, Stephen. *World Within World.* New York: Simon and Schuster, 1978.

Sperber, Manes. *Ces Temps-la,* especially *Le Pont inacheve,* and *Au-dela de l'oubli: Les Porteurs d'eau.* Paris: Calmann-Levy, 1979.

Stewart, Donald Ogden. *By a Stroke of Luck!* London: Paddington Press, 1975.

Straight, Michael. *After Long Silence.* New York: Norton, 1983.

Strasser, Otto. *Hitler and I.* Translated by Gwenda David and Eric Mosbacher. Boston: Houghton Mifflin, 1940.

Tabouis, Geneviève. *They Called Me Cassandra.* New York: Scribner's, 1942.

Tanenhaus, Sam. *Whittaker Chambers: A Biography.* New York: Random House, 1997. (Modern Library Paperbacks, 1998.)

Tchoukovskaia, Lydia. *Entretiens avec Anna Akhmatova.* Translated from the Russian by Lucille Nivat and Genevieve Liebrich. Paris: Albin Michel, 1980.

Thomas, Hugh. *John Strachey.* New York: Harper and Row, 1973.

——— *The Spanish Civil War.* Third revised edition. London: Hamish Hamilton, 1977.

Thompson, Dorothy. *The. New Russia.* New York: Henry Holt, 1928.

Thornberry, Robert. *Malraux et l'Espagne.* Geneva: Librairie Droz, 1977.

Tobias, Fritz. *The Reichstag Fire.* Translated from the German by Arnold J. Pomerans. London: Secker and Warburg, 1963; New York: Putnam's, 1964.

Tolstoy, Nikolai. *Stalin's Secret War.* London: Cape, 1981.

Trepper, Leopold. *Le Grand Jeu.* Paris: Albin Michel, 1975.

Trilling, Lionel. *The Middle of the Journey.* New York: Viking, 1947.

Troyat, Henri. *Maxim Gorky: A Biography.* Translated from the French by Lowell Bair. New York: Crown, 1989.

Tuck, Jim. *Engine of Mischief: An Analytical Biography of Karl Radek.* New York: Greenwood Press, 1988.

Tucker, Robert C. *Stalin in Power: The Revolution from Above 1928–1941* New York: Norton, 1990.

Vaksberg, Arkady. *Hotel Lux: les Partis Frères au Service de l'Internationale Communiste.* (Translated from the Russian by Olivier Simon.) Paris: Fayard, 1993.

Vaksberg, Arkady. *Le Mystère Gorki.* (Translated from the Russian by Dimitri Sesemann.) Paris: Albin Michel, 1997.

Valtin, Jan. *Out of the Night.* New York: Alliance Book Corporation, 1941.

Vernon, Betty. *Ellen Wilkinson.* London: Croom Helm, 1982.

Viertel, Salka. *The Kindness of Strangers: A Theatrical Life.* New York: Holt, 1969.

Voros, Sander. *American Commissar.* Philadelphia: Chilton, 1961.

Weinstein, Allen. *Perjury: The Hiss-Chambers Case.* New York: Knopf, 1978.

Weinstein, Allen, and Vassiliev, Alexander. *The Haunted Wood: Soviet Espionage in America—The Stalin Era.* New York: Random House, 1999.

Weintraub, Stanley. *The Last Great Cause*. New York: Weybright, 1968.

Wessel, Harald. *Münzenbergs Ende*. Berlin: Dietz Verlag, 1991.

West, Anthony. *H. G. Wells: Aspects of a Life*. New York: Random House, 1984.

West, Rebecca. *The New Meaning of Treason*. New York: Viking, 1964.

West, W. J. *Truth Betrayed*. London: Duckworth, 1987.

Willett, John. *The Theater of Erwin Piscator*. New York: Holmes & Meier, 1969.

Wilson, Edmund. *Classics and Commercials*. New York: Farrar, Straus, 1952.

Winks, Robin. *Cloak and Gown: Scholars in the Secret War, 1939–1961*. New York: Morrow, 1987.

Wolf, Markus (with Anne McElvoy). *Man Without a Face: The Autobiography of Communism's Greatest Spymaster*. New York: Public Affairs, 1999.

Wolfe, Bertram. *The Bridge and the Abyss*. New York: Praeger, 1967.

Wolton, Thierry. *Le Grand Recrutement*. Paris: Grasset, 1993.

—— *Le KGB en France*. Paris: Grasset, 1986.

Wright, Peter, with Paul Greengrass. *Spycatcher: The Candid Autobiography of a Secret Intelligence Officer*. New York: Viking, 1987.

Wright, William. *Lillian Hellman: The Image, the Woman*. New York: Simon and Schuster, 1986.

Zelt, Johannes. *Proletarischer Internationalismus im Kampf um Sacco und Vanzetti*. Berlin: Dietz Verlag, 1958.

Pamphlets

Kerbs, Diethart, and Walter Uka. *Willi Münzenberg*. Zeitgenossen I. Berlin: Editions Echolot, 1988.

Perreault, Gilles, et al. *Willi Münzenberg, 1889–1940: D'Erfurt a Paris, im komme contre*. Published in conjunction with an international Conference held in Avignon, March–April 1992.

Articles

Andrew, Christopher, and Harold James. "Willi Münzenberg, The Reichstag Fire. and the Conversion of Innocents." In *Deception in East West Relations*, edited by David Charters and Maurice Tugwell. London: Pergamon, Brassey, 1990.

Binder, David. Article on Alexander Orlov. *New York Times,* June 26, 1991, p. A11.

Carew-Hunt, R. N. "Willi Münzenberg." *Saint Anthony's Papers,* no. 9, (1960).

Deak, Istvan. "Hungary: The New Twist." *New York Review of Books,* August 18, 1988, p. 47.

Draper, Theodore. "The Man Who Wanted to Hang." *Reporter,* January 6, 1953.

Fejtö, François. "Letter from Paris: The Real Louis and Elsa." (A review of Dominique Desanti's *Les Yeux des d'Elsa.) Encounter,* 1983.

Gellhorn, Martha. "On Apocryphism." *Paris Review,* no. 79 (1981), p. 301.

Gruber, Helmut. "Willi Münzenberg: Propagandist for and against the Comintern. *International Review of Social History,* vol. 10 (1965), part 2, pp. 188–210.

Kersten, Kurt. "Das Ende Willi Münzenbergs." *Deutsche Rundschau* (May 1957).

Klehr, Harvey, and John Haynes. "The Comintern's Open Secrets." *The American Spectator,* December 1992, pp. 34–36.

Münzenberg, Willi. "Die Dritte Front." Berlin: 1930.

—— "Five Years of Workers' International Relief." *Inprecorr,* vol. 6, no. 61, September 9, 1926, English edition, pp. 1044–1045.

—— "Mit Lenin in der Schweiz." *Inprecorr,* August 27, 1926. German edition, p. 1838.

Oak, Liston. Report on Communist Party work in Spain. *Call,* December 18, 1937.

Schliemann, Jörgen. "The Life and Work of Willi Münzenberg." *Survey,* no. 55 (April 1965), pp. 62–91.

Schmidt, Maria. "The Hiss Dossier." *New Republic,* November 8, 1993, pp. 17–18.

Wollenberg, Erich. *Echo der Woche,* August 12, 1949.

Interviews and Correspondence

Mary Bancroft
Ralph Bates
Nina Berberova
Sir Isaiah Berlin
Rae Bernstein
Pierre Bertaux
Patricia Bosworth
Michael Burke
Andrew Cockburn
John Costello
Alan Cullison
Robert Crowley
Roald Dahl
Manuella Dobos
François Fejtö
Babette Gross
Peter Gross
Norman Hackforth
John Hunt
Joris Ivens
Kot Jelinski
Karel Kaplan
Catherine Károlyi
Harvey Klehr
Peter Kurtz
Melvin Lasky
Leo Lerman
Ruth Levine
Eugen Loebl

Peter Lübbe
Jean Malaquais
Frieda Marshall
Herbert Marshall
Mary McCarthy
Naomi Mitchison
Steve Nelson
Henriette Nizan
Allen Oak
Ruth Price
Margaret Regler
Herb Romerstein
Jörgen Schliemann
Maria Schmidt
Peter Semerdjiev
Carlotta Shipman
Janka Sperber
Herman Starobin
Michael Straight
Sam Tanenhaus
Tzvetan Todorov
Robert Towers
Diana Trilling
Gus Tyler
Ruth von Mayenburg
Sir Dick White
Paul Willert
Helen Wolff
William Wright

FOIA Dossiers

Julio Alvarez del Vayo, FOIA Dossier # 100-11688.

Louis Gibarti, FOIA Dossier # 61-6629.

Lillian Hellman, FOIA Dossier # 100-26858.

Otto Katz, FOIA Dossier # 65-9266.

Willi Münzenberg, FOIA Dossier # 105-54056.

NOTES

Chapter 1
LYING FOR THE TRUTH

1. The life and death of Willi Münzenberg has been treated by many writers. The most important memoir is Babette Gross, *Willi Münzenberg: A Political Biography*. The best full biography is Sean McMeekin, *The Red Millionaire*. Other useful books are Wessel, *Münzenbergs Ende*, and Kerbs, *Münzenberg*. Also noteworthy are Carew-Hunt, "Münzenberg, and Kersten, "Das Ende Willi Münzenbergs." Indispensable articles are Schliemann, "Münzenberg," and Gruber, "Münzenberg." A significant, if controversial, text is Leo, *Frühzug nach Toulouse*.

   Noteworthy personal and political memoirs of Münzenberg appear in Koestler's autobiographical volume, *Invisible Writing*, in Regler, *The Owl of Minerva*; and in Sperber, *Ces Temps-la*, especially in *Le Pont inacheve*. Also important to the events and people around Münzenberg is Buber-Neumann, *Von Potsdam nach Moskau*. The Count and Countess Károlyi in their memoirs, *A Life Together*, and *Memoirs*, both include revealing portraits. Münzenberg himself wrote an autobiographical article "Die Dritte Front" and an account of the founding of WIR: "Five Years of Workers' International Relief." Information on Münzenberg revealed through the Freedom of Information Act (dossier #105-54056), regarding information to be in the files of the United States State Department, or the FBI, is surprisingly meager and ill informed, in notable contrast to similar records about many personalities close to him. American officials seem to have known vastly more about Münzenberg's lieutenants than they ever knew about him. (I should note that a large number of files on Münzenberg remain classified, and inexplicably so.) Still, a very useful and well-informed "Memorandum on the Workers' International Relief: Based Exclusively on Communist and Soviet Sources," was prepared for the Division of Eastern European Affairs of the United States Department of State, December 16, 1932, and one can hope, albeit wanly, that this excellent document was widely read in the government (National Archives of the United States).

   Information pertaining to Münzenberg in the archives of the Communist International in Moscow is massive. See McMeekin.

2. Gross, *Münzenberg*, p. 47.

3. See Jim Tuck, *Engine of Mischief: An Analytical Biography of Karl Radek*.

4. See Whittaker Chambers, *Witness*, p. 6. See also Slonim, Marc. *Soviet Russian Literature: Writers and Problems*, p. 68.

5. By far the best published account of Maly's life is Poretsky's *Our Own People* (London, 1969; Ann Arbor, 1970).
6. Information to the author from the late Diana Trilling.
7. For a discussion of Dzerzhinsky's role under Lenin, see Pipes, *The Russian Revolution.*
8. Koestler, *Invisible Writing*, pp. 250–251.
9. For the Kuczynski family's multifarious life in espionage, see Glees, *The Secrets of the Service.* Robert Rene Kuczynski's relation to Münzenberg is mentioned in Gross, *Münzenberg*, p. 158. The best scholarly volume on the Eisler family is by Peter Lübbe. Ruth Fischer's *Stalin and German Communism* is a major work.
10. Information to the author from Ms. Ruth Price. See also Markus Wolf, *Man Without a Face*, pp. 229–230.
11. Except where otherwise indicated, direct quotations from Babette Gross, as well as paraphrases of her views, are taken from my taped interviews of July 1989.
12. Information to the author from Mr. Paul Willert.
13. Münzenberg, "Mit Lenin in der Schweiz," *Inprecorr*, as cited by Gross, *Münzenberg*, p. 59.
14. With this assistance, Münzenberg wrote many articles and speeches. The only book under his signature is a remarkable study of Nazi propaganda techniques: *Propaganda als Waffe.* Willi was assisted in its composition by Kurt Kersten.
15. The Archives of the Central Party, on the Pushkinskaia in Moscow, are formally known as the "Russian Center for the Preservation and Study of Documents of Modern History." I will hereafter refer to them as the "Central Party Archives," or "CPA." The CPA's Third Division is devoted to the records of the Communist International and its successor organizations. It contains their own records, and records of those organizations' ties to various foreign communist and socialist parties. In addition, and as part of these liaisons to foreign parties, the Communist International maintained a working and very active secret Service, known as the OMS (the "Department of International Ties"). Many but not necessarily all records of the OMS are also in the Central Party Archives, though as of mid-1993 access to these flies remained restricted. Nonetheless it is very clear that Münzenberg worked in close, steady collaboration with the director of the OMS, Mirov-Abramov.

Münzenberg's political activities, both legal and illegal, even the simple management of fellow travellers such as Barbusse, were routinely referred for review in Moscow. (A typical example can be found in CPA fond 495.19.213, in a dossier of material from Henri Barbusse concerning management of fellow travellers connected to the Comintern in Spain, including Ellen Wilkinson.) The records are filled with budgetary requests for fellow-travellers' Propaganda trips, reports on relatively small glitches in press coverage, nuanced evaluations of work by "innocents," careful records on all front committees and their functioning, proposals for propaganda initiatives, both covert and overt, in every major country.

Familiar bromides about the supposed "independence" of Münzenberg's political work and that of his fronts must be laid to rest after examination of the Archives. When the work of the fronts became politically sensitive, as it did repeatedly, no detail seems to have been too small for Münzenberg to forward to the Executive Committee for direction "from Moscow," with financial records kept to the penny (e.g., CPA fond 495.292, files 242a, and 244a, among many other examples). Indeed, remarkably fine points of propaganda and organization were submitted for personal approval by Stalin himself (e.g., CPA fond 495.19.243).

As for Münzenberg's personal "independence," he was given some deference as a senior figure, but that he was a servant of the larger enterprise, that he was expected to be, and was, obedient to the commands of its leadership, is perfectly evident. (Typical examples along many of this kind can be found in CPA fond 495.19.337, and fond 495.73.26.) This dimension of Münzenberg's relation to the ECCI (Executive Committee of the Communist International) stands out in special relief after 1936, when other members of the German Communist Party, notably Wilhelm Pieck and Walter Ulbricht, set out to discredit him, and Münzenberg's response is filled with protestations of his long and obedient service (e.g., the Secretariat of G. Dimitrov, CPA fond 495.74; files on "the Case of WM.").

The interpenetration of Münzenberg's activities by the other intelligence Services of the Soviet State, especially the INO, or Foreign Wing of the Soviet Secret Police (OGPU-NKVD-KGB), and the Intelligence Wing of the Red Army (GRU), is evident throughout the records of the Central Party, frequently showing high-level intelligence officers, such as Abram Slutsky (director of the INO), present at meetings in which his activities were under discussion. (A typical example can be found in the minutes of a meeting of the Executive Committee of the Comintern on the German Situation conducted under conspiratorial conditions—with most participants using pseudonyms—with Slutsky in attendance, September 7, 1933. Multiple other examples can be found, *inter alia*, in the Secretariat of Osip Piatnitsky, Central Party Archives fond 495.19, files 216a, 217, 347, 357. All these show Slutsky, or some other representative of the GRU or NKVD secret service, repeatedly in attendance.) For a detailed account of Münzenberg's financial dealings and bureaucratic work, and their documentation, see McMeekin.

16. Regler, *The Owl of Minerva*, p. 170.
17. Anne Applebaum, *Gulag. A History*, pp. 14-15.
18. Gross, p. 220.
19. Sam Tanenhaus, *Whittaker Chambers. A Biography* (New York: Modern Library Paperbacks, 1998), p. 91.

20. For Münzenberg's use of this phrase, see Gross, *Münzenberg*, p. 133.
21. Koestler, *Invisible Writing*.
22. The most reliable account of the Comintern in its early stages is Lazitch and Drachkovitch, *Lenin and the Comintern*, vol. 1. An indispensable volume by the same writers is *The Comintern: Historical Highlights: Essays, Recollections, Documents*. Likewise essential, compiled by Lazitch and Drachkovitch, is *The Biographical Dictionary of the Comintern*. For a useful survey of its activities and role, see Heller and Nekrich, *Utopia in Power*. I have relied as well on Krivitsky, *In Stalin's Secret Service*, and Kennan, *Russia and the West*.
23. Robert Payne, *The Life and Death of Lenin*, p. 213.
24. That Otto Katz was a member of the NKVD, or the GRU (Soviet Military Intelligence), as well as of the Comintern secret service is a conclusion widely shared by those who were close to his activities. Certainly he was so regarded by Babette Gross; such was also the view held of him by many others, including Koestler, Regler, and Ruth Fischer. Koestler claims that Münzenberg spoke openly of Otto having been planted "to spy on Willi for the *apparat*" (*Invisible Writing*, p. 236), noting that this recognition contributed to the generally patronizing tone Willi adopted toward his right-hand man. Certainly from the time of his original mission from Moscow to Paris in 1933, Katz was entrusted with work far more characteristic of the NKVD than of the Comintern. The secret work in the Reichstag Fire campaign required undercover technique and witting involvement at a high level. More significantly, Katz rose to the apex of his influence after 1935, the date after which the familiar distinction between the Comintern secret service and the NKVD and GRU ceases to have practical meaning. That Katz belonged to one of these Services strikes me as probable to a very high degree.

Though Katz's involvement in the illegal enterprises of the Communist International were intricate, prolonged, and not infrequently quite public, files documenting his movements turn out to be rather meager—at least in the Central Party Archives. This scarcity is itself suggestive. The most probable is that the files were purged of material dealing with Katz. What remains seems to be material that is either innocuous, and in which Katz played a minor role (cf. CPA 495.73.26), or he is engaged in highly sensitive work, but under one of his cover names, which might have been missed by those indexing the files (cf. Katz engaged in secret conversations with Torgler's attorney, Alfonse Sachs, September 8, 1933: CPA 495.292.244a, in which Katz participates under his cover name "Breda"). One might contrast the scarcity of records on Katz to the expansive paper trail found there on his more visible master Münzenberg: Willi's thick dossiers line the dusty fonds. Another plausible reason for this paucity of Comintern paper is that Katz was a GRU or NKVD agent, and part of the Comintern only in the eyes of outsiders. If so, we may not see his dossiers soon. The records of those agencies remain obdurately shut away. In fact, the work of Otto's unseen hand may well have been of such sensitivity that his records may be kept in the "Presidential Archives," where the most sensitive documents of the regime are kept in rooms that once served as Stalin's private Kremlin apartment—certainly an *occultum occultorum* chosen with uncanny symbolism.

The question of whether Louis Gibarti (or to use his real name, Ladislas Dobos) was in the NKVD as well as being a "Münzenberg-man" is more debatable. When I met Babette Gross, she did *not* view Gibarti as having been an NKVD agent. She viewed him as temperamentally unsuited to secret work. "He was much too outgoing." Nonetheless, when I outlined information about Gibarti's activities in New York during the 1930s assembled through the Freedom of Information Act and at the National Archives of the United States, she came to the conclusion that Gibarti, like Katz, had worked for' 'the Russian service," or as she sometimes called it, "the other service," by which I take it she meant the GRU or NKVD. Though she found the fact "astonishing," she seemed to view it as quite clearly the case. In addition, I am informed by Mr. John Costello, whose research on the senior NKVD operative Alexander Orlov is based upon access to the relevant archives in Moscow, that the archives support my inference that Kim Philby began his secret service work in Europe through Gibarti's World Committee for the Relief of the Victims of German Fascism. For that reason, the Committee plainly served as an NKVD as well as Comintern front, with Gibarti a witting participant in espionage recruitment.

25. Knightley, *The Master Spy: The Story of Kim Philby*, pp. 36–37. The World Committee for the Relief of the Victims of German Fascism, the organization which dispatched Philby to Vienna immediately after he left Cambridge, was run by Gibarti. The World Committee was a legal front, as we shall see, for illegal activities. (See also note 23.) Philby was referred to Gibarti by a Cambridge don, Maurice Dobb, who was a talent-spotter for the Soviet services and was active in another of Gibarti's fronts, the League Against Imperialism. (See John Costello, *Deadly Illusions*, pp. 126–128.) In fact, Philby's trip through Paris on his way to Vienna serves as a useful illustration of how the stages in the recruitment system worked.

26. An example of this fusion of bookselling and espionage is recounted by the noted New York bookseller Walter Goldwater, a former communist who during his days with the Party was asked to open a bookstore near Columbia University to serve as a front for espionage activity. (Walter Goldwater, interview in a series of interviews on the advanced intellectual culture of New York, courtesy of Diana Trilling.) The rationale for using a "Press Agency" as a cover for espionage work is easily seen: Both are in the business of transmitting information. The "independent reporters" filing their stories can be made difficult to distinguish from other kinds of informants, while mingling legal with illegal information can be inconspicuously done. Ex-

amples of this are the Continental News Service in which Kim Philby worked with the Austrian Soviet agent Peter Smolka (also known as Peter Smolka-Smollett) and the American Feature Writers Syndicate, which Whittaker Chambers founded in New York at roughly the same time. FOIA information suggests that a pioneer in this particular device may have been Münzenberg's man Louis Gibarti.

27. Gross, *Münzenberg*, p. 220.
28. See Caute, *The Fellow Travellers*.
29. Gross, p. 133.
30. Gross, *Münzenberg*, pp. 216–221.
31. The phrase is taken from an unreliable portrait of Gibarti found in a book called *Crime Without Punishment*, by Günther Reinhardt. Reinhardt was a decidedly unsavory character, a stringer for the FBI, who did manage to insinuate himself into Gibarti's Company in the late 1930s. It is clear that he knew Gibarti; it is likewise clear that his portrait is sensational and false in a number of demonstrable ways. The quotation about "rabbit breeding" is, however, at least plausible. I should in fairness add that Mrs. Gustav Regler assures me that Reinhardt's account of her own husband in this book is entirely accurate, and indeed it was Margaret Regler who recommended the book to me.
32. Gross, *Münzenberg*, p. 219.
33. Berberova, *Histoire*, p. 260.
34. An excellent example is a dossier of letters of Romain Rolland and Henri Barbusse on the preparation of the Amsterdam Congress in CPA fond 495, which can be compared to the revealing letter from Rolland to Barbusse published by Babette Gross, op. cit., pp. 224–225.
35. Koudachova's role in Rolland's intellectual life has been extensively documented, sometimes sympathetically, as in David James Fischer, *Romain Rolland*. Her managerial role guiding Rolland's Stalinism was noted very early by insiders (Eugene Lyons, *Assignment in Utopia*.) By the time of Koudachova's death it was quite widely assumed that she was a member of the apparatus. (Information to the author from M. François Fejto.) In her conversations with me, Babette Gross unequivocally stated that Koudachova was a member of the apparatus, explicitly assigned to managing Rolland's life. A glimpse of Rolland's working relation to Gibarti may be had in Rolland's journal, *Inde*, though the reader should note that this volume was edited by Koudachova herself, and the entry tends to demonstrate Rolland's "independence." A less attractive side of Gibarti's relation to Rolland is documented by Gross *(Münzenberg*, pp. 224–225). The claim that Koudachova was trained in Moscow for her role in Rolland's life is found in Guillbeaux, *La Fin des Soviets*, in a chapter entitled "Romain Rolland's Marriage of State: Prisoner of the Kremlin." But Guillbeaux is a very dubious character; an obviously compromised reporter and a distasteful personality to boot. In his

book of 1937, he gives the impression of having very nearly become a fascist fellow traveller. In any case, he cannot be viewed as reliable, though he plainly knew Koudachova well in their early days in the USSR. He claims to base his account in part on Information from Gide and Victor Serge.

36. Gross, *Münzenberg*, pp. 224–225.
37. See Desanti, *Les Yeux d'Elsa*.
38. See Justin Kaplan, *Lincoln Steffens*. For the challenges to Steffens's support of the Terror, see Hook, *Out of Step*, pp. 204–205, 569.
39. Stewart, *By a Stroke of Luck*, pp. 233–242, esp. 234.
40. FOIA dossier on Louis Gibarti, #61-6629, section 3. Deposition of Louis Gibarti before Special Counsel to the United States Senate Robert Morris, Esq., and United States Senators Willis Smith and Homer Ferguson, Paris, August 28, 1951. Question 72. Ella Winter's tie to Katz can be seen below, in my discussion of Katz's role in founding the Hollywood Anti-Fascist League.
41. Stalin's epithet is reported by Krivitsky, *In Stalin's Secret Service*, p. 74.

Chapter 2
THE PATH TO HITLER

1. On Münzenberg leaving the Communist Youth International, see Gross, *Münzenberg*, pp. 99–109.
2. Paul Johnson, *Modern Times*, p. 714.
3. Nicolas Werth, "From Tambov to the Great Famine," *The Black Book of Communism: Crimes, Terror, Repression*, translated into English by Jonathan Murphy and Mark Kramer (Cambridge, Massachusetts) Harvard University Press, 1999, p. 123.
4. Gross, *Münzenberg*, p. 118.
5. Payne, *The Life and Death of Lenin*, p. 538.
6. Conquest, *Harvest of Sorrow*, p. 53.
7. Gross, *Münzenberg*, p. 113.
8. Willi Münzenberg, as quoted in Schliemann, "Münzenberg," p. 71.
9. *Saint Anthony's Papers*, no. 9. Issue on International Communism, chapter on Willi Münzenberg by R. N. Carew-Hunt, p. 75. For Gorky's relation to Münzenberg, see Gross, passim.
10. Conquest, *Harvest of Sorrow*, pp. 55–56; and *The Black Book*, Werth, p. 122.
11. Werth, loc. cit.
12. Werth, pp. 122–123.
13. Bertram D. Wolfe, *The Bridge and the Abyss* (New York: Praeger, 1967), pp. 114–115.
14. Bertram Wolfe was under the mistaken impression that this explanation was made by Kamenev. It real author was Josif Unshlikht, a key aide to Dzerzhinsky. Werth, 123.

15. Payne, *The Life and Death of Lenin*, pp. 537–538. An account of the lower-level political forces surrounding the famine can be found in Conquest, *Harvest of Sorrow*.
16. Werth, 124.
17. Gross, *Münzenberg*, pp. 120–121.
18. Koestler, *Invisible Writing*, pp. 207–208.
19. Gross, p. 126.
20. Gross, p. 270.
21. The state of the American Party following the Bridgeman, Michigan, raids of 1922 is explored in Draper, *American Communism and Soviet Russia*, pp. 1–51 and passim, and Klehr, *The Heyday of American Communism*, pp. 3–27.
22. Russell, *Sacco and Vanzetti*, pp. 126–144.
23. In addition to Gross's comments on Münzenberg's role in the Sacco-Vanzetti case, Münzenberg himself pointed with pride to his achievement with Sacco-Vanzetti in *International Press Correspondence*, nos. 1, 8, and 42, August 1, 1928, "Five Years of Workers' International Relief," pp. 1044–1045. See also Russell, *Sacco and Vanzetti*. Against these claims, stands the categoric dismissal of Münzenberg's role in the case by McMeekin, pp. 202, 346–347.
24. Lyons, *Assignment in Utopia*, p. 32.
25. Russell, *Sacco and Vanzetti*, p. 13.
26. Lyons, *Assignment in Utopia*, p. 13.
27. Ibid., p. 31.
28. Russell, *Sacco and Vanzetti*, p. 222.
29. Ibid., p. 29.
30. An interesting although problematical account of the Red Aid's sweeping control of the Propaganda campaign over Sacco and Vanzetti has been documented, and in detail, from a communist source: Zelt's *Proletarischer Internationalismus*. Zelt wrote after being granted access to the archives of the Comintern in Moscow, and his purpose was to claim credit for the International in the campaign, downplaying the "bourgeois" contribution. His book's account of Red Aid's organization and control over the campaign is remarkably detailed. Interestingly, while the book outlines and lavishly praises the effectiveness of the Operation, it at no time let slip the name Münzenberg, who was not in good odor at Red Aid, and later, of course, was a non-person in the DDR.
31. Russell, *Sacco and Vanzetti*, p. 119.
32. Ibid. For Cannon's knowledge of Sacco's guilt, see p. 133. The Organizers' doubts are cited on p. 140.
33. Porter, *The Never-Ending Wrong*, p. 27. Rosa Baron is also discussed in Zelt.
34. Russell, *Sacco and Vanzetti*, p. 117. Russell relies, in part, on Zelt.
35. Gardner Jackson's close association with Louis Gibarti is documented in dossiers now in the National Archives of the United States, 800.00B, dossier on Louis Gibarti, document #37.

36. Murray Kempton, *Part of Our Time,* "The Dry Bones" (Simon and Schuster, New York, 1955), p. 50.

37. See Baker, *Brandeis and Frankfurter,* Chapter 12, for an account of Marion and Felix Frankfurter's relation to the Sacco-Vanzetti case.

38. See Russell, *Sacco and Vanzetti,* pp. 133–134.

39. Ibid., pp. 141–142.

40. Anne Applebaum, *Gulag: A History* (Doubleday: New York, 2003), pp. 64–65.

41. Ibid, p. 66.

42. Gross, p. 251; Paul Johnson, *Modern Times,* pp. 274–275.

43. Gross, pp. 262–263.

44. The orchestration of the "Peace Movement" through the Münzenberg fronts and their associated organization is very visible in the voluminous documentation of the Propaganda of the fronts in the period, culminating with Amsterdam-Pleyel. The process of this development, beginning with the League Against Colonialism, its transformation into the League Against Imperialism at the time of the Brussels Congress, and the increasing preoccupation with "peace" which had its culmination in Amsterdam is documented by Gross, *Münzenberg,* pp. 181–227. Confidential Information provided to me and pronounced roughly accurate by Babette Gross indicates that the author of the "peace" plan was a French Münzenberg-man named Guy Jerram, whose plan for an apparatus-sponsored pacifist movement was presented to Stalin in 1928, and revised by the dictator personally at that time. The phrase "peace conspiracy" apparently begins with Jerram.

45. CPA fond 495.292.242a. and 244a. These flies consist of correspondence concerning the Leipzig Trial with the Anti-War Commission of the ECCI, which in turn had been in charge of the Anti-War Congresses in Brussels and Amsterdam.

46. Nehru's speech at the Bandung Conference is referred to in Schliemann, Gross, p. 188.

47. Joachim Fest, *Hitler,* p. 395.

48. Information to the author from Mr. Herb Romerstein and Mr. Jörgen Schliemann.

49. The CPA contains many archives on preparation for the Amsterdam Congress, including many dossiers of correspondence between Münzenberg and Piatnitsky on the subject. These documents are found in the same fonds (Fond 495.19 especially) as are records of the Anti-Imperialist League, and later the sundry antifascist committees, including the World Committee against War and Fascism.

50. For the secret arrangements at Amsterdam, see Gross, *Münzenberg,* p. 227.

51. The Papen coup is discussed by Fest, *Hitler,* pp. 339–345. See also, and particularly, Gross, p. 229. It is very interesting to note that the CPA contains a secret Service report to Piatnitsky by a deep-coyer informant dated a week following the Papen coup (July 29), pointing out that events had caused a rift

in the Nazi ranks: That Röhm was pressing for a *coup d'état* for July 31, 1932, and that Hitler was holding out for a legal seizure of power. The letter's context makes plain that Piatnitsky has been steadily informed about high-level debate within the Nazi ranks from this source, whose code name was "your friend Teddy" (CPA fond 495.19.247). "Teddy's" identity is not known to me, but his file is in the fonds devoted to the Münzenberg apparatus.

52. François Furet, *The Passing of an Illusion: The Idea of Communism in the Twentieth Century*. (Translated into English by Deborah Furet.) Chicago: University of Chicago Press, 1999, p. 215.

Chapter 3
ANTIFASCISM AND FIRE

1. The standard work on the Reichstag Fire is Tobias, *The Reichstag Fire*.
2. Gross, *Münzenberg*, p. 240. Münzenberg's consultations at this time were with Iosif Piatnitsky, and focussed on the work of Amsterdam-Pleyel, though it should be recalled that Gibarti ran both Amsterdam-Pleyel and the World Committee for the Relief of the Victims of German Fascism. I should note that Babette Gross emphasized that Gibarti's work in Paris was always done away from Münzenberg's Paris offices, obviously to maintain an appearance of separation. The move to Paris was discussed, along with, presumably, the change in Amsterdam-Pleyel that would come with the antifascist campaign. Piatnitsky was very active in secret matters and espionage, and his influence ranged outside the Comintern to the other Services. See Poretsky, *Our Own People*, pp. 105–106.
3. Gross, *Münzenberg*, p. 232.
4. Furet, p. 224.
5. See Fest, *Hitler*, pp. 396–397.
6. Tobias, *The Reichstag Fire*, pp. 84–85.
7. Fest, *Hitler*, pp. 474–475.
8. See Paul Johnson, *Modern Times*, pp. 282–283; see also Gross, *Münzenberg*, pp. 227–233.
9. Gross, *Münzenberg*, p. 232.
10. Ibid., p. 235.
11. Hsi-Huey Liang, *The Berlin Police Force in the Weimar Republic*, Berkeley, U. of California Press, 1970.
12. Gross, *Münzenberg*, p. 235.
13. Ibid., p. 238.
14. Ibid., pp. 234–239.
15. Contacts with the OMS (the Comintern secret Service, *Otdel mezhdunarodnoi svyatzi*) in support of the antifascist campaign in Paris are discussed by Gross, p. 264. This supervision presumably was run by the OMS and the

secret Service of the Comintern, rather man any of the other Soviet Services. Yet such a presumption may be naive. In these years, the functions of the Comintern secret service were increasingly being drawn into the ambit of the other Services, usually covertly. If one concedes the probability that Katz was a liaison between the antifascist movement and the *apparat*, the thought that Alpari (and others) may have had similar bonds does not seem too loose a speculation. This would help explain Alpari's survival of the purges, in which most of his senior comrades in the OMS were put to death, and his curious behavior at the time of the fall of France.

16. See Tobias, *The Reichstag Fire*, on Lübbe's arrest.

17. Margarete Buber-Neumann, "Le Conspirateur Sans Mystère," *Preuves*, Avril, 1957, p. 44. [My translation.]

18. Central Party Archives, Moscow, File 495, 60, 242a. Memo from agent "Semko" to Moscow Center. May 11, 1933.

19. See ibid. on the arrests of Dimitrov, Popov, and Tanev.

20. *The Diaries of Georgi Dimitrov 1933–1949*: Ivo Banac, editor. XXV. See also the Semko memorandum.

21. Information to the author from Ms. Frieda Marshall. See also Gide, *Littérature Engagée*, pp. 20–25.

22. Regler, *The Owl of Minerva*, p. 170.

23. Gross, *Münzenberg*, pp. 242–243.

24. FOIA dossier on Louis Gibarti, #61-6629, section 3. Deposition of Louis Gibarti before Special Counsel to the United States Senate, Robert Morris, Esq., and United States Senators Willis Smith and Homer Ferguson, Paris, August 28, 1951.

25. The procedure for establishing Soviet authority over a local party and its officials was accomplished by a written order, known as a *mandat*, borne by a given Comintern official, such as Gibarti and presented to the local party. The *mandat* had the effect of a command, requiring full cooperation and indeed obedience from the local party officials with regard to the project at hand. According to Babette Gross, such a *mandat* was given to Vaillant for Münzenberg's Paris operations. Gibarti testified that he also had such a *mandat*, written on silk and signed by Münzenberg himself, which he presented to Earl Browder in New York in March 1934.

26. Gross, *Münzenberg*, pp. 240–242. It is possible that other hands were at work in this co-ordinated activity at a level higher up the *apparat* chain of command than Münzenberg. Who held this authority after Münzenberg's fall from grace is not entirely clear. One would look to Mikhail Koltsov for the more public face of it. There was also Louis Dolivet and the *Rassemblement Universel Populaire*, or RUP. See below.

27. CPA fond 495.292.244a. Documents of the Anti-War Commission on the Leipzig Trial and the London Counter-Trial.

28. Gibarti's life has rarely broken into the printed record, and the one volume in which he plays a large role, *Crime Without Punishment*, by Günther Reinhardt is not reliable. My principal sources come from interviews, and Gibarti's files in the National Archives of the United States, as well as my FOIA request.

29. See Gibarti, FOIA file.

30. For the League Against Imperialism as an Instrument for Sabotage and espionage, I am indebted to Deacon's unpublished *The British Connection* especially pp. 112–114. Deacon relies on revelations concerning Percy Glading over the Woolrich Arsenal Gase. Deacon's views have been confirmed by Mr. John Costello, in his work in Soviet archives. Mr. Costello has discovered that Maurice Dobb, of the Cambridge University branch of the League Against Imperialism, and Gibarti himself, played a fully witting role in the recruitment of Kim Philby. See Costello, *Deadly Illusions*, pp. 125–126.

31. See Schliemann, "Münzenberg."

32. Regler, *The Owl of Minerva*, p. 164.

33. A revealing account of such a clandestine Propaganda mission, ran for the apparatus in 1934, can be found in *A Life Together*, the memoirs of the Countess Catherine Károlyi. This account should be supplemented by a report on the same mission made by Count Michael Károlyi in his *Memoirs*. Note especially the two slightly differing accounts of the role played by the French embassy in Berlin.

34. Langer, *Josephine Herbst*, from the 1985 paperback edition, pp. 206–217.

35. See Sperber, *Au-dela de l'oubli: Les Porteurs d'eau*, chapter 1.

36. Karel Kaplan, *Report on the Murder of the General Secretary*, p. 276.

37. For the World Committee feeding disinformation to Winston Churchill, see Deacon, *The British Connection*, pp. 105–107. It should be noted that the Duchess of Atholl was a prime "innocent" for the World Committee.

38. The question of whether Michael Károlyi was or was not under the discipline of the apparatus is much debated. *Apparat* insiders in the United States during the late twenties report being told unequivocally that Count Károlyi was under Party discipline. (See Voros, *American Commissar*.)

I myself knew the late Countess Károlyi in the early 1980s. She was then in her great age—over 90—and still a woman of great charm. I owe her a debt of gratitude. I was twice a resident at the artists' foundation she created in the south of France and dedicated to her husband's memory. At that time, I was not in the least conscious of the Countess's special role in the issues under examination here, though I did read part of her memoirs and knew the gossip at the Károlyi Foundation that she had once been a spy. Though it made no particular impression on me at the time, I must have come across Münzenberg's name for the first time reading her book.

On the rare occasions when we discussed politics, the Countess invariably gave the impression of knowing more than she was prepared to say. Her thinking, though subtle and insightful, remained enthralled by the revolutionary myth. I once asked her, for example, whether she regarded the substance of Solzhenitsyn's *The Gulag Archipelago* as true. "It is true," she replied after a bleak, solemn pause. "It is exaggerated, but it is essentially true." I was (and I remain) astonished that a woman possessed of that knowledge could later say in my hearing that though Hungary was a communist country, "it is not communist enough for me." There was something invincible in her innocence.

The Countess made an instructive contrast to her no-less-intelligent but more politically hard-headed and more flexible contemporary Babette Gross, whom she somewhat resembled and had surely known well.

39. See Elizabeth Bentley's account of her work in the New York office of the League Against War and Fascism, in *Out of Bandage*.
40. See Costello, *Deadly Illusions*, pp. 125–126.
41. See Anthony Boyle, *The Climate of Treason*, p. 108.
42. Gross, *Münzenberg*, p. 264.
43. For Gibarti's contacts with Alpari and Fried, see the interview with Louis Gibarti in the David Dallin Papers, Special Collections of the New York Public Library.
44. Information to the author from the late Babette Gross.
45. Information from Babette Gross. See also interview with Louis Gibarti, in the Dallin Papers, New York Public Library.
46. Banac, Dimitrov, *Diary, 1933–1949*, pp. 83 and 93.
47. See entry on Alpari in Lazitch and Drachkovitch, *The Biographical Dictionary of the Comintern*.
48. Lucien Vogel was a major figure in the history of magazine publishing. He was also at this time a leading fellow traveller, and he appears in the events under discussion in many capacities. References to him appear in Gross, *Münzenberg*, in Gide, *Les Cahiers de la Petite Dame*, and in the memoirs of both the Count and Countess Károlyi. I am grateful to Mr. Leo Lerman for information concerning Vogel's career in New York, following his break with the Soviets. I am especially grateful to the late Pierre Bertaux for information concerning Vogel, and his daughter, Marie-Claude Vogel.
49. See *Les Cahiers de la Petite Dame*, referring both to Vogel's role in the offer coming from Mezhropohmfilm Russ to make a film of his novel *Les Caves du Vatican*, and the suggestion that Gide make a tour of the Soviet Union in 1932.
50. Count Michael Károlyi, *Memoirs*, pp. 286–287.
51. For a description of Vaillant-Couturier's role in Stalinizing French cultural life, see Ory, *Nizan*, pp. 127–130. For Münzenberg's meeting with Marie-Claude Vogel, Vaillant-Couturier, and Kurella, see Gross, *Münzenberg*, pp. 239–241. For a photograph of Vaillant-Couturier, see Desanti, *Les Yeux d'Elsa*, p. 231. For Alfred Kurella's history in the Comintern, see Lazitch and Drachkovitch, *A Biographical Dictionary of the Comintern*, pp. 207–208. For

Barbusse's and Rolland's lack of Standing in French cultural chic, as well as details of Vaillant's personality, see interview by the author with Pierre Bertaux, June 10, 1986.

52. Mann, *Diaries*, pp. 154–158. Also information to the author from the late Pierre Bertaux.

53. Pierre Bertaux, interview with the author, June 10, 1986.

54. Arkady Vaksberg, *Hotel Lux, Les parties Frères au Service de l'Internationale Communiste*. (Fayard: Paris, 1993), pp. 150–167. For a good account of Ilya Ehrenberg's general position, see Lottman, *The Left Bank*.

55. CPA. Various documents concerning Münzenberg's use of Henri Barbusse are scattered throughout fond 495. A typical example can be found in 495.19.337., documents 1, 3, and 9.

56. Information to the author from Babette Gross.

57. On sharing the fruits of espionage between Willi and the French, see Count Károlyi, *Memoirs*, p. 283, with endnote.

58. Pierre Bertaux, interview with the author, June 10, 1986.

Chapter 4
THE LIEUTENANT

1. I have relied upon many written sources for the life of Otto Katz. These include Gross, *Münzenberg*, Koestler, *Invisible Writing*, Regler, *The Owl of Minerva*, Kersten, "Das Ende Willi Münzenbergs," Wessel, *Münzenbergs Ende*, and Karel Kaplan, *Report on the Murder of the General Secretary*, inter alia. There is an important and quite reliable, albeit intensely hostile, footnote on him in Ruth Fischer's *Stalin and German Communism*. Voluminous information documenting his work in America is held in the National Archives of the United States, and in response to my request, a large FOIA file from the FBI has been assembled on his activities, FBI FOIA dossier #65-9266. He appears in all accounts of the Slansky Trials (Hodos, *Show Trials*, Karel Kaplan, *Dans les Archives du Comité Central*, Slanska, *Report on My Husband*, London, *The Confession*, and *The State of My Mind*, inter alia). Katz is discussed, albeit mendaciously in memoirs by Lillian Hellman, *An Unfinished Woman*, and Ella Winter, *And Not to Yield*. In addition, I am indebted for Interviews concerning his activities to Mr. Paul Willert, the late Mr. Pierre Bertaux, Mr. Herman Starobin, Mrs. Margaret Regler, Mrs. Rae Bernstein, Mr. Peter Lübbe, Mr. Robert Crowley, Mr. Gus Tyler, Mr. John Hunt, Mrs. Henriette Nizan, Ms. Manuella Dobos, and Mr. Steve Nelson, among others. Many conversations with Mr. John Costello, supported by documentation from his research, have been indispensable.

2. For Katz's earliest contacts with Münzenberg, see Gross, *Münzenberg*, p. 309.

3. Gross, *Münzenberg*, pp. 310–311. For the intellectual ambience of the era, see passages on Kafka's connections to Kisch in ibid., and Willett, *The The-*

ater of Erwin Piscator, along with the passages on the Piscatorbühne in Hayman's biography of Brecht, *Bertolt Brecht.* For a memoir of the era, see also Viertel, *The Kindness of Strangers,* with references to Katz on p. 101, and passim. An amusing fictional account of the era and its people can be found in Isherwood's *Prater Violet.*

4. See Gross, *Münzenberg,* p. 311. Katz's role in the joint Comintern-NKVD assassinations in Spain is discussed in my chapter 10 on Spain. Brecht's devotion to Stalinism in its cruelest aspects is summarized in Paul Johnson, *Intellectuals* (London: Weidenfeld, 1988; New York: Harper & Row, 1988).

5. Hook, *Out of Step,* pp. 491–496.

6. FOIA dossier on Otto Katz, #65-9266.

7. Draper, essay on Otto Katz, "The Man Who Wanted to Hang," *The Reporter,* January 6, 1953, pp. 26–30.

8. For Hollywood fellow travelling prior to 1935, see Schwartz, *The Hollywood Writers' War,* the memoirs of John Howard Lawson, Ella Winter, and many others.

9. See Meade, *Dorothy Parker,* pp. 253–254. See also Stewart, *By a Stroke of Luck.* See also Schwartz, *The Hollywood Writers' Wars,* p. 83, and passim. Katz's presence in Hollywood is mentioned by a number of other memoirists, among them Viertel, *The Kindness of Strangers.*

10. Katz's close association with Eisler is documented in the FOIA dossier on Otto Katz, Section #1; FBI memorandum of Feb. 4, 1943. Also information to the author in an interview with Mrs. Rae Bernstein, July 1991. That Lillian Hellman worked with Katz is indicated by Mrs. Bernstein's assertion to me that her husband Joseph Bernstein, who gave extensive editorial assistance to Katz in his writing, had been introduced to Katz by Lillian Hellman.

11. Information on Otto Katz and Fritz Lang, FOIA dossier on Otto Katz. Reference is also made to Katz's social life in Hollywood in the memoirs of Viertel, *The Kindness of Strangers.* Note especially pp. 101–102 and 211–220.

12. Information to the author from Mrs. Rae Bernstein.

13. See CPA fond 495.72.26. A document on the World Committee Against War and Fascism," addressed to Otto Katz, in which "active [presumably legal] work in America" is discussed. See also, CPA fond 495.19.336 and 337.

14. See Otto Katz FOIA dossier, on his expulsion from the United States in November 1940.

15. Confidential information to the author.

16. Claud Cockburn, *A Discord of Trumpets,* Willett, *The Theater of Erwin Piscator,* and Koestler *Invisible Writing,* all testify to Katz's skill as a rapid writer in several languages. I should add that Mrs. Rae Bernstein, widow of Joseph Bernstein who collaborated with "André Simon" on *Men of Europe,* tells me that Katz's English, while fluent, was far from perfect, and required intensive editorial help. Since many of the books by "Simon" or "Simone" appeared first in English, probably all had editorial assistance of the kind sup-

plied by Joseph Bernstein—who was incidentally also the literary right hand, in English, of Julio Alvarez del Vayo.

17. Hellman, *An Unfinished Woman,* p. 68.

18. For Hellman's relation to Katz and his activities in New York in 1939 and 1940, I am indebted to information from Mrs. Rae Bernstein, Mrs. Ralph Bates, and Margaret Regler. No account, document, or memoir in the many hundreds I have seen mentions any imprisonment or arrest of Katz in Spain. He was in America, Paris, and the Riviera during the final phases of the Spanish Civil War. As the reader will see below, I think it highly likely (but not certain) that Katz was quietly involved in *P.M.,* in the creation of which Hellman and Hammett were intimately involved, as both William Wright and Carl Rollyson show in their biographies of Hellman.

19. Koestler, *Invisible Writing,* p. 209.

20. For Cockburn's introduction to Münzenberg, see *A Discord of Trumpets,* p. 232, and for a fairly candid account of fabricating disinformation for Katz in Spain, see pp. 306–309.

21. Cockburn, *A Discord of Trumpets,* p. 306.

22. Cockburn, *A Discord of Trumpets,* p. 305.

23. Information to the author, interview with Mr. Paul Willert, London, June 6, 1986.

24. Hellman, *An Unfinished Woman,* pp. 68–69.

25. Koestler, *The Invisible Writing,* p. 211. Geneviève Tabouis was a famous French political Journalist; Ellen Wilkinson, a sometime fellow traveller, was a leading personality in the British Labour Party.

26. Confidential interview with the author.

27. Information to the author from the late Eugen Loebl (spelling is an anglicized version of the original Löbl).

28. For Blunt's and Burgess's claims to be "Comintern" agents, see Rees, *A Chapter of Accidents,* and Straight, *After Long Silence,* in the passages describing Burgess and Blunt attempting to recruit them. That Maly and Orlov were among the first controls of the Cambridge ring has been established by John Costello. See *The Mask of Treachery,* and the *New York Times,* June 26, 1991, p. 11.

29. On apologists for the Popular Front, see Alpern, *Freda Kirchway,* Louis Fischer, *Men and Politics,* et al.

30. The penetration of the Comintern by the NKVD and the GRU in 1935 has been explored by a number of reliable authors, chief among them Conquest, *The Great Terror,* pp. 399–408, and passim. I am grateful to Mr. Herb Romerstein for revealing to me the actual identity of "Comrade Moskfin" (or "Moskvin"). "Moskfin" was the man in Charge of liquidating the Münzenberg Trust in 1935; he was in truth a founding senior officer of the NKVD, Mikhail Trilliser, who by 1935 seems to have been attached to the GRU. This information was confirmed during June 1992 by research in the

Comintern archives in Moscow by Mr. Harvey Klehr, to whom I am indebted here. For "Moskfin's" role liquidating Münzenberg's enterprises, see Gross, *Münzenberg*, p. 277.

31. Information to the author from Mr. Paul Willert.
32. Information to the author from Mrs. Rae Bernstein.
33. Radek's competence in German matters was an indispensable factor in his place within the Soviet hierarchy. The best available consideration of this, as of 2003, is Arkady Vaksberg, in *Hotel Lux*. See also Tucker, *Stalin in Power*, pp. 232–238. See Heller and Nekrich, *Utopia in Power*, pp. 232–233. Also Lazitch and Drachkovitch, *Lenin and the Comintern*, and many other authorities.
34. See Willett, *The Theater of Erwin Piscator*.
35. A reliable sketch of Katz's relations with Piscator can be found in ibid. Babette Gross supplies much information as well. It is Cookridge who reports (without citation) the information not found elsewhere that Katz contributed to Piscator's sets, in *The Net That Covers the World*.
36. Willett, *The Theater of Erwin Piscator*, pp. 67–71.
37. Ibid.
38. Gross, *Münzenberg*, p. 311.
39. Ibid.
40. Koestler, *Invisible Writing*, p. 211.
41. Information to the author from Mr. Herbert Marshall.
42. Ibid.
43. Karel Kaplan, *Report on the Murder of the General Secretary*, p. 276.
44. Gross, *Münzenberg*, p. 311.
45. For Katz and his connection to Batista, see FOIA report.
46. Information to the author from Mr. Herman Starobin.
47. Information to the author from Mrs. Margaret Regler.
48. Information to the author from the late Eugen Loebl.

Chapter 5
ANTIFASCISM ON STAGE: TRIAL AND COUNTER-TRIAL

1. Thomas Mann, *Diaries 1918–1939*, Selection and Forward by Herman Kesten. Translated from the German by Richard and Clara Winston. (New York, 1982: Harry N. Abrams), p. 137.
2. Georgi Dimitrov, *The Diary of Georgi Dimitrov: 1933–1939*, Ivo Banac, editor (New Haven and London. Yale University Press, 2003), p. 5.
3. Central Party Archives, Moscow Fond 495, file 60, Document 242a. Letter from Agent "Semko," May 21, 1933.
4. Furet, pp. 211–212.
5. Catherine Károlyi, *A Life Together: The Memoirs of Catherine Károlyi* George Allen & Unwin (Ruskin House, Museum Street) 1966.

6. See Hilger and Meyer, p. 252; Conquest, *Terror,* p. 197.

7. Furet, p. 211.

8. Thomas Mann, *Diaries,* p. 137.

9. Ruth Fischer, Arkady Maslow, *Abtrünnig wider Willen: Aus Briefen und Manuscripten des Exils,* Herausgegeben von Peter Lübbe (R. Oldenbourg Verlag, München 1990), p. 465.

10. Fischer and Maslow, op. cit., p. 467.

11. Catherine Károlyi, *A Life Together,* p. 271.

12. Regler, *The Owl of Minerva.*

13. Lerner, *Karl Radek,* pp. 8–30.

14. Gross, *Münzenberg,* p. 179.

15. From within the Trotskyist camp, a perspective on Blumkin's demise and his relation to Trotsky is found in van Heijenoort's book, *With Trotsky in Exile.*

16. See Krivitsky, pp. 9–15.

17. See Heller and Nekrich, *Utopia in Power,* pp. 324–326.

18. For the creation of the Podlipki "Eighth International Sports Base," see Gross, *Münzenberg,* pp. 264–266, 267. For the downfall of Mirov-Abramov, see Conquest, *The Great Terror,* p. 408.

19. For Münzenberg's planning at this stage, see Gross, *Münzenberg,* pp. 239–270.

20. Ibid., p. 249.

21. Goebbels is cited in Shareen Brissac, *Resisting Hitler,* p. 124.

22. Babette Gross, interview with the author, Munich, Germany, July 6, 1989.

23. Regler, *The Owl of Minerva.*

24. Ibid., pp. 160–161.

25. *The Brown Book of the Hitler Terror and the Burning of the Reichstag,* and *The Second Brown Book of the Hitler Terror,* went through many editions and were very widely translated. Gustav Regler, Arthur Koestler, and Manes Sperber, in their memoirs, all write vividly about work in the collective that produced the books. Otto Katz himself produced a book on their composition called *Der Kampf um ein Buch.* (I have found no record of a translation.) After the war, Dimitrov himself wrote a version of the event in *Das Reichstagsbrandprozess.*

26. See Gross, *Münzenberg,* p. 251. See also Regler, *The Owl of Minerva,* and Costello, *The Mask of Treachery,* p. 298.

27. For a useful summary of Torgler's place in German communism, see Borkenau, *European Communism.* Tobias naturally discusses Torgler's case extensively, though Torgler's tangled connection to the entire event has never been fully explored. Indispensable to that exploration would be Ruth Fischer, *Stalin and German Communism,* and especially the correspondence of Ruth Fischer with Maria Reese now on deposit in the papers of Ruth Fischer in the Houghton Library at Harvard. Many of these documents, along with other relevant documents, have been published by Peter Lübbe in his collection of the Ruth Fischer-Arkady Maslow papers, *Abtrünnig wider Willen,* in

particular pp. 219, 248, and 273. Gisevius, in *To the Bitter End*, also provides some discussion of Torgler's role.

28. An important document for understanding this phase of Katz's career in his letter to Klement Gottwald, written on the day of his execution in Prague, and found in Karel Kaplan, *Report on the Murder of the General Secretary.* Katz's contact with Ellen Wilkinson and others is also reported in Vernon, *Ellen Wilkinson.*

29. Stewart, *By a Stroke of Luck!*

30. See Hays, *City Lawyer.*

31. Göring's performance at the trial is reported by Tobias, *The Reichstag Fire,* pp. 221–228.

32. Rhysselberghe, *Cahiers d'André Gide #5. Les Cahiers de la Petite Dame. Notes pour l'histoire authentique d'André Gide, 1929–1937.* See also Gide, *Litterature engagée,* especially the very useful chronology.

33. I have used many sources to reconstruct Gide and Malraux's trip to Berlin with their petition: The notebooks of Maria van Rhysselberghe; Gide*Litterature engagée;* Malraux, *Anti-Memoirs;* Lacouture, *André Malraux,* and others.

34. Lacouture, *André Malraux,* p. 182.

35. See the notebooks of Maria van Rhysselberghe, and the letters of André Gide to Roger Martin du Gard.

Chapter 6
BEHIND THE SMOKESCREEN

1. Arthur Koestler, *The Invisible Writing, An Autobiography* (New York, Macmillan, 1954), p. 194.

2. Thomas Mann, *Diaries,* entry for November 24. 1933, p. 181.

3. In this context, I might cite two letters to me from Fridrikh Firsov, the former Soviet archivist who served as principle archival advisor to Yale University Press's "Annals of Communism" series. In 1998 Mr. Firsov had recently read Valtin for the first time. In a letter to me of November 8, 1998, he wrote: "Valtin's book made a strong impression on me. It has been necessary for me to become familiar with quite a bit of material connected with the events of the fall of 1923 in Germany. Anyway, Valtin described these events in 1923 with such accuracy that I was simply stunned, and he so thoroughly and accurately recreated them in his book. In a second letter, of October 15, 1998, Mr. Firsov added, "This book impressed me greatly, and not only by its contents. Many facts and names mentioned in this book are familiar to me through the archival material. And in many cases what Valtin has written corresponds to these archival documents." Mr. Firsov then proceeds to analyze various documents in his possession in these terms.

4. Jan Valtin [Richard J. H. Krebs], *Out of the Night* (New York, Alliance Book Corporation, 1941), pp. 492–493.
5. Central Party Archives, Moscow. Fond 495, file 60, document 242a. Letter from agent "Semko" to unnamed Comintern officials, "Semko," May 21, 1933.
6. Central Party Archives, Moscow. Fond 495, file 60, document 244a. Letter from Karl Radek to Boris Vinogradov, May 20, 1933.
7. Shareen Brissac. *Resisting Hitler* (New York: Oxford University Press, 2000), pp. 155–158.
8. Brissac, p. 157.
9. The best discussion of the Vinogradov-Dodd love affair is in Brissac, chs. 9 and 10. It is also discussed in Weinstein, *The Haunted Wood*, ch. 3.
10. See Gisevius, *To the Bitter End*.
11. A useful summary of this well-known and crucial juncture in Hitler's planning can be found in Paul Johnson, *Modern Times*, pp. 296–300.
12. Ibid.
13. Ibid.
14. Carlton, *Anthony Eden*, p. 46.
15. For Hitler's planning and behavior on the Night of Long Knives, see Gisevius, *To the Bitter End*, and Fest, *Hitler*.
16. Gross, *Münzenberg*, p. 248. A more detailed of Katz's maneuvers fabricating the story of Lübbe's "homosexuality" can be found in Hans Schoots, *Living Dangerously: A Biography of Joris Ivens*, translated from the Dutch by David Colmer (Amsterdam University Press: Amsterdam, 2000), pp. 85–90.
17. Koestler, *Invisible Writing*, p. 196.
18. Tobias, *The Reichstag Fire*, p. 57.
19. The intrigues with the Berlin police department are mentioned by both Koestler, *Invisible Writing*, and Regler, *The Owl of Minerva*. The most thorough eyewitness account from within the Prinz Albrechtstrasse Police Headquarters is Gisevius, *To the Bitter End*.
20. Relations between Gisevius and Diels are complex, and worthy of sustained separate examination. Torgler figures in them significantly, as Torgler's letters to Ruth Fischer make clear. We know that one week after the London Counter-Trial ended, Hitler (in real or feigned anger) suddenly removed Rolf Diels, presumably over the leaks and breaches of security that had been used by Münzenberg in the London propaganda. Diels seemed disgraced; Hitler seemed enraged. Diels fled to Czechoslovakia, from which it was rumored that he threatened "embarrassing revelations" if he was not restored to power. This restoration promptly followed. To Gisevius and Nebe, who had been leaking as much negative SA information as possible, this seemed the end: they had been found out, and were finished. Yet on the day of Diels's return, Gisevius was summoned to his office and greeted with a sudden warmth and friendliness. Astonishing! Gisevius was not to be shot

but promoted. To a big new job! Gisevius was to become the Gestapo's special liaison. Where? To the Reichstag Fire Trial!

Diels had had his crucial meeting with Hitler the day before, when this leading officer of the fledgling Gestapo was given his new marching orders. Those orders clearly entailed Gisevius's promotion, rather than dismissal.

21. Malraux confided his general suspicions on this subject in an interview with Jean Lacouture, as they worked together preparing Lacouture's biography of Malraux. Lacouture, *André Malraux*, p. 182.

22. Fischer, *Stalin and German Communism*, pp. 308–309.

23. Arthur Koestler, *The Invisible Writing*, pp. 247–249.

24. Mann, *Diaries*, November 1, 1933, p. 179.

25. Ruth Fischer und Arkady Maslow, *Abtrünnig wider Willen: Aus Briefen und Manuskripten des Exils*. Heraugegeben von Peter Lübbe (R. Oldenbourg Verlag. München, 1990).

26. Babette Gross, interview with the author, July 4, 1989.

27. Fischer-Maslow, *Abtrünnig*, p. 248. See also letter to Sidney B. Fay, December 30, 1947, p. 217.

28. Dimitrov, Georgi, *The Diary of Georgi Dimitrov: 1933–1949*. Edited and Introduced by Ivo Banac (Yale University Press: New Haven and London, 2003), p. 69.

29. Preface, Popov, *Ot lajpzigskija prozes v sibirskite lagen*. I am exceedingly grateful to M. Tzvetan Todorov for having brought this important piece of evidence to my attention, and for supplying me with the literal translation of Semerdjiev's introduction, which with his kind permission I am including here.

30. Mr. Semerdjiev's claim that Pieck acted as the intermediary between the Nazi and Soviet governments is sustained by a cable found in the Central Party Archives, written by Pieck, sent to Piatnitsky, and translated from the German for Stalin's eyes only. This document conveys a proposal from the German government to Stalin suggesting that the dictator offer "Dimitrov and the Bulgarians" political asylum "in any form." Exactly as Ruth Fischer understood, Ernst Torgier was not to be included in the deal. The cable in question was received by Piatnitsky four days after the Leipzig acquittal, December 28, 1933, Christmas having intervened (CPA 495.19.248).

31. Both Regler, *The Owl of Minerva*, and Koestler, *Invisible Writing*, recall Dimitrov's access to *The Brown Book* while in prison.

32. Information to the author from Mr. Peter Semerdjiev: a letter dated November 6, 1992, and an extended telephone interview, November 13, 1992.

33. *The White Book on the Executions of June 30, 1934.*

34 *The White Book on the Executions of June 30, 1934.*

35. National Archives of the United States, 800.00B, dossier on Louis Gibarti, document #73. Memorandum from the Visa Division, Department of State,

dated January 29, 1940, unsigned but annotated VD; AMW: MLS. For Bredow's role with the Guchkov circle, see Deacon, *The British Connection*, p. 107.

36. Toland, *Hitler*, p. 465.

37 Information citing Gibarti as the probable author of the Oberfohren Memorandum can be found in his FOIA dossier, #61-6629. A careful account of the Oberfohren Memorandum is found in Tobias, *The Reichstag Fire*, p. 104.

38. CPA fond 495.73.26.

39. See letter from Radek to Vinogradov, already cited.

40. See Tobias, *The Reichstag Fire*, appendix C.

41. Ibid., pp. 144–146.

42. The fantasy that Hitler was merely a front man in danger of losing control of the Nazi government to the SA led the conservatives to seek covertly to assist him in resisting that threat.

It's worth noting that after the event, and once the United States was in the war, this Version of early Nazi history was believed at high levels of American intelligence. In Geneva in 1942, Mary Bancroft, an OSS operative who was simultaneously intimate with Allen Dulles and Gisevius, acted as the liaison between both men in preparing the attempted assassination of Hitler in the von Stauffenberg plot—a final shot at salvation on the part of anti-Nazi German conservatives and their beloved army, this time covertly assisted by the United States. In conversations with me, Ms. Bancroft made it quite plain that Allen Dulles accepted more or less whole Gisevius's version of the early struggle within the Nazi government, and of the Reichstag Fire.

The tragedy of the conservatives' effort to ruin the SA is that it did nothing to rescue the honor of either German politics or the German army, and instead played into the hands of both Hitler and Stalin. By underestimating Hitler's own importance and (perhaps) overestimating the hated SA, they solidified Nazi power and thereby promoted the aims of both the dictators they despised.

43. See Gisevius, *To the Bitter End*.

Chapter 7
THE POPULAR FRONT: PROPAGANDA AND PROPHECY

1. Gross, p. 277.

2. Walter Krivitsky, *In Stalin's Secret Service*, p. 8.

3. Krivitsky, pp. 60–61.

4. Ibid., p. 61.

5. See Gisevius, *To the Bitter End*.

6. Krivitsky, chapter 1.

7. Krivitsky, pp. 2–3.

8. Ibid.

9. Robert Tucker, *Stalin in Power: The Revolution from Above. 1928–1941*. (New York: Norton, 1992), p. 345.

10. Both Conquest, *The Great Terror*, and Heller and Nekrich, *Utopia in Power*, discuss Stalin's willingness to see damage done to the German communists in 1933.

11. Heller and Nekrich, *Utopia in Power*, pp. 251–258. See also Krivitsky, *In Stalin's Secret Service*, pp. 1–25.

12. Arkady Vaksberg, *Hôtel Lux: Les partis frères au service de l'Internationale communiste*. Translated into French from the Russian by Olivier Simon. (Fayard: Paris, 1993), p. 135.

13. Hilger and Meyer, *The Incompatible Allies*, pp. 267–268.

14. One such incident from January 1934 is described in Tucker, pp. 255–256.

15. Heller and Nekrich, *Utopia in Power*, pp. 309–311, citing Gnedin, *Iz istorii otnoshenii mezhdu SSSR ifashistskoi Germanii. Dokumenty i sovremennye kommentarii*, pp. 22–27.

16. Dimitrov, *The Diary of Georgi Dimitrov, 1933–1949*. Ivo Banac, ed. Entry for September 1, 1939, p. 115.

17. For Radek's relation to the antifascist campaign, see Krivitsky, pp. 8–15, as well as Heller and Nekrich, *Utopia in Power*, p. 325. Gross, *Münzenberg*, pp. 179–180. See also Dziak, *Chekisty*, p. 83.

18. Krivitsky, *In Stalin's Secret Service*, pp. 8–15.

19. Ibid., pp. 1–25, noting especially pp. 10–11, and all references to Radek.

20. Conquest, *The Great Terror*, pp. 62–63.

21. Krivitsky, p. 163.

22. Furet, *The Passing of an Illusion*, p. 220.

23. Furet, op. cit., pp. 212–213.

24. Koltsov's role in the 1935 Culture Congress is noted by Lottman, *The Left Bank*. It was confirmed to me by Babette Gross. That Katz played a leading role in the Left Book Club was first pointed out to me by Mr. Paul Willert, who noted especially that "Katz had a lot of Negrin money" (that is, money from the Stalinist Spanish government) to spend on Propaganda in both Europe and England. Katz speaks of his role with Gollancz and Laski in his letter to Klement Gottwald; see above, chapter 4, note 2.

25. Tucker, p. 341.

26. For a thorough analysis of the movement toward the pact, see Nekrich and Heller, *Utopia in Power*, pp. 316–369. For Stalin's general strategic thinking prior to the European war, see Paul Johnson, *Modern Times*, p. 359. The reader is also directed to Dziak, *Chekisty*, chapters 4, 5, and 6.

27. Tzvetan Todorov, "Staline vu de Pres" (my translation).

28. Conquest, *Stalin and the Kirov Murder*, p. 104.

29. Ibid., p. 146.

30. Gross, p. 290.

31. Conquest, *Great Terror*, pp. 145–147.
32. The best account of the 1937 purge of the Red Army general staff can be found in Conquest, *The Great Terror*, chapter 7, "The Assault on the Army." Conquest's range of reference is too wide to summarize here, but he does rely, as I do, on both Orlov and Krivitsky. Among other notable historians of this well-known incident, I have used Robert C. Tucker's account in *Stalin in Power: Revolution from Above. 1928–1941*, particularly the sequence of chapters called "The Forging of Autocracy." For a useful and incisive summary of the affair, and various positions that have been taken over it, see also Laqueur, *Stalin: The Glasnost Revelations*. For an intensive re-examination of Orlov's role and Information, see Costello, *Deadly Illusions*. Another book which I have found useful is Blackstock, *The Secret Road to World War II*. See also Hilger and Meyer, *The Incompatible Allies*.
33. Krivitsky, *In Stalin's Secret Service*, "Why Stalin Shot His Generals."
34. Conquest, *The Great Terror*, pp. 195–205.
35. Ibid.
36. Krivitsky, *In Stalin's Secret Service*, "Stalin's Hand in Spain."
37. Conquest, *The Great Terror*, p. 199.
38. For Katz's links to the Miller organization and the Guchkov circle, see Costello, *The Mask of Treachery.*
39. I should note that according to Mrs. Rae Bernstein, during the period he spent in New York in 1940, Katz made frequent reference (when speaking within reliably communist circles) to his past privileged link to President Beneš. Information to the author from Mrs. Rae Bernstein.
40. Willi's suspicions of Otto on this score may be the context for his attack on Katz in their last encounter, as reported in Gross, 312—though Willi's scorn on this occasion was primarily focused on Katz's acceptance of the new alliance with Hitler, which had been accompanied by Hitler's expulsion of the Beneš government, with which Katz had until then sedulously ingratiated himself.
41. Sir Isaiah Berlin, interview with the author, January 24, 1992.
42. Conquest, *The Great Terror*, p. 195.
43. Conquest, *Stalin and the Kirov Murder*, pp. 182–183. Solzhenitsyn, *The Gulag Archipelago*, vols. 1–2, see glossary entry p. 631, and in the text, pp. 410–416.

Chapter 8
THE POPULAR FRONT AND ESPIONAGE

1. The best study of the Washington activities of the Cambridge group is found in *The Cambridge Spies*, by Verne Newton.
2. Boyle, *The Climate of Treason*, pp. 400–10.

3. Ibid., pp. 271–273, and passim.
4. Ibid., pp. 400–405.
5. Mr. Paul Willert, phone interview with the author, June 25, 1987.
6. Costello, *The Mask of Treachery*, p. 208.
7. Arthur Martin's account of this scene is quoted and paraphrased in *Conspiracy of Silence*, by Penrose and Freeman, pp. 415–420.
8. Malraux, *Anti-Memoirs*, p. 89.
9. Leo Long is quoted in Miranda Carter, *Anthony Blunt: His Lives*, p. 191. The quotation is taken from a longer citation in Barrie Penrose and Simon Freeman, *Conspiracy of Silence*, pp. 118–120.
10. Maly's role is best established by Costello in *The Mask of Treachery*, especially pp. 278–285.
11. See Hede Massing, *This Deception*.
12. The chapter of *This Deception* entitled "Assignment America" describes Massing's meetings with Maly. Hede Massing died before Maly was identified as the Cambridge recruiter and control, and she did not know his real name when she wrote her book. She did correctly identify *"der Lange"* however with "Paul Hardt," without knowing that name to be one of Maly's aliases. Her description of *"der Lange"* is exactly appropriate to Maly in every detail. Indeed, Massing's precise description of him and his role is in itself persuasive evidence for the general veracity of *This Deception*.
13. Langer, *Josephine Herbst*, pp. 206–207.
14. Massing, *This Deception*, pp. 115–138, and passim.
15. Poretsky, *Our Own People*, p. 144.
16. The best source of information on Noel Field is Flora Lewis's book of 1965, *Red Pawn*. Its conclusions about Field's work for the Soviets are very conservatively formulated and at no point go beyond the evidence then available. Much more has become available since that time, though it is rather scattered, especially through information released by Dr. Karel Kaplan, a member of the Dubcek government who saw much of the documentation of the period. (See Weinstein, *Perjury*.) See also Hodos, *Show Trials*. Copious information about Field's work as a secret Service agent, both in Europe and in espionage with Alger Hiss in Washington, has been examined in the Archives of the Ministry of Information, Budapest, by Ms. Maria Schmidt, notably in the archives of the Hungarian Secret Police. According to testimony of Louis Budenz, accepted by Flora Lewis, and confirmed by my own research in the National Archives of the United States, Noel Field was a member of the Communist Party by 1927.
17. Flora Lewis, *Red Pawn*. Also information to the author from Ms. Maria Schmidt.
18. The essential outline of Noel Field's relation to Allen Dulles, beginning immediately after World War I, and ending in the murderous hysteria of the

Slansky Trials, can be found in Flora Lewis's *Red Pawn*, which, while excellent, is now quite dated. The entire subject of Noel Field calls out for new, post-Cold War research.

19. Field's disappearance is described in *Red Pawn*.
20. The successive waves of arrests are reported in Hodos, *Show Trials*.
21. Information to the author from Ms. Maria Schmidt, Budapest, January 24, 1993.
22. Peter Wright, *Spycatcher*, pp. 225–226.
23. The indispensable source on Maly's life is Poretsky, *Our Own People*. See also Costello, *The Mask of Treachery*, and very interesting references to Maly's rehabilitation with the KGB in Andrew and Gordievsky, *The KGB*.
24. Michael Straight, *After Long Silence*. For a description of his recruitment, see pp. 100–106.
25. Ibid., p. 102.
26. The Straight family's connections to Dolivet are treated in *After Long Silence*. See also Newton, *The Cambridge Spies*.
27. Straight, *Silence*, p. 110.
28. Chambers, *Witness*, p. 14.
29. Orlov, *The Secret History of Stalin's Crimes*, pp. 229–232.
30. For the relation between Orlov and Maly, see Costello, *Deadly Illusions*.
31. Orlov, *The Secret History of Stalin's Crimes*.

Chapter 9
THE BLOOMSBURY SPIES

1. Bell, *Virginia Woolf*, pp. 48, 54, 63.
2. Bell, *Virginia Woolf*, vol. l, pp. 129–130.
3. Paul Johnson, *Modern Times*, p. 168. Reference to "the Method" is from Allen, *The Cambridge Apostles*, p. 71.
4. See Deacon, *The Cambridge Apostles*. See also Costello, *The Mask of Treachery*.
5. I am indebted in this passage, and throughout this chapter, to John Costello's study of Blunt, *The Mask of Treachery*.
6. Quoted in Paul Johnson, *Modern Times*, p. 167, citing ibid., pp. 211–212.
7. Conquest, *The Great Terror*, p. 317. For Arnold Deutsch's shrewd assessment of Burgess' homosexuality, see Costello, *Deadly Illusions*, p. 226.
8. Catherine Károlyi, *A Life Together*.
9. An excellent summary of the activities of Pascal and Dobb can be found in Costello, *The Mask of Treachery*.
10. Katz refers to this British surveillance in the letter to Klement Gottwald, written hours before he was hanged and published in Karel Kaplan, *Report on the Murder of the General Secretary*.

11. Wilkinson's visit to Katz on the Riviera is mentioned by Louis Fischer in *Men and Politics.*

12. Otto Katz's relation to Claud Cockburn figures quite prominently in Cockburn's memoir, *A Discord of Trumpets,* and in Patricia Cockburn's *Figure of Eight,* as well as Patricia Cockburn, *The Years at "The Week."*

13. Cockburn. *A Discord of Trumpets.*

14. Roy Hoopes, *Ralph Ingersoll.*

15. William Warner, *Lillian Hellman: The Image, the Woman* (New York: Simon and Schuster 1986), pp. 167–169.

16. Otto Katz's role at *Ce Soir,* and in Parisian political journalism generally, was quite well known within the apparatus during the Popular Front. *Ce Soir* was a forthrightly communist publication, and its directors were all people close to Katz, but in addition to that, Katz was directly involved in purchasing the services of journalists. (Information to the author from Mr. Paul Willert. See also Poretsky, *Our Own People.*) That *Ce Soir* was subsidized by the Propaganda apparatus is plain from the discussion of it that appears in Ory, *Paul Nizan,* pp. 172–173.

17. Information to the author from Ms. Patricia Bosworth.

18. Wright, *Spycatcher,* pp. 288 and 339. Wright's exact phrase is to describe Cockburn as a man "of interest to the Service as a prominent left-winger and Comintern agent" (p. 339). Cockburn was closely enough associated with the International to adopt an alias or "Party name": "Frank Pitcairn." This is however not quite the same as saying that Cockburn was a witting member of the Comintern secret Service.

19. The Tetuan story appears in Claud Cockburn, *A Discord of Trumpets.*

20. Thomas, *John Strachey,* p. 149. For Strachey's appointment as Director of the World Movement Against Fascism and War, see p. 138.

   That John Strachey was a witting member of the Soviet apparatus seems to me plainly demonstrated by his position in the Anti-War International, and Strachey's action (as described by John Lehmann in a letter to Andrew Boyle), at the time of the attempt to recruit Lehmann for work in espionage during the Viennese Propaganda campaign of 1934. (See Boyle, *The Climate of Treason,* paperback revision, pp. 105–106.) But few observers would doubt Strachey's deep involvement at this late date. The case of Gollancz is perhaps more controversial. During the years of the LBC, Gollancz was at the very least a fellow traveller who was very reliably responsive to the needs of the Party, and to Strachey's direction. My guess, based on two recent studies, is that he was more than that (see Paul Johnson, *Intellectuals,* and Edwards, *Victor Gollancz*).

21. A good summary of LBC politics can be found in Paul Johnson, *Intellectuals,* pp. 269–287.

22. For Strachey's consultations with the leaders of the British Communist party over selections for the Left Book Club, see Thomas, *John Strachey.* For the

LBC generally, see S. Samuels, "The Left Book Club," *Journal of Contemporary History* (N.Y.) v. 2, 1966.

23. For Olden's relation to Münzenberg, see Gross, *Münzenberg*, pp. 229, 232.
24. Information to the author from Mr. Paul Willert.
25. I am indebted to Mr. Herbert Marshall for this observation, which he first made working in the English-language wing of Münzenberg's Mezhropohmfilm Russ in the late 1920s and 1930s.
26. Information to the author from M. François Fejto.
27. For Hewlett Johnson's relation to Gibarti, Information to the author from M. François Fejto. For Johnson's role as a Stalinist Propagandist in general, see David Caute, *The Fellow Travellers*, passim.
28. For Julian Bell's friendship with Guy Burgess, see Andrew Boyle, *The Climate of Treason*, p. 110.
29. Lehmann, *The Whispering Gallery*, p. 212. Lehmann's account of this phase of his life, especially the relation to Virginia and Leonard Woolf, can be found on pp. 184–228.
30. Costello, *Deadly Illusions*, chapter 6.
31. Dollfuss was assassinated by the Nazis in 1934.
32. See Krivitsky, *In Stalin's Secret Service*.
33. See Heller and Nekrich, *Utopia in Power*.
34. Mitchison, *You May Well Ask*, p. 195.
35. Boyle, *The Climate of Treason*, pp. 105–106.
36. Ibid., p. 106.
37. See Rees, *A Chapter of Accidents*, pp. 117–128.
38. For the quotation and the preceding one, see ibid., p. 155.
39. Muggeridge, *The Infernal Grove*, pp. 106–107.
40. For the fascinating list of his social contacts, provided by Burgess to the NKVD, see Costello, *Deadly Illusions*. Nicolson is on the list.
41. Glees, *The Secrets of the Service*, p. 149. See also W. J. West, *Truth Betrayed*, pp. 52–58, and passim.
42. Nicolson, *Diaries and Letters*, p. 435. Cited by Glees, *The Secrets of the Service*.
43. W. J. West, *Truth Betrayed*.
44. Information to the author from M. François Fejto.
45. Nicolson, *Diaries and Letters*, p. 349. (Entry for June 7, 1951.)

Chapter 10
IN AMERICA

1. Peter Kurth, American *Cassandra: The Life of Dorothy Thompson* (New York: Little Brown, 1990).
2. See Sheean, *Dorothy and Red*. The incident is also reported in Kurth, *American Cassandra*.

3. Kurth, *American Cassandra*, p. 109.

4. Information to the author from Babette Gross.

5. That Vincent Sheean was a much-used fellow traveller at least until September 1, 1939, is proved by his signature on an open letter attacking Krivitsky, and published in major newspapers across the United States in August 1939. That he quite clearly understood Rayna Prohme's position within the apparatus is suggested in *Dorothy and Red*, and confirmed in the memoirs of John Dos Passos, *The Best of Times: An Informal Memoir*. For the role of Samson Raphaelson among the Hollywood fellow travellers, see Schwartz, *The Hollywood Writers' Wars*.

6. See Dorothy Thompson's letter to Sinclair Lewis on this event, in Sheean, *Dorothy and Red*, p. 67. Also Sheean's account of the relationship, pp. 74–77, as well as in his *Personal Memoir*, chapter 6.

7. See Sheean, *Dorothy and Red*, p. 77.

8. That Soong Chin'ling was a Münzenberg agent, see Gross, *Münzenberg*, p. 183, and the FOIA dossier of Louis Gibarti, # 61-6629, section 3. Deposition of Louis Gibarti before Special Counsel to the United States Senate, Robert Morris, Esq., and United States Senators Willis Smith and Homer Ferguson, Paris, August 28, 1951.

9. See Sheean, *Dorothy and Red*.

10. See the letters of Dorothy Thompson to Sinclair Lewis, reprinted in ibid.

11. See Thompson's book about her trip, *The New Russia* (1928).

12. Sheean, *Dorothy and Red*. Letters of Thompson to Lewis.

13. On January 29, 1940, the Visa Division of the United States Department of State filed a memorandum on Otto Katz referring to information from "an unnamed but reliable source" (National Archives of the United States, 800.00B, dossier on Louis Gibarti, document #73). Other correspondence from this episode can be found in the National Archives, 800.00B, dossier on Katz-Breda.

14. Ibid.

15. A. A. Berle's letter of reply to correspondence was produced in an FOIA request on Katz. It is dated May 8, 1940.

16. William Wright, *Lillian Hellman*.

17. Karel Kaplan, *Report on the Murder of the General Secretary*, p. 276.

18. See Langer, *Josephine Herbst*.

19. Hemingway, *Selected Letters*, p. 120. Also p. 114.

20. The founding of the New Playwrights' Theater, and its debt to Piscator, is discussed in the memoirs of Harold Clurman.

21. The role of Trachtenberg and Jerome is indicated in Schwartz, *The Hollywood Writers' Wars*, pp. 89–90.

Though much research remains to be done, the focussed and intrusive interest of the Soviet propaganda apparatus in the Los Angeles film colony has been amply documented. Lawson and Faragoh's work among the Hollywood fellow travellers and for the special unit of the Communist Party USA specifically created for work in the film colony is treated, admiringly but revealingly, in Schwartz's *The Hollywood Writers' Wars*. Following the common line of such works, Schwartz seeks to promote the fantasy that the American Communist party was in some way independent from the International and from Soviet political control generally, so that the "idealistic" enterprises of its front groups somehow were not co-ordinated to serve the Stalinist tyranny. This is a notion that present evidence uniformly contradicts: The American Communist party was always financed and ideologically controlled by the Soviet Union.

22. The dossier on Em Jo Basshe is found in the National Archives of the United States, 800.00B.

23. The sources on the life of Basshe are thin. There is a rather condescending entry on him in Kunitz and Haycroft, *Twentieth Century Authors* (1942). His plays are *Earth* (1927, New Playwrights' Theater) and *Centuries* (1928); *Portrait of a Tenement House* (1928) and *Doomsday Circus* (1938). They are not in print. He is mentioned by all memoirists of the New Playwrights' Theater, and he played a role in the Lafayette Theater of Harlem in the Negro Theater Division of the WPA, in which he worked as a director. He appears in *Most Likely to Succeed,* Dos Passos's novel, as "Eli."

24. National Archives of the United States, 800.00B, dossier on Em Jo Basshe, document #5.

25. Woolcott's review is quoted in the article on Basshe in *The Biographical Dictionary of the American Theater.*

26. Dos Passos, *Most Likely to Succeed* (1954).

27. The documents recounting this story are memoranda from the U. S. Embassy in London, based on Information supplied by British intelligence. The probable source would have been Guy Liddell. They are on file in the National Archives of the United States, 800.00B, dossier on Em Jo Basshe.

28. There have been numerous accounts of this episode. See Schwartz, *The Hollywood Writers' Wars,* and David Caute, *The Great Fear* (New York: Simon and Schuster, 1978).

29. V. J. Jerome and Alexander Trachtenberg's role in New Playwrights' appear in Dos Passos, *Most Likely to Succeed.* Katz's remark about Columbus and Hollywood is cited in Draper, "The Man Who Wanted to Hang."

30. National Archives of the United States, 800.00B, dossier on Katz-Breda.

31. See Viertel, *The Kindness of Strangers,* pp. 101–102.

32. An excellent albeit "innocent" eyewitness account of the founding of the Hollywood Anti-Nazi League can be found in Stewart, *By a Stroke of Luck.*

33. Ibid., p. 225.

34. Ibid., pp. 225–226.

35. Mann, *The Letters of Thomas Mann: 1889–1955,* pp. 330–332.

36. Schwartz, *The Hollywood Writers' Wars.* pp. 82–83 (my emphasis).

37. Wright, *Lillian Hellman, p.* 162. Wright is quoting Hellman from the *New York Times,* January 20, 1940. For an analysis of Hellman's own account of her response to the Finnish Invasion, both at the time and in *An Unfinished Woman,* see Rollyson, *Lillian Hellman,* pp. 149–152. Rollyson concludes that Hellman's Version of these events is "an outrageous piece of nonsense."
38. Lyons, *Red Decade,* p. 374.
39. A leading personage in West Coast communism who was invited to step inside the magic circle of the Hollywood Stalinists and their celebrity elite was Harry Bridges, who by 1936 was a dominating figure in the CIO, the great labor union of the era on the West Coast of the United States. The Central Party Archives now show that Bridges was a member of that apparatus, and under Soviet control. See Klehr and Haynes, *The American Spectator,* December 1992, pp. 34–36. The legal and Propaganda struggle fought for decades over Bridges's presence in the United States is a saga marked by interminability. For years, the American government made every conceivable effort to expose Bridges's links to the Soviets. For years, the apparatus responded with every conceivable effort to discredit that effort and protect the more or less open secret of his subordination to Stalin and his government.

  In Washington, communists within the Roosevelt administration, including almost certainly Alger Hiss's brother Donald Hiss, were in continuous maneuver to derail and discredit the government's inquiry and challenge to Bridges's power on the San Francisco docks. Meanwhile, with numbing immunity to ennui, the Propaganda apparatus lionized and defended Bridges year after weary year. Among the Hollywood Stalinists, Bridges was viewed as a saintly figure. (Schwartz, *Hollywood Writers' Wars.*)
40. Lyons, *Red Decade,* p. 51.
41. Stewart, *By a Stroke of Luck.*
42. Meade, *Dorothy Parker,* p. 254.
43. See Justin Kaplan, *Lincoln Steffens.*
44. Stewart, *By a Stroke of Luck,* pp. 230–236.
45. See FOLA dossier on Louis Gibarti.
46. Justin Kaplan, *Lincoln Steffens,* p. 312. Ella Winter was a leading figure in the Committee for the Relief of the Victims of Fascist Oppression, the American branch of the World Committee for the Relief of the Victims of German Fascism, which was, of course, under Gibarti's direction.
47. Ibid., pp. 311–312.
48. Ibid., pp. 321–324.
49. Langer, *Josephine Herbst, p.* 79.
50. See ibid.
51. Though the evidence before me is vague, my impression is that Radek was probably the guiding spirit behind the Kharkov Writers' Congress. Its cultural politics seem to show his hand. Radek at this time has just (but only

just) returned to Stalin's good graces, assuming the leading role in Stalinist cultural politics he would hold until he was purged.

As for the phrase, "ladies of the Kremlin," it can be found in Berberova, *Histoire,* and was used in my presence by Nina Berberova during my interview with her on January 10, 1991. The "ladies"—Russian women toiling for Stalin in European cultural life—included Baroness Budberg, Princess Koudachova, Elsa Triolet, Nunsch Eluard, and a number of others.

52. See Herbst, *The Starched Blue Sky of Spain,* pp. 121–122.
53. That Maxim Lieber was Katz's literary agent is mentioned in Weinstein, *Perjury,* pp. 322–324.
54. I am grateful to Ms. Elinor Langer for useful information regarding Josephine Herbst's contacts at this time.
55. Weinstein, *Perjury,* pp. 134–145. For Herbst and Herrmann's link to Otto Katz, see Otto Katz, FOIA dossier #1, 65-1763. Arriving in New York on September 10, 1935, Katz cites a "friend," Mrs. John Herrmann, 10 Fifth Avenue. Katz's cover at this time, according to the report of the American authorities, was that he was researching a book on Arctic explorations. This may well be linked to Peter Smolka-Smollett's work being done at the same time on the same subject, for the apparatus. See Andrew and Gordievsky, *KGB: The Inside Story,* pp. 325–335.
56. Hemingway, *Selected Letters,* p. 548.
57. Information to the author from the late Mr. Robert Towers.
58. Langer, *Josephine Herbst.*
59. John Herrmann's bond to Harold Ware is discussed extensively in Langer, *Josephine Herbst.*
60. Langer, *Josephine Herbst,* p. 171.

Chapter 11
AN END TO INNOCENCE

1. The role of Otto Katz in the founding of the Hollywood Anti-Nazi League figures in many memoirs and biographies, notably Stewart's *By a Stroke of Luck,* and in Meade's *Dorothy Parker.*
2. Lottman, *The Left Bank,* chapter 12.
3. *Cahiers d'André Gide # 5. Les Cahiers de la Petite Dame. Notes pour l'histoire authentique d'André Gide. 1927–1937* (Paris: Gallimard, 1974), p. 205.
4. Ibid., p. 155.
5. Ibid.
6. Ibid., p. 152.
7. For Herbart's link to publications supervised by Vaillant, see *Cahiers d'André Gide,* and its reports of Herbart's journalistic work between 1932 and 1935, and his trip to the USSR.

8. Lottman, *The Left Bank*, p. 84.
9. Arkady Vaksberg. *Le Mystère Gorki*, translated from the Russian by Sesemann, Dimitri, Albin Michel, Paris 1997.
10. Ibid. For a more detailed account, see Berberova, *Histoire de la baronne Boudberg*, pp. 259–263.
11. Regler, *The Owl of Minerva*, pp. 232–233.
12. Lottman, *The Left Bank*, pp. 92–93.
13. Ibid., p. 91.
14. Ibid., p. 93.
15. Gide, *Litterature engagée*. The text of Gide's letter is found on pp. 97–98. For the account of these events as seen from within Gide's household, see *Cahiers d'André Gide*, pp. 445–449. See also Lottman, *The Left Bank*.
16. Alix Guillain's attack on the letter is noted in *Cahiers d'André Gide*, p. 469.
17. Conquest, *The Great Terror*, p. 464.
18. For Gorky's financial lies to the pre-revolutionary Party, see Pipes, *The Russian Revolution*, pp. 369–371.
19. For Gorky's political history and his early links to revolutionary thought, see Troyat, *Maxim Gorky*, pp. 92–99. See also Pipes, *The Russian Revolution*, pp. 350–352, 369–378.
20. Pipes, *The Russian Revolution*, p. 351. This citation includes the passage from Gorky on Lenin.
21. Ibid., p. 351.
22. Ibid., p. 255. See also Vaksberg, 317.
23. Berberova, *Histoire*, pp. 250–254.
24. My discussion of Maxim Gorky in this chapter is indebted both in its broad outlines and especially its details to Arkady Vaksberg's absorbing book, *Le Mystère Gorki*. In the first edition of *Double Lives*, I relied on Nina Berberova's *Histoire de la Baronne Budberg*. That book is still useful for its memoir of Nina Berberova's own life in Gorky's household. But unlike Berberova, Vaksberg has had excellent post-Soviet access to the Gorky archives, and his book supersedes Berberova's account in most other aspects of the relation between Gorky and the Baroness.
25. Vaksberg, p. 255.
26. The relation between Lockhart and Moura Budberg is most famously told in Lockhart's *Secret Agent*. It is also discussed and analyzed in Berberova, *Histoire*.
27. Berberova's account of the arrest of Moura Budberg and Lockhart, which closely follows Lockhart's own account, is found in her *Histoire*, *"Amour et Prison,"* pp. 67–106.
28. Ibid., p. 266.
29. Anthony West, *H. G. Wells*, pp. 72–76.
30. Ibid., p. 145.
31. Ibid., pp. 144–147.

32. Troyat, *Maxim Gorky*, p. 189. See also Berberova, *Histoire*, p. 279.
33. The account of Stalin and Gorky's developing mutual distrust following the Kirov murder is recounted in Orlov, *The Secret History of Stalin's Crimes.*
34. In addition to Berberova, *Histoire*, see Conquest, *The Great Terror*, p. 388.
35. See Conquest, *The Great Terror*, pp. 375–398.
36. *Cahiers d'André Gide*, pp. 602–610.
37. Vaksberg, pp. 400–407; Berberova, *Histoire*, p. 264, especially footnote.
38. For Gide's preparations for departure, see *Cahiers d'André Gide*, pp. 539–550. I am grateful for M. Jean Malaquais, who gave me the benefit of his memories of being present in Gide's household as these events took place.
39. See *Cahiers d'André Gide*, p. 457.
40. Ibid.
41. Ibid., p. 547.
42. See Troyat, *Maxim Gorky*, p. 193.
43. See Berberova, *Histoire*. Information on this visit also appears in Desanti, *Les Yeux d'Elsa.*
44. See Berberova, citing Aragon, in *Histoire*, p. 263.
45. Ibid. Also Desanti, *Les Yeux d'Elsa.*
46. *Les Cahiers de la Petite Dame*, p. 542.
47. *Cahiers d'André Gide*, 5, p. 542.
48. An account of Bukharin's visit to Gide's hotel room appears in Desanti, *Les Yeux d'Elsa*, p. 253.
49. Information to the author from Mme. Nina Berberova.

Chapter 12
THE SPANISH STRATAGEM

1. Gross, *Münzenberg*, p. 276.
2. CPA, fond 495.19.337.
3. Gross Ibid., pp. 275–282.
4. Ibid., pp. 286–288.
5. Ibid., p. 277.
6. Ibid.
7. Ibid.
8. The masked identity of Mikhail Trilliser within the Comintern at this moment in the history of the Stalinist secret Services is a key and revelatory fact. I am grateful to Prof. Harvey Klehr for his assistance in identifying this imposture during his visit to the archives of the International in Moscow in June 1992; I am grateful in particular for the information, new to me, that in his guise as "Comrade Moskfin," Trilliser was under the discipline of the GRU, and not (as I had supposed) the NKVD, even though he had been a founder of the latter Service. I am also most grateful to Mr. Herbert

Romerstein, who first alerted me to Trilliser's clandestine role within the Comintern, and for Mr. Romerstein's original research, performed long before the archives opened, establishing that fact.

9. Gross, *Münzenberg*, pp. 282–289.
10. The reader is directed to an interesting study by M. Thierry Wolton on the work of Dolivet, Pierre Cot, Olof Aschberg, and sundry senior politicians in the Popular Front gathered around RUP: *Le Grand Recrutement*. M. Wolton's study is particularly informative about the links of RUP to the Soviet secret Services, information greatly enriched by archival material newly acquired.
11. Information to the author from Mr. Michael Straight.
12. Gross, *Münzenberg*, p. 288. See also Desanti, *Les Yeux d'Elsa*.
13. Lynn, *Hemingway*, p. 449.
14. Such a photograph is reproduced in Marion Meade, *Dorothy Parker: What Fresh Hell Is This?*
15. A good description of this Conference, noting the oddity of its lavishness, can be found in Stephen Spender, *World Within World* (New York: Simon and Schuster, 1978).
16. Gross, *Münzenberg*, p. 287.
17. CPA, fond 495.73.26, item #2: Letter from Münzenberg to Dimitrov.
18. Ibid., p. 290.
19. Ibid., pp. 290–293.
20. Ibid., p. 290.
21. Ibid., p. 291.
22. Ibid. For the military and secret Service background of this decision, see also Krivitsky, *In Stalin's Secret Service*, pp. 82–90.
23. Krivitsky, *In Stalin's Secret Service*, pp. 82–84.
24. For Münzenberg's role in the earliest days of supplying Spain, see Gross, *Münzenberg*, p. 291. For a more detailed account of the role of Münzenberg's people in procuring arms for Spain in the early stages of that conflict, see Thornberry, *Malraux et l'Espagne*, chapter 1.
25. Gross, *Münzenberg*, p. 291.
26. Ibid., pp. 290–291.
27. CPA, fond 495.19.243 and especially 495.19.337.
28. Gross, ibid.
29. Ibid. See also Buber-Neumann, *Under Two Dictators*, pp. 4–5.
30. Buber-Neumann, *Under Two Dictators*, part II, pp. 167ff.
31. Buber-Neumann's book on Milena Jasenska is a major document and has been translated into many languages. See *Milena* (New York: Schocken, 1988).
32. Buber-Neumann, *Under Two Dictators*, p. 324.
33. Arkady Vaksberg, *Hotel Lux*, p. 188.
34. Gross, *Münzenberg*, pp. 291–292.

The historical literature on the Spanish Civil War is of course massive, and since 1975 has been undergoing considerable revision. The most compendious and reliable, though not always most readable, account is Burnett Balloten, *The Spanish Civil War: Revolution and Counterrevolution* (Chapel Hill: Univ. of N. Carolina Press, 1991). Ronald Radosh and Mary Hobeck's *Spain Betrayed: The Soviet Union in the Spanish Civil War* (New Haven: Yale 2001) is indispensable. The standard volume of 1961, Hugh Thomas's *The Spanish Civil War*, should be read in its revised edition of 1977, and supplemented by the large body of Spanish scholarship emergent since the death of Franco. The tone and direction of Thomas's first edition extended general approbation to the Popular Front and the moral credit it claimed for itself. In that spirit, he treated the accounts of both Krivitsky and Orlov with undisguised and entirely dismissive contempt. I know of no reputable authority working since the death of Franco who would adopt such an attitude. The revelations of Walter Krivitsky have been the subject of almost uninterrupted journalistic invective and pseudo-scholarly attack from the moment they appeared; their subsequent history has been one of steady confirmation in virtually all substance and most detail, though some of Krivitsky's assertions about the Soviet role in arming the Spanish Republic need qualification in the light of Gerald Howson's *Arms for Spain* (New York: St. Martin's Press, 1999). I would direct the reader to the bibliographical note of *The Great Terror*, in its 1968 edition, p. 570, and to Conquest's comment on that note in his introduction to the 1990 *Reassessment*, p. viii. (An interesting attack on Krivitsky in matters of detail can be found in Poretsky, *Our Own People*, p. 171n, and passim.) I am especially grateful to Mr. John Costello, whose research into Orlov based on Information from the Soviet archives promises to revise this entire discussion, and shows Krivitsky's account of Orlov's role in Spain is generally supported by the documents. See also Costello, *Deadly Illusions*, chapter 12.

35. Katz's presence in Valencia was widely known. See Gross, *Münzenberg*, p. 312.
36. Information to the author from Babette Gross.
37. See Krivitsky's *In Stalin's Secret Service*, chapter 3, "Stalin's Hand in Spain," pp. 75–116. A useful overview of the Spanish War can also be found in Johnson, *Modern Times*, chapter 9, "The High Noon of Aggression."
38. See Krivitsky's *In Stalin's Secret Service*, chapter 3, "Stalin's Hand in Spain," pp. 75–116. A useful overview of the Spanish War can also be found in Johnson, *Modern Times*, chapter 9, "The High Noon of Aggression."
39. See Johnson, *Modern Times*, p. 329, and his sources, especially Salas, *Intervención extrajeras*. The question of how Stalin financed his assistance to the Spanish Republic is raised there, and a great deal of supporting material is to be found in Krivitsky, *In Stalin's Secret Service*.
40. Johnson, *Modern Times*, pp. 324–325.
41. Ibid., pp. 324–327. An interesting political account by an eyewitness can be found in Buber-Neumann's *Von Potsdam nach Moskau*, in her discussion of Heinz Neumann's Comintern work in Spain, and especially events with Alvarez del Vayo in 1936.

42. See Buber-Neumann, *Von Potsdam nach Moskau.*
43. Johnson, *Modern Times,* pp. 326, 328.
44. Krivitsky, *In Stalin's Secret Service,* p. 76.
45. Thomberry, *Malraux et l'Espagne,* pp. 33–34. Thomberry's account is by far the best and most detailed in existence. Malraux's activities were both on the level of clandestine military sales and propaganda.
46. Krivitsky, *In Stalin's Secret Service,* pp. 76–78.
47. Ibid., pp. 80–85.
48. The work of Alvarez del Vayo as a Münzenberg-man is mentioned in Gross, *Münzenberg,* pp. 272, 311. Note that Otto Katz's close link to del Vayo is mentioned in 311. It was common knowledge to all high-level witnesses, such as Louis Fischer (see *Men and Politics*). I am grateful to Mrs. Rae Bernstein for the information that del Vayo and Otto Katz remained associates in New York following the Spanish War. Alvarez del Vayo's influence over Largo Caballero figures in most Standard histories of the war. As to his lifelong claim to being an "independent leftist," it should be viewed in the light of his deeds.
49. Johnson, *Modern Times,* p. 333. See also Krivitsky, *In Stalin's Secret Service.*
50. Ronald Radosh, Mary R. Hobeck, and Grigory Sevostianov, *Spain Betrayed: The Soviet Union in the Spanish Civil War* (New Haven and London: Yale University Press, 2001), pp. 22–98, "The Advisors Begin Their Work." I would direct the reader's attention especially to "Document 16," a memorandum for Vladimir Gorev to Voroshilov, dated September 25, 1936. This memorandum is resonant here not only because it frankly reveals Soviet intentions, but because it was around this time that Jose Robles Pazos was assigned to Vladimir Gorev as his Spanish adjutant and interpreter.
51. Krivitsky, *In Stalin's Secret Service,* pp. 83–85.
52. See Bolloten, *Spanish Civil War,* Part II, Chapter 14.
53. For more on Malraux's role, see Thomberry, *Malraux et l'Espagne.* For the general gathering of cultural personalities in Spain, see Weintraub's *The Last Great Cause.*
54. Krivitsky, *In Stalin's Secret Service,* p. 82.
55. Ibid., pp. 32–83.
56. Krivitsky, *In Stalin's Secret Service,* chapter 3.
57. Ibid., pp. 96–99. Berzin's previous history and role in Spain is also discussed in Conquest, *The Great Terror.*
58. Conquest, *The Great Terror,* p. 410.
59. Krivitsky, *In Stalin's Secret Service,* pp. 99–115.
60. For these events of October 1936, with *Pravda* declaring purges essential and Berzin's awareness of them, see Krivitsky, *In Stalin's Secret Service.*
61. Ibid., p. 115.
62. See Johnson, *Modern Times,* p. 333, citing Hugh Thomas, *The Spanish Civil War* (London, 1977), and also citing Salas, *Intervention extrajera.*

63. See Martha Gellhorn, "On Apocryphism," *Paris Review*, no. 79 (1981), p. 301.
64. Information to the author from Mrs. Margaret Regler.
65. Information to the author from the late Joris Ivens.
66. Lynn, *Hemingway*, pp. 465–466. See also Lash, *Eleanor and Franklin*, chapter 38, p. 567.
67. Ivens relation to Münzenberg and his work as a Münzenberg man is explored in detail in Hans Schoots, *Living Dangerously, A Biography of Joris Ivens* (Amsterdam University Press, translated from the Dutch by David Colmer, Amsterdam, 2000). Chapters 9–11 are especially relevant to the story of Ivens and the *apparat's* relation to *The Spanish Earth*.
68. Information to the author from the late Joris Ivens, Paris, July 1986. In his interview with me, Ivens was equivocal on this point. He told me that he knew Katz well, but that Katz had "nothing to do" with the film. Nonetheless, Ivens added that Contemporary Historians had been set up to avoid any suspicion about a role for Otto.
69. Virginia Spencer Carr, *Dos Passos*, pp. 359–363.
70. Ibid., pp. 262–263. See also the biographies of Hellman and Hemingway.
71. Virginia Spencer Carr, *Dos Passos*, pp. 366–367.
72. Ibid.
73. Ibid., p. 367.
74. Virginia Spencer Carr, *Dos Passos*. It is perhaps worth mentioning that in later life Liston Oak tended to keep the story of his experiences in Spain limited to a narrow circle of his intimates. Many people very close to him were unaware that he had ever been in Spain at all, or that the pivotal event of his political life had taken place there.
75. Information to the author from Mr. Allen Oak.
76. Hemingway's line about "my second war," was mentioned by the late Joris Ivens in an interview with the author.
77. A standard biographical account of Herbst's movements and action in this affair is in Langer, *Josephine Herbst*, pp. 219–233. Langer relies heavily on Herbst's essay "The Starched Blue Sky of Spain," which appeared in the *Noble Savage*, no. l, and is reprinted in Herbst, *The Starched Blue Sky of Spain*.
78. Herbst, *The Starched Blue Sky of Spain*, p. 154.
79. Ibid.
80. I am most grateful to Mrs. Margaret Regler for the gift of a typescript of Gustav Regler's war diary during these events. The diary entries for March and April provide vivid accounts of the journalistic atmosphere in Madrid at the time, especially reports of treason by "fascist spies" among the Republican ranks. These specific provocations, and an example of the response to it by a literary man whom Herbst would regard as one of the "best men" she met in Spain, can be found in the typescript entries for April 15, 16, and 17, 1937. These are precisely the days of the events in the Hotel Florida under discussion here.

81. Fifty years later, Joris Ivens, who was present and integral to the entire event, repeated the falsehood that designated Robles as a fascist spy, and did so with the apparent confidence that the charge was true. While disclaiming unequivocal personal knowledge, Ivens even added operational details: He claimed that Robles had been sending light signals to the fascist lines by night. Ivens must have been given these details by someone, and he must have been told them during the events under discussion here. Joris Ivens, interview with the author, June 1986.

82. Herbst, *The Starched Blue Sky of Spain*, p. 154.

83. Ibid.

84. Ibid., p. 155. Note Herbst's remark about Hemingway's agreement to the deceptive course of action she had suggested: "Perhaps he agreed with too cheerful a readiness."

85. Regler's war diary speaks of the celebrations around Thaelman Day, though he himself does not seem to have been present at the castle. See also Virginia Spencer Carr, *Dos Passos*, p. 368.

86. See both ibid. and Herbst, *The Starched Blue Sky of Spain*.

87. Herbst, *The Starched Blue Sky of Spain*, pp. 156–157.

88. Otto Katz's presence at the Hotel Florida is established by Regler's war diary, entry of April 17, 1937. The specific passage reads: "In Madrid, Simon [Katz's alias] digs up some English countesses. Franco fires shells under their beds. Wilkinson also there." That Wilkinson was staying with Otto Katz in the Hotel Florida at this time is confirmed in Vernon, *Ellen Wilkinson*. The reader might also note that Claud Cockburn, whom Herbst describes as her friend, was likewise in the hotel that day, and that Cockburn was at this time deep in his political collaboration with Katz.

89. Virginia Spencer Carr, *Dos Passos*, p. 370.

90. Shipman and Hemingway's claims of Dos Passos's cowardice are summarized in ibid.

91. Ibid., p. 371. Carr relies in part on Dos Passos's *The Theme Is Freedom*.

Chapter 13
MÜNZENBERG'S END

1. The Popular Front was of course universally jettisoned with the Nazi-Soviet Pact. But it was already in decline in the apparatus by the spring of 1937. See Krivitsky, *In Stalin's Secret Service*, conversation with Slutsky reported on pp. 214–215.

2. Ibid., p. 215.

3. Münzenberg's illness is described in Gross, *Münzenberg*. Note that Gross misspells the name of the clinician: it is Dr. Le Savoureux, not Savouret.

4. Ibid.

5. Bukharin's visit to Paris is described in Cohen, *Bukharin and the Bolshevik Revolution*, pp. 365–367. See also Medvedev, *Nikolai Bukharin*, p. 122. The incident with Dr. Le Savoureux is reported in Gross, *Münzenberg*.

6. Bukharin's meetings with Nicholaevsky are extensively discussed in Nicholaevsky, *Power and the Soviet Elite*.

7. Kennan's comment is found in his introduction to *Power and the Soviet Elite*.

8. See Gross, *Münzenberg*.

9. See FOIA dossier on Otto Katz, # 65-9266, section 7, Report of the FBI, file # 100-15865, July 13, 1944.

10. Károlyi and Fischer's efforts are mentioned in Gross, *Münzenberg*.

11. Beletsky's visit to Münzenberg is mentioned in Krivitsky, *In Stalin's Secret Service*, p. 62. Gross accepts Krivitsky's account.

12. Gross, *Münzenberg*.

13. Ibid.

14. The history of *Die Zukunft* is reported in many memoirs: Gross, *Münzenberg*, Sperber, *Ces Temps-la*, Koestler, *Invisible Writing*, inter alia. It became a model for *Der Monat* and other Journals.

15. Gross, *Münzenberg*, pp. 289–292.

16. See ibid. and Schliemann, "Münzenberg." Also information to the author from Babette Gross.

17. See Schliemann, "Münzenberg," p. 80. See also Wessel, *Münzenbergs Ende*, p. 333.

18. Schliemann, "Münzenberg," p. 82.

19. Information to the author from Mr. Paul Willert.

20. The warning to Wilkinson about British intelligence is mentioned in Deacon, *The British Connection*, p. 173.

21. Philby's relation to Liddell is discussed in Costello, *The Mask of Treachery*, pp. 418, 438, 605.

22. See Gross, *Münzenberg*.

23. The presence of the apparatus in the internment camps of the period is discussed by Regler, *The Owl of Minerva*, pp. 331–354.

24. *Le Peuple*, Brussels, January 30, 1940.

25. Information to the author from Babette Gross.

26. Glees, *The Secrets of the Service*, pp. 127–132, and all other references to Sefton Delmer. Glees examines the war-time activities of Sefton Delmer—who was, if anything, closer to Münzenberg in this period than Willert—and comes to the conclusion that Delmer was under Soviet control. I find Glees's meticulously researched case interesting but too much based in inference to carry me even to moral certainty.

27. Gross, *Münzenberg*.

28. Münzenberg's hopes for help from Marcu are raised in Carew-Hunt, "Münzenberg," p. 87.

29. On Münzenberg's mood, note the small difference between Gross's account (*Münzenberg*, p. 324) and Schliemann's ("Münzenberg," p. 89).

30. A description of these penetrations of the internment camps by the apparatus can be found in Regler, *The Owl of Minerva*.

31. The story of the "Red-Headed Youth" appears in Kersten, "Das Ende Willi Münzenbergs," Gross, *Münzenberg*, Wessel, *Münzenbergs Ende*, and Schliemann, "Münzenberg."

32. See Wessel, *Münzenbergs Ende*, p. 333.

33. Ibid.

34. Schliemann, "Münzenberg," pp. 88–89.

35. Ibid., and also Gross, *Münzenberg*.

36. Gross, *Münzenberg*.

37. The departure from Chambarran is discussed in all authorities: Kersten, "Das Ende Willi Münzenbergs," Gross, *Münzenberg*, Schliemann, "Münzenberg," Carew-Hunt, "Münzenberg," Gruber, "Münzenberg," and Wessel, *Münzenbergs Ende*. Note that my information from Helen Wolff contradicts the belief common to many that Kurt Wolff was in the group moving on foot. He left Chambarran by bus.

38. Wessel, *Münzenbergs Ende*, pp. 234–235.

39. Siemsen is quoted in both Kersten "Das Ende Willi Münzenbergs" and Schliemann, *Münzenberg*, p. 87.

40. In 1987, a controversial book made a large impact at a Münzenberg Congress, which took place in Zurich. A man named Gerhart Leo, who held a quite high-level journalistic position in the Honecker journalistic world, published the book in the East German Republic. It claims that Gerhart Leo's father, a certain Wilhelm Leo, was one of the two young men with Willi— whether he was red-headed or not is unclear—and that Wilhelm had confided the whole truth of the events in Montagne to Gerhart in 1945, when the family returned to Stalinist East Germany to take up residence.

According to Gerhart Leo, once Hartig had left the group and Münzenberg was left alone in the Montagne cafe with his two companions, Willi was in despair. He also claimed to be ill, and in such a state of demoralized exhaustion that he could not possibly go on without a rest. He urged his two companions to strike out into the forest ahead of him, and he would try to catch up. They obediently left him, though precisely how Willi was to pick up their path through the woods is quite unclear. More to the point, strike out for what destination? The Swiss border? The men were exhausted. Night was falling. They had no car. Hartig had not returned, and he may have had their money. Obviously, the only sensible action would have been to return to their fellow refugees, still camped out, ready to spend the night beneath the stars, a very few kilometers away—fellow refugees who in fact all, every one, eventually reached safety. But there was not even a message sent to the people still waiting in Saint Antoine. Instead, madly, the two young men struck out into the woods.

Leo claims that his father and the other youth waited in the woods for their improbable rendezvous with the "rested" Willi. Except he did not come. After the appointed hour was long past, Leo claims the Red-Headed Youth and the other man returned to the edge of the wood. There they found Münzenberg. He had hanged himself with some rope used for baling the local tobacco, found on the ground.

Babette Gross had read this book several times, very carefully. She viewed it with the utmost suspicion. First of all, she viewed its source, a committed communist journalist publishing with a state-sponsored house in the DDR, as rendering it unreliable on its face. Moreover, she claimed to have no knowledge of any Wilhelm Leo among the German exiles, though her knowledge was encyclopedic. That the elder Leo had been known to Münzenberg she flatly denied. Moreover, she could not believe that Münzenberg would ever have trusted his life to these two obviously untested and unknown men. It obviously would have been far, far better to take his chances with the long column of refugees, trudging south to safety. Münzenberg always intended to return to his friends in Saint Antoine, either with a car or without one, either to pick up passengers or to spend the night under the stars and then rejoin the march. Why then, in the midst of his despair and possible illness, would he reverse himself and say he would try running, on foot, to Switzerland? The idea that a man so utterly grounded in reality as Münzenberg would have even considered embarking on such a trek, walking, at nightfall, without a clear path, in a state of complete exhaustion, unprotected, and in the company of two young communists, struck Babette as preposterous. And so it strikes me. Add to this the mystery of long silence. Why did the younger Leo and his family wait for almost half a century to clarify one of the most persistent mysteries of the Second World War? Rather lamely, Gerhart Leo claims that the Ulbricht regime disliked former German exiles like his father and disliked Münzenberg even more: Willi was a non-person in the DDR virtually until the younger Leo published his book. Leo claims the regime would have opposed letting this story be known. This is a little difficult to believe. In the West, that the apparatus had murdered Münzenberg was almost universally believed during the Cold War, a famous black mark against the NKVD and the German Party. An incontestable demonstration that the assassination theory was false, false and better yet paranoid, could only have been welcome propaganda for the East German government. Yet it took until 1987, after Hartig and many other witnesses were safely dead, for Leo's story to be allowed to surface.

Babette Gross regarded the Leo book as worthless. Though she did not use the word with me, I think it fair to say she saw it as disinformation.

41. See Gross, *Münzenberg*.

42. The size of the stand of woods can be estimated by maps made by the United States Corps of Engineers of the region during the Second World War, and available in the map collection of the New York Public Library.

EPILOGUE

1. Information to the author from Mr. Herman Starobin.
2. Otto's role in the Masaryk government is discussed in many sources. See Costello, *The Mask of Treachery*, p. 298. I am also grateful to Mr. Herman Starobin for information about his work in Czechoslovakia.
3. "There is no tree high enough to hang me from." This line was cited by Eugen Loebl in an interview with me. The actual words to the peroration of Katz's "confession," are these: "I have joined the U.S., British, and French anti-Semites against the Soviet Union. Therein lies my crimes. I am a writer, supposedly an architect of the soul. What sort of architect have I been, I who have poisoned people's souls? Such an architect of the soul belongs to the gallows. The only Service I can still render is to warn all who, by origin or character, are in danger of following the same path to hell. The sterner the punishment..." But at this point Katz's voice sank to a whisper, and he could not be heard.
4. Koestler, *The Invisible Writing*, p. 405.

Index